ADVANCES IN
Experimental
Social Psychology

VOLUME 27

ADVANCES IN

Experimental Social Psychology

EDITED BY

Mark P. Zanna

DEPARTMENT OF PSYCHOLOGY
UNIVERSITY OF WATERLOO
WATERLOO, ONTARIO, CANADA

VOLUME 27

ACADEMIC PRESS
San Diego   New York   Boston
London   Sydney   Tokyo   Toronto

This book is printed on acid-free paper. ∞

Copyright © 1995 by ACADEMIC PRESS, INC.

All Rights Reserved.
No part of this publication may be reproduced or transmitted in any form or by any means, electronic or mechanical, including photocopy, recording, or any information storage and retrieval system, without permission in writing from the publisher.

Academic Press, Inc.
A Division of Harcourt Brace & Company
525 B Street, Suite 1900, San Diego, California 92101-4495

United Kingdom Edition published by
Academic Press Limited
24-28 Oval Road, London NW1 7DX

International Standard Serial Number: 0065-2601

International Standard Book Number: 0-12-015227-4

PRINTED IN THE UNITED STATES OF AMERICA
95 96 97 98 99 00 BB 9 8 7 6 5 4 3 2 1

CONTENTS

Contributors ix

Inferences of Responsibility and Social Motivation

Bernard Weiner

I.	Introduction	1
II.	A Short Story about Responsibility Inferences	6
III.	The Responsibility Process	7
IV.	Consequences of Judging Another Responsible	21
V.	Help Giving (Altruism)	26
VI.	Aggression	30
VII.	Rejection	32
VIII.	Impression Management (Excuse Giving)	34
IX.	Theoretical Comparisons	40
X.	Concluding Theoretical Notes	42
	References	44

Information Processing in Social Contexts: Implications for Social Memory and Judgment

Robert S. Wyer, Jr., and Deborah H Gruenfeld

I.	Motivational Influences on the Communication of Pragmatic Meaning	52
II.	Informational Influences on Pragmatic Information Processing: The Role of Expectancy Deviations	68
III.	Individual Differences in Pragmatic Information Processing	80
IV.	The Mental Representation of Information Conveyed in a Social Context	83
V.	Final Comments	85
	References	87

The Interactive Roles of Stability and Level of Self-Esteem: Research and Theory

Michael H. Kernis and Stefanie B. Waschull

I.	Nature and Assessment of Stability of Self-Esteem	94
II.	Why People Vary in the Extent to Which Their Self-Esteem Is Unstable	97
III.	The Roles of Stability and Level of Self-Esteem in Self-Enhancement and Self-Protective Strategies	108
IV.	Self-Esteem and Depressive Symptomatology	121
V.	Domain-Specific Evaluations, Pride, and the "Big Five"	127
VI.	Summary	131
VII.	Future Directions	134
	References	135

Gender Differences in Perceiving Internal State: Toward a His-and-Hers Model of Perceptual Cue Use

Tomi-Ann Roberts and James W. Pennebaker

I.	Introduction	143
II.	Gender Differences in Perceiving Internal State: Toward a His-and-Hers Model of Perceptual Cue Use	144
III.	Gender Differences in Self-Reports of Symptoms, Emotions, and Physical Exertion	154
IV.	Gender Differences in the Use of Internal and External Cues	156
V.	Why Women and Men Might Rely on Different Sources of Information in Judging Their Internal States	160
VI.	Discussion	166
	References	170

On the Role of Encoding Processes in Stereotype Maintenance

William von Hippel, Denise Sekaquaptewa, and Patrick Vargas

I.	Introduction	177
II.	Perceptual Processes	181
III.	Conceptual Processes	195
IV.	Prejudice as Encoding Processes	224
V.	Conclusions	237
	References	242

Psychological Barriers to Dispute Resolution

Lee Ross and Andrew Ward

I.	Introduction	255
II.	Types of Barriers	256
III.	More Detailed Examination of Five Specific Psychological Barriers	263
IV.	Sources of Misattribution and Mistrust: Broader Theoretical Perspectives	275
V.	Implications for Mediators, Facilitators, and Other Third Parties	288
	References	298

Index	305
Contents of Other Volumes	313

CONTRIBUTORS

Numbers in parentheses indicate the pages on which the authors' contributions begin.

DEBORAH H GRUENFELD (49), Kellogg School of Management, Department of Organizational Behavior, Northwestern University, Evanston, Illinois 60201

MICHAEL H. KERNIS (93), Department of Psychology, University of Georgia, Athens, Georgia 30602

JAMES W. PENNEBAKER (143), Department of Psychology, Southern Methodist University, Dallas, Texas 75275

TOMI-ANN ROBERTS (143), Department of Psychology, The Colorado College, Colorado Springs, Colorado 80903

LEE ROSS (255), Department of Psychology, Stanford University, Stanford, California 94305

DENISE SEKAQUAPTEWA (177), Department of Psychology, Ohio State University, Columbus, Ohio 43210

PATRICK VARGAS (177), Department of Psychology, Ohio State University, Columbus, Ohio 43210

WILLIAM VON HIPPEL (177), Department of Psychology, Ohio State University, Columbus, Ohio 43210

ANDREW WARD (255), Department of Psychology, Stanford University, Stanford, California 94305

STEFANIE B. WASCHULL (93), Department of Psychology, University of Georgia, Athens, Georgia 30602

BERNARD WEINER (1), Department of Psychology, University of California at Los Angeles, Los Angeles, California 90024

ROBERT S. WYER, JR. (49), Department of Psychology, University of Illinois at Urbana–Champaign, Champaign, Illinois 61820

INFERENCES OF RESPONSIBILITY AND SOCIAL MOTIVATION

Bernard Weiner

I. Introduction

The story of Magic Johnson, the renowned basketball star who now carries the acquired immunodeficiency (AIDS) virus, pervaded the popular press and media in 1991, not just in the United States but around the world as well. I begin with an informal analysis of reactions to Magic Johnson, followed by an experimental study regarding this life event. I then turn to related issues that form the heart of this chapter—the process of inferring that another is responsible for an untoward act and the emotional and motivational consequences of this belief.

A. MAGIC JOHNSON AND PERCEIVED RESPONSIBILITY FOR AIDS

Magic Johnson first announced that he tested positive for the human immunodeficiency virus (HIV) in a press conference. Shortly thereafter, the popular magazine *Sports Illustrated* published a widely read article written by Johnson about his illness (Johnson, 1991). This article emphasized the reasons for his contracting the virus and discussed his responsibility. Johnson wrote, "To me, AIDS was someone's else disease. It was a disease for gays and drug users. Not for someone like me" (p. 10). He then went on to state:

> Not that being HIV-positive has been easy to accept. Not when I could easily have avoided being infected at all. All I had to do was wear condoms. I am certain that I was infected by having unprotected sex with a woman who has the virus. The problem is that I can't pinpoint the time, the place, or the woman. It's a matter of numbers. Before I was married, I truly lived the bachelor's life. . . . I was never far from admiring women. . . .

> I did my best to accommodate as many women as I could—most of them through unprotected sex. (pp. 21–22)

It is evident, then, that Magic Johnson accepted some personal responsibility for getting the AIDS virus—he admittedly engaged in frequent casual sex. However, he did suggest that this was not entirely his responsibility in that he was pursued by women. Furthermore, in another place in the article he states that his behavior was typical of his celebrity circle, thus prompting a situational rather than a personal attribution (see Kelley, 1967).

The immediate reactions to Magic Johnson's announcement were shock, sorrow, and sympathy. A public outpouring of grief ensued. Magic Johnson was greeted with applause on a popular talk show and people were seen weeping and expressing genuine concern for him. Yet there soon followed more accusing voices with a different affective tone. An editorial from the *New York Times,* for example, stated,

> Magic Johnson is hardly a model or ideal to anyone with a sense of sexual morality. . . . Anyone with a sense of heterosexual responsibility isn't likely to get the HIV virus. . . . Magic apparently never pretended to be responsible for his sex life. . . . Earvin Johnson of the Fast Lane . . . finally got caught for speeding" (Anderson, 1991, p. B-7).

And a reader wrote:

> The real tragedy is how one man's refusal to exercise discretion, self-discipline and just plain common-sense can bring so much pain. . . . Worse has been [the press's] blatant recklessness and irresponsibility in placing this on the same level as Lou Gehrig [a baseball star] being stricken with amyotrophic lateral sclerosis [ALS]. ALS is not dictated by personal behavior: HIV/AIDS, for the most part, is. Magic Johnson asks us to feel sorry for him. Believe me, I don't. ("Letters to the Editor," C-3).

B. AN EXPERIMENTAL INVESTIGATION CONCERNING MAGIC JOHNSON

Along with a colleague and two students (Graham, Weiner, Giuliano, & Williams, 1993), the affective consequences of responsibility judgments in regard to Magic Johnson were examined more systematically. Two types of respondents participated in this research. One group consisted of college students; the second sample was composed primarily of adults, all of African-American descent. This sample was desired because Magic Johnson is believed to be a particularly important figure in the African-American community, which could influence inferences about his responsibility for carrying the AIDS virus as well as affect the emotional reactions this elicits. Both groups were tested within days following Magic's announcement.

The groups responded to a questionnaire about Magic Johnson. One part of this questionnaire involved a manipulation of five known causes of AIDS. The participants were asked to assume that each of five disparate causes resulted in Magic Johnson becoming infected. The causes provided were (1) a blood transfusion (during one of his knee operations); (2) normal (i.e., conventional) sexual behavior with a woman he knew; (3) frequent casual (promiscuous) sex with many women, which was his stated reason; (4) homosexual behavior; and (5) using drugs with a contaminated needle. Each cause was given, followed by questions about responsibility and affective reactions. Specifically, the respondents indicated how responsible Magic Johnson was for contracting this illness,

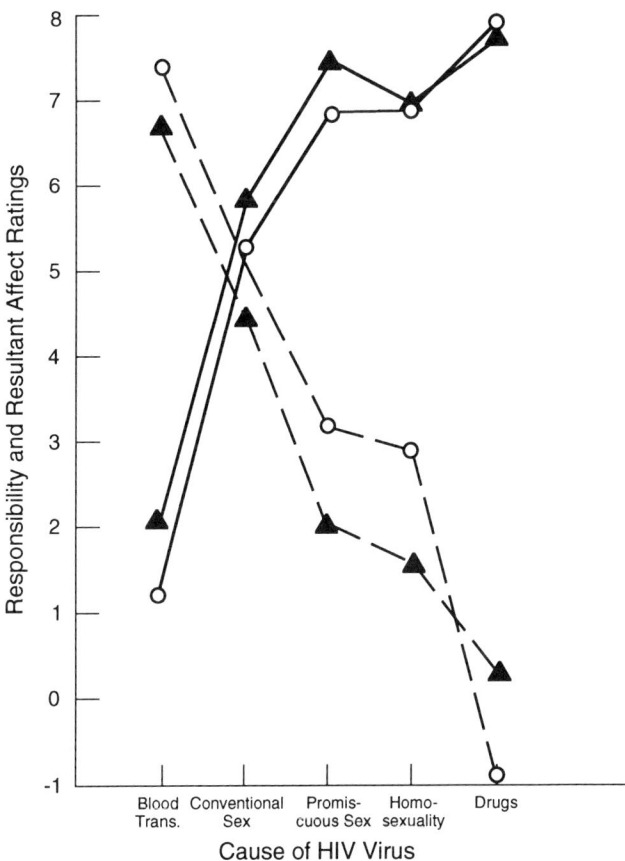

Fig. 1. Responsibility and resultant affect (sympathy minus anger) ratings as a function of the imagined cause of Magic Johnson having the AIDS virus. Unbroken line (—), responsibility; broken line (--), affect; ▲, adult subjects; ○, college subjects. (From Graham, Weiner, Giuliano, & Williams, 1993.)

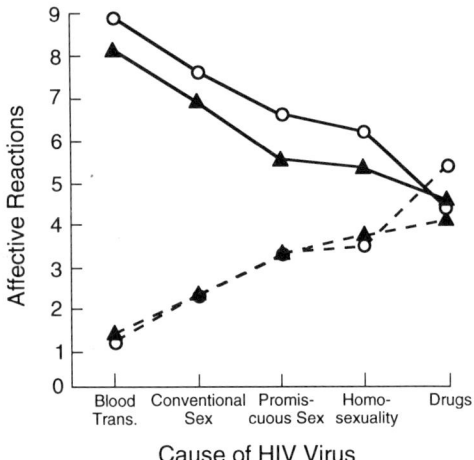

Fig. 2. Sympathy and anger ratings for college students and African-American adults as a function of the imagined cause of Magic Johnson having the AIDS virus. Unbroken line (—), sympathy; broken line (--), anger; ▲, adult subjects; ○, college subjects. (From Graham, Weiner, Giuliano, & Williams, 1993.)

as well as how much sympathy and anger they felt toward him if this was the real reason for his illness. A nine-point scale followed each of these questions, anchored with "not at all" and "as much as possible."

Figure 1 (see the solid lines) shows the responsibility ratings as a function of the manipulated cause. There is least responsibility when the HIV-positive condition was caused by a blood transfusion, followed by conventional sexual behavior. The next highest responsibility ratings were given equally for promiscuous sex and homosexual behavior. Most responsibility was assigned given drug use as the cause. The data from the two samples were quite consistent, with somewhat higher responsibility ratings given by the adult African-American sample than by the college students.

Figure 2 depicts the sympathy and anger ratings for the two samples as a function of the hypothetical cause of Magic's AIDS. Sympathy and anger are inversely related, with sympathy greatest and anger least given a blood transfusion as the cause, and anger greatest with sympathy least when drug use with a shared needle was the reason for Magic's infection with the AIDS virus. Again, trends from both samples were identical, although college students reported somewhat more sympathy than did the African-American adults.

A "resultant affect" index was created by Graham et al. (1993) by subtracting the anger ratings from the sympathy ratings. This index reflects the relative positivity of the emotional reactions toward Magic Johnson (see the broken lines in Fig. 1). Inspection of Figure 1 reveals an inverse relation between perceptions

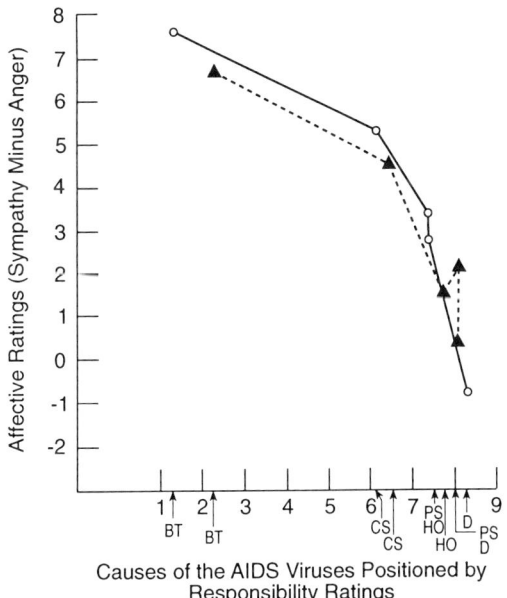

Fig. 3. Resultant affect (sympathy minus anger) ratings as a function of the imagined cause of Magic Johnson having the AIDS virus, with spatial arrangement of causes determined by the linked responsibility ratings. Short arrows on the figure indicate ratings for college (○) subjects; long arrows represent ratings for the African-American adults (▲). (BT = blood transfusion; CS = conventional sex; PS = promiscuous sex; HO = homosexual behavior; D = drug use). (From Graham, Weiner, Giuliano, & Williams, 1993.)

of responsibility for a negative state (or action) and the positivity of the reported feelings. Reactions were most favorable given a blood transfusion as the cause of AIDS and least favorable in the case of drug use.

The results of a somewhat more sophisticated procedure examining the association between responsibility inferences and affective reactions are shown in Figure 3. In contrast to Figures 1 and 2, in Figure 3 the distances between the causes on the horizontal axis are determined by their responsibility ratings. That is, rather than equally spacing the causes, as in the prior two figures, they are set at intervals according to their psychological meaning (i.e., their implications for perceptions of responsibility). The resultant affect ratings are again depicted for the five manipulated causes. Figure 3 reveals that the large increment in responsibility between blood transfusion and normal sexual behavior as the cause of AIDS is accompanied by relatively little (albeit some) decrease in resultant positive affect. That is, although one is held much more responsible for contracting AIDS by means of normal sexual behavior rather than through a blood transfusion, nevertheless there is a great deal of sympathy and relatively little anger given either cause. After that, however, there is an inflection point, or a point on the curve where change takes place. Now small increases in perceived responsibility are accompanied by large decreases in positive responses. Thus, for example, although people report that others are almost as responsible for AIDS due to promiscious sexual behavior as when drug use is the cause, there is much less relative sympathy for the drug user. The function relating responsibility to reported affect is nearly identical for both respondent populations.

C. CHAPTER GOALS

Of course, responsibility judgments and their consequences are not confined to celebrities, or to those with AIDS. In everyday life, one is constantly confronted with issues related to responsibility for actions, particularly when they are negative, and subsequent reward or punishment. Indeed, so prevalent is the tendency to find if others are responsible for an event or a personal difficulty that religious tenets advise us to forego such judgments (e.g., "Let him who is without sin among you cast the first stone," John 8:7; "Judge not that ye not be judged, for with what judgment ye judge ye shall be judged," Matthew, 7:1). But this advice has not been heeded, as will be documented in this chapter. In addition to pointing out the extensity of responsibility judgments in everyday life, my goals in this chapter are to analyze the responsibility inference process and to relate responsibility to emotional and social behavior. Considering the data just presented, why is it that blood transfusion and drug use as causes of AIDS differ so greatly on judgments of responsibility? What is it about these causes that produce such disparate beliefs? And why are the participants more sympathetic toward Magic Johnson when blood transfusion was the cause, and more angry given drug use as the reason for AIDS? Furthermore, what are the behavioral consequences of these emotional reactions, and how do beliefs about responsibility, emotions, and actions interrelate? And finally, what strategies are available to decrease judgments of responsibility?

II. A Short Story about Responsibility Inferences

To answer the questions that were just raised, let me first introduce a very common scenario that further directs the reader to thinking about perceived responsibility and its linkage with emotion and conduct. Imagine that one evening you are carefully driving home when suddenly there is a bang and a crash at the rear of your car. The trunk flies open and the car is pushed forward. Given this incident, you are likely to emerge from your automobile and immediately initiate a negative exchange with the driver of the car in the rear.

I believe that the process intervening between this aversive event and the behavioral reaction is quite complex, with many component parts. The temporal sequence is not readily discernable in the situation that was described, for the reaction may have been automatic (scripted), or the process took place so rapidly that you, as well as any observers, were unaware of the sequential contingencies. However, it is possible to logically as well as experimentally demonstrate the psychological steps intervening between the crash (the external stimulus) and the shouting at the rear driver (the behavioral response).

The notion that a psychological reaction has multiple inputs or sequential antecedents that are only discernable with experimental procedures or dialectical analyses that decompose the process is not new in social psychology or in motivation. For example, the influential Schachter and Singer (1962) conception of emotion postulates that the fear one experiences at the sight of a gun is generated by two elements: arousal and the perceived situational cause of that arousal. The individual experiencing the fear, as well as onlookers, are unaware of these multiple and sequential influences. Schachter and Singer (1962), however, crafted an experimental situation to separate the component parts. Regardless of what one believes about the success of this attempt, their analysis is valuable in pointing out that one can isolate parts of an integrated process that is outside of the conscious awareness of the involved individual.

Let me, then, logically alter some of the conditions in the car crash scenario and intuit how this might change the reader's reaction to this event were he or she the driver of the car. I will focus attention first on the responsibility process, or the dynamics involved when another is found to be culpable.

The scenarios that are introduced might be considered *Gedankenversuchen* (thought experiments) and were Fritz Heider's (1958) dominant method of scientific inquiry. The conditions that will be varied were guided by beliefs voiced by three psychologists particularly active in exploring the pertinent issues—Frank Fincham (e.g., Fincham & Roberts, 1985; Fincham & Schultz, 1981), Kelly Shaver (e.g., Shaver, 1985; Shaver & Drown, 1986), and Thomas Shultz (e.g., Shultz, Schleifer, & Altman, 1981; Shultz & Wright, 1985), as well as by the thoughts of philosophers and experts in jurisprudence (e.g., Hart, 1968; Hart & Honoré, 1959; Morse, 1992).

III. The Responsibility Process

A. PERSONAL VERSUS IMPERSONAL (SITUATIONAL) CAUSALITY

Imagine that as you come out of your car, shouting and ready to engage in battle with the driver of the auto in the rear, you discover that a rock from a nearby hill has fallen on your back bumper. Anger and confrontation now give way to a search for where the rock had come from and for other causal information pertinent to your fate. You are still feeling "bad,"—demoralized, knowing that the car has to be repaired yet again; despair at the anticipated cost; frustrated because of the time delay; and so on. But the moral judgment of holding another responsible is no longer being called forth by the situation (unless you begin to wonder if the rock may have been thrown or pushed by someone on the hill).

An assignment of responsibility therefore appears to require human or personal agency (although, on some occasions, other self-initiating agents such as a cat or dog may be held responsible for wrecking the couch, and even God can be considered responsible for moving the rock). Given the above premise, it would be appropriate to state that the rock *caused* the damage to the car, but not that the rock was *responsible* for that damage, although the latter usage may be heard in daily discourse. Similarly, a transfusion with contaminated blood may have caused Magic's HIV-positive state, but was not responsible for it.

Considering examples in which inferences of personal causality are made, a picnic canceled because of poor planning, a business failure ascribed to insufficient effort or trying, HIV or AIDS because of sexual behavior, and an accident caused by another driver's speeding do result in ascriptions to human agents. Responsibility judgments then *may* be reached (i.e., the responsibility process continues). Responsibility inferences therefore require causal beliefs about human involvement, or personal causality, but not all causal beliefs implicate personal responsibility. Hence, in distinction to a position voiced by some psychologists (e.g., Brewer, 1977), a responsibility judgment is not to be equated with a causal judgment.

In sum, it is contended that an assignment of responsibility has as a first step a distinction between person versus situation causality, or thoughts about what is called the locus of causality (Heider, 1958; Weiner, 1986). It again and again has been documented that causal location is one of the main dimensions or properties of causal thinking. Implicit in the automobile vignette was that the driver of the smashed car assumed that the rear driver was causally involved (prior to finding the rock). This might have been revealed in an accusation such as, "Look what *you* have done."

A large degree of literature documents the tendency to infer dispositional attributions for the behaviors of others (e.g., Sedikides & Anderson, 1992), as opposed to ascribing their actions to situational factors. Of course, contexts do exist in which the immediate causal appraisal is situational (see Krull, 1993). Finding a large rock on top of the trunk of your car would be one of these (although this does relate to the cause of car damage rather than to the cause of conduct of another person).

There are many determinants of the ascription of an event or a state of another to personal versus impersonal causes. Here I will call attention to two very disparate antecedents I have examined that bear upon responsibility judgments and their consequences: (1) affective states and (2) political ideology.

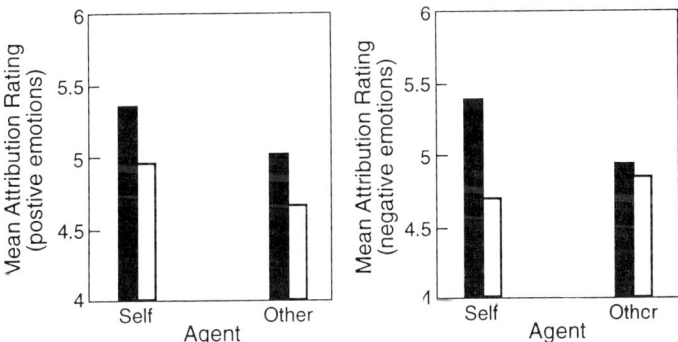

Fig. 4. Mean situational (filled bar) and dispositional (open bar) attribution ratings for positive and negative emotions. (From Karasawa, 1994, in press.)

1. Positive versus Negative Affective States

In one of a series of studies by Karasawa (in press), situational and dispositional causality were rated for a number of positive and negative emotions described as being experienced by the self or by another person. The positive emotions included happiness, excitement, and pride, whereas among the negative emotions were unhappiness, guilt, and shame.

Specifically, for example, subjects were simply told that "John is happy." They then rated how likely it was that something good had happened and how likely it was that John is a happy person. The findings revealed that for positive emotions (left half of Fig. 4), the situation was judged as causally more important in eliciting the emotion than was disposition, both for the self and for others. Happiness therefore generally is believed to be due to something that has happened, rather than to something about the person experiencing this feeling.

The pattern of responses for the negative emotions also are shown in Figure 4 (right half). When, for example, the rater is described as unhappy, that emotional state is most ascribed to the situation, or to something that has happened. On the other hand, if another person is characterized as unhappy, then there is about equal ascription to the person and to something about the situation.

Liu, Karasawa, and Weiner (1992) then elaborated Karasawa's research (which, although published later, had been conducted prior to Liu et al., 1992). A situational cause was provided for an emotion, and subjects were then asked if additional causes might have produced this feeling. For example, in vignettes it was stated that "Tom felt excited when starting a new job," or that "Tom felt angry when his roommate left a pile of dishes in the sink." The subjects then indicated if three other categories of causes might have contributed to the emotional reaction: disposition ("something about the kind of person he is also caused or contributed to the emotional reaction"), situation ("something else

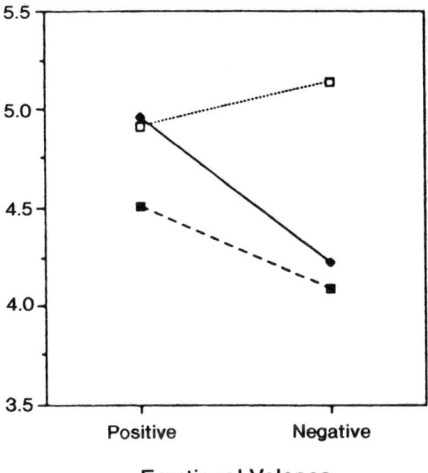

Fig. 5. Mean likelihood of additional causal inferences as a function of emotional valence and causal inference type (□, disposition; ■, mood; ●, situation). (From Liu, Karasawa, & Weiner, 1992, p. 609.)

about the immediate situation or recent past also caused or contributed to this emotional reaction"); and current mood state.

The data from one investigation reported by Liu et al. (1992) are shown in Figure 5. Figure 5 reveals that when a positive emotion is experienced by another, all three other potential causes of this feeling state are considered somewhat high (the ratings were made on 7-point scales) and nearly equal. On the other hand, when the emotion is negative, perceptions of disposition as an additional cause are elevated, whereas situation and mood judgments are relatively low.

Taken together, these investigations document that when others express negative emotions such as unhappiness, there is a proclivity to believe that something about them caused this feeling (also see Rippere, 1977). Additional research reported by Karasawa (in press) documents that responsibility is perceived as much greater when something about the other person rather than the situation is inferred to be the cause of an individual's emotional state. Hence, people are viewed as more responsible for feeling bad than for feeling good.

Although discussing the consequences of these judgments would take us ahead of the story to be unfolded, I want to alert the readers to future directions. I believe that the rejection and active social distancing that are displayed toward the depressed (see Coates & Wortman, 1980; Coyne, Kahn, & Gotlib, 1987; Gurtman, 1986) are in part due to the belief that depressed persons cause their own unhappy state and are responsible for their misery. This inference, which tends to elicit anger from others (as will soon be examined), disrupts needed social relationships and social support, thereby exacerbating the depression. Thus, a dysfunctional cycle is established.

2. Political Ideology Related to the Perceived Causes of Poverty

A second antecedent of judgments of perceived causality that in turn relates to perceptions of responsibility is political ideology. Here I will examine these attitudes only in relation to beliefs about poverty.

Opinions differ about the causes of poverty. On the one hand, the Protestant ethic dominates the beliefs of many Americans. It is thought that through industriousness and dedication the American Dream will be fulfilled. However, this ethic began to be questioned several decades ago. At that time the welfare system was introduced, in part stimulated by the impersonal forces of the economic system. Thus, both society and the person came to be considered plausible causes of poverty.

There have been many studies examining lay beliefs about the causes of poverty (e.g., Feagin, 1972; Feather, 1974; Furnham, 1982). Usually, somewhat more than ten dominant perceived causes of poverty are identified—the personal causes include laziness and poor spending habits, whereas the social causes entail no available jobs, lack of educational opportunities, and the like.

Political ideology has been found to have a significant effect on causal perceptions of poverty. As Lane (1962) has pointed out, "At the roots of every ideology are premises about the nature of causation, the agents of causation, and the appropriate ways of explaining complex events" (p. 318). In support of this contention, it has been found that conservatives rate individualistic causes of poverty as more important than do liberals, whereas liberals consider social factors as being more important influences on poverty than do conservatives (see, for example, Kluegel & Smith, 1986; Skitka & Tetlock, 1992; Zucker & Weiner, 1993). Hence, it follows that conservatives are more likely than liberals to consider the poor as responsible for their own plight. As Dionne (1991) expressed so well:

> Since the 1960s, American politics has been at war over which set of sins should preoccupy government. Conservatives preached that the good society would be created if individuals could be made virtuous. Liberals preached that the good society would create virtuous individuals.

It certainly is likely that the immediate causal judgments about poverty that are offered by liberals and conservatives are largely governed by automatic processes requiring few cognitive resources and not needing awareness or effort. On the other hand, explaining why another is unhappy may necessitate greater effort and causal search, more controlled processing, and more consciousness. In general, the consciousness and effortfulness of the initial decision in the responsibility process is likely to vary considerably across content domains, whether the event was or was not personally relevant, the typicality of the outcome in need of causal explanation, and on and on (see Anderson, Weiner, & Krull, in press).

B. CONTROLLABLE VERSUS UNCONTROLLABLE CAUSALITY

As already indicated, in the initial car crash vignette the damaged party implicitly assumed that the driver in the rear was the cause of the crash. In the absence of this belief, it is contended that inferences of responsibility, followed by shouting and confrontation, would not have followed. But human involvement is merely the first step in this process and does not necessarily result in an assignment of personal responsibility.

To clarify why personal causality is a necessary but not a sufficient antecedent for an assignment of responsibility, let us return to the automobile incident and add more information as well as a second *thought experiment*. Assume that the accident was indeed caused by the rear driver, but prior to the crash that person had a heart attack and fainted. This fact may not be available to the driver of the hit car. If it were, however, then it is postulated that a responsibility judgment would not be rendered.

In other situations, the uncontrollability of a cause, that is, its nonamenability to volitional change or willful regulation, is quite evident and known by others. For example, if failure at math is caused by lack of aptitude, or if obesity is caused by a thyroid problem, then the cause is located within the person but cannot be controlled. Teachers are likely to be aware of the low aptitude of a student, and parents are likely to be knowledgeable about the thyroid condition of their child. In these instances, it is proposed that the person will not be judged as responsible for a negative event or for a personal plight because accountability requires that the causes of these conditions can be willfully changed. Responsibility therefore is intimately linked with freedom and choice.

On the other hand, failing because of lack of effort, obesity due to overeating, and causing a car accident because of fast driving all can result in the assignment of responsibility because one can try or not, overeat or not, drive fast or slowly, and so on. Responsibility inferences thus necessitate *internal and controllable* causality. In the case of Magic Johnson, sexual behavior and drug use are perceived as under volitional control of the person. These behaviors are presumed to be freely chosen. For this reason, the responsibility judgments were high. Just as causal locus is known to be a basic property of phenomenal causality, so is causal controllability (see Weiner, 1986).

An inability to inhibit one's actions also can result in the cause of a negative event being perceived as uncontrollable and therefore the person is not judged as responsible. So-called crimes of passion produced judgments of nonresponsibility because it was presumed that the revengeful individual could not inhibit the retaliation (passion has the same linguistic root as passive—thus, one is "overcome with passion"). However, the supposed "irresistable impulse" was often used as a false pretext for very controllable acts against women!

1. The Causal Controllability of Stigmas

Evidence of the significance of perceptions of causal controllability (and by implication responsibility) is particularly manifest in the study of reactions to the stigmatized. A discussion of stigmas already has been introduced, for in the prior pages both AIDS and poverty were examined. These "social marks" are considered stigmas because they define one as "flawed, limited, spoiled, and generally undesirable" (Jones et al., 1984, p. 6). Stigmatization provides a good opportunity to study responsibility, for stigmatized persons such as the physically handicapped often raise the existential question of "Why me?", while observers inquire, "Why is he drinking so much?" or "What caused the nervous breakdown?"

In many instances, the stigma itself implies or connotes a cause, thus negating the need for further information. Along with two colleagues (Weiner, Perry, & Magnusson, 1988), we examined ratings of responsibility for a variety of stigmatizing conditions. The stigmas included in this research were AIDS, Alzheimer's disease, blindness, cancer, child abuser, drug addiction, heart disease, obesity, paraplegia, and Vietnam War syndrome. Responsibility judgments were made on 9-point scales anchored at the extremes with "not at all responsible" and "entirely responsible."

The data from one study reported by Weiner et al. (1988) are given in Table I. Table I shows that persons with Alzheimer's disease, blindness, cancer, paraplegia, Vietnam War syndrome and heart disease were judged as low on responsibility for these stigmas, whereas the remaining four stigmas (AIDS, child abuser, obesity, and drug addiction) elicited high responsibility inferences.

The relatively bifurcated set of responses revealed in Table I suggests that individuals are not held responsible for physical (somatic, biologically based) problems, but are inferred to be responsible for behaviorally based deficiencies (with the arguable exception of Vietnam War syndrome). Hence, psychologists study and help those perceived as personally responsible for their frailties; medical doctors, on the other hand, examine (for the most part) individuals who are not responsible for their exhibited flaws!

TABLE I
MEAN RESPONSIBILITY RATINGS
OF VARIOUS STIGMAS[a]

Stigma	Responsibility rating[b]
Alzheimer's disease	0.8[a]
Blindness	0.9[a]
Cancer	1.6[ab]
Paraplegia	1.6[ab]
Vietnam War syndrome	1.7[ab]
Heart disease	2.5[b]
AIDS	4.4[c]
Child abuser	5.2[c]
Obesity	5.3[c]
Drug abuse	6.5[d]

[a]Adapted from Weiner, Perry, and Magnusson (1988), p. 740.
[b]Means not sharing a superscript differ at the $p < .01$ level.

The fact that individuals are held accountable for some stigmas but not for others brings to mind a distinction between "sin" and "sickness" (see Weiner, 1993). Consider, for example, the following analysis by Sarbin (1990) of the defense provided an accused witch during the Middle Ages:

> Teresa of Avila (1515–1582) declared that the unwanted conduct, the reported visions, should be treated as if they were symptoms of illness . . . accounted for by natural causes. . . . Since the person is not the agent of action in sickness, he or she cannot be held responsible. . . . Teresa effectively sidetracked the Inquisitors from their usual practice of locating the cause of unauthorized visions in the visionary's intentional commerce with the devil. (p. 301)

Teresa clearly was arguing that the accused was "sick" rather than a "sinner." Thus, controllability-responsibility-sin tend to be linked, as do uncontrollability-not responsible-sickness (but see Brickman et al., 1982, for a distinction between onset and offset control that would take me too far afield here).

Although it is evident from Table I and the discussion that persons are judged as more responsible for some stigmas than for others, the Weiner et al. (1988) research thus far examined does not document that stigma controllability actually gives rise to inferences of responsibility. To provide such proof, a controllable versus an uncontrollable cause for the stigmas already listed was provided in another investigation reported by Weiner et al. (1988). For example, heart disease was described as due to leading an unhealthy lifestyle (causal controllability) or because of a genetic deficit (uncontrollable causality); obesity was characterized as due to overeating (controllable) or a thyroid dysfunction (uncontrollable), and so on. As anticipated, this information influenced the responsibility judgments in the anticipated manner: controllability information increased beliefs about responsibility, whereas uncontrollability information lessened these judgments.

However, not all stigmas are amenable to such alterations. For example, it is apparently not possible to convince others that Alzheimer's disease is controllable by the sick individual. There is sufficient media coverage for the public to realize that the cause of this illness is not subject to volitional alteration. In addition, the type of symptoms do not lend themselves to a controllable interpretation. Conversely, it is very difficult to bring others to the belief that beating a child is not controllable. Image reparation and escape from personal responsibility (a judgment of sin) is near impossible for this violation of conduct.

Just as was true for opinions about poverty, political ideology also influences perceptions regarding the controllability of a variety of stigmas. For example, conservatives are more likely to view homosexuality as a free choice or a preference than are liberals, who endorse biological causality and regard homosexuality as an "orientation" (an unusual position for an ideology focused on environmental causality; see Mallery, 1991; Whitley, 1990). Similar findings are reported in regards to obesity: Conservatives are more likely to ascribe obesity to overeating than are liberals (see Crandall, in press; Crandall & Biernat, 1990).

Scientific reports that brain areas are different for gays and lesbians than for heterosexuals, that the metabolism rates differ between obese and normal-weight individuals, and that alcoholism runs in families and thus has a genetic component therefore not only have implications for medical science, but they are of importance for perceptions of the public in regards to accusations of personal responsibility and sin. As Millman (1980) has commented:

> It is especially the case that an overweight woman is assumed to have a personal problem. She is stereotypically viewed as . . . out of control . . . being overweight is fundamentally viewed as an *intentional* act. In the case of women, being fat is considered such an obvious default or rebellion against being feminine that it is treated as a very significant, representative . . . characteristic. (p. xi)

C. MITIGATING CIRCUMSTANCES

To review the chapter thus far, it has been contended that two antecedents of perceived personal responsibility are internal causality and controllable causality. These, in turn, are influenced by many factors including the affective state of the target, the political ideology of the observer, the type of stigma under consideration, and specific causal information.

The above discussion assumes that causal controllability differs from personal responsibility. There are two major reasons for this distinction. First, controllability refers to the characteristics of a cause—causes, such as the absence of effort versus low ability, or sexual behavior versus a transfusion with contaminated blood—either are or are not subject to volitional alteration. Responsibility, on the other hand, refers to a judgment about a person: She "should" or "ought to have" done otherwise, such as trying harder, not engaging in unprotected sexual behavior, and the like. Hence, it is proposed that the responsibility process initially focuses on causal understanding and then shifts to, or provides evidence about, the person. In a manner akin to the well-known sequence going "from acts to dispositions" (Jones & Davis, 1965), here it is being suggested that thoughts progress from a causal understanding to an inference about the person. Responsibility therefore is not viewed as an attribution, as others, including Fincham and Shaver, have contended (see prior references). I prefer instead to use the terms assignment, inference, or judgment of responsibility, reserving attribution to an exclusive linkage with causality.

There is a second, more compelling reason to differentiate causal controllability from personal responsibility. Even if the cause of an aversive event is located within the person and that cause is deemed to be controllable, it still is possible that a judgment of responsibility will not be rendered. This is because there may be mitigating circumstances that negate moral responsibility. To mitigate means to soften or alleviate; hence, mitigating circumstances soften, alleviate, or totally eliminate responsibility judgments about a person.

In the auto accident scenario, consider now another thought experiment. In this situation, picture the rather far-fetched possibility that the driver bumped into your car because it was headed toward an embankment that could not be seen by you and this was her only means of stopping the car, thereby saving your life. I presume that this would result in the offset of a negative response from you, once this fact was accepted.

In other situations, mitigating circumstances are somewhat easier to introduce. Consider, for example, a business failure that is due to insufficient job-related effort. Inasmuch as goal-directed effort is located within a person and is controllable, the conditions have been met to reach a verdict of personal responsibility for the failure. But now assume that the lack of job effort was due to the competing time needed to care for a sick child. Because of this justification (the act serves a higher moral goal), an adult would not hold the person responsible for the business decline (it might be said that the personal role in producing the failure is discounted). But perhaps the most common example of a mitigating circumstance is when the police intentionally harm a person to protect others!

Mitigating circumstances also are present when there is incapacity on the part of the wrongdoer. Inability to comprehend the "wrongness" of an act or to discriminate right from wrong (which differs from an inability to control the behavior), as might be the case with very young children, the mentally handicapped, the insane, a "brainwashed" cult member, or even in the case of persons from other cultures maintaining contrary belief systems, could reduce or totally do away with judgments of responsibility. In cases of wills or contracts, these are termed "invalidating conditions." Thus, an adult does not hold an infant responsible for bed-wetting if that child could not prevent this (causal uncontrollability) or does not yet recognize this as "wrong" (mitigating circumstances). But if the child were older, then responsibility would be assigned. Evidence has been reported that some types of child abuse are instigated because the caretaker considers children responsible for acts they may not be able to control or do not perceive as transgressions (see, for example, McKinnon-Lewis, Lamb, Arbuckle, Baradaran, & Volling, 1992).

As might be imagined, what circumstances absolve one from responsibility because they are considered mitigating can be a difficult judgment to make, one hotly debated in courts of law as well as by philosophers. For example, assume that a social engagement is broken and the individual states that she must take her mother grocery shopping. Will the receiver of this information release the person from responsibility, or will it be thought that she should have managed her time better? As in legal contexts, it is difficult for the accused to prove the presence of mitigating circumstances that result in a social transgression. But the onus of proof is on the accused, or the defendant (whereas proving that the act was committed by the defendant is the goal of the prosecutor).

One controversy regarding mitigating circumstances that is of great public debate concerns alcoholism and being involved in an accident when drunk. Excessive alcoholic consumption is known to give rise to cognitive deficits, confusion, and thought disorder, all of which function to reduce perceptions of responsibility. MacAndrew and Edgerton (1969) have suggested that due to alcohol's effects, the drink, rather than the drinker, is considered to be the cause of untoward behavior. They go on to argue that disinhibited behavior is displayed because the drinker can "get away with it."

On the other hand, there is much evidence in everyday life that individuals want to increase (rather than decrease) the punishment of those committing crimes when under the influence of alcohol, as illustrated in the position of Mothers Against Drunk Drivers (known as MADD).

Thus, two opposing tendencies appear to be elicited if a crime or a social transgression is committed when the violator is drunk. In accord with this, some researchers report that punishment is reduced when a crime such as wife abuse is completed when the abuser is drunk (e.g., Richardson & Campbell, 1980),

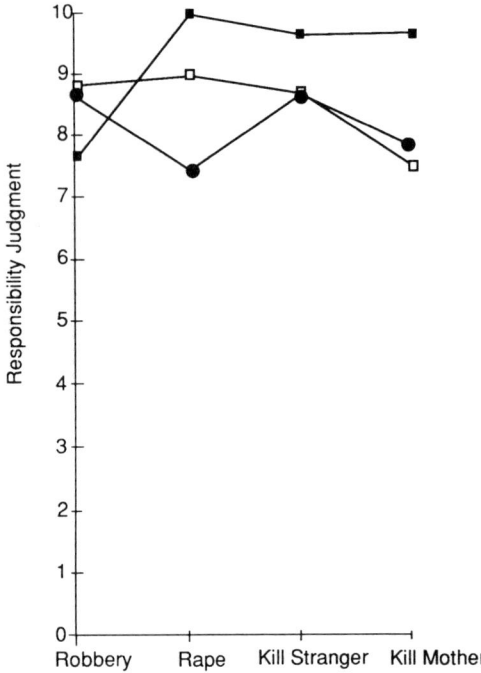

Fig. 6. Responsibility judgments as a function of the type of crime and type of mitigating circumstance (■, poverty; □, physical abuse; ●, sexual abuse). (From Li & Weiner, 1993.)

whereas others report increases in responsibility (e.g., Aramburu & Leigh, 1991). Thus, it is likely that the effects of intoxication on inferences of responsibility will depend on many factors such as the type of crime, pattern of drinking behavior, the perceived cause of drinking, and on and on (including, of course, the time in history of the action and the cultural context).

The above discussion seems to suggest that a mitigator in one situation will not necessarily act as a mitigator in a different context. In one study of responsibility (Li & Weiner, 1993), we presented vignettes of four crimes to our subjects: one of robbery, a second of rape, and a third and fourth vignette in which a stranger or a mother was killed. These crimes were factorially crossed with three potential mitigators: the person was in poverty, had been physically abused as a child by the mother, or was sexually abused by the mother.

Responsibility ratings in these conditions are shown in Figure 6. Figure 6 reveals that poverty lessens responsibility judgments when the crime is robbery, but not for killing or rape. On the other hand, if the crime is rape, then sexual abuse is most mitigating, whereas for murder both sexual and physical abuse somewhat relieve one of moral culpability. This latter finding substantiates what is apparent in current court cases, where the so-called abuse excuse is increasingly being put forth to absolve clients of responsibility for acts of violence against abusive spouses and parents.

Legal scholars (e.g., Morse, 1992) have argued that there are two basic categories of mitigators—diminished capacity and compulsion. However, compulsion appears (to me) to be a determinant of causal controllability and therefore conceptually may be useful to distinguish from mitigators, whereas other states of the person such as poverty also lessen judgments of responsibility for particular acts. It is evident that we are far from a complete understanding of the concept of mitigation!

D. SUMMARY AND UNSETTLED ISSUES

To review once again the discussion, it has been contended that responsibility judgments require human causality. In addition, the cause must be controllable for the person to be held responsible. And finally, responsibility can be reduced or entirely lifted if there are mitigating circumstances. The process activated in situations that give rise to judgments of responsibility therefore can be represented with a treelike diagram that includes a series of on–off judgments (see Figure 7). As shown in Figure 7, three separate stages are hypothesized to intervene between the onset of an event and the inference that another person is held accountable for that occurrence.

Although the process that has been depicted seems quite reasonable, a number

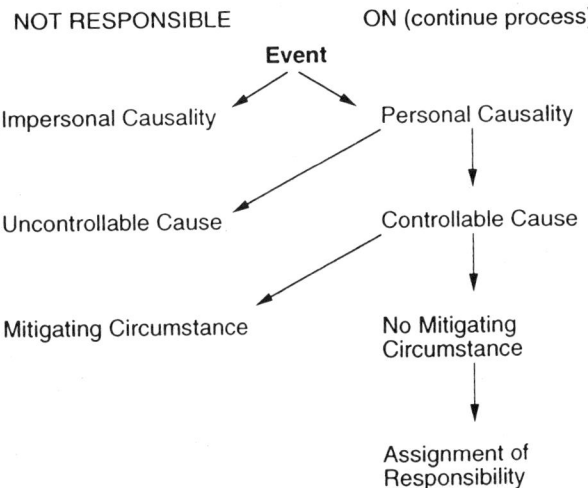

Fig. 7. The responsibility process.

of questions remain unanswered. One issue concerns whether this is an invariant sequence. Must individuals first seek out information about person versus situation causality, determine if the cause was or was not controllable, search for mitigating circumstances, and then decide about responsibility (with the stipulation that a negative answer at any stage terminates the process)? The answer to this is an unequivocal no. As already suggested, it is probable that responsibility is immediately presumed in the car crash context. Only later might this be changed if it is determined that a rock was causal, that the person had a heart attack prior to the accident so that the cause was not controllable, or that the crash was to prevent a more serious accident. Furthermore, one may already be aware that the person who performed a social transgression is a child, or mentally handicapped, so that mitigating circumstances are immediately available.

It also is evident that under some conditions personal causality and controllability are combined. For example, failure of a pupil may be ascribed to lack of effort (internal and controllable) or to lack of aptitude (internal and uncontrollable). However, such joint determination need not always be the case. For example, if an individual drops a cup at a party, it may only later be learned that she has hand tremors, which results in the cause being judged as internal and uncontrollable, in contrast to the prior inference of carelessness, which is internal but controllable.

It also might be argued that causal controllability is nothing other than a mitigating circumstance. However, in response to this position, given a mitigating circumstance, such as a moral justification for an act, there nonetheless still is control over the action and freedom of choice. In contrast, a student failing because of lack of aptitude has no such "freedom." One psychological issue this analysis raises is whether one failing at school because of time spent caring for a sick mother nonetheless had freedom of choice to do otherwise. Obviously, questions of sequence and the conceptual distinctions raised give rise to difficult, if not Herculean, problems to resolve.

Thus, what has been advanced is one possible sequence that is activated in some situations, most likely those in which controlled processing is operative. What does characterize a judgment of responsibility is that most of the component parts depicted in Figure 7 are included. The reader will note that I wrote "most of," for the degree of responsibility is influenced by still other factors. Foremost among these is whether the act was intentionally carried out or was due to negligence. It is well accepted that a purposeful action results in judgments of higher responsibility than an act caused by negligence or unintentional factors (as exemplified in the distinction between murder and manslaughter). I would most likely capture this central distinction within the umbrella of causal controllability. However, this as well as other determinants of judgments of responsibility must be ignored in this context, for it is time to move on to the second part of the title of this chapter—social motivation.

IV. Consequences of Judging Another Responsible

It was sometimes explicitly and sometimes implicitly implied that finding another responsible for being unhappy, poor, or having some other stigma has negative consequences for that individual. For example, it was suggested that the depressed might be avoided because they are held responsible for their unhappiness. In this section of the chapter, the emotional and behavioral significance of inferences of responsibility are addressed. In addition, the relations between responsibility judgments, feelings, and social action are considered. As was true of the responsibility process, answers to these motivational questions are complex, and more than one process is likely, depending on the particular circumstances under study. Following this, I examine account giving and strategies that reduce perceptions of personal responsibility.

A. EMOTIONAL REPERCUSSIONS

Imagine your feelings when an employee is not performing well because of a lack of trying, when your child is doing poorly in school because of a refusal to do homework, and when an athlete on your favorite team is "loafing" during a loss. Not only are there thoughts about controllability and responsibility, but there also are feelings of anger. You are mad at the lazy employee, the rebellious child, the lackadaisical athlete, and angry at Magic Johnson for engaging in promiscuous sex and at the daydreaming driver for bumping into the back of your car.

Of course, the more that you are involved with this individual or situation, the greater the anger is likely to be; there will be greater irritation with your child than with some distant athlete (see Brown & Weiner, 1984). But anger can be experienced even with minimal personal involvement, as evidenced by some of the reactions to Magic Johnson. As long as a moral code has been broken and an individual is perceived as responsible for some negative action or outcome, then anger may be experienced toward the "sinner."

Now imagine your feelings about the retarded child who fails an exam in spite of putting forth great effort, or your emotions about Magic Johnson if he had contracted AIDS because of a transfusion with contaminated blood. There is more than the dispassionate reaction that these individuals are not responsible for their plights. As shown in Figures 2 and 3, compassion and sympathy will be experienced. Because the emotions of anger and sympathy are so closely linked with perceptions of responsibility, one cannot discuss moral accountability and social reactions to this judgment without also considering these feelings.

1. Anger

As already suggested and documented in Figures 2 and 3, anger is generated by inferences about responsibility (see Averill, 1982, 1983; Frijda, 1986; Weiner, 1986). Anger is an accusation, or a value judgment, that follows from the belief that another person "could and should have done otherwise."

In one of many studies supporting this position, college students were asked to describe a recent situation in which they became angry (Weiner, Graham, & Chandler, 1982). The students most often reported that they felt angry when their boyfriend or girlfriend lied to them, when their roommate did not clean up a mess that was made, or when they could not study because an inconsiderate person made excessive noise. In all these contexts, there was controllable causality without apparent mitigating circumstances (i.e., the other was construed as responsible).

Anger can be altered if the person undergoing that feeling were to receive information that decreased other-perceptions of responsibility. Thus, one can be "talked into" or "talked out of" anger, which further reveals the close association between this emotion and specific thoughts. If, for example, it was learned that the roommate did not clean up the room because of an electricity blackout or broken vacuum cleaner (impersonal causality), because he became ill (lack of control), or because he had to drive a sick friend to the hospital (a mitigating justification), then anger would quite surely dissipate.

Anger, then, communicates that one "should have" done or not done something. The moral aspect of anger is even more evident when it is recognized that if the communicated anger is "accepted" or perceived as justified, then the recipient of this emotional message will feel guilty (see Weiner, 1986). This is because guilt follows from a self-perception of responsibility (Davitz, 1969), and at times is considered self-directed anger. This is one illustration of the interconnection between self- and other-directed emotions.

a. Unresolved Issues. A number of questions are associated with this conception of anger that are not readily resolvable. Is anger felt if and only if another is held responsible? This seems contradicted by the observation that dogs and young infants give the appearance of expressing anger, although they surely do not have the cognitive capacities to make responsibility judgments. In addition, it seems that people are often "mad" at their nonstarting cars or flat tires (see Berkowitz, 1993). Yet, given the definition of anger just proposed, cars and tires cannot be held responsible (as opposed to being causative) because they do not have agency.

The necessity of responsibility inferences for anger is a difficult issue and a definitive answer cannot be provided. On the one hand, it could be contended that dogs, young infants, and those about to remove a rock from the top of their car trunk do not feel (are not feeling) anger. Rather, they are experiencing or expressing some other emotion, such as frustration or unhappiness. These other emotions may be evoked by a threat in the environment, pain, the blockage of a desired goal, and so forth.

A different position is to accept that anger may be evoked by events and cognitions other than perceptions of responsibility. That is, responsibility is a sufficient but not a necessary condition to evoke anger. Hence, pain from a diaper pin or having a flat tire also can elicit anger.

Of these two alternatives, I am more attracted to the necessary (responsibility must be an antecedent) rather than to the sufficient (responsibility may be the antecedent) explanation. This position is not based on empirical data (although reports of anger do typically include situations in which responsibility inferences are evident). Rather, I consider this to be a more parsimonious path for the direction and the organization of the field of emotion. The only way to settle this issue empirically is to identify the criteria that differentiate affects such as anger, frustration, and unhappiness from one another. Then what contextual and cognitive antecedents are linked with which affects can be determined.

But if someone is responsible for personal harm, must the wronged party feel angry? Again a definitive answer cannot be supplied, and at least two points of view are feasible. On the one hand, it could be contended that we may learn to "turn the other cheek" so that either no emotion is experienced or perhaps some other affect, even compassion, is felt toward the responsible person. Plato accomplished this by considering all crimes against others a product of disease, thus freeing the criminals from responsibility (they are sick rather than sinners) and reducing anger. However, one might also accept that others are responsible yet experience no anger.

Conversely, it might be claimed that even though compassion is expressed following volitional harm by another, the original or initial feeling nonetheless was anger. However, this atavistic reaction, which is likely to be a product of our evolutionary heritage (Fox, 1992; Trivers, 1971), can be masked or superceded by other learned reactions. Given this interpretation, a response of anger must follow an inference of responsibility for a personally relevant negative event, although that reaction may be transient and need not be displayed nor perhaps consciously experienced.

My position on this issue, and again it is without empirical confirmation, is that one indeed can learn not to feel angry following an assignment of responsibility to another for a personally relevant aversive outcome. But this is quite atypical, perhaps evident only among our most religious people.

2. Sympathy and the Ethos of Pathos

In contrast to the linkage between responsibility and anger, the absence of responsibility given the personal plight of another is associated with sympathy and the related emotions of pity and compassion. Thus, a person confined within a totalitarian state (impersonal causality), failure of another because of a physical handicap (uncontrollable causality), or lack of effort because one has to take care of a sick child (a mitigating justification) are prototypical predicaments that elicit sympathy inasmuch as the person is perceived as not responsible for his or her plight.

There has been relatively little research on this emotion, although there are some pertinent data. For example, Weiner et al. (1982) asked college students to report instances in their past when pity and sympathy were experienced. The most frequently reported contexts were when observing others with handicaps and personal interactions with the very aged. More broadly conceived, Wispé (1991) speculated that "one will sympathize more with a brave sufferer, in a good cause, in which one's afflictions are beyond one's control" (p. 134).

Inasmuch as sympathy and pity are evoked by the absence of responsibility, if these emotions are communicated to others, then the receiver of this affective message is led to believe that the negative condition in which he or she is in is one for which responsibility cannot be assumed (see Graham, 1984, 1991). That is, the plight is not amenable to personal intervention and change. This in itself is aversive.

As in the discussion of anger, a number of unanswered questions can be raised regarding this conception. It is uncertain if lack of responsibility is a necessary antecedent of sympathy, and it is not known if, given lack of responsibility for a negative personal plight, sympathy must be experienced. For the purposes of this chapter, answers to these questions are not necessary. What is essential is the uncontestable fact that perceptions of responsibility and nonresponsibility for events and plights have respective linkages to the emotions of anger and sympathy. This is central in the analysis of social conduct.

B. FROM EVENT TO ACTION: THE MOTIVATIONAL PROCESS

I now will consider two sequences that illustrate the psychological process and the mechanisms proposed to intervene between the onset of an event, such as a school failure or a car crash, and the behavioral reactions to that event, such as helping the failing student or shouting at the driver of the car in the rear.

Consider, for example, two students who are failing in school. Following failure at the exam, the teacher will search for information that allows him or her to infer the causes that gave rise to these outcomes. In achievement contexts, two personal causes are particularly dominant—ability and effort. Assume that, on the basis of evidence that is available such as past success history, the teacher reasons that one student failed because of lack of effort. This cause is construed as personal and controllable, inasmuch as effort can be volitionally altered. Because of these characteristics, the student may be held responsible. The teacher might then have a conference with this student to ascertain if mitigating circumstances, such as the need to be earning money at a job, might be operating that absolve the student from all or some of the responsibility. Perhaps the pupil might offer an excuse, such as the noise in his home (external causality) or an inability to understand the material (personal but uncontrollable). If there are no apparent mitigating circumstances and the excuses are not accepted, then the teacher will be angry and offer no sympathy.

It is postulated here that anger provides a bridge between thinking and conduct. Anger directs the experiencer of this emotion to "eliminate" the wrongdoer—to go toward that person and retaliate with some form of aggressive action, or go away from that person to withhold some positive good (see Averill, 1983). Anger therefore is a "goad" that pushes the individual to undertake actions. The anger also has the function of "frightening" the offender by communicating potential harm. And the punishment that is driven by anger provides both the doer and onlookers with a "moral education," as well as decreasing the likelihood that the "sin" will again be committed. Hence, the action driven by the anger is utilitarian and rehabilitative, two of the major positions in the philosophy of punishment.

The sequence that has been reviewed briefly may be outlined as follows:

Event (exam failure) → Causal search → Causal decision (lack of effort) → Causal properties (personal and controllable) → Inference of responsibility (responsible) → Emotional reactions (anger, no sympathy) → Behavioral response (punish)

Alternately, the teacher may conclude that this student is without aptitude. Or, perhaps the mitigating circumstance of the need to work is accepted. Assuming that lack of aptitude is the inferred cause, then sympathy is elicited because this cause is internal but uncontrollable. In contrast to anger, which is presumed to evoke aversive social responses, it is contended that pity and sympathy give rise to positive social behaviors (see review in Eisenberg, 1986). As noted by Trivers (1971), "sympathy has been selected to motivate altruistic behaviors" (p. 49). This sequence may be summarized as follows:

Event (exam failure) → Causal search → Causal decision (lack of aptitude) → Causal properties (personal and uncontrollable) → Inference of responsibility (not responsible) → Emotional reactions (sympathy, no anger) → Behavioral response (help).

Similar analyses can readily be supplied to explain reactions given in a car crash. If the driver of the front car notices that a rock rather than the rear driver is causal, then a responsibility judgment will not be rendered or, if already reached, there will be an offset of this judgment. This will then be followed by the nullification of anger and shouting. In a similar manner, if the driver is aware that the driver in the rear had a heart attack, then this same sequence is postulated to transpire. On the other hand, if the driver in the rear is a teenager, wearing headphones, and shrugging his shoulders as you advance toward his car, then perceptions of responsibility, anger, and shouting surely will prevail.

1. Alternative Motivational Sequences

Of course, other models are possible in addition to those described above (see Reisenzein, 1986). In the prior discussion, it was presumed that thoughts about responsibility give rise to affect, which then generates action. This assumes that emotions are proximal determinants of conduct and that thoughts are distal influences. That is, what is thought determines feelings, and what is felt determines action.

Alternatively, one might postulate that thinking determines both feeling and acting, and that emotions have no direct influence on action; or that both thinking and feeling have independent and proximal influences on behavior; or that an eliciting stimulus itself affects the behavioral response, without mediation of attributions and affects; and so on.

Just as with the responsibility process, it is quite likely that there is no "one" motivational sequence, but rather that this varies as a function of many factors, including the amount of emotionality that the event elicits, the centrality of the event, and on and on. I will now examine the viability of this conceptual approach in three contexts: help giving (going toward), aggression (going against), and rejection (going away from).

V. Help Giving (Altruism)

A number of investigations have demonstrated directly or indirectly that perceptions of responsibility for a need of help influence whether a needy person is aided or neglected (see review in Schmidt & Weiner, 1988). In addition, perhaps more than any other area within the field of social motivation, investigators of helping behavior have documented that emotions play an important motivational role (see review in Carlson & Miller, 1987).

Consider, for example, an experiment by Schmidt and Weiner (1988). In that study, subjects were given the following scenario (based on a "field" study by Barnes, Ickes, & Kidd, 1979):

> At about 1:00 in the afternoon you are walking through campus and a student comes up to you. . . . He asks if you would lend him the class notes from the meetings last week. He indicates that he needs the notes because he was having difficulty with his eyes, a change in glasses was required, and during the week he had difficulty seeing because of eye drops and other treatments. You notice that he is wearing especially dark glasses and has a patch covering one eye. (p. 615) [Alternate condition: He says he needs the notes because he went to the beach instead of class]."

These two conditions capture an internal uncontrollable cause (eye problems) and an internal controllable cause (not trying).

In addition, each of these conditions was accompanied by experimental instructions that altered the set or attention focus of the subjects. Prior to reading the vignette, the subjects were instructed to pay attention to the facts ("try to be as objective as possible"), versus emotional self-focus ("imagine how you would react in this situation") and emotional other-focus ("imagine how the other person feels"). After reading each scenario, the subjects rated the controllability of the cause of the need (and, by implication in this context, the responsibility of the needy person), affective reactions of anger and sympathy (pity), and the likelihood of help giving.

The left columns in Table II show the correlations between the responsibility, affective, and behavioral judgments. It is immediately evident that in all conditions (including the control group) the identical pattern prevailed—perceived responsibility related positively to anger and negatively to sympathy; responsibility and anger were negatively associated with help; and sympathy related positively to helping judgments.

Turning next to the within-condition path analyses shown in the right-hand columns, Table II documents that in all four conditions there were significant paths or relations between affective reactions and judgments of help, but not from controllability (here considered also as responsibility) to aid. A multigroup path analysis combining the data in all four conditions ($N = 496$) is shown in Figure 8. It is quite evident from Figure 8 that a responsibility-emotion-action conception is strongly supported by these data—feelings (anger and sympathy) are tied to causal beliefs, and in turn give rise to intended action (also see Betancourt, 1990; Dooley, in press; Reisenzein, 1986; Weiner & Graham, 1989). There also was a direct path from the eliciting stimulus to behavior capturing the nonattributional determinants of help giving.

Conceptually similar studies also were conducted by Zucker and Weiner (1993). In that research, college students and adult respondents classified as liberals and conservatives rated thirteen dominant causes for their importance in

TABLE II
CORRELATIONS AND STRUCTURAL PATHS IN FOUR EXPERIMENTAL CONDITIONS[a]

Condition	N	Correlation coefficient[b]					Path coefficient		
		R × A	R × S	R × H	A × H	S × H	R → H	A → H	S → H
Control	127	.41	−.58	−.37	−.55	.56	NS[c]	−.48	.55
Self-focus	126	.28	−.70	−.25	−.64	.36	NS	−.67	.14
Other-focus (empathy)	123	.38	−.62	−.23	−.58	.41	NS	−.62	.37
Objective	120	.33	−.66	−.29	−.54	.52	NS	−.49	.52
X̄	—	.35	−.64	−.29	−.58	.47	NS	−.55	.42

[a]Adapted from Schmidt and Weiner, 1988, p. 617.
[b]R = responsibility; A = anger; S = sympathy; H = help.
[c]NS = not significant.

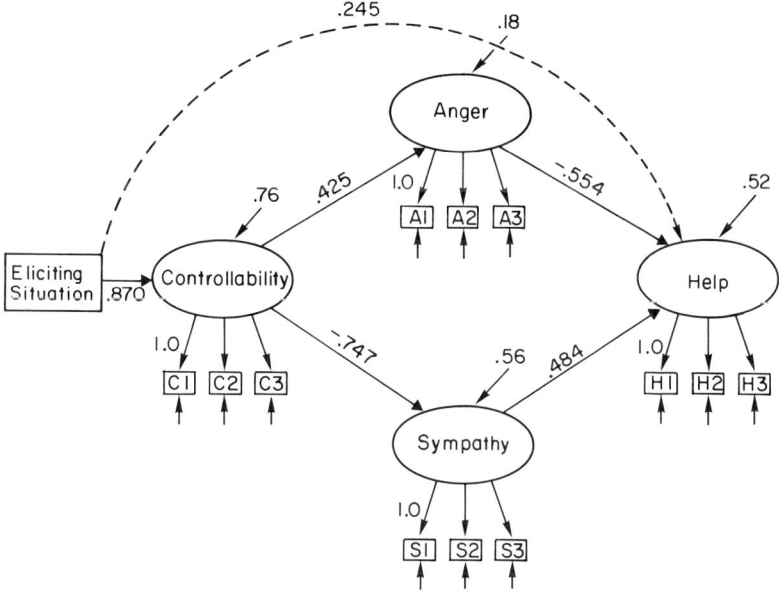

Fig. 8. Structural model combining all subjects in all conditions relating the situation, causal controllability, and affective reactions to judgments of help. (From Schmidt & Weiner, *Personality and Social Psychology Bulletin,* **14** 610–621, copyright ©, 1988, p. 618. Reprinted by permission of Sage Publications, Inc.)

giving rise to poverty. In addition, guided by the responsibility inference process as well as the proposed models of social motivation, subjects indicated how controllable was poverty, the degree to which the poor are personally responsible for their problems, affects of pity and anger toward these individuals, and judgments of help giving. Two types of help were distinguished that varied in the degree of individual involvement ("How likely would you be to help those who are poor for this reason?" and "How deserving are they of governmental assistance, such as welfare?").

Figure 9 shows the structural equation analysis of these data. Figure 9 reveals that conservatism relates negatively to the endorsement of social (uncontrollable) determinants of poverty and positively to beliefs about individual controllable causality, as often has been reported and was discussed earlier in this chapter (see Skitka & Tetlock, 1992; Williams, 1984). Social causes, in turn, are negatively associated with judgments of personal responsibility (inasmuch as they are impersonal), whereas individual controllable causes relate positively to inferences of responsibility, inasmuch as the person can choose otherwise. Thus, for example, the more one endorses "laziness" as a cause of poverty, and the less one agrees with the statement that "the government does not provide jobs," then the

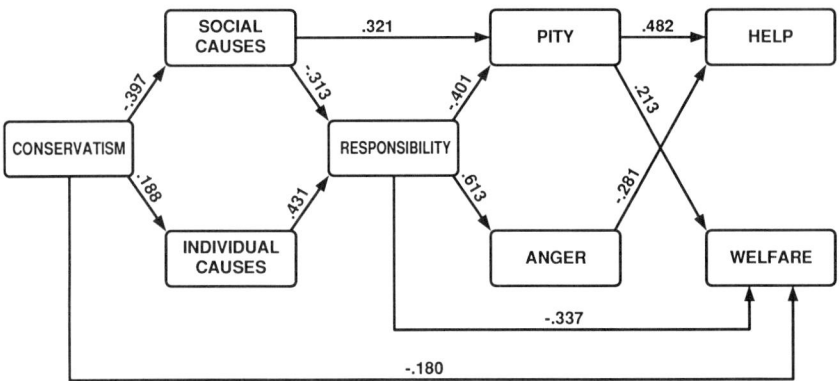

Fig. 9. Structural equation model of help and welfare. (From Zucker & Weiner, 1993.)

greater the perceived personal responsibility for poverty. Responsibility, in turn, correlates negatively with pity and positively with anger (also see Skitka & Tetlock, 1992). Furthermore, pity increases personal help, whereas anger decreases this helping judgment. Hence, this set of data is quite consistent with the findings reported by Schmidt and Weiner (1988).

However, the determinants of the welfare judgments tell a somewhat different story. In addition to welfare being augmented by pity, Figure 9 reveals that endorsing welfare relates negatively to both conservatism and perceived responsibility. That is, thoughts even more than affect directly influence action. It therefore appears that the less one is directly involved in an action or relates this action to the self, then the greater the contribution of "cold" thoughts to the intended behavior. Conversely stated, the more that one is personally involved in help giving (and, by implication, in other social behaviors as well), the greater the influence of emotions in guiding conduct. Thus, as already indicated, just as there is no single "responsibility process," there may be no single "motivational process." However, for both I assume that the basic components addressed here—personal causality, controllability, mitigating circumstances, personal responsibility, pity, and anger—are included in the determinants of behavior. This position has the advantage of not requiring a rigid sequence that is invariant over situations, yet it does not forego theoretical parsimony.

VI. Aggression

Just as I was neither smart nor foolish enough to think that I have proposed a general theory of helping, so in this section of the chapter I am not outlining a general theory of aggression. It is known that helping is determined by a multitude of factors, ranging from the number of others available to help to the genetic relationship between the help giver and the recipient of help. In a similar manner, it is known that aggression is determined by an equally wide number of factors, including environmental temperature and population density. Because of the great diversity and number of antecedents of social motivation, I do not believe it is possible to construct a viable theory of helping or aggression. Rather, an alternative theoretical route is to ask if there is a mechanism or process that can be applied to a variety of motivational phenomena. This process then becomes the basis for a general theory, although it is acknowledged that only a small percentage of the variance of any social behavior can be accounted for by that process.

Guided by this line of reasoning, I believe that some types of hostile behavior are subject to the same conceptual analysis as helping behavior. The general motivational process in this case begins with an apparently hostile action, such as being shoved while waiting in line. This person then determines if the "shover" should be held responsible for this action. Hence, it is determined (either with automatic or controlled processes), whether the act was caused by the other person, was under personal control, and was without mitigating factors. The other person would not be held responsible if the shove was caused by crowded conditions (impersonal causality), because of a leg problem that did not permit the accused to stand in one place (uncontrollability), or if in that person's culture shoving was considered a playful game (a mitigating circumstance). As already discussed, responsibility for a negative action then gives rise to anger, which promotes retaliation (see Ferguson & Rule, 1983). This motivational process in the domain of aggression can be depicted as follows:

Aversive (hostile) action → Inference of responsibility → Anger →
Aggressive retaliation (or reactive aggression)

In a study guided by this line of reasoning, Betancourt and Blair (1992) presented subjects scenarios of a "rock throwing" contest. In one condition, the losing contestant appears to intentionally throw a rock that breaks the windshield of the car of the wining thrower; in a second condition the rock misses the target and veers to the side, also breaking the windshield of this competitor. Subjects then rated the controllability and intentionality of the action (indicators of responsibility), the amount of anger, sympathy, and pity they experienced when reading the story, and what their most likely response to the instigation would have been.

A simplified path analysis of these data is shown in Figure 10. Figure 10 reveals that thoughts both directly influence affect and behavior (aggression), and affects also directly determine aggressive retaliation. In this case, the magnitude of the responsibility effect exceeds that of the contribution of affect in predicting reported aggression. To repeat what has been stated earlier, the relative effects of

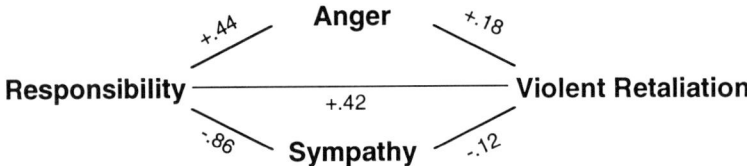

Fig. 10. Simplified structural equation model relating perceptions of responsibility and affect to aggression. (Data from Betancourt & Blair, 1992.)

thinking and feeling on action will be determined by any number of factors, many of which remain unspecified and unknown.

A. AGGRESSION AND AT-RISK CHILDREN

These ideas also have been applied to the study of aggressive children, or children at risk for crime and other negative actions when they become adults. A number of investigators have reported that aggressive children display a marked bias to infer hostile intent (responsibility) following an other-instigated negative event. This bias is particularly in evidence when the cause of that event is ambiguous (see Dodge & Crick, 1990; Graham, Hudley, & Williams, 1992; Hudley & Graham, 1993). This would then produce anger and, in turn, aggression.

In one test of this hypothesis, Graham et al. (1992) had both aggressive and nonaggressive children respond to vignettes that depicted individuals as varying in their responsibility for harming another (damaging a school assignment). The adolescent aggressive and nonaggressive boys then indicated whether the harmdoer engaged in this action "on purpose," the amount of anger they would experience had they actually been in that situation, and the likelihood that they would engage in aggressive retaliation.

Consistent with the hypothesis, the aggressive children perceived the action as more intentionally undertaken, particularly when the cause was ambiguous, reported more anger, and also indicated that they would be more likely to retaliate aggressively than would the nonaggressive respondents. Furthermore, a structural equation analysis strongly supported the position that thoughts about the cause of the action relate to anger, and anger is directly linked with action.

VII. Rejection

Two broad categories of behavior have been examined: going toward (help giving) and going against (aggression). I now turn to the third behavior of the

Karen Horney taxonomy—going away from (rejection). Of course, it would be shocking to the reader if I did not argue that the responsibility–affect mediators championed thus far are again applicable.

Research conducted by Coie and his colleagues (e.g., Coie, Dodge, & Coppotelli, 1982; Coie & Kupersmidt, 1983) has shown that children who are unpopular tend to be aggressive, unattractive, or socially withdrawn. However, although children tend not to accept peers who display nonnormative characteristics, their reactions do vary according to the type of deviance. Children displaying aggressive, antisocial, or hyperactive behaviors are judged as least liked, whereas the physically handicapped, mentally disturbed, and socially withdrawn are apt to be "preferred" among the deviant groups (see Sigelman & Begley, 1987). Juvonen (1991, 1992) therefore contended that rejection also is determined by peers' reactions to deviant characteristics, and particularly to their beliefs about responsibility.

To examine this hypothesis, Juvonen (1991, 1992) gathered peer-nomination data to identify deviant and rejected sixth-grade children. Then these sixth-grade respondents (Americans in one sample, Finnish children in another) rated how responsible the deviant classmates were for their differences, the positive (sympathy and pity) and negative (anger and irritation) affects that they felt toward these deviants, and how willing they would be to provide various types of social support.

The findings were consistent with the data that already have been reported. That is, the greater the perceived responsibility, the less the sympathy and the more the anger. In addition, with more sympathy, more support would be given and the other was rejected less, whereas with greater anger, less social support would be given and the tendency to reject was greater. Finally, affect but not inferences about responsibility linked directly with social support and rejection (see Figure 11).

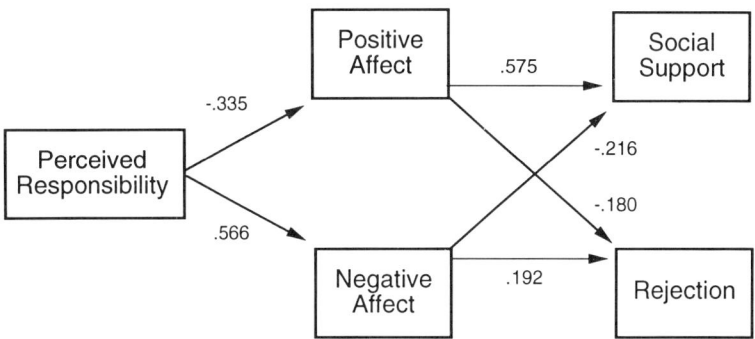

Fig. 11. Simplified structural equation model relating perceptions of responsibility for deviance to affect and both social support and rejection. (Adopted from Juvonen, 1991.)

Examining the specific categories of deviance, Juvonen (1991, 1992) reported that peers were perceived as responsible for bragging, rule breaking, and hyperactivity, and that these categories of deviance (sin) elicit anger and dislike. On the other hand, peers were perceived as least responsible for deviances of shyness and physical anomalies (e.g., epilepsy), and these conditions (sicknesses) evoked sympathy and little anger.

VIII. Impression Management (Excuse Giving)

Being responsible for a negative event has damaging consequences. Failure at an achievement task ascribed to lack of effort generates reprimand; stigmatization due to overeating, excessive drinking, sexual permissiveness, lack of financial care, and the like promote adverse reactions from others; unhappy mood states can give rise to criticism even by family members if it is believed that the depressed person is "not trying" to get better; being perceived as responsible for a hostile event can generate aggressive retaliation; and so on. It is reasonable to assume that the charged party wants to avoid such inferences, and does not want to be judged as responsible for failing at an exam, or for bumping into the rear of another car. What strategies are available, what techniques of impression management can be used, that will result in a lessening or the offset of assignments of responsibility?

Figure 7, which outlined the (or *a*) responsibility process, provides a foundation for the classification of accounts (see Table III). The responsibility process is initiated by a negative occurrence. First, then, the person can deny the very event or the meaning of that event for which she is being held accountable. It could be effective to explain to one's parents that, for example, a math test was not taken or that it was not failed (when, in fact, the test results were poor), that the

TABLE III
THE RESPONSIBILITY PROCESS RELATED TO STRATEGIES THAT PROMOTE NONRESPONSIBILITY

Stage in the responsibility process	Strategy
Negative outcome occurs	Disavow outcome (denial)
Outcome ascribed by others to the self	Ascribe to external factors (excuse)
Outcome ascribed by others to causes controllable by the self	Ascribe to uncontrollable causes (excuse)
No perceived mitigating circumstances	Indicate mitigating circumstances (excuse and justification)
Responsibility inference	Apology and confession

allowance was saved and not spent foolishly (when indeed the latter was the case), or that the unkempt appearance that characterizes oneself is fashionable in school and is not considered repugnant by others. This strategy often is referred to as denial, which in this case is one type of lie.

Continuing with the responsibility process as repeated in Table III, one might admit that the aversive outcome did take place, but that it was caused by an external agent or circumstances rather than by oneself. That is, there was no personal agency. For example, it could be conveyed that teacher bias was the cause of test failure or that a prank in the lunchroom or a malfunctioning juice machine is the reason that one's clothes are dirty. In these instances, the act or state is acknowledged but the explanation of it is altered from the true cause (self) to an external source.

Yet another tactic to reduce responsibility perceptions and, by implication, anger, is to accept that the cause of the negative event was the self but to convey that this cause was not controllable. For example, exam failure could be said to be due to lack of math aptitude rather than to the absence of effort, or that the poor attire is caused by a lack of native ability to have a "good eye" for clothes rather than sloppiness or lack of care. Ascriptions shifted from the true causes of lack of studying and personal negligence to external or internal factors not controllable by the self often are referred to as excues (ex = from, cuse = cause, or from one cause to another).

Still further in the responsibility process, it can be accepted that the cause of a negative outcome was due to internal, controllable factors yet the presence of mitigating circumstances are communicated. Telling a teacher that failure to study for a test because of the need to provide aid to a sick mother illustrates one such mitigator. As already indicated, this often is referred to as a justification—a higher moral goal was served. Other mitigators, such as inability to differentiate right from wrong, can be considered excuses.

Finally, even if self-responsibility for an action is admitted, there are still strategic devices used to foster positive impression management. These include apology and confession. Confession represents a paradox in that the individual publicly accepts responsibility for an act, yet this apparently decreases anger and punishment. The relations between the responsibility process and strategies or maneuvers used to "repair the broken and restore the estranged" (Scott & Lyman, 1968, p. 46) are summarized in Table III.

It should be noted that if the communication strategies that individuals use fit within the categories portrayed in the responsibility process (Figure 7), then some understanding of this process is part of naive psychology, or is shared by the "person on the street." It could then be said that the appropriate tactics, as well as some of the scientific analysis, are "common sense."

A number of research investigations indeed confirm that persons do understand the rules regarding inferences of responsibility and in many instances act to

TABLE IV
CATEGORIES OF EXPLANATIONS AND FREQUENCIES AS A FUNCTION
OF THE EXPERIMENTAL CONDITION[a]

	Experimental condition		
	Bad	Good	Any
Categories of explanation	($n = 17$)	($n = 18$)	($n = 19$)
Sudden obligation	1	6	3
Transportation, distance, space	1	5	3
School demand	0	4	5
Negligence	7	0	2
Free choice	6	0	0
Something missing	1	2	2
Miscellaneous or multiple categories	1	1	4

[a] From Weiner, Amirkhan, Folkes, and Verette (1987), p. 321.

reduce how responsible others perceive them to be. Here I will focus attention only on excuse giving, leaving aside denial, justification, and confession (although these are common tactics used to diffuse responsibility).

In one pertinent investigation reported by Weiner, Amirkhan, Folkes, and Verette (1987), subjects were detained by the experimenter so that they would arrive late for an experiment in which another subject was participating. In three experimental conditions, the instructions to the tardy subject were to (1) give an excuse that was "bad"; (2) give a "good" excuse; and (3) give any excuse.

Table IV shows the excuses that were communicated. When asked to give a bad excuse, negligence ("I forgot") and free choice ("I stopped to talk to some friends") were dominant. In these instances, there is personal causality, controllability, and no mitigating circumstances. It might be thought that negligence or forgetting are considered uncontrollable. But, to use a phrase from Chief Justice Holmes, a "person of ordinary intelligence and reasonable prudence" would be expected not to forget about the experiment; that is, forgetting tends to be perceived as controllable. Thus, responsibility is not absolved given that explanation.

On the other hand, for the good excuses the subjects communicated transportation problems ("The bus was late," an external cause), a school demand ("My midterm exam took longer than expected," also an external cause), or a sudden obligation ("I had to take my mother to the hospital," a mitigating circumstance). When asked to give any excuse, the pattern was very much like the good excuses.

TABLE V
EXCUSE CLASSIFICATION AS A FUNCTION OF EXPERIMENTAL CONDITION[a]

Excuse classification	Experimental condition		
	Bad excuse	Good excuse	Any excuse
Not responsible	2	15	11
Accept responsibility	13	0	2

[a]Data from Weiner, Amirkhan, Folkes, and Verette, 1987.

These excuses were then classified according to whether the participant had accepted or denied personal responsibility. As documented in Table V, the function of a good excuse is to deny responsibility.

In other research, my associates and I have examined excuse giving with a different methodology. In three investigations, we asked the research participants (college students) to recall a time when they gave an excuse and to report this incident as well as the real (withheld) cause and the falsely communicated cause (the excuse; Weiner et al., 1987; Weiner, Figueroa-Munoz, & Kakihara, 1991). In each of these studies, groupings were made of the withheld reasons and the excuses. Eight categories were sufficient to describe virtually all of the causes (see Table VI). Considering first the withheld or true causes, Table VI reveals that

TABLE VI
CONTENT OF TRUE (WITHHELD) AND FALSE CAUSES (EXCUSES) IN THREE INVESTIGATIONS (%)[a]

Content categories	Weiner et al., 1991 (Exp. 1)		Weiner et al., 1991 (Exp. 2)		Weiner et al., 1987	
	True	Excuse	True	Excuse	True	Excuse
Parents	1	7	0	0	0	14
Friends	4	7	0	0	0	6
Illness	0	21	4	16	0	5
Other commitment	2	24	4	3	1	19
Transportation	0	2	2	16	0	11
Work or study	2	15	4	27	0	12
Forget or negligence	12	2	28	6	34	8
Intent	70	2	53	1	60	1
Misc.	9	24	5	0	5	24

[a]Data from Weiner, Amirkhan, Folkes, and Verette, 1987; Weiner, Figueroa-Munoz, and Kakihara, 1991.

across three studies, 85% of the reasons that were withheld were forgetting or negligence or intentional ("I did not want to . . ."). Table VI also reveals that the communicated causes fall within six general categories: parents ("My parents would not let me go"), friends ("I had to help Mary"), illness, other commitments ("I had to take my mother to the airport"), transportation problems, and work or study ("My boss made me work overtime"). The excuses given are rather mundane, most likely out of fear that any unusual explanation will not be believed, and they predominantly convey external, uncontrollable causality.

It should be recognized that this approach to excuse giving differs from the position of Snyder and Higgins (1988). They define excuses as "the motivated process of shifting causal attributions for negative personal outcomes from sources that are relatively more central to the person's self to sources that are relatively less central" (p. 23). Thus, the cause of a negative event is shifted from personal to impersonal causality, which is Stage 1 of the responsibility process that has been outlined.

On the other hand, if the excuse goal is to free oneself from responsibility (rather than to protect self-esteem), then a shift within internal causality from controllability to uncontrollability also is quite functional. Thus, even though perceptions of ability may be very central to the self, an excuse to the teacher that "I cannot" often is communicated (see Juvonen & Murdock, 1993). Furthermore, I tend to view excuses as quite conscious *social* tactics, rather than unconscious mechanisms that are akin to defense mechanisms (see Weiner, 1992b).

A. AT-RISK CHILDREN AND EXCUSES

Earlier in the chapter, aggression was examined from a responsibility perspective. Another approach to the understanding of aggression in children derived from the present conceptual analysis relates to their knowledge about the logic and significance of excuses. My colleagues and I (Caprara, Pastorelli, & Weiner, 1994) tested at-risk (for aggression) and normal functioning children in an investigation concerned with excuse giving. Scenarios were presented that depicted broken social contracts. For example, in one vignette a boy did not show up at a friend's house when he had promised to do so (from Weiner & Handel, 1985). Controllable and uncontrollable reasons were provided for the transgression (e.g., "He watched TV instead" versus "His mother would not let him go"). The subjects then rated the extent to which the victim of this social transgression would be angry if these causes were known to him or her. The children also were asked if they would or would not reveal these causes.

Following the logic of the prior discussion, controllable causes were expected to elicit anger and therefore would not be revealed, whereas uncontrollable causes were not expected to evoke anger and therefore should be communicated.

TABLE VII
RATED ANTICIPATED ANGER AND INTENTION TO WITHHOLD OR REVEAL THE CAUSE OF A SOCIAL TRANSGRESSION AS A FUNCTION OF THE CONTROLLABLITY OF THE CAUSE AND THE SUBJECT POPULATION (AT-RISK VS. NORMAL CHILDREN)[a]

	At-risk children		Normal children	
	Controllable cause	Uncontrollable cause	Controllable cause	Uncontrollable cause
Anticipated anger	3.82	2.38	3.39	1.29
Intention to reveal	3.95	5.13	3.57	5.36

[a]Data from Caprara, Pastorelli, and Weiner (1994).

However, we wondered if this pattern would be less in evidence for the at-risk children. This deficiency could then contribute to aggression inasmuch as the at-risk children would be, for example, more likely to expect others to respond inappropriately with anger and would be more likely to communicate controllable causes that do arouse anger. Such beliefs and behaviors could then initiate a sequence of aggression.

Table VII shows the mean anticipated anger and revealing judgments as a function of the subject population and the controllability of the cause of the broken social contract. Examining first judgments of anticipated anger, the data replicate the established finding that controllable causes are perceived to elicit more anger than uncontrollable causes of a broken social contract. In addition, there is an effect of subject population, with at-risk children anticipating more anger than do normal children. Hence, not only are these children more aggressive, but they also expect others to be aggressive. Of most importance, there was a Cause × Population interaction. This interaction is traced to the finding that, given controllable causes, the difference in anticipated anger between the two subject populations is relatively equal (3.82 versus 3.39). On the other hand, given uncontrollable causes of the social transgression, there was much greater anticipated anger by the at-risk (2.38) than by the normal children (1.29). Hence, at-risk children have comparatively incorrect expectations regarding the actions of others when the excuse is "good" in that it lessens personal responsibility.

Turning next to the data regarding excuse revealing, also shown in Table VII, there again is a highly significant effect due to the transgression attribution—controllable causes were more likely to be judged as being withheld than uncontrollable causes (or, stated in the converse manner, uncontrollable causes were more likely to be revealed than controllable causes). But at-risk children were marginally more likely to reveal the controllable reasons than were the normal children (3.95 vs. 3.57), whereas the normal children were more likely to reveal uncontrollable causes of the transgression than were the at-risk children (5.36 vs. 5.13). This interaction is consistent with the more adaptive picture that has been painted of normal than the at-risk children (also see Graham, Weiner, & Benesh-Weiner, in press).

In sum, it was documented by Caprara et al. (1994) that at-risk children anticipate more anger from others, particularly when the cause of the transgression is uncontrollable and therefore not the "fault" of the transgressor. In addition, there was a tendency for children at-risk for aggression to reveal more controllable or "bad" reasons and fewer of the uncontrollable or "good" reasons than the normal functioning children. Thus, at-risk children appear to be less functional in their use and understanding of excuses (although they certainly still adhere to the general responsibility-affect-behavior patterns). These data contribute to the proposal that dysfunctional cognitive interpretations of the social world provide clues to the understanding of aggressive behavior in children (see Dodge & Crick, 1990).

IX. Theoretical Comparisons

It was indicated at the beginning of this chapter that the contributions of three psychologists—Frank Fincham, Kelly Shaver, and Thomas Schultz—have been especially important in guiding my thinking. However, I have rather blithely skipped along without sufficiently acknowledging their contributions and without pointing out the similarities and differences between what has been proposed here and what they already have written. I will turn to this topic next, although even now I will not differentiate between their individual positions.

Among the major points of agreement between what Fincham, Shaver, and Shultz have proposed and what has been contended here are the following:

1. Causality must be distinguished from responsibility. Shultz and Schleifer (1983), for example, use the notion of presupposition: "A judgment of responsibility presupposes one of causation" (p. 53). This distinction also is guided by their linkage of responsibility, but not necessarily causality, with moral concerns.

2. When thinking about the interrelationships between the concepts of causality, responsibility, and punishment, these theorists also suggest that a temporal sequence seems to best capture the motivational process.

3. When considering relations between causality, responsibility, and punishment, causality is more distal from punishment than is responsibility. Shultz et al. (1981), for example, report that a causal model from causality to responsibility to punishment is not improved with the addition of a relation or path going directly from causality to punishment.

On the other hand, the position advocated in this chapter also contains some major differences from the prior points of view.

A. BLAME AS A SEPARATE CONCEPT

Blame has not been included as a separate concept in the motivational process. The other theorists often consider blame an attribution, and research subjects are asked the extent that the other is to be "blamed for" an event. Furthermore, when blame is included in the motivational process, it is considered a more proximal determinant of punishment than is responsibility (see Fincham & Shultz, 1981). Hence, building on the prior paragraphs, the following motivational process is often intimated:

$$\text{causation} \rightarrow \text{responsibility} \rightarrow \text{blame} \rightarrow \text{punishment}$$

There indeed are compelling reasons to differentiate blame from responsibility, even though in everyday language these might at times be used interchangeably (e.g., "He is responsible for . . ." "He is to be blamed for . . ."). But if it is stated that "she is responsible for," then this could be followed either by "our success" or "our failure." However, if it is said, "she is to be blamed for," then this can only be concluded with a negative phrase.

Another possible reason to separate responsibility from blame is that a person may be perceived as very responsible for an outcome, although there might be little blame. This is because the outcome may be trivial, and outcome magnitude could influence blame but not responsibility. For example, assume that one individual, with foresight and planning, murders another; a second person, with the exact same foresight and planning, robs another. Both are fully responsible for their conduct. However, the murderer is likely to be blamed more than the robber. Or, to consider a more mundane example, imagine that a friend fails to show up to go to a movie. In one case, only the two of you were going, while in the second situation a party of four was to meet. There may be greater blame in the former than in the latter instance because only in the two-person situation might you return home rather than going to the movie. Blame, therefore, appears to be in part determined by the magnitude of the consequences of one's actions, whereas this may not be true regarding inferences of responsibility.

Thus, responsibility is not the same as blame. The difference appears to reside in their emotional connotations or components: responsibility is more a "pure" thought, and affectively neutral, whereas blame always conveys emotional negativity. Because of this I do not consider blame an attribution, which refers exclusively to a thought about causality.

B. BLAME AS A PROXIMAL MEDIATOR

But is blame the proximal mediator of subsequent social responses, as Fincham and Shultz (1981) have proposed? I take issue with this position, and instead argue that anger and sympathy mediate between responsibility and action. My reasoning is that blame appears to be a cognition similar to responsibility, as well as an affect akin to anger. Thus, when blame is proposed or demonstrated to mediate between responsibility and action, it is precisely because of its dual components, and particularly its affective meaning (anger).

This disagreement may represent a regression to an earlier, Titchnerian era in psychology when one psychologist argued that green is neither yellow nor blue, whereas another contended that green is precisely a combination of the two and is not a distinct color. Others maintain that blame is distinct from responsibility (and most likely anger) and have not differentiated or considered its cognitive and affective components. I am contending that blame is precisely a blend or combination of these two (with perhaps some unique meaning) and therefore does not warrant independent status when considering the sequence of cognitions and emotions that result in social action. For conceptual clarity, I therefore replace blame with the less ambiguous emotions of anger (and sympathy).

There is another important advantage in having the linkage between responsibility and action be (at times) mediated by anger and sympathy. Given these emotional mediators, both negative or antisocial responses and positive or prosocial reactions may be included within the same conceptual system. As already noted, blame can only be imposed to account for sanctions. This obviously limits the generality of the analysis.

X. Concluding Theoretical Notes

The history of the study of motivation can be described as a succession of metaphors used to capture disparate aspects of human and subhuman behavior (see Weiner, 1990, 1992a). Drive theory, the first dominant theory of motivation derived from experimental data, was guided by the metaphor that all living organisms are machines. Hence, behavior is not guided by cognitions or consciousness, there is no volition, energy is required to instigate action, and the direction of behavior is determined by rigid connections between stimuli and responses.

The next dominant metaphor in the history of motivation was linked with expectancy-value theories of behavior. Here a godlike metaphor proved useful in which individuals were assumed to be all-knowing: they realized the value of each available goal and were able to calculate the expectancy of success of all the behaviors resulting in goal attainment. Then the worth of each behavioral choice could be determined by multiplying the expectancy of goal attainment and the value of the associated goal. After comparing the alternatives, the all-knowing, perfectly rational person would select the behavioral alternative with the maximum utility.

The drive and expectancy X value approaches, although differing in many essential respects, shared some common assumptions about the study of motivation. First, motivation primarily was conceived as an intrapsychic process. Second, hedonism was the main determinant of action. And third, emotions other than pleasure and pain played little role in deciding conduct. After all, machines are not very emotional, nor is a completely rational organism (although these conceptions did accept the pleasure-pain principle).

Two overlapping metaphors guided the conception of motivation presented in this chapter. One of the metaphors includes the image of persons as godlike. However, rather than stressing the all-knowing God which directed expectancy-value theory, the judging aspect of God is the focus. The presumption is that individuals assume the right and legitimacy to judge others, deciding if they are innocent or guilty for personal conduct (e.g., not studying for an exam, shoving someone, committing a crime) as well as for personal states and plights (e.g., AIDS, poverty, needing class notes, being shy). In so doing, others tend to be perceived as "sinners" or as "sick." The defendants are allowed to plead their cases, provide evidence, and offer excuses and justifications that can influence the decision of the judge. Finally, following a moral evaluation, the judge experiences anger or compassion and bases social behavior on the moral decisions that have been reached or the affects that these generate.

A related metaphor guiding this chapter embraces the view that not only are all individuals godlike judges, they also are defendants. Hence, life is a courtroom (the motivational metaphor) where dramas are played out regarding moral culpability. Each person can influence this process, ask for forgiveness, confess, offer an excuse, and so on. Then the individual is "sentenced," and even may be "paroled" for good behavior.

Given the metaphor that the person is a godlike judge, or that life is a courtroom, then motivation is not purely an intrapsychic process. Rather, behavior and the determinants of behavior reside in a social context with significant others who influence this process. Furthermore, specific emotions directed toward others such as anger and sympathy guide behavior, and one's conduct has social implications. Finally, hedonism is not necessarily the mainspring of action. In part, the motivational process is initiated by a desire to know and reach causal understanding (i.e., to attain some cognitive mastery of the social world). And a central goal of action is to maintain the social system, ensuring that others attain their "just due" and that the scales of justice remain in balance. Given this view, interpersonal behavior interacts with the system of legal procedures and the tenets of theology. These intersect and influence one another in mysterious and intricate ways that provide questions for the future.

Acknowledgment

This chapter was written while the author was supported by grant DBS-9211982 from the National Science Foundation.

References

Anderson, C. A., Weiner, B., & Krull, D. S. (in press). The process and consequences of explanation. In E. T. Higgins & A. Kruglanski (Eds.), *Social psychology: Handbook of basic mechanisms and processes*. New York: Guilford.

Anderson, D. (1991, November). Sorry, but Magic Johnson isn't a hero. *New York Times*, p. B-7.

Aramburu, B. F., & Leigh, B. C. (1991). For better or worse: Attributions about drunken aggression toward male and female victims. *Violence and Victims, 6*, 31–41.

Averill, J. R. (1982). *Anger and aggression: An essay on emotion*. New York: Springer-Verlag.

Averill, J. R. (1983). Studies on anger and aggression. *American Psychologist, 38*, 1145–1160.

Barnes, R. D., Ickes, W. J., & Kidd, R. (1979). Effects of perceived intentionality and stability of another's dependency on helping behavior. *Personality and Social Psychology Bulletin, 5*, 367–372.

Berkowitz, L. (1993). *Aggression*. New York: McGraw-Hill.

Betancourt, H. (1990). An attribution-empathy model of helping behavior: Behavioral intentions and judgments of help-giving. *Personality and Social Psychology Bulletin, 16*, 573–591.

Betancourt, H., & Blair, I. (1992). A cognition (attribution)–emotion model of violence in conflict situations. *Personality and Social Psychology Bulletin, 18*, 343–350.

Brewer, M. (1977). An information processing approach to attribution of responsibility. *Journal of Experimental Social Psychology, 13*, 58–69.

Brickman, P., Rabinowitz, V. C., Karuza, J., Jr., Coates, D., Cohn, E., & Kidder, L. (1982). Models of helping and coping. *American Psychologist, 37*, 368–384.

Brown, J., & Weiner, B. (1984). Affective consequences of ability versus effort ascriptions: Controversies, resolutions, and quandaries. *Journal of Educational Psychology, 76*, 146–158.

Caprara, G. V., Pastorelli, C., & Weiner, B. (1994). A social-cognitive approach to the understanding of at-risk children. *European Journal of Personality, 8*, 31–43.

Carlson, M., & Miller, N. (1987). Explanation of the relation between negative mood and helping. *Psychological Bulletin, 102*, 72–90.

Coates, D., & Wortman, C. (1980). Depression maintenance and interpersonal control. In A. Baum & J. Singer (Eds.), *Advances in environmental psychology, Vol. 2* (pp. 149–182). Hillsdale, NJ: Erlbaum.

Coie, J. D., Dodge, K. A., & Coppotelli, H. (1982). Dimensions and types of social status: A cross-age perspective. *Developmental Psychology, 18*, 557–570.

Coie, J. D., & Kupersmidt, J. B. (1983). A behavioral analysis of emerging social status in boys' groups. *Child Development, 54*, 1400–1416.

Coyne, J. C., Kahn, J., & Gotlib, I. H. (1987). Depression. In T. Jacob (Ed.), *Family interaction and psychopathology* (pp. 509–533). New York: Plenum.

Crandall, C. S. (in press). Symbolic anti-fatism: Ideology, experience, and anti-fat attitudes. *Journal of Personality and Social Psychology*.

Crandall, C. S., & Biernat, M. R. (1990). The ideology of anti-fat attitudes. *Journal of Applied Social Psychology, 20*, 227–243.

Davitz, J. R. (1969). *The language of emotion*. New York: Academic Press.

Dionne, E. J., Jr. (1991). *Why Americans hate politics*. New York: Simon & Schuster.

Dodge, K. A., & Crick, N. R. (1990). Social information-processing bases of aggressive behavior in children. *Personality and Social Psychology Bulletin, 16*, 8–22.

Dooley, P. A. (in press). Perceptions of the onset controllability of AIDS and helping judgments: An attributional analysis. *Journal of Applied Social Psychology*.

Eisenberg, N. (1986). *Altruistic emotion, cognition, and behavior*. Hillsdale, NJ: Erlbaum.

Feagin, J. (1972). Poverty: We still believe that God helps them who help themselves. *Psychology Today, 6*, 101, 129.

Feather, N. (1974). Explanations of poverty in Australian and American samples: The person, society, or fate? *Australian Journal of Psychology, 26,* 199–216.

Ferguson, T., & Rule, B. (1983). An attributional perspective on anger and aggression. In R. Geen & E. Donnerstein (Eds.), *Aggression: Theoretical and empirical reviews, Vol. 1. Theoretical and methodological issues* (pp. 41–74). New York: Academic Press.

Fincham, F. D., & Roberts, C. (1985). Intervening causation and the mitigation of responsibility for harm doing. *Journal of Experimental Social Psychology, 21,* 178–194.

Fincham, F. D., & Shultz, T. R. (1981). Intervening causation and the mitigation of responsibility for harm. *British Journal of Social Psychology, 20,* 113–120.

Fox, R. (1992). Prejudice and the unfinished mind: A new look at an old failing. *Psychological Inquiry, 3,* 137–152.

Frijda, N. (1986). *The emotions.* Cambridge: Cambridge University Press.

Furnham, A. (1982). Why are the poor always with us? Explanations for poverty in Britain. *British Journal of Social Psychology, 21,* 311–322.

Graham, S. (1984). Communicated sympathy and anger to black and white children: The cognitive (attributional) consequences of affective cues. *Journal of Personality and Social Psychology, 47,* 40–54.

Graham, S. (1991). A review of attribution theory in achievement contexts. *Educational Psychology Review, 3,* 5–39.

Graham, S., Hudley, C., & Williams, E. (1992). Attributional and emotional determinants of aggression among African-American and Latino young adolescents. *Developmental Psychology, 28,* 731–740.

Graham, S., Weiner, B., & Benesh-Weiner, M. (in press). An attributional analysis of the development of excuse giving in aggressive and nonaggressive African-American boys. *Developmental Psychology.*

Graham, S., Weiner, B., Giuliano, T., & Williams, E. (1993). An attributonal analysis of reactions to Magic Johnson. *Journal of Applied Social Psychology, 23,* 996–1010.

Gurtman, M. B. (1986). Depression and the responses of others: Reevaluating the reevaluation. *Journal of Abnormal Psychology, 95,* 99–101.

Hart, H. L. A. (1968). *Punishment and responsibility.* Oxford: Clarendon Press.

Hart, H. L. A., & Honoré, A. M. (1959). *Causation in the law.* Oxford: Clarendon Press.

Heider, F. (1958). *The psychology of interpersonal relations.* New York: Wiley.

Hudley, C., & Graham, S. (1993). An attributional intervention to reduce peer-directed aggression among African-American boys. *Child Development, 64,* 124–138.

Johnson, E. (1991, November). I'll deal with it. *Sports Illustrated,* pp. 18–26.

Jones, E. E., & Davis, K. E. (1965). From acts to dispositions: The attribution process in person perception. In L. Berkowitz (Ed.), *Advances in experimental social psychology* (Vol. 2, pp. 219–266). New York: Academic Press.

Jones, E. E., Farino, A., Hastorf, A. H., Markus, H., Miller, D. T., & Scott, R. A. (1984). *Social stigma.* New York: Freeman.

Juvonen, J. (1991). Deviance, perceived responsibility, and negative peer reactions. *Developmental Psychology, 27,* 672–681.

Juvonen, J. (1992). Negative peer reactions from the perspective of the reactors. *Journal of Educational Psychology, 84,* 314–321.

Juvonen, J., & Murdock, T. B. (1993). How to promote social approval: The effects of audience and outcome on publicly communicated attributions. *Journal of Educational Psychology, 85,* 365–376.

Karasawa, K. (in press). An attributional analysis of reactions to negative emotions. *Personality and Social Psychology Bulletin.*

Kelley, H. H. (1967). Attribution theory in social psychology. In D. Levine (Ed.), *Nebraska symposium on motivation* (pp. 192–238). Lincoln: University of Nebraska Press.

Kluegel, J. R., & Smith, E. R. (1986). *Beliefs about inequality.* New York: Aldine.
Krull, D. S. (1993). Does the grist change the mill? The effect of the perceiver's inferential goal on the process of social inference. *Personality and Social Psychology Bulletin, 19,* 340–348.
Lane, R. (1962). *Political ideology: Why the American common man believes what he does.* New York: Macmillan.
Letter to the Editor. (1991, Nov. 16). *Los Angeles Times,* p. C-3.
Li, A., & Weiner, B. (1993). *The specificity of mitigating circumstances.* Unpublished manuscript, University of California, Los Angeles.
Liu, J., Karasawa, K., & Weiner, B. (1992). Inferences about the causes of positive and negative emotions. *Personality and Social Psychology Bulletin, 18,* 603–615.
MacAndrew, C., & Edgerton, R. B. (1969). *Drunken comportment: A social explanation.* Chicago: Aldine.
Mallery, P. (1991). *Attributions and attitudes toward AIDS.* Unpublished manuscript, University of California, Los Angeles.
McKinnon-Lewis, C., Lamb, M. E., Arbuckle, B., Baradaran, L. P., & Volling, B. L. (1992). The relationship between biased maternal and filial attributions and the aggressiveness of their interactions. *Development and Psychopathology, 4,* 403–415.
Millman, M. (1980). *Such a pretty face: Being fat in America.* New York: Norton.
Morse, S. J. (1992). The "guilty mind": Mens Rea. In D. K. Kahehiro & W. S. Laufer (Eds.), *Handbook of psychology and law* (pp. 207–229). New York: Springer-Verlag.
Reisenzein, R. (1986). A structural equation analysis of Weiner's attribution-affect model of helping behavior. *Journal of Personality and Social Psychology, 50,* 1123–1133.
Richardson, D. C., & Campbell, J. L. (1980). Alcohol and wife abuse: The effects of alcohol on attributions of blame for wife abuse. *Personality and Social Psychology Bulletin, 8,* 468–476.
Rippere, V. (1977). Commonsense beliefs about depression and antidepressive behavior. *Behavioral Research and Therapy, 15,* 57–63.
Sarbin, T. R. (1990). Metaphors and unwanted conduct: A historical sketch. In D. E. Leary (Ed.), *Metaphors in the history of psychology* (pp. 300–330). Cambridge, England: University of Cambridge Press.
Schachter, S., & Singer, J. E. (1962). Cognitive, social, and physiological determinants of emotional state. *Psychological Review, 69,* 379–399.
Schmidt, G., & Weiner, B. (1988). An attribution-affect-action theory of behavior: Replications of judgments of help-giving. *Personality and Social Psychology Bulletin, 14,* 610–621.
Scott, M. B., & Lyman, S. M. (1968). Accounts. *American Sociological Review, 5,* 46–62.
Sedikides, C., & Anderson, C. A. (1992). Causal explanation of defection: A knowledge structure approach. *Personality and Social Psychology Bulletin, 18,* 420–429.
Shaver, K. G. (1985). *The attribution of blame: Causality, responsibility, and blameworthiness.* New York: Springer-Verlag.
Shaver, K. G., & Drown, D. (1986). On causality, responsibility, and self-blame: A theoretical note. *Journal of Personality and Social Psychology, 50,* 697–702.
Shultz, T. R., & Schleifer, M. (1983). Toward a refinement of attribution concepts. In J. Jaspars, F. D. Fincham, & M. Hewstone (Eds.), *Attribution theory and research: Conceptual, developmental and social dimensions* (pp. 37–62). London: Academic Press.
Shultz, T. R., Schleifer, M., & Altman, I. (1981). Judgments of causation, responsibility, and punishment in cases of harm-doing. *Canadian Journal of the Behavioural Science, 13,* 238–253.
Shultz, T. R., & Wright, K. (1985). Concepts of negligence and intention in the assignment of moral responsibility. *Canadian Journal of Behavioral Science, 17,* 97–108.
Sigelman, C. K., & Begley, N. L. (1987). The early development of reactions to peers with controllable and uncontrollable problems. *Journal of Pediatric Psychology, 12,* 99–115.
Skitka, L. J., & Tetlock, P. E. (1992). Allocating scarce resources: A contingency model of distributive justice. *Journal of Experimental Social Psychology, 28,* 491–522.

Snyder, C. R., & Higgins, R. L. (1988). Excuses: Their effective role in the negotiation of reality. *Psychological Bulletin, 104*, 23–35.
Trivers, R. L. (1971). The evolution of reciprocal altruism. *Quarterly Review of Biology, 46*, 35–57.
Weiner, B. (1986). *An attributional theory of motivation and emotion.* New York: Springer-Verlag.
Weiner, B. (1990). History of motivational research in education. *Journal of Educational Psychology, 82*, 616–622.
Weiner, B. (1992a). *Human motivation: Metaphors, theory, and research.* Newbury Park, Ca: Sage.
Weiner, B. (1992b). Excuses in everyday interaction. In M. L. McLaughlin, M. J. Cody, & S. J. Read (Eds.), *Explaining one's self to others* (pp. 131–146). Hillsdale, NJ: Erlbaum.
Weiner, B. (1993). On sin versus sickness. *American Psychologist, 48*, 957–965.
Weiner, B., Amirkhan, J., Folkes, V. S., & Verette, J. A. (1987). An attributional analysis of excuse giving: Studies of a naive theory of emotion. *Journal of Personality and Social Psychology, 52*, 316–324.
Weiner, B., Figueroa-Munoz, A., & Kakihara, C. (1991). The goals of excuses and communication strategies related to causal perceptions. *Personality and Social Psychology Bulletin, 17*, 4–13.
Weiner, B., & Graham, S. (1989). Understanding the motivational role of affect: Life-span research from an attributional perspective. *Cognition and Emotion, 3*, 401–419.
Weiner, B., Graham, S., & Chandler, C. C. (1982). Causal antecedents of pity, anger, and guilt. *Personality and Social Psychology Bulletin, 8*, 226–232.
Weiner, B., & Handel, S. (1985). Anticipated emotional consequences of causal communications and reported communication strategy. *Developmental Psychology, 21*, 102–107.
Weiner, B., Perry, R., & Magnusson, J. (1988). An attributional analysis of reactions to stigmas. *Journal of Personality and Social Psychology, 55*, 738–748.
Whitley, B. E., Jr. (1990). The relationship of heterosexuals' attributions for the causes of homosexuality to attitudes toward lesbian and gay men. *Personality and Social Psychology Bulletin, 16*, 369–377.
Williams, S. (1984). Left-right ideological differences in blaming victims. *Political Psychology, 5*, 573–581.
Wispé, L. (1991). *The psychology of sympathy.* New York: Plenum.
Zucker, G. S., & Weiner, B. (1993). Conservatism and perceptions of poverty: An attributional analysis. *Journal of Applied Social Psychology, 23*, 925–943.

INFORMATION PROCESSING IN SOCIAL CONTEXTS: IMPLICATIONS FOR SOCIAL MEMORY AND JUDGMENT

Robert S. Wyer, Jr.
Deborah H Gruenfeld

The last decade of research in social cognition has greatly advanced our understanding of information processing. This is evident from the substantial changes in the content of major texts and reference works that have emerged (cf. Fiske & Taylor, 1984, 1992; Wyer & Srull, 1984, 1994). Several theoretical formulations have been developed to account for both specific phenomena (Clore, Schwarz, & Conway, 1994; Fiske & Neuberg, 1990; Higgins, Bargh & Lombardi, 1985; Klein & Loftus, 1990; Srull & Wyer, 1989; Trafimow & Wyer, 1993; Wyer, Shoben, Fuhrman, & Bodenhausen, 1985) and social information processing more generally (Carlston, 1994; Smith, 1984, 1990; Wyer & Srull, 1986, 1989). These models have typically been quite successful in accounting for the behaviors to which they have been applied.

Somewhat ironically, however, much of our theoretical and empirical knowledge about social information processing has been obtained under laboratory conditions that only faintly resemble the social situations in which information is usually acquired in everyday life. In particular, highly controlled experimental situations have typically been constructed in which the influence of social contextual factors of the sort that surround the acquisition and use of information outside the laboratory is minimized. These factors can include (a) the ostensible purpose for which the information is transmitted, (b) the style in which it is conveyed, and (c) prior knowledge about both its source and its referents. In the absence of these contextual cues, subjects are necessarily disposed to focus on the semantic, literal meaning of the information in construing its implications and using it to make judgments and decisions. Unfortunately, contextual features are likely to interact with the literal meaning of the information in determining the implications that people derive from it. Consequently, a consideration of the semantic features of information that people receive in a social context is often insufficient to understand how the information is interpreted and how it is likely to influence judgments and behavior. Recipients' perceptions of the reasons why the information has been conveyed to them is likely to have additional explanatory value.

This observation recognizes that when communications are conveyed in a social situation by a specified source, these communications constitute social behaviors, or *speech acts* (Searle, 1969). The generation of these messages, and others' reactions to them, are likely to be governed by processes similar to those that underlie the generation and perception of other behaviors that occur in a social context. For example, communicative acts are typically goal directed. That is, they are generated for a particular purpose: to inform, to persuade, to self-aggrandize, or simply to entertain. A recipient's reaction to these communications may in turn be influenced by his or her own objectives, which could either be fairly specific (to form an impression of the speaker, to make a decision, or to acquire knowledge about the topic being discussed), or more general, such as simply to understand what the speaker is trying to say. The recipient's attainment of these objectives, however, can require a consideration of not only the literal, semantic meaning of the communication but also why the communication was transmitted.

A recognition of this fact becomes particularly important when the meaning that a speaker intends to convey to his or her audience does not correspond to the meaning that the recipient actually extracts from it. For example, a person who comments that "what America needs is another Ronald Reagan" might intend the statement as sarcasm, and thus as a disparagement of Reagan rather than praise. However, the recipient may not necessarily perceive this intention. Similarly, a colleague who announces that he or she is on the editorial boards of eight major journals may be perceived to be boastful and conceited, although the speaker's actual intention is to complain about being overworked.

Although the occurrence of phenomena similar to those described in these examples are commonplace, they usually do not come into play in the research paradigms used to investigate social information processing. Our own previous research on person memory and judgment (e.g., Srull & Wyer, 1989) provides an example. In this research, subjects are often asked to form an impression of an unknown person on the basis of descriptions of the person's traits and behaviors. The information is typically taken from an unfamiliar and often unspecified source, and is ostensibly selected by the experimenter for reasons that pertain to the particular issues being investigated. In these conditions, recipients are likely to take the information at face value, and, therefore, to base their judgments on the semantic implications of the information for the person it describes without questioning the validity of the information or the communicator's motives in transmitting it. In contrast, the same information might be processed quite differently if it is conveyed spontaneously about a person in the context of a conversation (Wyer, Budesheim, & Lambert, 1990). In this case, the recipient is likely to question why this particular information about the individual is being conveyed. As we will point out presently, recipients of the information conveyed in a conversation often believe it reflects as much on the speakers as on the person to whom the information refers.

The thesis of this chapter is that an understanding of information processing in a social context requires a consideration of not only the literal meaning of the information conveyed but also subjects' perceptions of *why* the information is communicated. We will refer to recipients' inferences of the reasons a message is transmitted as their perceptions of the *pragmatic* implications of the message, as opposed to its literal meaning. Note that our use of the term "pragmatic" in this context is broader than its use in linguistics, which is restricted to the meaning that the communicator *intends* to convey through his or her message. The pragmatic implications that recipients derive from a message can obviously be influenced by perceptions of the meaning that the communicator intends to transmit. Moreover, when recipients infer that the speaker intends to convey factual information, their perceptions of the message's pragmatic implications can include its literal meaning. However, these perceptions are not necessarily restricted to either the literal meaning of a communication or its intended meaning. In addition, they could pertain to more general feelings, attitudes, and personal characteristics that the speaker does not always wish to reveal.

As we have conceptualized them, the transmission and perception of pragmatic meaning can depend on not only the actual objectives of the communicator, but also characteristics of the recipient and the body of knowledge that the communicator and recipient have in common. Communicators' objectives can determine not only the content of their messages but the style in which the information is conveyed, and these factors, in turn, can affect recipients' interpretation of the information and its consequent impact. On the other hand, recipients' interpretation of a message can depend on at least two other factors. First, the recipients' own objectives in receiving information can lead them to consider its nonliteral implications. Second, characteristics of the information itself can stimulate attention to these implications. For example, when either the content or the style of a communication that is received in a social context deviates from normative expectations for the type of messages that are usually conveyed, recipients are likely to question why the deviation occurred. In the course of arriving at an explanation, they might construe the communicator's intentions, or might consider other reasons why the messages occurred. As a result of these considerations, recipients might reinterpret the message in a way that is not reflected by its literal meaning. Consequently, the communication affects recipients' judgments and behavior in ways that cannot be predicted from its semantic implications alone.

Examples of these effects are provided in the remainder of this chapter. We first consider motivational factors that affect both the content and style with which information is transmitted and its ultimate interpretation by the recipient. We then discuss informational factors that stimulate a recipient's attention to the nonliteral meaning of information conveyed in a social context, and address the implications of pragmatic information processing for (a) judgments based on the information presented, (b) recall of the information, and (c) the use of other available information that is encountered in the course of this processing. Individual differences in the tendency to take the pragmatic implications of information into account are also considered. Finally, we evaluate more generally the implications of pragmatic information processing for an understanding of the mental representation of social information, and consider the future directions that research in social information processing is likely to take.

I. Motivational Influences on the Communication of Pragmatic Meaning

A. EFFECTS OF COMMUNICATION OBJECTIVES ON INFORMATION TRANSMISSION

The content and style of a communicator's message, and consequently the pragmatic implications that recipients see in it, are governed in part by the motives of the communicator and, therefore, the meaning that he or she intends (either directly or indirectly) to convey. The indirect communication of meaning can involve the use of irony or indirect speech acts (Clark & Clark, 1977; Green, 1989; Searle, 1969; Sperber & Wilson, 1986). It can also involve nonverbal or paralinguistic behavior, such as facial expressions, eye contact, or tone of voice (Ellsworth & Carlsmith, 1968; Krauss, Geller, & Olson, 1976). The style in which a communication is transmitted, either orally or in writing, can also have pragmatic meaning. For example, it might reflect the communicator's concern about the issue at hand, or his confidence that the position expressed is valid. These attributions, in turn, can mediate recipients' responses to the communicator's message and the consequent influence of this message (for further discussion of this possibility, see Chaiken & Eagly, 1976; Higgins, 1981).

The stylistic features that affect perceptions of pragmatic meaning can often result from an intentional communication strategy that the communicator employs to attain a particular objective. In other cases, however, they can result from the communicator's inability to use a given strategy effectively, resulting in the appearance of uncertainty or ignorance. In both cases, the communication style that a communicator adopts is influenced by not only his or her communication objectives but also his or her perception of the audience and the implications that the audience is likely to draw from it.

1. Normative Influences on Communication Transmission

The exchange of information in a social context is often governed by normative principles of communication that are applied by both the communicator in deciding how to construct a message and by the recipient in interpreting it (Grice, 1975). Although these principles have been studied extensively by psycholinguists (Green, 1989; Sperber & Wilson, 1986), they have been less widely recognized by social cognition researchers (for exceptions, see Higgins, 1981; Kraut & Higgins, 1984; Schwarz, 1994).

For example, communications are generally expected to be informative, and to be relevant to the topic under discussion. Moreover, they are expected to convey the truth as the communicator perceives it. Therefore, communicators attempt to construct their messages in a way that conforms to these normative principles, and they assume that recipients will interpret them accordingly. Often, a communicator will intentionally generate a message with a literal meaning that violates one of these principles under the assumption that the recipient will recognize this violation and, therefore, will realize that the message's literal meaning is not its intended meaning. Thus, for example, a communicator may make a statement he or she considers to be obviously false (e.g., "What America needs is another Ronald Reagan"), assuming that the recipient will immediately realize this norm violation and recognize the statement as sarcastic. Alternatively, a communicator may make a statement that is completely uninformative (e.g., "Many people are dying of AIDS") under the assumption that the recipient is aware that the statement's literal meaning violates a normative principle to convey information and will interpret it as an implicit expression of attitude (i.e., as an indication that the speaker believes the situation to be deplorable and that something should be done to eliminate it). In such instances, however, the speaker's success in communicating the meaning intended depends on the accuracy of his or her perception of the audience's knowledge and ability to recognize the statement's semantic implications as counternormative. When the communicator's perception is incorrect, misinterpretations are likely. We return to these matters in later sections of this chapter. (For other reviews of the role of communication norms in social information processing, see Higgins, 1981; Kraut & Higgins, 1984; Schwarz, 1994; Strack, 1994).

2. Intended Effects of Communication Strategies

The preceding discussion implies that to be effective in transmitting the meaning they intend, communicators must be attuned to the pragmatic implications that their audience is likely to derive from their messages. This is particularly true when the communicator's objective is to influence the audience to adopt a particular point of view. The techniques that are most likely to succeed in influencing people to alter their opinions have of course been the subject of social psychological research and theory for decades (Eagly & Himmelfarb, 1978; Hovland, Janis, & Kelley, 1953; Petty & Cacioppo, 1981, 1986; for a recent review, see Petty, Priester, & Wegener, 1994). Much less frequently studied are the social contextual factors that actually stimulate communicators to employ a particular strategy.

In considering this latter issue, it seems reasonable to suppose that a determinant of the communicator's strategy is his or her assessment of the likelihood that an influence attempt will succeed. In group decision situations, for example, minority members may believe that in order to exert influence, they must take an extreme position and advocate it forcefully and persistently (Moscovici, 1985). In contrast, majority representatives are likely to adopt a broader perspective that permits the minority view to be acknowledged and perhaps reconciled with their own position. This implies that the opinion rationales communicated by majority representatives are likely to be more complex and multifaceted, and hence more comprehensive, than those conveyed by the minority.

Two studies by Gruenfeld (1993) support this general hypothesis. One, a field study, was based on content analyses of the decision rationales prepared by representatives of minority and majority factions in cases decided by the U.S. Supreme Court. The cases considered were selected over a 30-year period in such a way that both the issue domain (economics, civil rights, etc.) and the ideology reflected by the majority and minority positions (liberal vs. conservative) were controlled. The rationales prepared by both majority and minority representatives were scored for integrative complexity (Tetlock, 1986), an index of the extent to which the points of view expressed were both differentiated and integrated. As expected, the decision rationales prepared by minority representatives were less complex than those prepared by majority representatives, and this was true regardless of the ideology conveyed by the positions in question.[1] This was true even when individual differences in communication style were controlled (i.e., when each justice in the sample represented majority and minority positions the same proportion of times).

A laboratory study (Gruenfeld, 1993) confirmed this basic conclusion. Subjects were administered a pretest concerning their opinion on a hypothetical court case (specifically, the appropriateness of busing to ensure school integration). Based on this pretest, subjects were randomly assigned to 4–6-person groups in which they were members of either the majority or the minority. Then, following discussion, some subjects were asked to prepare a statement defending their

---

[1]Based on the results of earlier analysis of Supreme Court decision rationales, Tetlock (1986) postulated that conservatives were typically less integratively complex than were liberals. During the time period in which Tetlock's data were collected, however, the Supreme Court was predominantly liberal, and so conservatives were in the minority. Gruenfeld replicated these findings, but further found that during periods in which the Supreme Court was predominantly conservative, liberal judges wrote generally less integratively complex rationales than did conservatives.

position, much as they would if they were asked to represent the faction to which they belonged. Minority members' decision rationales conveyed less integrative complexity than majority members' rationales, confirming results of the Supreme Court study.

Gruenfeld's studies, conducted both in the field and in the laboratory, support the notion that communicators adopt strategies for conveying information that they believe will attain their communication objectives. Other factors can also affect these strategies and, therefore, the pragmatic implications that recipients actually draw from them. In some cases, for example, the integrative complexity of communicators' decision rationales is likely to reflect the nature of their underlying thoughts about the issue at hand rather than simply the style with which they communicate these thoughts. Suppose minority subjects feel more threatened, and, therefore, more emotionally aroused, than majority subjects. This arousal could interfere with cognitive processing and, therefore, decrease cognitive complexity for reasons similar to those suggested by Easterbrook (1959) and others. In fact, Gruenfeld found that minority members' communications were less complex than those of majority members when they conveyed their thoughts privately to the experimenter as well as when they prepared a public decision rationale. To the extent recipients perceive different pragmatic implications in messages that differ in complexity, this suggests that these implications can be transmitted unintentionally as well as intentionally. This possibility is further elaborated in the next section.

3. Unintended Influences of Communication Goals on Communication Style

a. Effects of Speech Style on the Communication of Uncertainty. The studies by Gruenfeld demonstrate that communicators construct their messages in ways that are useful for attaining their communication objectives. Because the actual impact of communicators' messages on recipients' beliefs was not assessed in their studies, the effect to which communicators' objectives were actually attained is of course unclear. However, a study by Gruenfeld and Wyer (1993, Experiment 2) provides more direct evidence that speakers' efforts to attain specific communication objectives can influence recipients' perceptions of their messages' pragmatic implications and, therefore, the impact that these messages have on recipients' beliefs. Moreover, the effects can occur when the transmission of these implications is not intended by the speaker.

In this study, subjects who were assigned the role of communicator read a passage describing a relatively unfamiliar disease. The passage was ostensibly taken from either a recent newspaper story or an encyclopedia article. The primary objective of newspapers is presumably to convey new and important information of general interest to the public. In contrast, an encyclopedia's principle function is to record archival knowledge in a way that is accurate although not necessarily of general interest. After reading the passage, communicators were asked to convey the information to a naive recipient in a way that was either as interesting as possible or as accurate as possible. In some cases, therefore, the communicator's goal and that of the original information source were similar, and in other cases they were dissimilar. After delivering the message, both communicators and recipients reported their general opinions concerning the seriousness of the disease and more specific beliefs associated with its incidence, prognosis, and treatment.

We expected that communicators whose objectives were congruent with those of the original information source (that is, speakers who were told to convey information from a newspaper in a way that was interesting, or information from an encyclopedia in a way that was accurate) would infer that they could attain their objective simply by transmitting the material in the same form in which it was originally presented, and would be relatively confident about their ability to do so. In contrast, speakers whose objectives were incongruent with those of the information source (speakers who were told to convey information from an encyclopedia in a way that was interesting, or to convey information from a newspaper in a way that was accurate) would be uncertain about how best to present the information, and this uncertainty should be reflected in their speech style. A content analysis of communicators' speeches supported this hypothesis. The actual amount of information contained in these speeches did not significantly depend on either the communicator's objectives or those of the original information source. However, two other factors were affected in the manner we expected. One, a general indication of poor speech style (e.g., the frequency of "uhhs" and "errs"), is shown in the first section of Table I as a function of the communicator's objectives and the original information source. The second, the time that speakers took to deliver their speech (a possible indication of the tendency to ramble), is shown in the second section of the table. As these data indicate, communicators' speeches were characterized by significantly poorer speech style, and took significantly longer to deliver, when the communicators' objectives were incongruent with those of the original information source than whey they were congruent. In other words, communicators' speech style conveyed less confidence in the validity of what they were saying in the former condition than the latter.

Moreover, recipients appeared to be sensitive to these pragmatic implications. Recipients' beliefs and opinions concerning the issue being discussed are shown in the last two sections of Table I. These judgments were both significantly less extreme when speakers' objectives were incongruent with those of the original information source than when they were congruent.

In interpreting these results, two additional findings should be considered. First, communicators' *own* beliefs and opinions were not influenced by either

TABLE I
Effects of Information Source and Communicators' Objectives on Speech Style Indices and Recipients' Beliefs and Opinions[a,b]

	Communicators' objective	
	Interesting improvisation	Accurate improvisation
1. Quality of speech style		
Newspaper source	−.00	−.47
Encyclopedia source	−.05	.53
2. Length of time spent delivering speech		
Newspaper source	−.26	.37
Encyclopedia source	.20	−.31
3. Recipients' specific beliefs		
Newspaper source	44.6	34.8
Encyclopedia source	38.1	44.7
4. Recipients' general opinions		
Newspaper source	28.6	24.8
Encyclopedia source	21.8	28.7

[a] Indices of speech style and the time spent delivering the speech in standard scores. More positive scores indicate (a) higher quality of speech (i.e., fewer "uhhs" and "errs") and (b) longer speaking time, respectively. Recipients' beliefs and opinions are the sum of relevant items rated along a scale form 0 (not at all likely) to 10 (extremely likely).
[b] Based on data from Gruenfeld and Wyer, 1993.

their own communication objectives or those of the original information source. Thus, the effects of these variables on communicators' speech style were apparently not a reflection of their *actual* uncertainty about the implications of the information they communicated, or the strength of their own beliefs and opinions about the issue being addressed.

Second, communicators' speech style was also independent of their ability to remember the original information they received. In a second study (Gruenfeld & Wyer, 1993, Experiment 1), communicators were exposed to conditions similar to those described above. However, rather than actually delivering their speech, they were asked to recall the information they had read. The ostensible objectives of the original information source and speakers' own communication goals had similar, additive effects on recall. Specifically, speakers who believed that the passage was taken from a newspaper recalled significantly fewer items of information, distorted the implications of these items to a greater extent, and made more intrusion errors, than speakers who believed that the passage came from an encyclopedia. Correspondingly, subjects whose *own* anticipated communication objectives were to be interesting remembered fewer details, distorted these details to a greater extent, and made more intrusion errors, than subjects whose anticipated objectives were to be accurate. This suggests that (a) subjects' perceptions of the pragmatic implications of the information they were given and (b) the pragmatic meaning they anticipated having to transmit to another had similar effects on subjects' cognitive responses to the information at the time they received it. Moreover, the independent effects of information source and speakers' own communication objectives on recall indicate that the difference in speech style observed in the first study (which was an interactive function of these variables) did not reflect a difference in the communicators' ability to remember the information they wished to transmit. Rather, it resulted from a difference in speakers' certainty about *how* they should transmit the information.

Considered in isolation, the finding that poor speech style decreases the impact of a communication is hardly surprising. However, the role of pragmatic inferences in this process is more noteworthy. That is, communicators in constructing their message took into account not only their own communication objectives but also the pragmatic implications of the original information source for how they should attain these objectives. The effects of these considerations mediated the pragmatic implications that were drawn from their speech by recipients who had no direct knowledge of either the communicators' own objectives or those of the original information source. Moreover, these implications (which pertained to the speakers' confidence in the validity of the information presented) were qualitatively different from those that the communicators intended to convey.

b. *The Detection of Deception.* In Gruenfeld and Wyer's study, the pragmatic implications that recipients saw in the message (i.e., its implications for the speakers' confidence in the validity of the position espoused) were not only inaccurate (as evidenced by the fact that communicators' own beliefs about the issue were unrelated to their speech style) but were totally unrelated to the implications that communicators wished to convey. Similar conclusions can be drawn from research on the detection of deception (e.g., DePaulo, 1992; Krauss, 1981; Kraut, 1978). To give but one example, Krauss et al. (1976) instructed subjects either to tell the truth or to lie in response to a series of questions about themselves. Their responses were recorded on videotape, and were later played to naive subjects who (a) predicted whether the speakers were lying or telling the truth and (b) evaluated the speakers along a number of other attribute dimensions. Several nonverbal and paralinguistic characteristics were correlated with communicators' actual truth-telling behavior, but few of them were correlated with recipients' perceptions of this behavior. On the other hand, although communicators were judged as no more deceitful when they actually lied than when they actually told the truth, they were often judged as less *attractive* in the former condition. Thus, recipients appeared to be sensitive to cues that were unintentionally elicited by speakers in the course of lying, but they misattributed these characteristics to other factors. These findings, therefore, confirm the general conclusion that although message recipients are often sensitive to cues elicited by communicators that have pragmatic implications, their perception of these implications may be unrelated to the factors that actually caused these cues to be transmitted

4. Effects of Communicators' Objectives on Their Own Beliefs and Opinions

Gruenfeld and Wyer's (1993) study showed that communicators' own beliefs and opinions may not be influenced by the pragmatic implications of messages when they are unaware of these implications. When the pragmatic implications of their communications are salient to them, however, they may construe these implications and, in some cases, may be affected by them in much the same way as recipients are affected. This possibility is of course a fundamental implication of self-perception theory (Bem, 1972). That is, communicators who deliver a message that promotes a particular point of view, and are later asked their personal opinion about the validity of this view, are likely to base their judgment not on the semantic content of the message they have delivered but rather on their perceptions of why the message was generated. Therefore, if subjects perceive that they were forced to prepare the message, they are likely to infer that their behavior has no implications for their opinions at all. If however, they perceive that they prepared the message voluntarily, which implies that they approve of the position they espoused, they report their opinion accordingly (Bem & McConnell, 1970; Festinger & Carlsmith, 1959).

This is not to say that semantic factors do not enter into the picture at all. A quite different series of studies by Higgins and his colleagues (Higgins & McCann, 1984; Higgins, McCann, & Fondacaro, 1982; Higgins & Rholes, 1978) suggest that they do. These studies investigated the extent to which subjects' modification of their messages to attain situation-specific communication objectives would affect their own beliefs in the position they espoused. In a representative study (Higgins & Rholes, 1978), subjects read a passage describing behaviors of a target person that could be interpreted in terms of either favorable traits (e.g., self-confident) or unfavorable ones (conceited). Then, they were asked to describe the target to someone who either liked the target or disliked him in a way that would permit the recipient to identify him. Subjects described the target in more favorable terms when the intended recipient liked the target than when he disliked the target—a tendency that could be stimulated by a desire to be either accurate or polite. Having done so, however, subjects based their own liking for the target on the communication they generated rather than the original information they had received. Thus, they liked the target more when they had communicated a favorable description than when they had not. In a control condition, in which subjects were aware of the audience's attitude toward the target and expected to write a message but did not actually do so, this effect did not occur. In summary, then, speakers' motivation to construct a message that would attain their pragmatic processing goals affected the *semantic* implications of their message, and they later used these latter implications as a basis for their own judgments of the target.

The question arises as to why such effects were not obtained by Gruenfeld and Wyer (1993). In that study, however, speakers' processing objectives did not affect the content of their speech but only their manner of delivering it. Moreover, the stylistic features that influenced recipients' beliefs were unintended by the communicators. Consequently, the communicators themselves might have been less aware of these features, and therefore less likely to use them as an indication of their beliefs in the position they espoused, than is usually the case under conditions in which self-perception phenomena have been detected.

B. EFFECTS OF RECIPIENTS' OBJECTIVES ON THEIR SENSITIVITY TO PRAGMATIC MEANING

Although most information that is conveyed in a social context has pragmatic implications over and above its literal meaning, recipients may not identify these implications unless they have reason to be sensitive to them. This sensitivity depends in part on their own objectives when they encounter the information. A complete evaluation of a communication's pragmatic implications requires cognitive effort. Therefore, people who receive information for no purpose other than to comprehend it may not always be motivated to expend the additional effort required to construe implications of the information over and above its literal meaning. That is, they may assume that the literal meaning is sufficient to comprehend the information and respond to it appropriately.

The conditions in which recipients are motivated to consider the reasons why a communication has been generated are nonetheless very common. Two quite different situations are described in this section. One situation arises when a recipient wishes to form an impression on the basis of information that people provide about themselves or others. A second situation arises in interviews or opinion surveys when a respondent is asked a question and must decide what information is actually being requested.

1. Pragmatic Influences on Impression Formation

The perception of pragmatic meaning is particularly important when one person's objective is to evaluate another. A personnel manager, for example, may need to know whether a job applicant's expression of interest in job-related activities is sincere or is stimulated by a desire to ingratiate. (For a well-known empirical demonstration of the effect of such assessments on judgments of a job applicant, see Jones, Davis, & Gergen, 1961.) A female graduate student may want to know whether her advisor's invitation to have lunch reflects an interest in her research project or an interest in her physical attractiveness. More generally, people in social interactions are often motivated to understand the traits and motives that underlie their behavior and the statements they make. Indeed, the assumption that this is true underlies much of the past research and theory on social attribution processes (Harvey, Ickes, & Kidd, 1976; Jones & Davis, 1965; Kelley, 1967, 1972). It is therefore somewhat surprising to realize that these considerations have usually not come into play in the impression-formation research that has been performed within a social cognition framework (for reviews, see Higgins & Bargh, 1987; Wyer & Srull, 1989; Wyer & Carlston, 1994).

In informal conversations, people not only convey information about other persons but exchange information about themselves. Both types of communications can have implications for characteristics of the speaker. Evidence that recipients are often attentive to these implications, and the consequences of considering these implications for reactions to the speaker, are described in turn.

a. Recipients' Reactions to Descriptions of Other Persons. The tendency for people to focus on the reasons for a communicator's statements about another person is particularly evident when their objective is to form an impression of this person. In such situations, the communicator's statements are often expressions of opinion, and therefore can reflect as much or more on the communicator as on the information's referent. For example, a man's description of a colleague as dumb and incompetent has negative implications for the person described. At the same time, the speaker's comments suggest that he is personally more unpleasant and dislikable than someone who describes colleagues in less disparaging terms. In short, people's statements about another person can affect impressions of the people themselves as well as the person to whom the statements refer.

In fact, an evaluation of a communicator may often be considered a precondition for interpreting his or her statements about the person the communicator is describing (Higgins, 1981; for evidence of similar mediating processes in the area of communication and persuasion, see Eagly, Wood, & Chaiken, 1978; Mills & Jellison, 1966). That is, subjects who hear the statements might first attempt to understand why the statements were made. In the course of doing so, they might attribute the statements to a general disposition of the speaker as well as to characteristics of the person to whom the statements pertain. The subjects' liking for these persons could depend on the nature of these attributions. This possibility was, in fact, raised by Asch (1952) in discussion of the effects of authorship on perceptions of a statement's "cognitive content."

A study by Wyer, Budesheim, and Lambert (1990) provides more direct evidence. Subjects listened to a taped conversation between two college students about a third. Before doing so, however, subjects received written trait descriptions of the target that the speakers had ostensibly provided prior to the discussion. Then, during the conversation, speakers exchanged anecdotal descriptions of the target's behavior. After hearing the conversation, subjects evaluated both the speakers and the target and then recalled the behaviors that each speaker had mentioned.

Subjects used the speakers' descriptions of the target to form impressions of the *speakers*. That is, they evaluated speakers more favorably when the speakers' trait descriptions of the target were favorable than when these descriptions were unfavorable (apparently reasoning that people who describe others favorably are more likable than people who disparage others). On the other hand, subjects evaluated the target *less* favorably when the speakers' trait descriptions of him were favorable. In other words, subjects spontaneously formed impressions of the speakers on the basis of the implications of the speakers' descriptions of the target for attributes of the speakers themselves (e.g., dispositions to be friendly or unfriendly). Later, they appeared to use these impressions as comparative standards in judging the individual the speakers were talking about.

Recall data supported this interpretation. That is, subjects appeared to organize the behaviors mentioned during the conversation around the concepts they had formed of the speakers rather than a concept of the target himself. Moreover, they had better recall of behaviors that confirmed the validity of these concepts (i.e., behaviors that supported their assumption that the speakers' trait descriptions of the target reflected general dispositions of the speakers to evaluate people favorably or unfavorably rather than characteristics of the target). Specifically, they remembered better the behaviors a speaker mentioned that were evaluatively inconsistent with the trait description of the target provided by the *other* speaker, and therefore implied that this description was inaccurate.

These data therefore provide further evidence that the statements people make in conversations do not merely convey descriptive information about the people and events to which they refer. In addition, they are interpreted as communicative acts that have pragmatic implications for characteristics of the speakers themselves. Although we have restricted our discussion to impression-formation processes, similar effects are likely to occur in other domains of information processing as well. For example, Newtson and Czerlinsky (1974) found that subjects attributed different attitude positions to communicators when their messages were directed toward an audience who held extreme opinions on the issue being discussed than when this was not the case. The effects of the communicators' speech on subjects' own attitudes seem likely to be influenced by such attributions (for evidence bearing on this possibility, see Eagly et al., 1978; Mills & Jellison, 1967). Newtson and Czerlinsky's study also calls attention to the fact that the audience to which a communicator's message is ostensibly directed can have an important influence on cognitive responses to this message. The following section provides further evidence of this influence.

b. Recipients' Reactions to Self-Descriptions. People in get-acquainted conversations sometimes make explicit references to their own traits and behaviors as well as to those of others. However, these self-descriptions are communicative acts that can have trait and evaluative implications quite apart from their literal meaning. Thus, a man who announces that he recently had his sixth paper accepted for publication in the past 12 months might on one hand be inferred to be productive or intelligent, based on the semantic implications of the statement for these traits. On the other hand, listeners who are stimulated to consider why this statement was made might interpret it as evidence that the speaker is arrogant or boastful. These trait inferences could influence evaluations of him over and above the effects of traits that are inferred on the basis of the statement's semantic implications.

Indirect evidence of this influence was obtained by Wyer, Budesheim, Lambert, and Swan (1994) in a series of studies to be described in more detail presently. In these studies, subjects listened to a tape-recorded conversation between two persons in which the topic of discussion was one of the speakers. As the tape began, subjects heard the experimenter ask one speaker to write down a set of trait descriptions of the other (target) person, and the target to write down traits that he personally considered himself to have. The tape was then stopped and these descriptions (which were either favorable or unfavorable) were passed on to the subjects. Later, after hearing the conversation, subjects evaluated both parties to the discussion. The favorableness of the nontarget's characterization of the target had a positive influence on subjects' liking for the communicator himself, thus replicating the findings reported by Wyer et al. (1990). However, the target's trait description of himself had no effect at all on subjects' liking for him. This suggests that the effects of the nonliteral implications of the target's self-description for his attributes offset the effects of its literal implications, leading to an overall evaluation of the target that was relatively neutral. (For example, the semantic implications of a target who described himself as intelligent may have contributed positively to evaluations of him, whereas its pragmatic implications that the target was boastful contributed negatively. Similarly, a target who described himself as unintelligent may have been inferred to have this attribute but also to be modest.)

In the impression-formation situations constructed by Wyer et al., the literal and nonliteral implications of communications, although evaluatively similar, were along different dimensions. When recipients' objective is to make a specific type of judgment rather than to form a global evaluation, the effects of semantic and pragmatic factors may be more easily separated. A study by Rosen, Cochran, and Musser (1990) is of interest in this regard. Subjects in this study evaluated job applicants on the basis of the applicants' self-descriptions and external letters of reference. When candidates' reference letters were positive, the favorableness of their self-descriptions had a positive influence on subjects' recommendations of them for the job. When candidates' reference letters were negative, however, candidates' self-descriptions had a negative impact on subjects' recommendations. Perhaps when subjects have external evidence that a communicator is credible (as was the case when the reference letters were favorable), they give weight to the semantic implications of the communicator's self-descriptions in making their judgments. When they have reason to believe that the communicator is not credible, however, subjects are relatively more attentive to the pragmatic implications of his or her self-description.[2]

A study by Wyer, Swan, and Gruenfeld (in press), in which subjects were themselves participants in a conversation with the persons they were asked to evaluate, provides further evidence that self-descriptions are evaluated on the basis of their pragmatic implications. In this study, however, these implications were drawn from the way in which self-relevant information was conveyed rather than the content of the information itself. Subjects engaged in a get-acquainted conversation with a partner of either the same or the opposite sex. Ostensibly for purposes of control, they were told to ask their partner five questions similar to those that college students typically ask one another when they meet for the first time (e.g., "Where are you from?" "Do you like school?", etc.) Partners (also experimental subjects who agreed to serve as accomplices) responded to these questions (a) by either elaborating or giving short (e.g., "yes" or "no") answers, and (b) by either asking a question in return or not doing so. Aside from these questions and responses, participants were instructed to carry on the conversation normally. Subjects after the conversation reported their liking for their partner and made other ratings of both their partner and the conversation.

Each subject in the study was assigned a different partner. Therefore, the content of the information that partners provided about themselves varied randomly over experimental conditions. Moreover, the semantic implications of their responses to subjects' questions were evaluatively neutral. However, the pragmatic implications of partners' responses were expected to vary over conditions as a function of experimental manipulations. Specifically, a partner's failure to elaborate or to reciprocate questions could indicate aloofness or self-centeredness. In addition, it could imply lack of interest in the subject personally, and a lack of desire to establish a social relationship with him or her. For either or both reasons, the behavior could decrease the partner's likableness.

---

[2]The relative influence of self-descriptions and others' descriptions on evaluations of a target could also depend on the relevance of these descriptions for the judgments at hand. In a study by Jones, Schwartz, and Gilbert (1984), for example, subjects anticipated bargaining with a partner who was described by either himself or another as either honest or deceitful. In this case, subjects' judgments of the partner's honesty (a trait that was directly relevant to subjects' interaction objectives) were more influenced by the partner's self-description than by the other's characterization of him.

This decrease occurred. That is, both males and females liked their partner less when he or she failed to elaborate or to reciprocate their questions than under other conditions. Contrary to expectations, however, these effects were not mediated by spontaneous inferences of the partner's aloofness or self-centeredness. (Although question reciprocation and elaboration had a nonsignificant influence on subjects' perceptions of these traits, these perceptions were not correlated with liking for the partner.) This is noteworthy in light of the common assumption that underlies much impression-formation research, that general trait attributions play an important role in person impression formation and evaluation (Anderson, 1981; Fiske & Neuberg, 1990; Wyer & Srull, 1989).

Rather, the effects of partners' behavior on subjects' liking for them were mediated by the pragmatic implications of this behavior for the quality of the relationship that subjects had established with the partners during the interaction. That is, subjects interpreted their partner's failure to elaborate or to reciprocate questions as an indication that the partner was not interested in them and did not particularly like them, and these pragmatic inferences decreased their liking for the partners. These inferences and their effects were significantly more evident among females than among males. This sex difference is consistent with Tannen's (1990) hypothesis concerning the differential importance that men and women attach to a sense of connectedness and community in their social interactions.

The effects of partners' behavior on subjects' liking for them were mediated by other factors as well (e.g., the difficulty that subjects had in conducting the conversation and, therefore, their enjoyment of it).[3] However, the results of the study support the hypothesis that people with an impression-formation objective evaluate the information they receive in conversations at least in part on the basis of its pragmatic implications for impression-related attributes as well as its literal meaning.

2. Pragmatic Influences on Opinion Surveys

A quite different set of circumstances in which people are motivated to construe the pragmatic implications of communications arises in interview situations. In such situations, a respondent must decide what information is being solicited by the questions he or she is asked, and then must decide how best to provide this information. However, the precise nature of the information being requested is often ambiguous. Moreover, the information must often be conveyed by selecting from among a restricted set of alternatives provided by the

---

[3]Specifically, when partners failed to elaborate or to reciprocate questions, subjects were required to come up with a new topic to discuss. This increased the difficulty they had in conducting the conversation, and consequently decreased their enjoyment of it. This negative evaluation of the conversation per se apparently generalized to the partner as well.

questioner, and the meaning of these alternatives is also subject to interpretation. In these conditions, a respondent must often use contextual cues that exist in the interview situation, or in the questionnaire being administered as a whole, to infer what the questioner actually wants to know and how best to convey it.

The way in which questionnaire respondents make these inferences has been the subject of an extensive program of research conducted by Norbert Schwarz, Fritz Strack, and their colleagues (Schwarz, 1994; Strack, 1994; Strack & Martin, 1987). These authors have typically likened an interview situation to a conversation in which respondents use normative principles of communication (e.g., Green, 1989; Grice, 1975; Higgins, 1981; Sperber & Wilson, 1986) to infer the sorts of responses that the questioner will consider to be informative, relevant, and accurate, and then respond accordingly. Because this research is reviewed in detail elsewhere (Schwarz, 1994; Strack, 1994), only a few examples will be provided here to convey the role of pragmatic information processing in these situations.

a. Pragmatic Influences on Question Interpretation. Opinion surveys are often constructed so that related questions occur together. Respondents who are motivated to respond appropriately to any given question may use the items accompanying it to infer the nature of the information they are expected to provide. In doing so, they may be guided by normative principles of communication—that is, to be informative, accurate, and relevant. Some implications of this possibility are somewhat ironic. That is, a survey researcher may sometimes include several highly related questions, differing only slightly in wording, for purposes of reliability. Respondents, however, may not appreciate this objective. Rather, they may infer that their response to each question should provide new and different information. Therefore, if they have already answered one of a series of related questions, they may assume that the later questions are intended to solicit information that they have not already conveyed in response to prior questions. Consequently, they use different criteria for responding to these questions than they might otherwise have done.

Thus, to use an example from a study by Strack, Martin, and Schwarz (1988), suppose college students are asked to evaluate their dating behavior and then, immediately afterwards, to judge their satisfaction with life as a whole. Dating is typically an important contributor to college students' general life satisfaction and would normally be used in part as a basis for evaluating it. However, respondents who are asked to report their life satisfaction immediately after reporting on their dating frequency may believe they are supposed to base the second judgment on criteria *other* than dating (i.e., to provide new information), and so they may exclude this criterion in computing their judgment. This means that responses to the two questions would be less highly correlated than they might otherwise be. Strack et al. (1988) found that this was indeed the case. That is, students' estimates of their life satisfaction were highly correlated with their dating frequency when these estimates were reported before their dating frequency had been judged. However, these estimates were uncorrelated with dating frequency when they were made immediately after dating frequency was reported.

Similar effects may occur in other domains. In a study by Ottati, Riggle, Wyer, Schwarz, and Kuklinski (1989), subjects reported their opinions on a variety of social issues. Some items concerned providing civil liberties to people in general (e.g., "People should be allowed to express their opinions in public"), and other items concerned providing these liberties to specific groups that subjects considered to be either desirable ("The ACLU should be allowed to speak on campus") or undesirable ("The Ku Klux Klan should be allowed to speak on campus"). When the group-specific item was presented several items before the general item in the questionnaire, responses to the general item were more favorable when the group specified in the related item was favorable than when it was unfavorable. When the group-specific item was presented immediately before the general one, however, subjects endorsed the general item more strongly when the preceding item referred to an undesirable group than when it referred to a desirable one. In this latter condition, subjects apparently inferred that the questioner intended them to use criteria for responding to the second item that differed from the criteria they had used in answering the first one (i.e., to provide new information). Consequently, they excluded the group specified in the first item from consideration, and this resulted in a contrast effect of the group-specific item on judgments of the general one.[4]

A perhaps more graphic example of subjects' use of context items to infer a criteria a questioner expects them to use is provided by Strack, Schwarz, and Wänke (1991, Experiment 1). German college students were asked their opinion about the desirability of an unspecified "educational contribution." The item was ambiguous, as it could refer either to a contribution that students would be required to make or a contribution from which they would benefit. When the item was preceded by an objectively irrelevant request to estimate the amount of money that Swedish college students receive from their government, subjects interpreted the item in the first way, and consequently expressed approval of the "educational contribution." However, when the item was preceded by an equally irrelevant request to estimate the average tuition fees that American college students have to pay, subjects interpreted the item in the second way and opposed the contribution.

[4]In other conditions of this study, in which subjects were instructed to base their responses on their affective reactions to the conditions described by the items they considered, contrast effects of group-specific items on the endorsement of general ones occurred even when the items were separated. Apparently, instructing subjects to focus on affect made the connection between the two items more salient, and so subjects excluded the implications of their responses to the first item from consideration in judging the general one regardless of their separation in the questionnaire.

b. Pragmatic Influences on the Interpretation of Response Alternatives. An equally important cue to the type of information a questioner is soliciting may be the response alternatives that he or she provides. To borrow an example from Schwarz, Strack, Mueller, and Chassein (1988), suppose subjects are asked the frequency with which they get "really irritated" along a scale with alternatives that range either (a) from "several times daily" to "less than once a week," or (b) from "several times a year" to "less than once every 3 months." Although "really irritated" is a household phrase, it is ambiguous in terms of the intensity of the irritation to which it actually refers. Consequently, respondents may use the response alternatives to disambiguate it. Thus, in the above example, they are likely to interpret it as pertaining to less extreme instances in the first case than in the second. Schwarz et al. found that this was indeed the case. That is, subjects who were asked to list examples of annoying experiences after responding to the item described above listed objectively less extreme experiences when the first set of response alternatives had been provided than when the second set had been provided.

Numerous other examples of respondents' use of contextual cues to infer the type of information they are expected to provide in opinion surveys are summarized by Schwarz (1994) and Strack (1994). However, the preceding examples suffice to point out that respondents who are motivated to communicate information to another not only rely upon the semantic implications of the questions they are asked. In addition, they use contextual cues as well as their general knowledge to infer what information the questioner wants to obtain, and these pragmatic inferences guide the responses they make.

II. Informational Influences on Pragmatic Information Processing: The Role of Expectancy Deviations

In the conditions we considered in the last section, the pragmatic implications of the information presented were particularly relevant to the purpose for which recipients acquired it (e.g., forming a person impression, or answering a survey question). In the absence of such objectives, subjects may not spontaneously expend the effort required to identify the pragmatic meaning of a message. This is particularly true if its literal meaning, and the style in which it is delivered, are consistent with expectations for what is appropriate under the circumstances in which the message occurs. If, however, the content or style of a communication deviates from expectations, subjects are more likely to seek an explanation for its occurrence. Then, they may construe the source's motive for conveying the information, and may reassess its meaning in light of this motive (Higgins, Monaghan, & Rholes, 1976, cited in Higgins, 1981). This latter, pragmatic meaning can often differ from the literal meaning of the information.

The factors that stimulate the spontaneous consideration of why a communication has been generated could be general or situation-specific, and could concern either the content of the communication or the style in which it is delivered. As noted earlier, normal conversation is governed by a number of implicit principles that are applied by both the communicator and the recipient in order to communicate effectively (Grice, 1975; see also Green, 1989; Higgins, 1981; Sperber & Wilson, 1986). For example, communications are usually intended to be informative, or nonredundant with recipients' prior knowledge. Thus, people expect that a communication they receive is intended to convey new information. Similarly, they assume that a communicator intends his or her statements to be accurate, and to be relevant to the topic of conversation.

Other normative principles of communication may be specific to certain types of interactions. In informal conversations, for example, communicators are expected to be polite, or not to offend intentionally the individuals with whom they are interacting. Moreover, people in such situations are usually expected to appear modest rather than boastful and self-aggrandizing. In these situations, as well as in the more general conditions considered by Grice and others, recipients are likely to expect communicators to adhere to these principles and interpret their communications accordingly. Finally, normative considerations can govern the style with which information is conveyed as well as its content. In the situation constructed by Wyer, Swan, and Gruenfeld (in press) and noted earlier, for example, participants in an informal conversation may expect their conversation partners to respond to their questions by elaborating rather than with simply a yes or no answers, and to express interest in the interaction by asking them questions in return.

Regardless of the particular norm involved, it seems reasonable to postulate that a violation of expectations based on this norm will stimulate recipients to question why the violation occurred and, therefore, to consider its pragmatic implications. Suppose, for example, that a recipient receives a message that is so redundant with his or her prior knowledge that it goes without saying (thus appearing to violate a principle that communications are intended to be informative). The recipient may attempt to understand why the statement was made. One possibility, of course, is that the statement does *not* in fact go without saying. That is, there could actually be some reason (of which the recipient is unaware) to suppose that the assertion is false, thus making its reaffirmation informative. Alternatively, the communicator could be unaware of the recipient's prior knowledge, and might believe that the statement does, in fact, convey new information. A third possibility is that the statement is intended as irony; that is, it is meant to convey the opposite of what it literally implies.

In summary, then, it seems reasonable to postulate that in the absence of objectives that require attention to a communication's pragmatic meaning, persons will tend to focus primarily on the literal meaning of the communication. If, however, the content or style of the communication violates normative expectations for information transmitted in the particular context in which it occurs, recipients will be stimulated to seek an explanation for it. This explanation-seeking activity could have three possible consequences:

1. Recipients will attempt to reinterpret the message in a way that is not reflected by its literal meaning, but is consistent with expectations for the type of communication that is normatively appropriate.
2. Recipients will think more extensively about the implications of the expectancy-deviant information than they otherwise would, and, as a result of this more extensive processing, may later be better able to recall it (Craik & Lockhart, 1972; Wyer & Hartwick, 1980).
3. Subjects are likely to seek *additional* information that will help them to understand why the communication occurred. As a consequence, information they encounter in the course of this search may have more impact on their later judgments than it otherwise would.

The studies we describe provide additional examples of each of these possible effects.

A. EFFECTS OF CONVERSATIONAL NORM VIOLATIONS ON THE INTERPRETATION OF INFORMATION

1. The Effects of Informativeness on Responses to Information in the Public Media

The role of informativeness in the construal of a communicator's intent, and its subsequent impact on subjects' beliefs and opinions, was demonstrated by Gruenfeld and Wyer (1992). Subjects read a series of statements that were ostensibly taken from either newspapers (a source with the primary objective of conveying new information) or an encyclopedia (a source with the primary function of recording archival knowledge). Some statements asserted the validity of target propositions that most subjects in the population we considered (first- and second-year college students) already believed to be false (e.g., "The CIA is engaged in illegal drug trafficking."). Other statements, however, denied the validity of these propositions. (Thus, affirmations were informative, whereas denials were uninformative.) After reading the statements subjects reported their own beliefs in both the target propositions and conceptually related ones (e.g., "The CIA is involved in illegal activities other than drug trafficking.").

We assumed that when statements were allegedly taken from encyclopedias, subjects would not necessarily expect the statements to provide new information. That is, they should attribute the statements' uninformativeness to the source's

TABLE II
EFFECTS OF ASSERTIONS ON BELIEFS IN TARGET
PROPOSITIONS AND RELATED PROPOSITIONS[a]

	Type of assertion[b]	
	Affirmation	Denial
Target propositions		
Newspaper source	1.16*	1.06*
Encyclopedia source	1.81*	.48
Related propositions		
Newspaper source	1.15*	1.20*
Encyclopedia source	1.62*	.91*

[a]Based on data from Gruenfeld and Wyer, 1992.
[b]Cell entries indicate differences between beliefs reported in experimental conditions and context-free beliefs reported in control conditions. Differences denoted by asterisks are significantly greater than 0, $p < .05$.

ostensible objective of conveying archival knowledge. Consequently, we expected that subjects in this condition would be primarily influenced by the literal meaning of the statements. This was in fact the case. The top half of Table II shows the difference between subjects' beliefs that the target propositions were true under each experimental condition and the beliefs of control subjects who were not exposed to assertions. Subjects who believed that the statements came from encyclopedias reported less strong beliefs in the propositions when the statement they read denied their validity than when they affirmed their validity. Beliefs in related propositions, shown in the bottom half of Table II, were similarly affected.

When the statements came from newspapers, however, we assumed that ostensibly uninformative statements (denials) would stimulate subjects to consider why the statements were made. In doing so, subjects might speculate that there were reasons to believe that the propositions being denied were actually true (thus making the denials of their validity informative). If so, these speculations should increase their beliefs in the propositions' validity rather than decreasing them. This appeared to be the case. As shown in Table II, subjects in these conditions increased their beliefs in the target propositions to just as great an extent when the statements they read denied the validity of the propositions as when they affirmed their validity. Subjects' beliefs in related propositions were affected in much the same way.

The boomerang effects of uninformative denials are similar to the effects of innuendo postulated by Wegner, Wenzlaff, Kerker, and Beattie (1981). However, the processes that underlie these effects are more general than Wegner et al. assumed. In an additional experiment (Gruenfeld & Wyer, 1992, Experiment 3), the target propositions that subjects considered were typically believed to be true. Therefore, affirmations of the propositions were uninformative and denials were informative. In this case, subjects who read statements that affirmed the propositions decreased their beliefs in the propositions' validity. Thus, the phenomenon is more general than would be predicted on the basis of innuendo effects alone.

The validity of some propositions, of course, is not open to question. For example, the statement "Americans are not allowed to vote until they reach the age of 18" is undeniably true, and so reading this statement in a newspaper is unlikely to affect beliefs in its validity. Readers might nevertheless be stimulated to consider why the statement was made. In such cases, they might interpret the statements as indirect expressions of opinion (e.g., "Americans are not allowed to vote until they are 18, and this situation is undesirable"), or as implicit statements of comparison ("Americans cannot vote until they are 18, but citizens of other countries can"). These interpretations could also affect recipients' beliefs in ways that are not implied by the literal meaning of the statements per se. Gruenfeld and Wyer (1992) provide some evidence of this as well.

The effects of deviations of statements' semantic meaning from expectations observed in the aforementioned studies were not examined in actual social interaction situations. However, similar deviations are likely to stimulate pragmatic information processing in these situations as well. This assumption is implicit in may current analyses of natural language understanding (e.g., Green, 1989; Sperber & Wilson, 1986). Two conditions that are of particular importance to a general conceptualization of social information processing concern (a) the elicitation of humor and (b) emotional communication in close relationships. Although the role of conversational norms in these contexts has been discussed elsewhere (Scott, Fuhrman, & Wyer, 1991; Wyer & Collins, 1992; Wyer & Gruenfeld, in press) certain aspects of this discussion are worth reiterating briefly in the present context.

2. *Humor Elicitation in Informal Interactions*

Although humor is often elicited by jokes, it is more frequently stimulated by witticisms that occur spontaneously in the course of informal conversation. Witticisms are of several types (Long & Graesser, 1988). The question is how witticisms are identified as such. How, for example, do people recognize a statement as ironic, and how do they distinguish between teases and sincere expressions of hostility? Facial expressions and other nonverbal behaviors can obviously provide cues as to whether or not a speaker is trying to be funny. However, other factors are likely to come into play as well.

Wyer and Collins (1992) postulate that the identification of a statement as a witticism is stimulated in part by the recognition that the statement's literal meaning violates a normative principle of conversation. This violation leads the recipient to infer that the literal meaning is not the meaning that the speaker intends to convey, but, in fact, may be quite the opposite. A second condition for humor elicitation is that the implications of a statement's intended meaning be more mundane (e.g., less extreme) than those of its literal meaning (for an elaboration of this contingency, see Wyer & Collins, 1992; see also Apter, 1992). Thus, for example, consider the statement "Central Illinois is a great place to spend the summer—all that lovely corn and high humidity." Residents of central Illinois are likely to recognize the statement's literal meaning as a violation of the conversational norm that communications are intended to be accurate. Therefore, for reasons suggested by Gruenfeld and Wyer (1992), they may be stimulated to consider the statement's pragmatic implications, and to conclude that the statement is intended as sarcasm. In contrast, a person who is unfamiliar with central Illinois and its climate would not be aware that the statement violates a conversational norm, and therefore would not identify its intended meaning.

Similarly, an individual's statement that "what America needs is another Ronald Reagan" is more likely to be interpreted as sarcastic, and therefore to be considered amusing, by a liberal Democrat than by an arch-conservative (who may well believe that the statement is true). However, the recipient must also believe that the *speaker* considers the statement to be inaccurate. In other words, the recipient must not only recognize that the statement's literal meaning violates a conversational norm but also must believe that the communicator is cognizant of this fact.

Violations of other conversational norms can also underlie the identification of witticisms. Suppose a person who has returned from a trip to Europe remarks that "Switzerland is even more beautiful than central Illinois." This statement is uninformative, and might elicit amusement to the extent the recipient recognizes that the statement is intended to disparage Illinois rather than to extol the virtues of Switzerland.

Statements could be recognized as teases as the result of their violation of two principles: accuracy and politeness. According to the politeness principle, communications are not intended to offend the recipient. Disparaging statements about a person appear to violate this principle when the statements are made in the person's presence, and so they are likely to stimulate a construal of the statement's pragmatic implications. These considerations might lead listeners to conclude that the speaker intended to tease the target rather than to disparage him or her. One implication of this reasoning is that statements are more likely to be recognized as teases if they are extremely disparaging (or alternatively, are grossly inaccurate) than if they are only moderately so. This is because they are more likely to be seen as violating a conversational norm in the former case than the latter.

As noted above, the mere recognition of a comment as in violation of a conversational norm is not sufficient to elicit humor. Both Wyer and Collins (1992) and Apter (1982) have attempted to circumscribe the necessary and sufficient conditions for humor elicitation. Unfortunately, relatively little research has been devoted to the cognitive processes that underlie humor elicitation in natural settings. This is as surprising as it is unfortunate in light of the preeminent role of humor in informal interaction.

3. Emotional Communication

The elicitation of humor theoretically requires recognition that a statement's intended meaning is more mundane than its literal meaning (Apter, 1982; Wyer & Collins, 1992). In some cases, a consideration of a statement's pragmatic implications can lead the statement to be interpreted as less innocuous than its literal meaning implies. The identification of these implications can also be mediated by the recognition that the literal meaning of a communication violates a conversational norm.

Thus, for example, suppose a woman remarks to her spouse, "I think it's cold in here." If she has rarely complained in the past about the temperature of the room, the husband may regard her statement as new information and take steps to correct the situation. However, if the wife's remark is one of many similar observations she has made in comparable situations over a period of time, the husband may regard it as uninformative. To this extent, he may construe its pragmatic implications. In doing so, he might interpret his wife's remark as an expression of anger over his desire to save energy by keeping the thermostat low. As this example implies, the identification of a statement's pragmatic meaning can often require a substantial amount of shared knowledge. Watzlawick, Beavin, and Jackson (1967) also note that partners in close relationships acquire a private meaning system that allows them to communicate thoughts, feelings and ideas to one another to which other listeners are not privy. These matters are largely communicated through the pragmatic implications of partners' comments to one another rather than their literal implications.

In fact, sensitivity to the pragmatic implications of communications is likely to be a major factor in emotional communication between persons who know one another well (for a more detailed discussion of this role, see Scott, Fuhrman, & Wyer, 1991). However, even persons with substantial knowledge of one another cannot always identify accurately the feelings that their partners intend to convey. In a study by Gaelick, Bodenhausen, and Wyer (1985), for example, married couples engaged in a videotaped discussion of a problem they were having in their relationship. Subsequently, each partner individually reviewed the tape, identified statements that were particularly significant, and made several ratings of these statements in terms of both (a) the emotions that the speaker intended to convey, and (b) the emotions that the recipient conveyed in return.

The emotional reactions that were transmitted by partners in this study were typically communicated through the pragmatic implications of their statements and not the semantic implications. Indeed, it was often very difficult for a naive observer to identify any intense feelings in the messages that partners identified as significant. In fact, partners themselves were not always accurate in identifying one another's feelings. Intentions to convey hostility, for example, were much more accurately perceived than intentions to convey love. This is particularly noteworthy in light of the fact that partners typically reciprocated the emotions that they perceived were conveyed to them. Therefore, because love was not accurately perceived, only expressions of hostility were actually reciprocated. As a consequence, expressions of hostility were more likely to escalate over the course of the interaction than were expressions of love.

A second finding of interest was that men but not women interpreted their partner's failure to communicate love as intentions to express hostility, whereas women but not men interpreted their partner's lack of hostility as expressions of love. Apparently, partners in close relationships have normative expectations for one another similar to those implied by sex-role stereotypes. That is, women expect their male partners to be generally aggressive, whereas men expect their female partners to be warm and nurturant. Therefore, partners' communications that violate these role-specific expectations stimulate a search for explanations of these violations, leading the statements to be interpreted as expressions of the opposite emotion rather than as simply neutral.

B. EFFECTS OF CONVERSATIONAL NORM VIOLATIONS ON MEMORY

To the extent that communications that deviate from normative expectations stimulate a consideration of their pragmatic implications, subjects should think more extensively about these communications than they otherwise would. This more extensive processing of norm-violating communications should increase their accessibility in memory and, therefore, the likelihood that recipients can later recall them (Craik & Lockhart, 1972; Wyer & Hartwick, 1980).

A series of studies by Wyer, Budesheim, Lambert, and Swan (1994) demonstrate these effects. In doing so, they call attention to the role of two conversational norms—politeness and modesty—that are of obvious importance in understanding the exchange of information in social interactions. In these studies, which were mentioned briefly earlier, subjects listened to a conversation between two male students in which the topic of discussion was one of the participants. Thus, over the course of the discussion, one participant, O, described both favorable and unfavorable behaviors that the target had performed, whereas the target conveyed both favorable and unfavorable things that he personally had done. In one study (Wyer et al., 1994; Experiment 3), subjects received this information under conditions in which they were asked either (a) to form an impression of O, based on O's descriptions of the target (*other-impression, other-focus* conditions); (b) to form an impression of the target, based on O's description of him (*target-impression, other-focus* conditions); or (c) to form an impression of the target, based on the target's descriptions of himself (*target-impression, target-focus* conditions).

We expected both politeness and modesty norms to operate in the conditions described above. Specifically, people in informal conversation are expected to try not to offend or antagonize the persons to whom they are communicating. To this extent, O's descriptions of the target's unfavorable behaviors should violate this normative expectancy, and therefore should be thought about more extensively in an attempt to explain their occurrence. Unfavorable statements the target makes about himself should of course not stimulate this cognitive activity. To the contrary, these statements are likely to be considered indications of modesty and, therefore socially appropriate. On the other hand, *favorable* descriptions of one's own behavior, particularly if carried to excess, may be considered counternormative. Thus, if behaviors that are thought about more extensively are better recalled, behaviors mentioned by O should be better recalled if they are unfavorable than if they are favorable, whereas behaviors mentioned by the target himself should be better recalled if they are favorable than if they are unfavorable.

This is in fact what happened. Table III shows the proportions of favorable and unfavorable behaviors recalled in each condition as a function of the speaker who mentioned them. Behaviors mentioned by O were recalled relatively better if they were unfavorable, whereas behaviors mentioned by the target were recalled relatively better if they were favorable. The recall advantage of unfavorable behaviors mentioned by O was least when the behaviors were irrelevant to subjects' processing objective (i.e., when they were told to form an impression of the target based on behaviors that he personally mentioned). Correspondingly, the recall advantage of favorable behaviors the target mentioned was least when these behaviors were goal-irrelevant (when subjects were told to form an impression of O based on the behaviors that O mentioned). However, these between-condition differences were not statistically significant. This suggests that subjects were at least somewhat sensitive to the counternormativeness of speakers' statements (and thus were stimulated to think about their pragmatic implications) even when the statements were not directly relevant to their primary information-processing goals.

Because an identification of the pragmatic implications of information requires processing over and above a consideration of its semantic implications, it may not occur when information processing demands are high. An additional study by Wyer et al. (1994, Experiment 2) suggests this. This study was similar to the first

TABLE III

PROPORTION OF FAVORABLE AND UNFAVORABLE BEHAVIORS RECALLED AS A FUNCTION OF TASK OBJECTIVES AND THE SOURCE OF THE BEHAVIORS[a]

	Task Objectives		
	Target impression, target focus	Target impression, other focus	Other impression, other focus
Behaviors mentioned by other (O)			
Favorable	.42	.40	.35
Unfavorable	.45	.54	.49
Behaviors mentioned by target (T)			
Favorable	.47	.50	.37
Unfavorable	.40	.41	.34

[a]Adapted from Wyer, Budesheim, Lambert, and Swan, 1994.

experiment described, except subjects were asked to consider the behaviors described by *both* speakers in forming an impression of either O or the target. A statement can usually be recognized as impolite independently of other statements that accompany it. However, favorable self-descriptions may not be identified as in violation of a modesty norm unless they occur repeatedly. That is, subjects may need to think about a favorable self-statement in the context of several similar statements in order to identify it as counternormative, and so their consideration of such statements in isolation may not stimulate pragmatic information processing. (Judgment data reported by Wyer et al. support this assumption. That is, subjects judged a single unfavorable statement about another to be counternormative if it was made in the other's presence, but they did not consider a single favorable self-description to be counternormative.) Consequently, when subjects are required to consider the behaviors mentioned by both speakers rather than only one, this increased processing load is likely to decrease their sensitivity to the counternormativeness of the target's self-descriptions. Results were consistent with this conjecture. That is, subjects had better recall of unfavorable behaviors mentioned by O than favorable behaviors, replicating results of the first experiment described. However, subjects' recall of favorable behaviors the target himself mentioned was only slightly higher than the recall of unfavorable ones, suggesting that these statements did not stimulate pragmatic information processing under these conditions.

C. THE EFFECTS OF CONVERSATIONAL NORM VIOLATIONS ON ATTENTION TO OTHER AVAILABLE INFORMATION

If statements made in a conversation that violate normative expectations stimulate subjects to identify their pragmatic implications, these statements should lead subjects not only to think more extensively about the norm-violating communications themselves, but also to seek other information that could provide an explanation for their occurrence. As a consequence of this greater attention, the latter information may have greater impact on judgments to which it is relevant than it otherwise would.

This hypothesis is supported by a second study we conducted on impression formation in informal conversations (Wyer, Swan, & Gruenfeld, in press). The study was similar in many respects to an experiment we described earlier. That is, female subjects engaged in a get-acquainted conversation with another subject who responded to their questions by either (a) both elaborating their answers and asking the subject questions in return, (*normative-behavior* conditions) or (b) neither elaborating nor reciprocating the subject's questions (*counternormative-behavior* conditions). However, subjects in some conditions, ostensibly by mistake, were given access to a description of their partner that another subject had provided during a previous experimental session. This description indicated that the partner was either (a) sociable (an attribute that was relevant to the partner's conversational style) or (b) high in integrity (an attribute that was irrelevant to the partner's behavior). In a third, control condition, no trait information was provided.

We expected that when the partner's response to subjects' questions was typical of behavior manifested in informal conversations (e.g., when partner elaborated and reciprocated questions), subjects would pay little attention to explicit trait descriptions of her. When the partner's behavior was counternormative, however, subjects were expected to seek an explanation for it and, in the course of this search, to become more sensitive to the trait information.

Results were consistent with this reasoning. Table IV shows subjects' evaluations of the partner as a function of the partner's conversational style and the implications of the trait information presented. When the partner elaborated and reciprocated subjects' questions, subjects' evaluations did not depend on whether trait descriptions of her were provided or not. When the partner's conversational style was counternormative, however, providing favorable trait descriptions increased subjects' evaluations of her. In other words, explicit trait descriptions had a positive influence on subjects' evaluations of their partner only when her conversational style deviated from expectations. Moreover, these effects occurred regardless of whether the trait description was relevant to the partner's

TABLE IV
SUBJECTS' LIKING FOR THEIR PARTNER AS A FUNCTION OF THE PARTNER'S CONVERSATIONAL STYLE AND TRAIT DESCRIPTIONS[a]

	Trait desription			
	Conversation-relevant	Conversation-irrelevant	None	M
Normative conversational style	8.78	8.56	8.95	8.76
Counternormative conversational style	6.78	6.63	3.88	5.89
M	7.78	7.50	6.56	—

[a]Based on data from Wyer, Swan, and Gruenfeld, in press.

conversational behavior or not. Thus, the information search that was stimulated by pragmatic information processing increased subjects' sensitivity to all available information, regardless of its actual relevance to the behavior they were attempting to explain.

Other factors that could contribute to these results should be considered. For example, the failure for favorable trait descriptions to increase evaluations of the partner when her conversational style was normative might be attributed to ceiling effects. The fact that evaluations were actually (nonsignificantly) less when trait descriptions were provided than when they were not (Table IV) argues against this possibility. A related possibility, however, is simply that once a favorable initial impression is formed, the addition of other favorable information has generally less impact. Whether unfavorable trait information would also have less impact when the target's conversational behavior was normative (i.e., favorable) is unclear from this study.[5] Trait descriptions were conveyed to subjects before the conversation took place. Therefore, if subjects had simply based their judgments of the target on the initial trait information independently of her behavior, this information should have had similar impact regardless of the nature of this behavior, and it did not. Nevertheless, caution should be taken in accepting the conclusions we have drawn from this study pending replication.

[5]The failure to run conditions in which trait adjective descriptions of the partner were unfavorable was a result of ethical considerations. Because partners in the study were themselves subjects, we thought it would be inappropriate to convey bogus unfavorable information about them to another without their informed consent. On the other hand, attaining this consent prior to the conversation seemed likely to influence their behavior, and therefore, to affect the interaction that occurred. Consequently, these conditions were not run despite their theoretical importance.

III. Individual Differences in Pragmatic Information Processing

Most of the factors we have postulated to influence the perception of a communication's pragmatic meaning have been situational. However, more general individual differences can also exist both in the tendency to extract pragmatic meaning from people's statements and behavior and in the particular type of meaning that is extracted. These differences can often be traceable to differences in the purpose for which recipients expect to use the information they receive, and in the importance they attach to the specific attributes to which the information is relevant (e.g., Wyer et al., in press). In addition, people's general values and social orientation could lead them to respond differently to the pragmatic implications of others' statements and behaviors. These differences could surround both the perception of these implications and the importance that is attached to them.

In this regard, the study by Wyer et al. (1994) cited earlier indicates that subjects have better recall of behaviors that violate normative expectations for communicators to be (a) polite and (b) modest. Violations of other norms could also stimulate more extensive processing. For example, people may generally think more extensively about statements and behaviors that they consider to be untrue and, therefore, to violate normative expectancies for a communication to convey objectively accurate information. On the other hand, individual differences are likely to exist in perceptions that communications actually violate this norm (i.e., in beliefs that the information conveyed is objectively true or false). These differences are particularly likely when the information reflects personal opinions.

A study by Wyer, Lambert, Budesheim, & Gruenfeld (1992) bears on this possibility. Subjects received information about a target person's opinions on a number of familiar social issues with instructions to form an impression of the person. The research paradigm was similar to that employed in other studies of person memory and judgment (Srull & Wyer, 1989) in that the opinions were communicated out of their social context. Nevertheless, we expected that subjects would vary in the extent to which they perceived the statements to be objectively valid. Moreover, because the statements concerned issues of social and personal relevance, they were expected to stimulate subjects to think about why a person might make the statements. (For evidence that statements that violate normative expectations can stimulate these considerations even when they are presented out of their social context, see Gruenfeld & Wyer, 1992, in a study described earlier.) This more extensive processing should lead the statements to be better recalled than statements that subjects perceived to be objectively true. Subjects varied, of course, in the extent to which they considered any given opinion statement to be true. As implied by the above considerations, however, subjects had better recall of those statements they personally believed to be false than those they regarded as correct.

Our interpretation of this difference assumes that subjects with an impression-formation objective spontaneously considered the reasons why the target person might have expressed opinions with which they personally disagreed, and that this more extensive cognitive activity increased their later recall of these opinions. However, there may be individual differences in the extent to which subjects are motivated to engage in this cognitive activity. Moreover, these differences, which could reflect differences in the importance that subjects attach to the reasons that underlie expressions of opinion when they are asked to form a person impression, could occur even when subjects are explicitly told to take these reasons into account. This possibility was investigated by Wänke and Wyer (1994). These authors speculated that the motivation to consider the underlying causes of statements and behaviors would be predictable from subjects' more general political ideology. Several studies (e.g., Emler, Renwick, & Malone, 1983; Fishkin, Keniston, & MacKinnon, 1973; Nassi, Abramowitz, & Youmans, 1983) suggest that liberals have a relatively high level of moral development, as defined by Kohlberg (1976). That is, they are relatively more apt than conservatives to consider the general principles that underlie social behavior. This assumption was confirmed by Wänke and Wyer, who found that subjects with a liberal social and political orientation reported being more inclined than conservatives to consider the underlying causes of a person's behavior when evaluating the person, and also manifested a greater level of attributional complexity as defined by Fletcher, Danilovics, Fernandez, Peterson, and Reeder (1986). Based on this assumption, Wänke and Wyer reasoned that explicit instructions to focus attention on the reasons why a target person's opinion-related behavior occurred when forming an impression would have greater influence on liberals' cognitive responses to this behavior than on conservatives' responses.

To examine this possibility, liberal and conservative subjects were told to form an impression of a target person on the basis of a series of social behaviors, each of which reflected an underlying opinion on a social issue (e.g., "picketed an abortion clinic," "organized free legal aid for low income families," etc.). The behaviors varied in their ideological implications and, therefore, in the likelihood that subjects would consider them (or the opinions they reflected) to be desirable. Subjects in *behavior-focus* conditions were simply told to form their impressions on the basis of the behaviors themselves, whereas subjects in *opinion-focus* conditions were explicitly told to consider the opinions reflected by the behaviors. Later, subjects were asked to recall the behaviors they had read. Subjects were expected to have better recall of opinion-relevant behaviors of which they disapproved than ones of which they approved, consistent with findings obtained earlier by Wyer et al. (1992). However, explicit instructions to focus attention on

TABLE V
MEAN PROPORTION OF BEHAVIORS RECALLED AS A FUNCTION OF THEIR DESIRABILITY, SUBJECTS'
IDEOLOGY, AND INSTRUCTIONS[a]

	Liberal subjects		Conservative subjects	
	Opinion-focus conditions	Behavior-focus conditions	Opinion-focus conditions	Behavior-focus conditions
Desirable behaviors	.37	.46	.39	.35
Undesireable behaviors	.64	.54	.33	.66

[a]Adapted from Wänke and Wyer, 1994.

the attitudes underlying these behaviors were expected to increase the magnitude of this difference among liberal subjects but not conservatives.

Results clearly confirmed these speculations. The proportion of behaviors that subjects recalled under each instructional condition is shown in Table V as a function of subjects' ideology and the desirability of the behaviors (based on each subjects' own postexperimental evaluations of these behaviors and the opinions they reflected). Liberal subjects had better recall of behaviors they considered undesirable than behaviors they considered desirable, and this difference increased when they were told explicitly to focus their attention on the opinions that underlie the behaviors. In contrast, although conservatives had better recall of undesirable than desirable behaviors under behavior-focus conditions, instructing them to consider the opinions reflected by the behaviors nonsignificantly reversed this difference. Perhaps when conservative subjects were told to take the antecedents of behaviors into account, their normal processing of these behaviors was disrupted. Consequently, their cognitive responses to the behaviors differed from those they would make in the absence of these external demands. Alternatively, conservatives might simply not have considered the judgmental criterion they were told to use under opinion-focus conditions to be important, and so they did not engage in the more extensive processing of opinions with which they disagreed.

Although the opinion-relevant information in Wänke and Wyer's study was presented under somewhat artificial experimental conditions, it seems likely that similar differences in responses would occur if similar information was conveyed in a social context. That is, both liberals and conservatives are apt to think more extensively about the behaviors and opinion statements they consider to be undesirable than about those they regard as desirable. However, liberals might focus their attention on the factors that underlie these acts, whereas conservatives might be more inclined to take them at face value. In any event, Wänke and

Wyer's study obviously provides only one example of the possible individual differences that might underlie pragmatic information processing. Other factors, such as need for cognition (Petty & Cacioppo, 1986) or integrative complexity (Tetlock, 1986) are likely to play a role as well. A general conceptualization of these differences is an objective of future research.

IV. The Mental Representation of Information Conveyed in a Social Context

It seems clear that any complete conceptualization of social information processing must be able to specify not only the cognitive activities that occur in response to information but also the mental representations that are formed from this information and how these representations are later used to make judgments and decisions. A specification of these processes and the representations that are formed has been a focus of much of our past research on person memory and judgment (Srull & Wyer, 1989; Wyer & Carlston, 1994; Wyer & Srull, 1989) and event memory (Fuhrman & Wyer, 1988; Trafimow & Wyer, 1993; Wyer et al., 1985).

In fact, certain of the effects discussed in this article might potentially be captured by a model similar to that proposed by Hastie (1980) and elaborated by Srull and Wyer (1989; see also Wyer & Srull, 1989). According to this model, individual items of information are organized around a central evaluative concept of the person to whom the information is relevant. In addition, items that are inconsistent with the central concept are thought about more extensively in relation to others, thus forming interitem associations that facilitate its later recall. If the information conveyed in a conversation can be viewed as a sequence of communicative acts, it might be organized around concepts of the speaker rather than concepts of the referent (Wyer et al., 1990). Moreover, the cognitive activity that stimulates interitem associations may result from the inconsistency of these communicative acts with more general conversational norms as well as their inconsistency with a concept of the speaker per se. One implication of this is that statements that violate normative principles of communication should be remembered. Evidence that this is true when a politeness norm is violated was obtained by Wyer et al. (1994) in the study described earlier.

Having said this, the conditions in which an associative network model can capture the mental representations that are formed in informal interaction are likely to be limited. The utility of such a model is greatest when the communications in question comprise a set of relatively independent statements. The messages investigated in the studies by Gruenfeld (1993) and Gruenfeld and Wyer (1993) were not of this type, nor are many communications that occur in informal conversations. That is, the tendency to provide only one- or two-sentence descriptions of oneself and others in conversations is more likely to be the exception than the rule. More generally, people who exchange information about themselves and others convey this information in the form of a *narrative*, or temporally and thematically related sequence of events. A narrative might be a personal history (e.g., the events leading up to one's decision to become a psychologist). Or, it might be a story about a specific experience one has had or heard about. The pragmatic implications that people extract from these narratives may be as or more important in understanding interpersonal perception in social situations than is the pragmatic meaning of single statements of the sort considered in our research thus far.

More generally, narratives (or cognitive representations of them) may be fundamental ingredients of social memory that are used in comprehending the new information one receives as well as in communicating to others. For one thing, everyday life experiences are inherently temporal, and mental representations of these experiences are likely to share this temporal character. Many narratives may consist in part of a verbal or nonverbal coding of a sequence of events that one has personally experienced. However, it can also contain thoughts, inferences, or emotional reactions that accompanied the occurrence of these events.

Others' accounts of their experiences are likely to be comprehended in terms of a previously formed narrative concerning experiences one has personally had or heard about. Schank (1992; Schank & Abelson, in press) has also argued that "stories" are the principle basis for comprehending information acquired outside the laboratory. In conceptualizing these comprehension processes, Schank points out that both the stories one hears and those that one retrieves for use in comprehending them are often incomplete. That is, certain features that are necessary in order to understand fully the determinants and effects of the events described in a story are not specified. When such "gaps" occur in one story, they are often filled by inserting features analogous to those contained in the other. Thus, comprehension is a two-way street, with each story being used to understand the other.

Note that the missing events in one story can occur either before, during, or after the sequence of events that compose the other. Thus, the second story might be used to infer either (a) the factors that gave rise to the sequence of events specified in the first story, (b) future consequences of these events, or (c) how the events contained in the story are causally related to one another. Moreover, thoughts and feelings that accompanied the events that compose a personal narrative may be attributed to characters in another's story, giving rise to feelings of empathy. By the same token, the relations among events on one's personal life may be inferred in the course of comprehending others' account of his or her experiences in which the causal links between the events are specified.

It is conceivable that narratives provide the primary basis for the impressions one forms of others. It is interesting to speculate that the ability to identify a personal narrative that is applicable for understanding another person's life experience is the primary basis for the perception that one "knows" and "understands" the other. An identification of the pragmatic meaning of another's description of his or her experience or life history may likewise be affected by the extent to which the narrative resembles those that one considers to be applicable under the social circumstances in which they occur. If this is so, abstract trait and behavior descriptions of the sort that provide the basis for impressions formed in many studies of person memory and judgment (Hamilton, Driscoll, & Worth, 1989; Klein & Loftus, 1990; Srull & Wyer, 1989) are likely to be of limited relevance to impressions formed in social contexts.

A clear conceptualization of the role of narratives in comprehension and communication will require substantial theoretical and empirical work. The manner in which a narrative is represented in memory is of course central to such a conceptualization. Research in both our laboratory (Trafimow & Wyer, 1993; Wyer & Bodenhausen, 1985; Wyer et al., 1985) and elsewhere (Black, Galambos, & Read, 1984; Graesser, 1981; Schank & Abelson, 1977; Stein & Glenn, 1979) has investigated the mental representations of temporally related sequences of events. However, the stimulus materials used have often been presented out of any social context and have typically been of little personal relevance to subjects. Therefore, the implications of this work for a conceptualization of the structure of personal narratives of the sort communicated in social situations is not entirely clear.

One must also develop a typology that permits narratives to be systematically compared. A solution to this problem is a prerequisite for understanding the manner in which narratives are indexed in memory and, therefore, the factors that lead any particular story to be spontaneously retrieved and used either to comprehend another's experience or to communicate information to others. An explication of these retrieval processes could have implications for the cognitive organization of information that challenge existing models of social memory (Carlston, 1994; Wyer & Carlston, 1994; Wyer & Srull, 1986, 1989). Research in our laboratory is just beginning to evaluate more generally the role of narratives in person impression formation and self-judgments and the semantic and pragmatic meaning that is likely to be drawn from them. However, we are a long way from attaining answers to the questions we are addressing.

V. Final Comments

In this chapter, we have summarized a very diverse body of research, conducted in a variety of experimental paradigms and addressing many different topics. However, the research converges on four related conclusions.

1. The interpretation of information that is received in a social context, and therefore its impact on judgments and decisions, is likely to be guided as much by perceptions of its pragmatic implications (i.e., *why* the information was conveyed) as by its semantic meaning. These implications can be conveyed either through the content of the information itself or the style in which it is delivered. In either event, recipients use contextual cues as well as their general world knowledge to infer why the information is transmitted and what it is intended to convey as well as what it literally means. These inferences, in turn, determine subjects' reactions to both the information and its source.

2. The pragmatic implications that recipients extract from a communication are often intended by the communicator. That is, communicators attempt to construct their messages in a way that will attain a particular objective. This objective could concern not only the communication's referents but also the communicators themselves (e.g., the strength of their convictions about the position being espoused, their feelings about the recipient, or more general abilities or personality characteristics that they possess). In many cases, however, the pragmatic implications that recipients draw from a communication may be conveyed unwittingly. As a result, recipients construe meaning in messages that the communicators did not intend.

3. The cognitive effort that recipients expend in construing the pragmatic implications of a message can be affected by their own desire to attain specific or general goals to which these implications are relevant. It can also be stimulated by deviations of the communication content or style from general or situation-specific expectations concerning the type of communications that are appropriate in the situation in which it occurs. These expectations can result in part from normative principles of conversation (e.g., Grice, 1975; Sperber & Wilson, 1986). On the other hand, they can also be specific to particular types of interactions in which well-established communication patterns have been developed, and to particular persons involved in these interactions (e.g., married couples). Moreover, the expectations can pertain not only to the content of the information exchanged but also to the style in which it is conveyed.

4. Recipients who are stimulated to construe the pragmatic implications of information that violates normative expectations often reinterpret the information in a way that is not reflected by its literal meaning but is consistent with the normative principle that gives rise to these expectations. In doing so, however, they are likely to think more extensively about the norm-violating message, with the result that the message is more likely to be recalled than is norm-consistent information. Moreover, they may seek additional information that bears on the interpretation of norm-violating communications, with the result that this information has more influence on later judgments than it otherwise would.

Although these conclusions are perhaps not surprising, their implications have not been considered in much prior research on social information processing, in which information is conveyed out of its social context. The failure for social cognition researchers to take contextual factors into account has been increasingly recognized by researchers in the area (e.g., Fiske, 1992; Schneider, 1991). Criticisms of the failure for social cognition research to be "social," however, are vacuous unless one can pinpoint specific differences between the processes that operate when information is conveyed in a social context and those that occur when it is not. However, a concern with the pragmatic implications of information is clearly among these differentiating factors, and further theoretical and empirical advances in our understanding of social information processing will have to take them into account.

Acknowledgments

Much of the research reported in this chapter was supported by grant MH3-8585 from the National Institutes of Mental Health. The authors are indebted to the University of Illinois Social Cognition Group for insightful comments on all phases of this research and for many of the ideas conveyed in this article, and to Tory Higgins for valuable comments on an earlier version of the manuscript.

References

Anderson, N. H. (1981). *Foundations of information integration theory.* New York: Academic Press.
Apter, M. J. (1982). *The experience of motivation: The theory of psychological reversals.* London: Academic Press.
Asch, S. E. (1952). *Social psychology.* Englewood Cliffs, NJ: Prentice-Hall.
Bem, D. J. (1972). Self-perception theory. In L. Berkowitz (Ed.), *Advances in experimental social psychology* (Vol. 6). New York: Academic Press.
Bem, D. J., & McConnell, H. K. (1970). Testing the self-perception explanation of dissonance phenomena: On the salience of premanipulation attitudes. *Journal of Personality and Social Psychology, 14,* 23–31.
Black, J. B., Galambos, J. A., & Read, S. J. (1984). Comprehending stories and social situations. In R. S. Wyer & T. K. Srull (Eds.), *Handbook of social cognition.* 1st ed. (vol. 3, pp. 45–86). Hillsdale, NJ: Erlbaum.
Carlston, D. E. (1994). Associated Systems Theory: A systematic approach to cognition representations of persons. In T. K. Srull & R. S. Wyer (Eds.), *Associated Systems Theory: Advances in social cognition* (vol. 7). Hillsdale, NJ: Erlbaum.
Chaiken, S., & Eagly, A. H. (1976). Communication modality as a determinant of message persuasiveness and message comprehensibility. *Journal of Personality and Social Psychology, 34,* 605–614.
Clark, H. H., & Clark, E. V. (1977). *Psychology and language.* New York: Harcourt, Brace, Jovanovich.
Clore, G. L., Schwarz, N., & Conway, M. (1984). Affective causes and consequences of social information processing. In R. S. Wyer & T. K. Srull (Eds.) *Handbook of social cognition,* 2nd ed. (Vol. 1). Hillsdale, NJ: Erlbaum.

Craik, F. I., & Lockhart, R. S. (1972). Levels of processing: A framework for memory research. *Journal of Verbal Learning and Verbal Behavior, 11,* 671–684.
DePaulo, B. M. (1992). Nonverbal behavior and self-presentation. *Psychological Bulletin, 111,* 203–243.
Eagly, A. H., & Himmelfarb, S. (1978). Attitudes and opinions. *Annual Review of Psychology, 29,* 517–554.
Eagly, A. H., Wood, W., & Chaiken, S. (1978). Causal inferences about communicators and their effect on opinion change. *Journal of Personality and Social Psychology, 36,* 424–435.
Easterbrook, J. A. (1959). The effect of emotion on cue utilization and the organization of behavior. *Psychological Review, 66,* 183–201.
Ellsworth, P. C., & Carlsmith, J. M. (1968). Effects of eye contact and verbal content on affective responses to a dyadic interaction. *Journal of Personality and Social Psychology, 10,* 15–20.
Emler, N., Renwick, S., & Malone, B. (1983). The relationships between moral reasoning and political orientation. *Journal of Personality and Social Psychology, 45,* 1073–1080.
Festinger, L., & Carlsmith, J. M. (1959). Cognitive consequences of forced compliance. *Journal of Abnormal and Social Psychology, 58,* 203–210.
Fishkin, J., Keniston, K., & MacKinnon, C. (1973). Moral reasoning and political ideology. *Journal of Personality and Social Psychology, 27,* 109–119.
Fiske, S. T. (1992). Thinking is for doing: Portraits of social cognition from daguerreotype to laserphoto. *Journal of Personality and Social Psychology, 63,* 877–889.
Fiske, S. T., & Neuberg, S. L. (1990). A continuum of impression formation, from category-based to individuating processes: In M. Zanna (Ed.) *Advances in experimental social psychology* (Vol. 23, pp. 1–74). New York: Academic Press.
Fiske, S. T., & Taylor, S. E. (1984). *Social cognition.* New York: Random House.
Fiske, S. T., & Taylor, S. E. (1992). *Social cognition.* New York: McGraw-Hill.
Fletcher, G. J. O., Danilovics, P., Fernandez, G., Peterson, D., & Reeder, G. D. (1986). Attributional complexity: An individual differences measure. *Journal of Personality and Social Psychology, 51,* 875–884.
Fuhrman, R. W., & Wyer, R. S. (1988). Event memory: Temporal-order judgments of personal life experiences. *Journal of Personality and Social Psychology, 54,* 365–384.
Gaelick, L., Bodenhausen, G. V., & Wyer, R. S. (1985). Emotional communication in close relationships. *Journal of Personality and Social Psychology, 49,* 1246–1265.
Graesser, A. C. (1981). *Prose comprehension beyond the word.* New York: Springer-Verlag.
Green, G. M. (1989). *Pragmatics and natural language understanding.* Hillsdale, NJ: Erlbaum.
Grice, H. P. (1975). Logic and conversation. In P. Cole & J. L. Morgan (Eds.), *Syntax and semantics: 3. Speech acts* (pp. 41–58). New York: Academic Press.
Gruenfeld, D. H. (1993). Status and integrative complexity in decision-making groups: Evidence from the U.S. Supreme Court and a laboratory experiment. Unpublished doctoral dissertation, University of Illinois, Urbana-Champaign.
Gruenfeld, D. H., & Wyer, R. S. (1992). Semantics and pragmatics of social influence: How affirmations and denials affect beliefs in referent propositions. *Journal of Personality and Social Psychology, 62,* 38–49.
Gruenfeld, D. H., & Wyer, R. S. (1993). *A two-set flow model of social communication: The influence of information source and communication objectives on memory, message content and delivery, and recipients' beliefs.* Unpublished manuscript, University of Illinois, Urbana-Champaign.
Hamilton, D. L., Driscoll, D. M., & Worth, L. (1989). Cognitive organization of impressions: Effects of incongruity in complex representations. *Journal of Personality and Social Psychology, 57,* 925–939.
Harvey, J., Ickes, W., & Kidd, R. (1976). *New directions in attribution research* (vol. 1). Hillsdale, NJ: Erlbaum.
Hastie, R. (1980). Memory for behavioral information that confirms or contradicts a personality

impression. In R. Hastie, T. M. Ostrom, E. B. Ebbesen, D. L. Hamilton, & D. E. Carlston (Eds.), *Person memory: Cognitive basis or social perceptions* (pp. 155–177). Hillsdale, NJ: Erlbaum.

Higgins, E. T. (1981). The "communication game": Implications for social cognition. In E. T. Higgins, C. P. Herman, & M. P. Zanna (Eds.), *Social cognition:* The Ontario symposium (Vol. 1, pp. 343–392). Hillsdale, NJ: Erlbaum.

Higgins, E. T., & Bargh, J. A. (1987). Social cognition and social perception. *Annual Review of Psychology, 38,* 359–425.

Higgins, E. T., Bargh, J. A., & Lombardi, W. (1985). The nature of priming effects on categorization. *Journal of Experimental Psychology: Learning, Memory and Cognition, 11,* 59–69.

Higgins, E. T., & McCann, C. D. (1984). Social encoding and subsequent attitudes, impressions, and memory: "Context driven" and motivational aspects of processing. *Journal of Personality and Social Psychology, 47,* 26–39.

Higgins, E. T., McCann, C. D., & Fondacara, R. A. (1982). The "communication game": goal-directed encoding and cognitive consequences. *Social Cognition, 1,* 21–37.

Higgins, E. T., Monaghan, R. A., & Rholes, W. S. (1976). *Judgments of communicators as a function of communicator status and message style.* Unpublished manuscript, Princeton University, Princeton, NJ.

Higgins, E. T., & Rholes, W. J. (1978). "Saying is believing": Effects of message modification on memory and liking for the person described. *Journal of Experimental Social Psychology, 14,* 363–378.

Hovland, C. I., Janis, I. L., & Kelley, H. H. (1953). *Communication and persuasion.* New Haven: Yale University Press.

Jones, E. E., & Davis, K. E. (1965). From acts to dispositions: The attributional process in person perception. In L. Berkowitz (Ed.), *Advances in experimental social psychology* (Vol. 2, pp. 220–266). New York: Academic Press.

Jones, E. E., Davis, K. E., & Gergen, K. J. (1961). Role playing variations and their informational value for person perception. *Journal of Abnormal and Social Psychology, 63,* 302–310.

Jones, E. E. Schwartz, J., & Gilbert, D. T. (1984). Perception of moral expectancy violation: The role of expectancy source. *Social Cognition, 2,* 273–293.

Kelley, H. H. (1967). Attribution theory in social psychology. In D. Levine (Ed.), *Nebraska symposium of motivation* (Vol. 15). Lincoln, Nebraska: University of Nebraska Press.

Kelley, H. H. (1972). *Causal schemata and the attribution process.* Morristown, NJ: General Learning Press.

Klein, S. B., & Loftus, J. (1990). Rethinking the role of organization in person memory: An independent trace storage model. *Journal of Personality and Social Psychology, 59,* 400–410.

Kolhberg, L. (1976). Moral stages and moralization: The cognitive developmental approach. In T. Lickona (Ed.), *Moral development and behavior: Theory, research and social issues.* New York: Holt, Rinehart & Winston.

Krauss, R. M. (1981). Impression formation, impression management, and nonverbal behaviors. In E. T. Higgins, C. P. Herman, & M. P. Zanna (Eds.), *Social cognition: The Ontario Symposium.* (Vol. 1, pp. 323–241). Hillsdale, NJ: Erlbaum.

Krauss, R. M., Geller, V., & Olson, C. (1976, September). Modalities and cues in the detection of deception. Paper presented at American Psychological Association Convention.

Kraut, R. E. (1978). Verbal and nonverbal cues in the perception of lying. *Journal of Personality and Social Psychology, 36,* 380–391.

Kraut, R. E., & Higgins, E. T. (1984). Communication and social cognition. In R. S. Wyer & T. K. Srull (Eds.), *Handbook of social cognition* (vol. 3, pp. 87–128). Hillsdale, NJ: Erlbaum.

Long, D. L., & Graesser, A. C. (1988). Wit and humor in discourse processing. *Discourse Processes, 11,* 35–60.

Mills, J., & Jellison, J. M. (1967). Effect on opinion change of how desirable the communication is to the audience the communicator addressed. *Journal of Personality and Social Psychology, 6,* 98–101.

Moscovici, S. (1985). Social influence and conformity. In G. Lindzey & E. Aronson (Eds.), *Handbook of social psychology* (3rd ed., Vol. 2, pp. 347–412). New York: Random House.

Nassi, A. J., Abramowitz, S. I., & Youmans, J. E. (1983). Moral development and politics a decade later: A replication and extension. *Journal of Personality and Social Psychology, 45,* 1127–1135.

Newtson, D. A., & Czerlinsky, T. (1974). Adjustment of attitude communications for contrasts by extreme audience. *Journal of Personality and Social Psychology, 30,* 829–837.

Petty, R. E., & Cacioppo, J. T. (1981). *Attitudes and persuasion: Classic and contemporary approaches.* Dubuque, IA: W. C. Brown.

Petty, R. E., & Cacioppo, J. T. (1986). *Communication and persuasion: Central and peripheral routs to attitude change.* New York: Springer.

Petty, R. E., Priester, J. B., & Wegener, D. (1994). In R. S. Wyer & T. K. Srull (Eds.), *Handbook of social cognition,* 2nd ed. (Vol. 2, pp. 69–142). Hillsdale, NJ: Erlbaum.

Ottati, V. C., Riggle, E. J., Wyer, R. S., Schwarz, N., & Kuklinski, J. (1989). The cognitive and affective bases of opinion survey responses. *Journal of Personality and Social Psychology, 57,* 404–415.

Rosen, S., Cochran, W., & Musser, L. M. (1990). Reactions to a match versus a mismatch between an applicant's self-presentational style and work reputation. *Basic and Applied Social Psychology, 11,* 117–129.

Schank, R. C. (1992). *Tell me a story: A new look at real and artificial memory.* New York: Scribner's.

Schank, R. C., & Abelson, R. P. (1977). *Scripts, goals, plans and understanding.* Hillsdale, NJ: Erlbaum.

Schank, R. C., & Abelson, R. P. (in press). Knowledge and memory: The real story. In R. Wyer (Ed.), *Knowledge and memory: Advances in social cognition* (Vol. 8), Hillsdale, NJ: Erlbaum.

Schneider, D. J. (1991). Social cognition. *Annual Review of Psychology, 42,* 527–561.

Schwarz, N. (1994). Judgment in a social context: Biases, shortcomings, and the logic of conversation. In M. Zanna (Ed.), *Advances in experimental social psychology* (Vol. 26, pp. 123–162). San Diego: Academic Press.

Schwarz, N., Strack, F., Mueller, G., & Chassein, B. (1988). The range of response alternatives may determine the meaning of the question: Further evidence on informative functions of response alternatives. *Social Cognition, 6,* 107–117.

Scott, C. K., Fuhrman, R. W., & Wyer, R. S. (1991). Information processing in close relationships. In G. Fletcher & F. Fincham (Eds.) *Cognition in close relationships.* Hillsdale, NJ: Erlbaum.

Searle, J. (1969). *Speech acts.* Cambridge, England: Cambridge University Press.

Smith, E. R. (1984). Model of social inference processes. *Psychological Review, 91,* 392–413.

Smith, E. R. (1990). Content and process specificity in the effects of prior experiences. In T. K. Srull & R. S. Wyer (Eds.), *Advances in social cognition* (vol. 3). Hillsdale, NJ: Erlbaum.

Sperber, D., & Wilson, D. (1986). *Relevance: Communication and cognition.* Cambridge, MA: Harvard University Press.

Srull, T. K., & Wyer, R. S. (1989). Person memory and judgment. *Psychological Review, 96,* 58–83.

Stein, N., & Glenn, C. G. (1979). An analysis of story comprehension in elementary school children. In R. O. Freedle (Ed.), *New directions in discourse processing.* Norwood, NJ: Ablex.

Strack, F. (1994). Response processes in social judgments. In R. S. Wyer & T. K. Srull (Eds.), *Handbook of social cognition,* 2nd Ed. (Vol. 1, pp. 287–322). Hillsdale, NJ: Erlbaum.

Strack, F., & Martin, L. L. (1987). Thinking, judging, and communicating: A process account of context effects in attitude surveys. In H. J. Hippler, N. Schwarz, & S. Sudman (Eds.), *Social information processing and survey methodology* (pp. 123–148). New York: Springer-Verlag.

Strack, F., Martin, L. L., & Schwarz, N. (1988). Priming and communication: The social determinants of information use in judgments of life satisfaction. *European Journal of Social Psychology, 18,* 429–442.

Strack, F., Schwarz, N., & Wänke, M. (1991). Semantic and pragmatic effects of context effects in social and psychological research. *Social Cognition, 9,* 111–125.
Tannen, D. (1990). *You just don't understand: Women and men in conversation.* New York: William Morrow.
Tetlock, P. (1986). Integrative complexity of political reasoning. In S. Krauss & R. Perloff (Eds.), *Mass media and political thought* (pp. 267–289). Beverly Hills, CA: Sage.
Trafimow, D., & Wyer, R. (1993). The cognitive representation of mundane social events. *Journal of Personality and Social Psychology, 64,* 365–376.
Wänke, M., & Wyer, R. S. (1994). *Individual differences in person memory and impression formation: The effects of socio-political ideology and ingroups vs. outgroup membership on responses to socially relevant behavior.* Unpublished manuscript, University of Illinois, Urbana Champaign.
Watzlawick, P., Beavin, J. H., & Jackson, D. D. (1967). *Pragmatics of human communication.* New York: Norton.
Wegner, D. M., Wenzlaff, R., Kerker, R. M., & Beattie, A. E. (1981). Incrimination through innuendo: Can media questions become public answers? *Journal of Personality and Social Psychology, 40,* 822–832.
Wyer, R. S., & Bodenhausen, G. V. (1985). Event memory: The effects of processing objectives and time delay on memory for action sequences. *Journal of Personality and Social Psychology, 49,* 304–316.
Wyer, R. S., Budesheim, T. L., & Lambert, A. J. (1990). Person memory and judgment: The cognitive representation of informal conversations. *Journal of Personality and Social Psychology, 58,* 218–238.
Wyer, R. S., Budesheim, T. L., Lambert, A. J., & Swan, S. (1994). Person memory and judgment: Pragmatic influences on impressions formed in a social context. *Journal of Personality and Social Psychology, 66,* 254–267.
Wyer, R. S., & Carlston, D. E. (1994). The cognitive representation of people and events. In R. S. Wyer & T. K. Srull (Eds.), *Handbook of social cognition,* 2nd Ed. (Vol. 1, pp. 41–98). Hillsdale, NJ: Erlbaum.
Wyer, R. S., & Collins, J. E. (1992). A theory of humor elicitation. *Psychological Review, 99,* 663–688.
Wyer, R. S., & Gruenfeld, D. H. (in press). Information processing in interpersonal communication. In D. E. Hewes (Ed.), *The cognitive bases of interpersonal communication.* Hillsdale, NJ: Erlbaum.
Wyer, R. S., & Hartwick, J. (1980). The role of information retrieval and conditional inference processes in belief formation and change. In L. Berkowitz (Ed.), *Advances in experimental social psychology* (Vol. 13, pp. 242–284). New York: Academic Press.
Wyer, R. S., Lambert, A. J., Budesheim, T. L., & Gruenfeld, D. H. (1992). Theory and research on person impression formation: A look to the future. In L. Martin & A. Tesser (Eds.), *The construction of social judgments.* Hillsdale, NJ: Erlbaum.
Wyer, R. S., Shoben, E. J., Fuhrman, R. W., & Bodenhausen, G. V. (1985). Event memory: The cognitive representation of social action sequences. *Journal of Personality and Social Psychology, 49,* 857–877.
Wyer, R. S., & Srull, T. K. (Eds.) (1984). *Handbook of social cognition.* Hillsdale, NJ: Erlbaum.
Wyer, R. S., & Srull, T. K. (1986). Human memory in its social context. *Psychological Review, 93,* 322–359.
Wyer, R. S., & Srull, T. K. (1989). *Memory and cognition in its social context.* Hillsdale, NJ: Erlbaum.
Wyer, R. S., & Srull, T. K. (Eds.) (1994). *Handbook of social cognition,* 2nd ed. Hillsdale, NJ: Erlbaum.
Wyer, R. S., Swan, S., & Gruenfeld, D. H. (in press). Impression formation in informal conversations. *Social Cognition.*

THE INTERACTIVE ROLES OF STABILITY AND LEVEL OF SELF-ESTEEM: RESEARCH AND THEORY

Michael H. Kernis
Stefanie B. Waschull

"Hit it between the shortstop and second baseman!"
One of us uttered the above statement many years ago while watching a group of friends play "box-ball," the city version of softball. Upon hearing this, the shortstop rushed toward the speaker, yelling "What are you doing—saying I can't field?", and landed a right hook that knocked the speaker clear off the fence and onto the ground. Somewhat dazed, and much confused, the speaker explained that no harm was intended. Rather, the intention was to call attention to the gaping hole between the two fielders. Satisfied, the shortstop returned to his position and the game continued.

Why do some people, like the shortstop in the above scenario, react with hostility and aggression to events that on the surface appear to be rather innocuous? Why do some people seem especially likely to exaggerate their accomplishments? What are the ways in which people deal with events that potentially have positive or negative self-esteem-relevant implications? For many researchers, a key to providing answers to such questions is to examine how individuals high and low in global self-esteem differ from one another. In recent years, this work has proliferated to the point that there are numerous, well-elaborated and important frameworks from which one can choose (see Baumeister, 1993a, for a compendium of these views; also Solomon, Greenberg, & Pyszczynski, 1991).

However, a close look at this literature reveals that there are differing views on the essence of both high and low self-esteem. For example, some researchers and theorists assert that high self-esteem reflects favorable feelings of self-worth that are secure and hence not easily threatened. Others, however, point to myriad self-protective and self-enhancement strategies that individuals high in self-esteem are prone to exhibit. Implicit in this latter view is the notion that high self-esteem may be a precious commodity that must be zealously defended and promoted in order to survive. Likewise, there are considerable differences of opinion on the extent to which low self-esteem is indicative of maladjustment. According to some researchers, low self-esteem is associated with highly negative self-feelings and a wide variety of maladaptive cognitive, affective, motivational, and behavioral patterns. Others, however, take a somewhat more benign view of low self-esteem, suggesting that it reflects self-feelings that are better characterized by uncertainty and neutrality than by negativity. Furthermore, low self-esteem is thought to reflect cautiousness that is directed toward minimizing exposure of one's deficiencies, rather than pervasive maladjustment per se.

Our major goal in this chapter is to demonstrate how consideration of both *level* and *stability* of self-esteem can provide a vehicle for reconciling these differing views. Specifically, we will provide a framework and review evidence that suggests that a full understanding of self-esteem processes requires a consideration of both self-esteem components. We begin by discussing what is meant by stability of self-esteem and how it can be (and has been) measured. We then consider the question of why people vary in the extent to which their self-esteem is unstable, focusing on both contemporaneous and early childhood influences. Next, we review theory and research that address the interactive roles of stability and level of self-esteem in reactions to evaluative events as well as in broader aspects of psychological functioning. Specifically, we will describe important differences that emerge between and within high and low self-esteem individuals (SEs) as a function of stability of self-esteem. In addition, we elaborate upon the different views of low and high self-esteem and discuss in detail the relevance of self-esteem instability for reconciling them. We conclude with a brief summary of directions for future research.

I. Nature and Assessment of Stability of Self-Esteem

Self-esteem instability has been conceptualized in terms of either long-term or short-term fluctuations (Rosenberg, 1986). Viewed as long-term fluctuations, self-esteem instability reflects change in one's baseline level of self-esteem that occurs "slowly and over an extended period of time" (i.e., baseline instability; Rosenberg, 1986, p. 126). Research with children and adolescents has shown, for example, that many children show a decrease in global self-esteem as they leave the relatively safe environment of elementary school for the more turbulent environment of middle school, followed by a steady, but gradual increase in self-esteem through the high-school years (Bachman, O'Malley, & Johnston, 1978; Demo and Savin-Williams, 1983; McCarthy & Hoge, 1982; O'Malley and Bachman, 1983; Savin-Williams & Demo, 1984).

Alternatively, self-esteem instability can be conceptualized as short-term fluctuations in one's contextually based global self-esteem (which Rosenberg, 1986, referred to as barometric instability). These fluctuations may be tied to specific external events such as a compliment or a failing grade, or to more internally generated events, such as reflecting on one's social life. According to some researchers (e.g., Rosenberg, 1986) these fluctuations must be dramatic (i.e., fluctuating between feelings of worthiness and worthlessness) for self-esteem to be considered unstable. In fact, one self-report measure of self-esteem stability, the Stability of Self Scale (Rosenberg, 1965) requires individuals with unstable self-esteem to endorse items such as, "Some days I have a very good opinion of myself; other days I have a very poor opinion of myself."

In contrast, we believe that self-esteem instability takes various forms (see also Savin-Williams & Demo, 1983). Although some people with unstable self-esteem may experience dramatic short-term shifts from feeling very positively to very negatively about themselves, others may primarily fluctuate in the *extent* to which they feel positive (or negative) about themselves. The precise nature of such fluctuations (both for different individuals and the same individual at different points in time) will depend upon a variety of factors, including what aspect of the self is salient and the valence of recently experienced self-relevant events (cf. Markus & Kunda, 1986). As we have argued elsewhere (Kernis, Cornell, Sun, Berry, & Harlow, 1993), the essence of unstable self-esteem is the propensity to exhibit short-term fluctuations in global self-feelings. Stated differently, the tendency to exhibit fluctuations can be viewed as a dispositional characteristic that interacts with contextual factors to result in specific patterns of fluctuations.

Although both short-term and long-term self-esteem instability are likely to have important implications for psychological functioning, we have focused our efforts on short-term instability. Consistent with this focus, we obtain multiple (once or twice daily) assessments of individuals' *current* self-esteem in naturalistic contexts, for periods ranging from five days to one week. We then calculate the standard deviation (*SD*) of each individual's total scores across these multiple assessments; the greater the *SD*, the more unstable is the person's self-esteem.

At this juncture, it is important to raise the issue of whether self-esteem instability reflects merely unreliability in responding. As we have argued elsewhere (Kernis, 1993; Kernis, Cornell, Sun, Berry, & Harlow, 1993), we believe that it does not. Rather, we believe that self-esteem instability reflects the operation of important psychological processes. If we suppose for the moment that self-esteem instability reflects careless or random responding, the question arises as to why it then relates to the various outcome measures that we have examined and will present in this chapter. We return to this point later in the chapter. Conceptually, because people are asked to complete the multiple self-esteem assessments based on how they feel at that moment, there is ample reason to consider changes as reflective of the *true* score component of responding, and not the error component (see Tellegen, 1988, for a related discussion). In addition, other research substantiates the claim that current self-evaluations are responsive to specific instances of evaluative feedback (Kernis & Johnson, 1990; Linville, 1985). Thus, we see no reason to consider instability of self-esteem to reflect merely unreliable responding.

To assess level of self-esteem in adults, Rosenberg's (1965) Self-Esteem Scale is administered in group settings as part of a battery of self-report measures. Although not part of the original scale instructions, we now explicitly ask people to respond on the basis of how they *typically* feel about themselves. In our research with adults to date, the zero-order correlation between stability and level of self-esteem has ranged from .15 to the high .20s. Moreover, we have found no evidence that self-esteem instability is most extreme among moderate SEs (compared to high and low SEs). These two findings are important, because they indicate that stability and level of self-esteem are distinct dimensions along which individuals can be characterized.

Stability and level of self-esteem are treated as continuous variables in our research. To examine their separate and interactive effects, hierarchical regression analyses are conducted. To aid in the interpretation of significant interactions, predicted values are generated using values one *SD* above and below the mean to represent high and low scores. Table I displays representative means and *SD*s that we have obtained for level and stability of self-esteem in our adult samples.

To reiterate, stability of self-esteem (barometric or short-term) refers to the

TABLE I
REPRESENTATIVE MEANS AND STANDARD DEVIATIONS FOR LEVEL AND STABILITY OF SELF-ESTEEM[a]

Study	Level M	Level SD	Stability M	Stability SD
Kernis et al (1989)	40.47	6.57	5.20[b]	3.31
Kernis et al (1991)[c]	39.79	5.79	6.47	4.25
Kernis et al (1992)	39.78	5.89	6.79	4.22
Kernis et al (1993)[d]	38.77	7.91	5.77	4.04
Kernis et al (1993)[e]	39.44	6.38	6.04	4.54

[a]For self-esteem level, item responses are made on 5-point scales (total score range 10–50); for self-esteem stability, they are made on 10-point scales. The higher the mean for stability, the more unstable individuals' self esteem. Copyrights © 1989, 1991, 1993 by the American Psychological Association and 1992 by Duke University Press. Adapted by permission.
[b]In this study only, multiple assessments took place over 7 days.
[c]This sample constitutes a subsample drawn from Kernis et al. (1992).
[d]Study 1.
[e]Study 2.

magnitude of short-term fluctuations in people's contextually based feelings of self-worth. This component of self-esteem can be distinguished from level of self-esteem, which refers to people's characteristic or relatively stable baseline feelings of self-worth (see also Savin-Williams and Demo, 1983).

II. Why People Vary in the Extent to Which Their Self-Esteem is Unstable

Recently, we have begun to examine factors that may underlie or promote the possession of unstable self-esteem. Although we are still in the early phase of addressing this issue, the evidence we present in this section suggests that one important factor is a heightened tendency toward ego-involvement in everyday activities. In addition, we discuss the potential role that an impoverished self-concept may play in promoting unstable self-esteem.

A. EGO-INVOLVEMENT

1. Variability and Importance of Specific Self-Evaluations

Rosenberg (1986) suggested that an important factor in the development of unstable self-esteem is the tendency to rely excessively on social sources of evaluation as a basis for determining one's overall self-worth. He based this assertion on the fact that social evaluations are quite frequent, yet they often contain contradictory information. Hence, it follows that people who place substantial importance on such evaluations would be more susceptible to short-term fluctuations in perceived self-worth. While accepting this assertion, we believe that this overreliance on evaluative information extends to personal as well as social sources. For example, even in the absence of explicit feedback, the more people base their self-worth on how competently they complete a task (perhaps relative to past performance), the more unstable their self-esteem is likely to be (see also Franks & Marolla, 1976, and Gecas & Schwalbe, 1983, for general discussions of the relation between efficacious action and self-esteem).

Evaluative information pertaining to particular self-aspects (e.g., one's competence or social acceptance) has direct implications for one's self-evaluations along those particular dimensions (Kernis & Johnson, 1990). Consequently, if unstable self-esteem is associated with placing substantial weight on specific evaluative information, the magnitude of fluctuations along specific self-evaluative dimensions should be related to the magnitude of fluctuations in global self-esteem. Furthermore, the greater the importance placed on specific self-evaluations as determinants of overall self-worth, the more individuals' self-esteem should be unstable. Finally, variability in specific self-evaluations should be more strongly related to instability of global self-esteem if the self-evaluative dimension is important rather than unimportant (Pelham & Swann, 1989).

We (Kernis, Cornell, Sun, Berry, and Harlow, 1993, Study 2) recently tested these propositions in a study involving over one hundred women undergraduate students. In the first phase, participants completed measures that assessed the perceived importance of self-evaluations of *competence* (e.g., How much I like myself is not much influenced by whether or not I am doing well at things), *social acceptance* (e.g., The feedback that I get from others has a big impact on whether I feel good or bad about myself), and *physical attractiveness* (e.g., To what extent does my physical attractiveness contribute to the way that I feel about myself overall).

Approximately one week later, participants completed Rosenberg's (1965) Self-Esteem Scale Monday evening, Tuesday through Thursday mornings and evenings, and Friday morning, under instructions to base their responses on how they felt at the moment they were completing the form (i.e., current self-esteem). In addition, each evening (Monday–Thursday), participants responded to a series of statements that focused on their experiences that day. These statements related to perceived *competence* (e.g., I felt smart today), *social acceptance* (e.g., The people with whom I interacted today seemed to like me), and *physical attractiveness* (e.g., I felt pretty today).

Overall, the results strongly supported our hypotheses. Day-to-day variability along each dimension (i.e., competence, social acceptance, and physical attractiveness) was significantly correlated with self-esteem instability (rs ranged from .23 for attractiveness to .40 for competence). In addition, the importance placed on competence and physical attractiveness was significantly correlated with self-esteem instability ($rs = .29$), although the importance placed on social acceptance was not. In separate regression analyses, we examined the unique contributions first of variability and then of perceived importance to the prediction of stability of self-esteem. Significant unique effects of variability emerged for competence and social acceptance, but not for physical attractiveness. Note that if variability of specific evaluations and global self-esteem were merely indexes of unreliable responding, there is no reason to expect unique contributions of variability along specific dimensions to the prediction of global self-esteem instability (since they should all share the same variance attributable to careless responding). For importance, unique contributions emerged for the dimensions of competence and for physical attractiveness, but not for social acceptance.

Furthermore, greater variability in day-to-day perceived competence was related to more unstable global self-esteem, particularly if competence was perceived to be an important determinant of one's overall self-worth. Table II displays the predicted values. Again, note that if self-evaluation variability and

TABLE II
PREDICTING STABILITY OF SELF-ESTEEM FROM
VARIABILITY AND IMPORTANCE OF PERCEIVED
COMPETENCE[a]

Importance	Variability	
	Low	High
Low	3.75	5.70
High	4.35	10.13

[a]From Kernis, Cornell, Sun, Berry, & Harlow (1993, study 2). Copyright © 1993 by the American Psychological Association, Inc. Reprinted with permission.

self-esteem instability merely reflect unreliable responding, there is no reason to expect that *greater* self-rated importance would magnify the relation between them.

The same pattern emerged for physical attractiveness and social acceptance, but only among people who perceived themselves relatively favorably along these dimensions. Among people who perceived themselves relatively unfavorably, greater variability in specific self-evaluations related to high degrees of unstable self-esteem even when the dimensions were rated as unimportant. Although we cannot be sure why this occurred, it seems possible that the substantial interpersonal consequences associated with these dimensions may have been sufficient to override considerations of personal importance.

These findings suggest that unstable self-esteem is associated with a heightened tendency toward ego-involvement in everyday activities. That is, compared to individuals with more stable self-esteem, those with unstable self-esteem appear more likely to perceive that their self-worth is continually "on the line." Not only do they place more importance on such things as their day-to-day competence and physical attractiveness, they fluctuate more in their self-appraisals along these dimensions, and the combination of high importance and large fluctuations is related to especially unstable self-esteem. The notion that unstable self-esteem is associated with greater ego-involvement received additional support in two other recent studies.

2. Self-Esteem Instability, Reasons for Anger, and Intrinsic Motivation in Children

Among the most common reasons that adults report for becoming angry include interruptions of ongoing or planned actions (frustrations) and threats to self-esteem (Anastasi, Cohen, & Spatz, 1948; Averill, 1982; Gates, 1926; Meltzer, 1933). Similarly, Karniol and Heiman (1987) found that children most often reported becoming angry because either their actions were disturbed or they were being mocked or gossiped about. Waschull and Kernis (in press) examined the extent to which stability and level of self-esteem predicted reasons for anger and intrinsic motivation in a sample of fifth-grade children. Here we focus primarily on the findings for reasons for anger. From the current perspective, self-esteem instability should be associated with the reasons children give for becoming angry because it reflects a heightened sensitivity to the self-esteem-relevant aspects of various events (cf. Kernis, 1993). Stated differently, children with unstable self-esteem should be especially sensitive to the self-esteem threatening qualities of aversive events. Hence, we predicted that self-esteem instability would relate to reports of becoming angry more because one's self-esteem was threatened than because one's actions or goals were interfered with.

Level of self-esteem was assessed by the global self-worth subscale of Harter's (1985) Perceived Competence Scale for Children. To assess stability of self-esteem, we modified the items on the global self-worth subscale so that they reflected momentary self-esteem, and we administered it twice daily (once in the morning and once in the afternoon) for a period of five days. Each item contained the words "right now" or "at this moment" and the scale was entitled "What I am Like at This Moment."

Participants also read five scenarios of aversive peer-related interpersonal events, each of which constituted an instrumental thwarting as well as a potential threat to self-esteem. The perpetrator in each scenario was always of the same sex as the respondent. Two reasons for becoming angry were presented under each vignette, in the form of "Some kids would become angry because . . . but other kids would become angry because . . ." One reason reflected the self-esteem-threatening consequences of the behavior (e.g., because I would *feel* taken advantage of), whereas the other represented the instrumental thwarting consequences of the behavior (e.g., because I would have to wait longer). Children were asked to decide "which kid you are more like" and next, to decide if this was "really true" or only "sort of true" of them. An example of a scenario appears in Table III.

The results strongly supported our prediction. That is, compared to children with stable self-esteem, children with unstable self-esteem provided responses indicating that they were more likely to become angry because of the self-esteem threatening aspects of the events depicted in the scenarios, $r = .27, p < .01$. The same pattern emerged with respect to low self-esteem, $r = -.17, p < .05$. In this sample, instability and level of self-esteem correlated $-.41$, which is substantially greater than what has emerged in adult samples. Therefore, it was crucial to control for this overlap in a regression analysis. The results of this analysis indicated that only self-esteem instability was a significant predictor ($p < .05$; for level, $F < 1$).

TABLE III
EXAMPLE OF SCENARIOS USED TO ASSESS REASONS FOR ANGER[a]

You are really thirsty after playing outside with your classmates. Just when you are next in line to get a drink from the fountain, another boy pushes ahead of you, making you wait. Some kids would be mad mostly because they were really thirsty and needed a drink, but other kids would be mad mostly because they felt pushed around. How would you react?

Really true for me	Sort of true for me	Some kids would be mad mostly because they were really thirsty and needed a drink	BUT	Other kids would be mad mostly because they felt pushed around.	Sort of true for me	Really true for me
☐	☐				☐	☐

[a]From Waschull and Kernis, in press.

Turning briefly to the findings for intrinsic motivation, correlations indicated that self-esteem instability and low self-esteem each related significantly to lower scores on both the preference for challenge and curiosity/interest subscales (but not the independent mastery subscale) of Harter's (1981) Intrinsic versus Extrinsic Orientation in the Classroom Scale. Importantly, when stability and level of self-esteem were examined together in regression analyses, self-esteem instability remained predictive of both lower preference for challenge and curiosity/interest scores, whereas low self-esteem remained predictive of only lower preference for challenge scores. These findings are also consistent with the assertion that unstable self-esteem is associated with heightened ego-involvement (Grolnick & Ryan, 1987; Plant & Ryan, 1985; Ryan, 1982). However, in contrast to the findings for reasons for anger, negative self-perceptions of scholastic competence mediated the relations between unstable (and low) self-esteem and lower scores on the intrinsic motivation indices. Thus, it may be less important to invoke the notion of heightened ego-involvement in this context. We discuss the general issue of the relation between self-concept differences and motivational explanations later in the chapter. Also, in a later section, we present findings indicating that among adults, unstable self-esteem is related to lower perceptions of scholastic competence among low, but not among high, SEs. For now, we simply note that additional research on the processes that link unstable self-esteem to lower intrinsic motivation would be valuable.

3. Impact of Everyday Events on Feelings of Self-Worth

If unstable self-esteem is associated with heightened ego-involvement (i.e., perceiving that one's self-worth is continually "on the line"), it should relate to greater responsiveness of self-feelings to everyday events. To examine this hypothesis, Kernis, Greenier, Whisenhunt, Waschull, and Berry (1993) first had approximately 60 undergraduate students complete measures of stability and level of self-esteem. Next, these individuals recorded the most positive and the most negative event they experienced each day for a period of 11 days. After writing a description of each event, they indicated the extent to which it made them feel better or worse about themselves, the duration of the event's impact on their self-feelings, how personally important the event was, and how positive or negative the event was.

The results were consistent with our assertion that unstable self-esteem is associated with heightened ego-involvement in everyday activities. First, the most unstable individuals' self-esteem, the more negative events adversely affected the way they felt about themselves. Second, more unstable self-esteem was associated with perceiving the impact of these negative events to be of longer duration. Third, unstable self-esteem was associated with viewing negative events more negatively, and fourth, it was associated with viewing negative events as more personally important. Somewhat surprisingly, self-esteem instability related only to reactions to negative events. We are currently collecting more data; it will be interesting to see if this finding holds with the larger sample. If it does, it suggests that it may be more important to focus on why people react strongly to negative events rather than positive events as a key to understanding self-esteem instability. Finally, we should note that in contrast to previous research (Campbell, Chew, & Scratchley, 1991), no significant effects for level of self-esteem emerged.

We also conducted analyses to examine whether subjective assessments of event negativity and importance mediated the relationship between unstable self-esteem and the impact that negative events had on self-feelings. For the magnitude of impact on self-feelings, the analyses suggested that both importance and perceived negativity were partial mediators. That is, although the relation between instability and impact magnitude was reduced considerably when either importance or negativity was controlled, it remained significant. For the duration of impact, these mediational effects were somewhat stronger in that the effect of instability was no longer significant. These analyses suggest that at least part of the reason why negative events have a greater impact on individuals with unstable self-esteem (compared to individuals with stable self-esteem) is that they perceive these events to be more negative as well as more important. An obvious question is whether these perceptions are distortions or reflections of the actual quality of the events experienced by individuals with unstable self-esteem. Addressing this issue is quite complex, and some would argue that there is no adequate way to resolve it. Although this may ultimately be true, it seems useful to compare the ratings made by people who experienced the events with ratings made by "uninvolved" people who did not experience the events. We are currently in the process of doing this.

In sum, the results of these three investigations suggest that self-esteem instability is accompanied by a heightened concern about feelings of self-worth, which permeates individuals' involvement in everyday experiences. This heightened concern translates into such things as placing more weight on specific self-evaluative information, reporting greater tendencies to become angry because of the self-esteem threatening aspects of aversive interpersonal events, and greater reactivity to negative everyday events.

A similar analysis has recently been offered by Deci and Ryan (in press), in their discussion of the distinction between "contingent" and "true" self-esteem. Contingent self-esteem is based upon one's ability (or inability) to live up to one's (or important others') expectations or standards. As such, it involves a heightened sense of ego-involvement in the promotion of one's agendas, and is subject to the vicissitudes of one's successes and failures. In contrast, true self-esteem is based on feelings of worth that derive from one's authenticity, rather than the achievement of specific outcomes (Ryan, 1993) and thus is more stable and secure.

B. IMPOVERISHED SELF-CONCEPTS

Consideration of factors related to unstable self-esteem suggests one other candidate worthy of investigation—a poorly developed self-concept. That is, having an impoverished or uncertain self-concept (lack of self-concept clarity, to borrow Campbell's, 1990, terminology) could lead individuals to rely on, and be more affected by, specific evaluative information, thereby contributing to unstable self-esteem (e.g., Baumgardner, 1990; Campbell, 1990). In addition, Paulhus and Martin's (1988) distinction between functional flexibility (i.e., the capacity to perform various social behaviors as dictated by the situation) and situationality (i.e., viewing one's behavior as being dependent upon the situation) may be relevant. Specifically, to the extent that unstable self-esteem is associated with poorly defined self-concepts, it may relate to lower functional flexibility (because one is less sure of one's capabilities) and greater situationality (because one is likely to depend on the situation for guidance on how to act).

Although plausible, we have yet to systematically examine the extent to which unstable self-esteem is associated with poorly developed or impoverished self-concepts. However, such a relationship has great theoretical and intuitive appeal. Moreover, there are multiple ways of operationalizing such self-concept qualities that are of interest in their own right. Consequently, whether or not unstable self-esteem is associated with impoverished self-concepts should be considered an important agenda for future research.

The preceding discussion focused on "contemporaneous" factors that may promote, or underlie, unstable self-esteem. Such factors provide some insight into the "psychological worlds" of people who possess unstable self-esteem. Additional insight could be gained through a better understanding of developmental factors that contribute to unstable self-esteem. Specifically, are there early childhood experiences that promote unstable self-esteem, perhaps by fostering an ego-involved orientation or interfering with the development of a well-defined self-concept? In the following section, we consider this very important issue.

C. EARLY CHILDHOOD EXPERIENCES AND THE DEVELOPMENT OF UNSTABLE SELF-ESTEEM

Waschull and Kernis (in press) reported that meaningful individual differences in stability of self-esteem emerge in children as young as 10–11 years old. In this section, we offer some speculations as to why these differences emerge at such an early age. Our main focus will be on early childhood experiences that may promote unstable self-esteem. This is not to say that other factors, such as genetic and hormonal influences, may not be important also. Rather, we believe that apart from these biologically based influences, early familial experiences can substantially affect the extent to which children's self-esteem will be stable or unstable. Given what we know about the antecedents of high versus low self-esteem per se, this assertion seems quite plausible. For example, in a landmark study, Coopersmith (1967) reported that parents of high self-esteem children exhibited substantial warmth and acceptance toward them, while at the same time setting clearly defined limits (i.e., authoritative parenting style, Baumrind, 1971). Other studies have further documented the importance to children's high self-esteem and well-being of such things as parental involvement, acceptance, support, and clearly defined limits (e.g., Buri, Louiselle, Misukanis, & Mueller, 1988; Gecas and Schwalbe, 1986; Grolnick & Ryan, 1989).

We believe that early childhood environments that contain substantial amounts of feedback that is noncontingent and/or controlling (Deci & Ryan, 1987) are likely to promote the development of unstable self-esteem. As noted by Berglas (1985), the essence of noncontingent feedback is that it is not subject to personal control. Furthermore, noncontingent feedback is not a direct function of one's abilities and performances, but is instead based upon such things as the recipient's ascribed characteristics (e.g., being a member of the "right" family); criteria established by the evaluator, but unknown to the recipient; and the evaluator's mood (Berglas, 1985). In a sense, noncontingent feedback is "often understood to be as much a consequence of an evaluator's idiosyncratic perspective as the performer's stable, internal dispositions" (Berglas, 1985, p. 245). Noncontingent feedback can contribute to unstable self-esteem in several, related ways. First, because such feedback may cause children to wonder what it is they did to receive it, achieving a clear understanding and appreciation of their own capabilities and limitations may be circumvented. Second, the unreliability of the source's conveyed sentiments is likely to deprive children of consistent and clearly defined "reflected appraisals" of their self-worth (Felson, 1985; Mead, 1934). Moreover, because some forms of noncontingent feedback link specific evaluative information to one's overall self-worth and are therefore also controlling (e.g., "Good boys behave themselves in public"; see next paragraph), self-worth is more likely to fluctuate as a function of specific evaluative information. Over time, these factors (separately or in combination) are likely to interfere with the achievement of a well-developed sense of one's self-worth and instead promote unstable self-esteem.

Feedback that is experienced as controlling, that is, as "pressure to think, feel, or behave in specified ways" (Deci & Ryan, 1985, p. 95), also is likely to undermine a stable sense of one's self-worth (Berglas, 1985; Deci & Ryan, 1987, in press). As a consequence of such felt pressure, one's actions and internal states become governed primarily by specific contingencies, rather than by an awareness of one's organismic needs and the desire to fulfill them (Deci & Ryan, 1987). Over time, an excessive focus on one's ability (or lack of ability) to successfully play into these contingencies is likely to contribute to feelings of overall self-worth that are based upon performance-contingency (mis)matches. In Deci and Ryan's (in press) terminology, one's thoughts, feelings, and behavior will be regulated through introjects, and one's self-esteem is of the contingent variety.

Some years ago, Rogers (e.g., 1959) made a distinction between unconditional and conditional positive regard that is relevant to the present discussion. Unconditional positive regard involves "liking and accepting all of another person's feelings and self-concept; a nonjudgmental and nonpossessive caring for, and prizing of, another person" (Ewen, 1993, p. 381). In contrast, conditional positive regard involves "liking and accepting another person only if that individual's feelings and self-concept meet with one's own standards" (Ewen, 1993, p. 381), and thus is highly controlling (as well as potentially noncontingent). Conditional positive regard, like controlling feedback, promotes conditional positive *self-regard,* such that one's sense of self-worth becomes based on one's ability to meet these introjected standards for appropriate feelings and behavior.[1]

---

[1]Unconditional positive regard differs in important ways from what we and others mean by noncontingent feedback. In noncontingent feedback, the focus is on the evaluation of specific actions or performances using criteria that are not clear to the recipient (e.g., How can you be so stupid? My son should be able to do better!). In contrast, in unconditional positive regard, the focus is on one's acceptance and value as a person, and the criteria are clear: one is valued for who one is, not for one's actions or performances (e.g., I love and value you even if you do not perform well). Consequently, one's feelings of self-worth are likely to be secure in spite of any deficiencies. Moreover, whereas noncontingent feedback is likely to be inconsistent and unreliable over time because the evaluator's

Interestingly, we have encountered very few people in our research who experience no day-to-day fluctuations in their self-worth. This suggests that even the best of parents (i.e., those who typically are warm, accepting, supportive, and who provide adequate structure) may at times provide feedback that children experience as noncontingent and/or controlling. Moreover, it is unlikely that peers, teachers, and other significant figures encountered in early childhood always provide feedback that is contingent and noncontrolling. Thus, rather than focusing on the presence or absence of such feedback, it probably makes more sense to focus on their relative prevalence.

In an initial attempt to test the role of parental feedback in the promotion of unstable self-esteem, we devised a series of items to tap the extent to which college students recalled receiving as a child feedback that was either contingent or noncontingent. Items dealt with both positive and negative feedback. Examples of items tapping each of the four types of feedback are as follows: *positive/contingent*—When I was growing up, my parents often acknowledged that I was good at doing certain things; *positive/noncontingent*—Often when I was growing up, when my parents were nice to me it seemed to be mostly a function of the mood that they were in, rather than because of something about me or my behavior; *negative/contingent*—When my parents criticized me as I was growing up, it was usually in a constructive manner; and *negative/noncontingent*—When my parents were displeased with me when I was growing up, I often wasn't sure what I had done to upset them. Through factor and item analyses, a reasonably consistent set of twelve items (involving both positive and negative feedback) was retained. Approximately 150 undergraduate men and women completed the measure, and level and stability of self-esteem were assessed as in our other research previously described (e.g., Kernis, Cornell, Sun, Berry, & Harlow, 1993, Studies 1 and 2). A significant Sex × Stability interaction emerged, indicating that among men (but not women), self-esteem instability was related to recollections of receiving greater amounts of noncontingent feedback. In addition, a main effect for self-esteem level emerged, indicating that low SEs felt that they received more noncontingent feedback than did high SEs, and a marginal ($p < .07$) Stability × Level × Sex interaction emerged (accounting for less than 2% of the variance).

Examination of predicted values for the three-way interaction suggested that for men, instability was related to recollections of greater noncontingent feed-

---

mood and criteria are likely to fluctuate, unconditional positive regard is highly consistent and reliable. Our view is that consistent positive regard that is not dependent upon the performance of specific behaviors will promote stable self-esteem, whereas noncontingent (and inconsistent) feedback will promote unstable self-esteem.

back, especially among low SEs. Among women, the same pattern did not emerge. These findings should be considered preliminary, as more scale refinement is warranted. Nonetheless, they do point to the potentially important role of parental feedback in the development of unstable (perhaps low) self-esteem, especially among males. However, a full understanding of the critical components of early childhood experiences that promote unstable self-esteem awaits further research.

Additional, albeit indirect, support comes from an examination of the relation between self-esteem instability and perfectionism among college students. Three dimensions of perfectionism have been distinguished (Hewitt & Flett, 1991): *self-oriented,* which involves such behaviors as setting unrealistically high self-standards; *other-oriented,* which involves setting unrealistically high standards for others; and *socially prescribed,* which involves people's beliefs that others are setting unrealistically high standards for them and putting undue pressure on them to excel. Self-esteem instability correlated significantly with socially prescribed perfectionism ($r = .24$, $p < .05$), but not the other two types. Hewitt & Flett (1991) suggested that socially prescribed perfectionism is very controlling in nature, inasmuch as it is experienced as pressure to live up to another's standards. These data do not indicate that socially prescribed perfectionism promoted the development of unstable self-esteem in childhood. On the other hand, they do suggest that adults with unstable self-esteem are more likely to perceive that their important interpersonal relationships are characterized by excessive control.

In sum, we have suggested that early childhood environments that provide substantial noncontingent and/or controlling feedback are likely to promote the development of unstable self-esteem. Initial evidence supportive of this claim was presented. We recognize, however, that the evidence we have amassed to date is only indirect and that it may be subject to alternative explanations. What is needed is longitudinal research involving children and their parents in which the effects of various childhood experiences on the contemporaneous and subsequent manifestation of unstable self-esteem can be examined.

To recapitulate, we have suggested that overall, unstable self-esteem is associated with heightened concerns about one's feelings of self-worth that permeate one's involvement in everyday activities. In our view, however, these concerns do not necessarily play themselves out in the same ways for low and high SEs. We will now elaborate upon this point and describe a number of studies that show that the role of self-esteem instability is quite different for low than for high SEs. We begin by focusing on people's tendencies to engage in self-enhancement and self-protective strategies. We then address the more general issue of how stability and level of self-esteem relate to psychological difficulties, specifically the experience of depressive symptomatology.

III. The Roles of Stability and Level of Self-Esteem in Self-Enhancement and Self-Protective Strategies

Among the most central questions on which self-esteem researchers and theorists have focused is whether there are self-esteem differences in the enactment of self-enhancement and self-protective strategies. This is not surprising, given that engaging in such tactics appears to be an important component of self-regulation in daily life. Excuse making, denying responsibility for negative outcomes, boasting about one's skills, and taking undue credit for successful outcomes are all commonplace occurrences. Indeed, some have gone so far as to suggest that the absence of engaging in such strategies is associated with psychological disturbances such as depression (Alloy & Abramson, 1988; Taylor & Brown, 1988). Consequently, it is of considerable importance to understand when people do and do not engage in self-enhancing and self-protective strategies and what factors are associated with their occurrence or nonoccurrence. A substantial amount of research in recent years has provided pieces of the puzzle. For the most part, this work has focused on individual differences in *level* of self-esteem (e.g., Baumeister, Tice, & Hutton, 1989; Baumgardner, Kaufman, & Levy, 1989; Brown, Collins, & Schmidt, 1988; Crocker, Thompson, McGraw, & Ingerman, 1987; Gibbons & McCoy, 1991; Tice, 1991). We believe, however, that a more complete understanding can be achieved by focusing on the roles of both level and stability of self-esteem.

A. DEFINING SELF-ENHANCEMENT AND SELF-PROTECTION STRATEGIES

First, it will be useful to define what we mean by self-protective and self-enhancement strategies. By self-protective strategies, we mean cognitive, motivational, and behavioral reactions to evaluative events that are used in an attempt (whether successful or not) to minimize or avoid negative self-feelings or self-evaluations (see also Brockner, Wiesenfeld, & Raskas, 1993; Tice, 1991). Perhaps more importantly, we distinguish elements of self-protective strategies that are primarily "internally or self-directed" (i.e., that pertain to remedial possibilities such as attributions to lack of effort) from those that are primarily "externally" directed (e.g., attacks on the source of the threat). For the most part, this distinction has been glossed over in the self-esteem literature. This is unfortunate, because the two types of elements are likely to have very different implications for psychological functioning. Put simply, internally directed self-protective efforts are, by and large, more adaptive than those that are externally directed, because they (as well as the consequences they produce) are more under the actor's control. For example, attributing failure to a lack of effort signifies that future occurrences can be prevented through increased diligence, and it is associated with more sophisticated problem-solving strategies (Dweck & Leggett, 1988) and lower negative affect (Kernis, Brockner, & Frankel, 1989; Kernis & Grannemann, 1990). In contrast, attributing failure to an unfair exam provides little if any insight into remedial strategies that can prevent future failures (cf. Dweck & Leggett, 1988), and instead is likely to be associated with heightened negative affect (Arkin & Maruyama, 1981).

Self-enhancement strategies, on the other hand, are employed in an attempt (whether successful or not) to magnify positive self-feelings or self-evaluations (again, see also Brockner et al., 1993; Tice, 1991). In some circumstances, endorsing positive traits as self-descriptive is a straightforward self-enhancing strategy. Other strategies are not so straightforwardly self-enhancing in nature. Take, for example, the finding that following threat, outgroup members are more likely to be derogated relative to the ingroup. Some have labeled this a self-enhancing strategy (e.g., Blaine & Crocker, 1993). We do not believe that this is necessarily the case. To the extent that the relative self-favorability stems from less endorsement of negative traits for self than for outgroup, we believe that it more accurately reflects a self-protection strategy. More importantly, if outgroup derogation reduces negative affect, but does not increase positive affect, its status as a self-enhancement strategy seems dubious.

Although this discussion has taken us somewhat away from our central theme, we believe that it is important for researchers to pay greater attention to the precise nature of responses to positive and negative events, as well as their affective and motivational sequelae. In recent years, it has become increasingly clear that minimizing negative consequences (e.g., by denying the existence of negative self-characteristics) and maximizing positive consequences (e.g., by endorsing the existence of positive self-characteristics) are not merely two ends of the same continuum (Paulhus & Reid, 1991). Tice's (1991) research on the relation between self-esteem and the motives underlying self-handicapping shows this quite nicely. In a series of investigations, Tice found that high SEs will self-handicap in order to maximize the possibility that they will look good, whereas low SEs will self-handicap in order to minimize the possibility that they will look bad.

Another important consideration is that some self-esteem differences in reactions to feedback (e.g., judgments of the accuracy of feedback) which traditionally have been thought of as motivationally based (either from a self-enhancement or self-consistency perspective), may be more easily explained in terms of actual self-concept or ability differences (Blaine & Crocker, 1993). For a reaction to be considered self-protective or self-enhancing, it seems necessary to rule out, as best as possible, the exclusive operation of self-concept or ability factors. This is also an issue that deserves greater attention in the years to come, and it is one that we return to later in this chapter.

B. TOWARD A THEORETICAL MODEL

We will now present a preliminary model of how stability and level of self-esteem jointly relate to the use of self-protection and self-enhancement strategies. For simplicity, we will refer to stable and unstable low and high SEs. However, empirically and conceptually, stability of self-esteem is treated as a continuous dimension along which people vary. We then present the results of three studies that bear directly on the model. Because these studies have been presented elsewhere (Kernis, 1993), we discuss them only briefly here.

Note that stability of self-esteem, level of self-esteem, and self-enhancement and self-protective strategies are components of an interlocking system that are likely to have reciprocal influences upon one another. For example, just as unstable self-esteem may "lead" to greater self-enhancement and self-protective strategies (especially among high SEs, as will be described), the use of such strategies may enhance short-term shifts in self-esteem. We have chosen to enter the system by assessing naturally occurring fluctuations in self-esteem, treating them as an individual difference variable that can then be used to predict a wide range of cognitive, emotional, and behavioral phenomena that serve to self-enhance or self-protect.

We will now bring into sharper focus how consideration of stability of self-esteem can inform some of the controversies in the self-esteem literature. The nature of these controversies is different for high and low SEs, so we discuss them separately.

1. High Self-Esteem

One predominant view of high SEs, consistent with humanistically oriented theories (e.g., Rogers, 1961), is that they like and are satisfied with themselves, feel that they are worthy individuals, have confidence in their skills and abilities, yet are accepting of their weaknesses. Implicit in this view is that high SEs' feelings of self-worth are built upon a solid foundation that does not require continual validation (see also Deci & Ryan, in press). Moreover, their feelings of worthiness are thought to not be upended by the inevitable adversities of life. However, according to others, high SEs are threatened by a wide variety of negative events, and to ward them off, they employ various self-protective strategies. Moreover, in response to positive events, high SEs are thought to engage in a variety of self-enhancement strategies. Implicit in this view is the notion that high self-esteem is a precious commodity that must be zealously promoted and defended in order to survive. In fact, research indicates that, more so than individuals with low self-esteem, high self-esteem individuals (a) display self-serving attributions (Fitch, 1970), (b) self-handicap to enhance the potentially positive implications of good performance (Tice, 1991), (c) set inappropriately risky goals when ego-threatened (Baumeister, Heatherton, & Tice, 1993), (d) actively create less fortunate others with whom they can compare favorably (Gibbons & McCoy, 1991), and (e) derogate outgroup members especially when their ingroup has been criticized (Crocker et al., 1987). Findings such as these paint a picture of high SEs which suggests that they are not very secure in their feelings of self-worth and liking.

Although these types of reactions have formerly been ascribed to high SEs in general, we suggest that they will especially be manifested among unstable high SEs. That is, to the extent that unstable high SEs are highly ego-involved (and less certain of their self-worth and who they are), they have a very precious resource—their favorable feelings of self-worth—that is fragile and highly vulnerable to challenge. Consequently, unstable high SEs will be highly invested in maintaining and enhancing their favorable self-feelings, as well as in minimizing their negative self-feelings. In contrast, stable high SEs are thought to have a well-anchored sense of their self-worth that is not dependent upon the attainment of specific outcomes or on validation by others. These people should be little threatened by negative evaluative events, nor should they especially revel in their successes.

Thus, our model holds that among high SEs, self-esteem instability will relate to especially favorable (and often self-enhancing) reactions to positive self-relevant events. In addition, our model holds that unstable high SEs are likely to be highly threatened by negative self-relevant events. That is, given the precarious nature of their positive self-feelings, such events must be "neutralized" to avoid more permanent downward shifts in feelings of self-worth. In addition, invoking one's self-worth in everyday negative events, as ego-involved individuals are prone to do, magnifies whatever adverse self-relevant implications these events have. How will unstable high SEs deal with these self-relevant implications? Will they attempt to minimize the threat by recognizing, accepting, and working on whatever weaknesses they may possess? We see this as highly unlikely, because such reactions will only feed into their fragile feelings of self-worth. Rather, it seems more likely that they will locate the source of the threat external to themselves and attack it. In so doing, consciously experienced declines in self-worth can be attenuated or avoided altogether. In brief, in response to threats, individuals with unstable high self-esteem are expected to have strong adverse reactions, to be highly defensive, and to actively attempt to undermine the threat's legitimacy.

2. Low Self-Esteem

One perspective holds that low SEs have quite negative self-views, are readily accepting (cognitively, at least) of unfavorable feedback, are highly prone to experience negative affect, exhibit ineffective strategies in the face of adversity, and show little if any propensities to self-enhance and self-protect (e.g., Harter, 1993; Kernis, Brockner, & Frankel, 1989; Watson & Clark, 1984). Thus, low SEs can be characterized as exhibiting a wide variety of maladaptive cognitive, affective, motivational, and behavioral patterns. However, another perspective holds that the self-evaluations and self-concepts of low SEs are characterized more by uncertainty and neutrality than by negativity (Baumeister, 1993b; Baumeister et al., 1989; Campbell, 1990), that they will embrace positive self-aspects whenever possible (Swann, Pelham, & Krull, 1989), and that they will engage in some forms of self-protective strategies and "indirect" forms of self-enhancement (Brown et al., 1988; Tice, 1991). In this view, low SEs are best thought of as cautious and uncertain (rather than highly maladjusted) individuals whose behavioral styles are geared toward minimizing exposure of their deficiencies (Baumeister et al., 1989).

In support of the latter position, research suggests that low SEs are unlikely to engage in direct forms of self-enhancement (Baumeister et al., 1989; Brown et al., 1988) or to actively derogate others in response to threat (Gibbons & McCoy, 1991). Instead, the focus of (at least some) low SEs seems to be to minimize the "internal" damage caused by threats. For example, Gibbons and McCoy (1991) found that although low SEs do not actively derogate a less fortunate other when threatened, they nevertheless feel better when exposed to such a person. Gibbons and McCoy refer to this as "passive" downward comparison. Brown et al. (1988) showed that when threatened, low SEs were more favorable in rating a group of similar individuals than a group of dissimilar individuals ("indirect enhancement"); such favorability did not materialize in ratings of the groups in which they were a member ("direct self-enhancement"). Other research has shown that low SEs will self-handicap to protect themselves from the conclusion that they are incompetent (Tice, 1991), yet they will not self-handicap to facilitate the conclusion that they possess superior ability.

We concur with others (e.g., Baumeister et al., 1989; Brown et al., 1988; Tice, 1991) who have suggested that low SEs typically do not engage in direct self-enhancement strategies due to concerns about whether a positive identity can be successfully defended. Even among unstable low SEs, there seems to be a variety of environmental and individual constraints that place a positive self-view beyond their immediate grasp.

More importantly from the current perspective, the degree of maladjustment and the propensity to engage in self-protective strategies among low SEs is thought to vary substantially as a function of stability of self-esteem. Elsewhere

(Kernis, Cornell, Sun, Berry, & Harlow, 1993), we argued that individuals with truly stable low self-esteem will not engage in adaptive, internally directed self-protective strategies. The hallmark of stable low self-esteem is thought to be a chronic dislike for oneself. Given that self-protective strategies are employed in the service of protecting oneself against negative self-feelings, we argued that it is illogical that such strategies would be employed by people whose negative self-feelings are not likely to change. Instead, it seemed to us that the critical factor is the degree to which one's low self-esteem is unstable. Specifically, we believed that among low SEs, unstable self-esteem is a manifestation of a desire to avoid continuously negative self-feelings. As already discussed, unstable low SEs are probably reluctant to engage in self-enhancement strategies, particularly when they pertain to their own performances. They may, however, engage in more "indirect" or subtle self-enhancement strategies, such as aligning themselves with successful others (so-called basking in reflected glory; Cialdini & Richardson, 1980; Tesser, 1988). Perhaps more importantly, by engaging in self-protective strategies, they can minimize the degree and duration of the adverse impact of negative evaluative events. In support of this last point, our early research (to be described shortly) suggested that among low SEs, self-esteem instability is related to greater resiliency and more adaptive coping (i.e., internally directed self-protection) in the face of potentially threatening events. However, as will become clear to the reader, some of our more recent research on the role of self-esteem instability among low SEs has led us to question some of our (e.g., Kernis, 1993; Kernis, Cornell, Sun, Berry, & Harlow, 1993) previous assertions.

Before continuing, it is important to point out the implications that self-esteem stability has for the results of previous research in which greater self-enhancement and self-protection emerged as a function of level of self-esteem. Most importantly, it does not imply the absence of overall self-esteem differences in tendencies to engage in self-enhancement and self-protective strategies. Instead, it implies that most people are at least somewhat unstable in their self-esteem and that the greater the degree of instability, the more likely it is that many of the strategies formerly attributed to level of self-esteem per se will emerge. In fact, as noted earlier, we have found that the vast proportion of people are at least somewhat unstable in their self-esteem, whereas very few individuals do not exhibit any shifts at all.

In sum, the model that emerged from and guided much of our early work focused on how stability and level of self-esteem relate to individual differences in reactions to evaluative events. Among high SEs, instability was hypothesized to relate to more favorable reactions and greater self-enhancement tendencies in response to positive events, and to more adverse reactions and greater self-protective efforts (of an externalizing sort) in response to negative events. Such reactions can be attributed to the fragility with which unstable high SEs feel positively about themselves, as well as to their heightened tendencies toward ego-involvement in everyday activities. Among low SEs, instability was hypothesized to relate to less adverse reactions and greater self-protective efforts (adaptive, internally directed) in response to negative events, but not to direct self-enhancing reactions to positive events.

We now turn to some empirical work in which we examined how stability and level of self-esteem relate to (a) anger and hostility proneness, (b) reactions to subjectively based success and failure, and (c) reactions to positive and negative interpersonal evaluations. The results from these studies provided general support for our assertions regarding the role of self-esteem instability among high SEs. Among low SEs, however, the findings for self-esteem instability were considerably more complicated. In fact, they suggest the need for some revisions in that part of our conceptualization just presented. We touch on this issue at the end of this section, but we defer a full discussion of it until other, more recently collected data, are described.

C. ANGER AND HOSTILITY PRONENESS

Who are more likely to become angry and hostile, people with low self-esteem or people with high self-esteem? Some have argued that it is high SEs, because they are more likely to perceive slights as unjustified, and unjustified threats are especially potent elicitors of anger and hostility (cf. Averill, 1982). Others have argued just the opposite, that low SEs are quick to anger, because threats are likely to be experienced as especially aversive to people who already feel negatively about themselves (cf. Averill, 1982; Wills, 1981). Prior to our (Kernis, Grannemann, & Barclay, 1989) research, however, there appear to have been no published reports of how self-esteem relates to individual differences in the tendencies to become angry and/or hostile.

Stability and level of self-esteem were first assessed. Subsequently, participants completed a battery of standard anger and hostility inventories, including the Novaco Anger Inventory (NAI; Novaco, 1975), the Trait Anger Scale (TAS; Spielberger, Jacobs, Russell, & Crane, 1983), and the Buss-Durkee Hostility Inventory (BDHI; Buss & Durkee, 1957).

Contrary to each of the positions just stated, there was no general tendency for high SEs to report being more likely to become angry or hostile than low SEs (or vice versa). Rather, the results indicated that individuals with *unstable* high self-esteem reported being especially likely to become angry and hostile (and more so than stable or unstable low SEs), whereas individuals with *stable* high self-esteem reported especially low tendencies (and less so than stable or unstable low SEs). Thus, depending upon whether their self-esteem was unstable (or stable), high SEs were more (or less) prone to experience anger and hostility than low

TABLE IV
PREDICTED VALUES FOR ANGER AND
HOSTILITY MEASURES AS A FUNCTION OF
STABILITY AND LEVEL
OF SELF-ESTEEM[a]

Stability	Low SE[b]	High SE
	Novaco Anger Inventory	
Stable	317.5	262.8
Unstable	321.7	342.9
	Trait Anger Scale	
Stable	21.9	18.0
Unstable	21.3	25.2
	BDHI Motor[c]	
Stable	22.3	18.9
Unstable	23.9	29.0

[a]Adapted from Kernis et al. (1989). Copyright © 1989 by the American Psychological Association, Inc. Adapted by permission.
[b]SE, Self-esteem level.
[c]BDHI, Buss-Durkee Hostility Index.

SEs.[2] Predicted values for these Level × Stability interactions are displayed in Table IV.

Anger and hostility are often instigated by threats of an interpersonal nature, such as insults or undue criticism. In such instances, they often serve to ward off other negative self-feelings, or to restore one's damaged self-esteem or public self-image. Moreover, they are often associated with externalization, or assignment of blame to the instigator (Averill, 1982). Thus, anger and hostility often serve a defensive, self-protective function.

The fact that unstable high SEs reported such high tendencies to experience anger and hostility thus supports our contention that in response to self-threat, they will engage in externally directed defensive self-protective efforts. At the other extreme, stable high SEs have substantially fewer "nerves" to touch, and so they are unlikely to feel the need to defensively react to many of the threats that "set off" unstable high SEs.

[2]The BDHI consists of various subscales that can be combined to form two broad types of hostility: "attitudinal" (resentment, suspicion) and "motor" (assault, indirect, verbal, and irritability). Predicted values for the motor component reflect a marginally significant Stability × Level interaction ($p < .09$). For the attitudinal component, only a marginal main effect for self-esteem level emerged ($p < .08$), indicating that lower self-esteem was associated with greater attitudinal hostility.

The moderate tendencies to experience anger and hostility reported by low SEs (both stable and unstable) seems best explained in terms of the sheer aversiveness of frustrations and provocations to people who already feel badly about themselves (Averill, 1982; Kernis, 1993). However, there was no indication that unstable low SEs were less likely to become angry and hostile than stable low SEs. We return to this shortly.

D. EXCUSE MAKING

People make excuses in order to deflect the negative implications of aversive events away from themselves (Darley & Goethals, 1980; Kernis & Grannemann, 1990; Schlenker, 1980; Snyder & Higgins, 1988). In the realm of performance outcomes, excuses predominantly involve claims that inhibiting *power* (e.g., I didn't get enough sleep the night before the exam), *motivational* (e.g., I didn't care enough to study hard for this exam), and *task difficulty* (e.g., The amount of material covered on this exam was too much) factors interfered with one's performance (Darley & Goethals, 1980). Thus, excuse making serves a self-protective function. In addition, claiming the operation of performance-inhibiting factors can serve a self-enhancement function, if they are offered *after* knowing that one has performed quite well (Kernis, Grannemann, & Mathis, 1992). In such instances, the individual is in a position to feel even better about him or herself because success occurred *in spite* of the operation of these inhibitory factors (Kelley, 1972; Tice, 1991).

Kernis et al. (1992) examined whether stability and level of self-esteem predicted differential tendencies to make excuses in either a self-protective or self-enhancing manner. Participants in this study were students in a large introductory psychology class whose level and stability of self-esteem were assessed several weeks prior to their first exam. Also prior to the exam, participants indicated the minimal grade they could feel satisfied with. In conjunction with their actual performance, these ratings were used to place participants in either the success or failure category. Thus, success and failure were determined in relation to each individual's subjective frame of reference. On the day they received performance feedback, participants indicated the extent to which a variety of power, motivational, and task-difficulty inhibitory factors influenced their performance.

No differences in excuse making emerged as a function of level of self-esteem per se. However, significant Level × Stability × Performance interactions emerged for the indexes of short- and long-term motivational factors. Predicted values are displayed in Table V.

Among high SEs, self-esteem instability was related to greater endorsement of motivationally based inhibiting factors following success, but not following failure. Thus, unstable high SEs were especially likely to self-enhance following

TABLE V
PERFORMANCE × STABILITY × LEVEL OF SELF-ESTEEM:
PREDICTED VALUES FOR MOTIVATION-BASED EXCUSES[a]

Self-esteem level	Performance			
	Success		Failure	
	Low	High	Low	High
Stability	*Short-term motivation*			
Unstable	4.13	5.89	5.30	3.53
Stable	4.01	3.46	3.63	3.39
Stability	*Long-term motivation*			
Unstable	3.32	7.48	4.64	4.26
Stable	3.46	3.53	3.04	3.69

[a]Higher numbers indicate greater perceived influence on performance. Adapted from Kernis et al. (1992). Copyright © 1992 by Duke University Press. Adapted by permission.

success, but not to self-protect following failure. The latter finding could reflect either that unstable high SEs were not very threatened by the failure, or that, if threatened, they were not well versed in the use of excuse making in this context.

Among low SEs, self-esteem instability related to greater endorsement of motivationally based inhibiting factors following failure, but not following success. Importantly, such motivational factors are internal and controllable. Furthermore, of all the inhibitory factors, these are most likely to be related to less adverse reactions to poor performance (Kernis & Grannemann, 1990). Thus, it appears that unstable low SEs were engaging in a relatively adaptive form of self-protection.

E. REACTIONS TO INTERPERSONAL FEEDBACK

Are reactions to feedback directly received from others related to both stability and level of self-esteem? Previous theory and research suggest that it is important to differentiate cognitive (e.g., How accurate is the feedback?) from affective (e.g., How do I feel?) reactions to evaluative feedback. The growing consensus is that cognitive reactions conform to predictions derived from a self-consistency analysis (e.g., Shrauger, 1975; Swann et al., 1987). That is, high SEs are thought to believe that positive feedback is more accurate than negative feedback, whereas the reverse is true for low SEs. Some have attributed this to a need or desire to obtain self-confirming or verifying feedback (e.g., De La Ronde & Swann, 1993), whereas others suggest that these differences can be explained in terms of actual self-concept differences that exist between high and low SEs (Blaine & Crocker, 1993). On the other hand, affective reactions are thought to conform to predictions derived from a self-enhancement analysis. That is, since everyone presumably prefers positive over negative feedback, affective reactions (regardless of recipients' self-esteem level) will be more favorable following positive than negative feedback (Swann et al., 1987). For high SEs, cognitive and affective reactions are in harmony. However, low SEs are thought to be caught in a "crossfire" between their desires for negative feedback (which would be self-verifying) and positive feedback (which would be affectively pleasurable) (De La Ronde & Swann, 1993; Swann et al., 1987).

Although plausible, it should be noted that evidence for these specific claims is rather sparse. The study most often cited in support of them was conducted by Swann et al. (1987). Participants were administered the Texas Social Behavior Inventory (TSBI), which is primarily a measure of social confidence. Based upon their responses, individuals were characterized as either high or low in social confidence, and, within each group, half received positive feedback that they appeared socially confident and half received negative feedback that they appeared socially insecure. Subsequently, both cognitive reactions (i.e., judgments of feedback accuracy, the diagnosticity of the evaluation technique, the evaluator's competence, and the perceived cause(s) of the feedback), as well as emotional states and liking for the evaluator (the latter being a hybrid cognitive-affective reaction) were assessed. The findings for cognitive reactions were consistent with those derived from the self-consistency approach, whereas those for affective reactions were consistent with the self-enhancement approach. However, given that participants were selected on the basis of their self-perceived social confidence, these findings (especially for cognitive reactions) are perhaps not surprising. That is, there is no need to presume that a motive for self-consistency drove people's reactions (again, especially for cognitive reactions), because there were clear self-concept differences that can account for them (Blaine & Crocker, 1993).

Swann et al.'s demonstration that domain-specific self-perceptions relate to the perceived accuracy of interpersonal feedback is important. However, it seems to us that a more definitive test of the motivational role of self-esteem in cognitive and emotional reactions to feedback requires that people be selected on the basis of their global feelings of self-worth. Moreover, our framework suggests that self-esteem instability would also play an important role. To examine these issues, Kernis et al. (1993, Study 1) first assessed stability and level of self-esteem in a sample of women undergraduates. Subsequently, as part of a laboratory session, individuals received either positive or negative feedback regarding their degree of social confidence. A variety of affective and cognitive reactions were then assessed.

The results for level of self-esteem largely replicated the findings reported by Swann et al. (1987), with one major exception. Swann et al. reported that positive self-concept individuals (those with favorable self-conceptions of their social confidence) viewed positive feedback as more accurate than did negative self-concept individuals, whereas the reverse was true for negative feedback. In contrast, Kernis, Cornell, Sun, Berry, & Harlow reported no overall self-esteem differences in the perceived accuracy of either positive or negative feedback. As shown repeatedly (e.g., Marsh, 1986; cf. Harter, 1983), self-judgments along specific dimensions (in this case, social confidence) are at best imperfectly related to global self-esteem. If feedback accuracy judgments do have a strong cognitive component, this suggests that just as some globally high SEs do not view themselves as especially socially confident, some low SEs do not view themselves as socially insecure.

Even more central to the present concerns is the fact that stability of self-esteem further moderated the role of global self-esteem in reactions to feedback. Among high SEs, self-esteem instability was related to more favorable reactions to positive feedback, but to less favorable reactions to negative feedback. Specifically, among high SEs who received positive feedback, unstable self-esteem was related to viewing the feedback as somewhat more accurate, to viewing the evaluator as especially competent and likeable, and to experiencing especially high levels of positive affect. In stark contrast, among high SEs who received negative feedback, unstable self-esteem related to greater derogation of the evaluation technique and the evaluator, and to somewhat greater excuse making. In support of our framework, unstable high SEs appeared to be locating the cause of the negative feedback within the evaluator and the evaluation technique, rather than to any existing deficiency within themselves.

Among low SEs, self-esteem instability did not relate to more favorable reactions to positive feedback. This was as anticipated. However, among low SEs who received negative feedback, the role of self-esteem instability was more complicated. First, as anticipated, unstable self-esteem was related to less rejection of the negative evaluator. Unexpectedly, however, unstable self-esteem was related to perceiving negative feedback as more accurate and the evaluation technique as more diagnostic. Thus, contrary to our expectations that unstable low SEs would be more likely than stable low SEs to engage in strategies to minimize the adverse implications of negative feedback, they were actually more accepting of it (for a more detailed presentation of these findings, see Kernis, Cornell, Sun, Berry, & Harlow, 1993, Study 1).

A thorough discussion of the implications that these findings have for the self-consistency and self-enhancement approaches (to how self-esteem relates to reactions to feedback) is beyond the scope of this chapter. We do wish to note, however, that at least in their present forms, they both may be too simplistic because they fail to take into consideration the role of self-esteem stability. As but one example, neither approach appears to readily account for the finding that, in response to positive feedback, unstable high SEs reported greater levels of positive affect than did stable high SEs.

F. SUMMARY AND IMPLICATIONS FOR MODEL

The results of these three studies offer some support for the model presented earlier, yet they also reveal some potential inadequacies. Our findings are most supportive of the role of SE instability among high SEs. Specifically, among high SEs, instability was shown to relate to greater anger and hostility proneness and to greater defensiveness in response to negative interpersonal evaluations. In addition, among high SEs, self-esteem instability was related to greater self-enhancement following success and more favorable reactions to a positive evaluation. However, it did not relate to more self-protective excuse making following subjectively based failure, which raises the possibility that such events are not highly threatening to them. Because there are many reasons for obtaining a null effect, it seems somewhat premature to endorse such a conclusion. Nevertheless, it does point to a potentially important distinction between negative events that involve more subjectively based failures (as examined in Kernis, Cornell, Sun, Berry, & Harlow, 1992) from those that have a strong interpersonal component (as examined in Kernis et al., 1993, Study 1). Subjectively based failures are those that are explicitly defined from the performer's point of view. For example, depending upon people's subjective standards, receiving a grade of B on an exam could be considered either success or failure. In contrast, the role of subjective standards is much less critical in interpersonally based negative feedback. Specifically, it matters little what one's subjective standards for performance are if one is explicitly told that he or she is socially unskilled or stupid. In addition, subjectively based failures are inherently more private than interpersonally based failures because one need not disclose to others the extent to which one's performance was substandard.

Avoiding the future occurrence of subjectively based failures is in many ways more controllable than avoiding failures that are interpersonally based. Specifically, whereas one's own subjective standards can readily be modified, it is much more difficult to modify another's standards for the self. Moreover, if unstable high SEs typically perform up to their own personal standards, isolated instances of failure may not be very threatening. However, if they have received considerable noncontingent or controlling positive feedback, direct performance-based criticism may take on extreme ramifications that must be protected against.

Stated differently, such criticism may strike more at the core of their fragility and insecurity than subjectively based failures. Although these are only speculations, we include them so as to emphasize the need for future research and theory to address potential differences between evaluative events that vary in the extent to which they are subjectively or interpersonally based.

Among low SEs, the role of instability seems a bit more puzzling. On the one hand, it did not relate to more self-enhancing reactions to either subjectively based success or to a direct positive interpersonal evaluation of one's performance. Thus, consistent with the model, self-esteem instability among low SEs did not relate to more favorable reactions to positive events. However, with regard to negative events, the role of instability was less clear. In three studies, instability (a) had no effect (for anger or hostility proneness), (b) was related to greater internally directed self-protection (excuse making following subjective failure), and (c) was related to less self-protection (greater acceptance following a negative evaluation). Once again, the distinction between subjective and interpersonally based evaluative events may be important. To the extent that subjectively based failures are private events, they may more readily provide opportunities for unstable low SEs to engage in adaptive self-protective efforts (which may be more believable to them than to others). Another possibility is that among low SEs, instability is related to substantial variability in tendencies to engage in self-protective efforts. That is, depending on some as yet unknown factors, unstable low SEs may fluctuate between using self-protective strategies in an adaptive manner and a failure to do so, making them at times highly susceptible to negative affect and self-feelings.

Putting these issues aside for the moment, we now describe the results of several studies that examined how stability and level of self-esteem relate to depressive symptomatology. These studies are especially important because they focus more directly on how self-esteem relates to psychological well-being. Several issues will be brought into sharper focus. First, are the self-protective and self-enhancement efforts of unstable high SEs successful in protecting them against depressive symptomatology? Second, when using susceptibility to depressive symptomatology as a criteria for psychological difficulties, who fares better—stable or unstable low SEs? Because some of this work is being presented for the first time here, we describe it in relatively more detail.

IV. Self-Esteem and Depressive Symptomatology

Strong theoretical and empirical justifications exist for linking low self-esteem with heightened depressive symptomatology. For example, Beck's (e.g., 1967) theory of depression holds that low self-esteem is an important component (perhaps even a causal determinant) of depressive episodes. In addition, negative self-evaluations are one of the diagnostic criteria for clinical depression. In fact, some have suggested that there may be considerable overlap in the processes that underlie low self-esteem and depression (cf. Watson & Clark, 1984). In support of this contention, Kernis et al. (1989) found that low SEs, like those who are depressed (Carver & Ganellen, 1983) overgeneralize the negative implications of specific failures.

In addition to level of self-esteem, stability of self-esteem may also have important implications for depression. As Tennen and Affleck (1993) note, clinical theorizing has linked unstable self-esteem with increased vulnerability to depression (e.g., Bibring, 1953; Chodoff, 1973; Fenichel, 1945; and Jacobson, 1975). According to these theorists, people who are vulnerable to depression are prone to experience substantial fluctuations in their feelings of self-worth, particularly in response to negative events. Thus, rather than low self-esteem per se, the susceptibility to downward shifts in self-feelings is thought to be the more critical vulnerability factor (see also Roberts & Monroe, 1992).

Yet another view can be derived from the perspective and research we have presented in this chapter. Specifically, although low self-esteem may be related to greater depression than high self-esteem, this difference may be especially apparent among stable SEs. Stated differently, stable high SEs may be least vulnerable to depression, whereas stable low SEs may be most vulnerable. Furthermore, among high SEs, instability may be associated with greater depression because it reflects fragile self-feelings that are highly vulnerable to challenge. Among low SEs, the role of self-esteem instability in depressive symptomatology is less clear. One possibility is that it may be associated with lower depression because it reflects greater resiliency and ability to cope with negative events. As we have seen, however, there is some reason to doubt the viability of this hypothesis. In fact, there is reason to suspect that among low SEs, self-esteem instability may be related to more intense depressive symptoms.

In our first study relevant to these issues (Kernis et al., 1991), participants completed measures of level and stability of self-esteem, and, five weeks later, a measure of depressive symptoms (Center for Epidemiological Studies Depression Scale; Radloff, 1977). As expected, although there was an overall inverse relation between self-esteem and scores on the depression inventory, stability of self-esteem moderated this effect. Predicted values indicated that (a) stable low self-esteem was associated with the highest scores and stable high self-esteem the lowest, and (b) instability was associated with lower scores among low SEs, but higher scores among high SEs.

Roberts and Monroe (1992) also examined the role of self-esteem instability in depression, but they examined it as a potential diathesis for increases in depression after life stress. Stress was operationalized as failure on a college exam. Overall, self-esteem instability was related to greater depression. Also, stress predicted increases in depression, particularly among individuals with unstable SE. Additional findings indicated that this was only true among individuals who were initially asymptomatic of depression (who the authors presumed were mostly of high self-esteem). Among initially mildly depressed individuals (who were presumably characterized by low self-esteem), unstable self-esteem did not predict increases in depression following stress. Roberts and Monroe (1992) suggested that this last finding may reflect better coping on the part of unstable low SEs, although they did not specifically test this interpretation. Thus, across two studies, there is some indication that instability may relate to decreased depression in low SEs, but to increased depression in high SEs.

Kernis, Waschull, Greenier, Whisenhunt, and Berry (1994) extended these findings by looking at a more general index of stress (daily hassles), as well as factors that could potentially serve as mediators. At Time 1, participants completed two measures of depression (the CES-D, and the Beck Depression Inventory; Beck, Ward, Mendelson, Mock, & Erbaugh, 1961), and Rosenberg's (1965) Self-Esteem Scale. The next week, they completed multiple measures of current self-esteem. Approximately four weeks later, they returned to complete the same depression scales, a measure of daily hassles (Kanner, Coyne, Schaefer, & Lazarus, 1981) calibrated for the intervening time period, the Attributional Style Questionnaire (Peterson et al., 1982), and the Attitudes Toward Self Scale (Carver & Ganellen, 1983). The latter two measures were included to examine their potential roles as mediators of any effects involving stability and level of self-esteem that emerged. What follows is an initial summary of the major findings that emerged (for a full report, see Kernis, Waschull, Greenier, Whisenhunt, & Berry, 1994).

In order to simplify our presentation, we primarily focus here on the findings that emerged for the Beck Depression Inventory (although major differences in the results obtained for the two scales will be noted). For depression at Time 1, main effects for stability and level emerged, as did a Level × Stability interaction. The same effects emerged for depression at Time 2, as well as for change in depression from Time 1 to Time 2. Predicted values for the Level × Stability interactions (see Table VI) revealed that at both Time 1 and Time 2, instability was related to greater depression, but only among low SEs. For change in depression, it appears (from extrapolation) that for low SEs only, instability was related to increases in depression. For the CES-D, the Stability × Level interaction was not significant for change in depression from Time 1 to Time 2.

A. THE ROLE OF STRESSORS

We then looked at the extent to which the presence of stressors (i.e., daily hassles) interacted with the self-esteem variables to predict depression. Interestingly, a Level × Stability interaction emerged for experienced hassles, indi-

TABLE VI
PREDICTED VALUES FOR DEPRESSION
AT TIME 1 AND TIME 2 AS A FUNCTION
OF LEVEL AND STABILITY
OF SELF-ESTEEM[a]

Stability	Low SE[b]	High SE
	Time 1	
Stable	4.38	3.89
Unstable	10.90	3.09
	Time 2	
Stable	2.96	2.87
Unstable	12.56	2.91

[a]From Kernis, Waschull, Greenier, Whisenhunt, and Berry (1994).
[b]SE, Self-esteem level.

cating that unstable low SEs reported an especially high number of hassles. Even so, in predicting Time 2 depression, a significant Level × Stability × Hassles interaction emerged ($p < .05$). Predicted values indicated that the tendency for self-esteem instability to be related to greater depressive symptomatology was especially true for low SEs who reported numerous hassles. Among high SEs, the same pattern did not emerge. When Time 1 depression was controlled, the three-way interaction was no longer significant ($p < .10$). One reason for this weaker effect is that the perceived experience of daily hassles may have related to depression at Time 1, even though it was not assessed. Taken as a whole, these findings suggest that unstable low SEs were especially vulnerable to depressive symptomatology, particularly if they reported experiencing a substantial number of daily hassles.

For the CES-D, the three-way interaction was not significant. However, a significant Stability × Hassles interaction emerged for Time 2 depression, which remained significant when Time 1 depression was controlled. Predicted values indicated that unstable self-esteem was related to greater depressive symptomatology, especially among people who reported high numbers of daily hassles. Stated differently, when they reported frequent daily hassles, unstable high SEs as well as unstable low SEs appeared to be at greater risk for depressive symptomatology (as measured by the CES-D; see Kernis, Waschull, Greenier, Whisenhunt, & Berry, 1994, for further discussion of the role of daily hassles).

B. POTENTIAL MEDIATORS

Additional analyses focused on whether attributional styles and the tendency to overgeneralize following failure (a subscale of the Attitudes Toward Self Scale) mediated the relationships that emerged between stability and level of self-esteem and depression (i.e., the significant two-way interactions). That is, were unstable low SEs especially prone to depressive symptoms because they possessed particularly detrimental attributional styles or because they were especially likely to overgeneralize following failure? The first step in establishing mediation is finding that the predictors relate to the presumed mediator in the same way that they relate to the criterion (Baron & Kenny, 1986). In this case, this would mean finding Level × Stability interactions. For the attribution measures, we created summary indexes by combining responses on the internality, stability, and globality scales, separately for positive and negative events. Higher numbers on each scale reflect greater perceived internality, stability, or globality of the major cause summed across the events (of the same valence) depicted on the questionnaire. For the negative event summary index, the Level × Stability interaction was significant. As can be seen in Table VII, among high SEs, self-esteem instability was related to a slightly more self-protective attributional style for negative events (lower scores on the combined index). In contrast, among low SEs, instability was related to a less self-protective style (higher scores on the combined index). For the positive event index, the Level × Stability interaction was not significant, $p < .14$. However, it is of interest to note that predicted

TABLE VII
PREDICTED VALUES FOR THE NEGATIVE EVENT ATTRIBUTION SUMMARY INDEX[a] AS A FUNCTION OF LEVEL AND STABILITY OF SELF-ESTEEM[b]

Stability	Low SE[c]	High SE
Stable	66.70	70.94
Unstable	77.18	68.43

[a]Entries reflect sums of scores on the internality, stability, and globality indexes, which are keyed so that higher numbers reflect greater internality, stability, and globality.
[b]From Kernis, Waschull, Greenier, Whisenhunt, and Berry (1994).
[c]SE, Self-esteem level.

values indicated that unstable low SEs were the least self-serving in their attributional styles.

The second step in testing mediation involves showing that attributional styles were significantly related to scores on the depression inventories. In fact, less self-serving attributions for positive events (lower scores on the combined index) and less self-protective attributions for negative events (higher scores on the combined index) were both related to significantly greater depressive symptomatology. Note also that these types of attributional styles were most apparent among unstable low SEs.

The next step would be to show that the Level × Stability interaction predicting depression is substantially reduced when the presumed mediator is included in the prediction equation. However, in all cases, inclusion of the attribution indexes did not substantially affect the magnitude of the Level × Stability interaction. The conclusion to be drawn, then, is that attributional style did not mediate the relationships between stability and level of self-esteem and depression. Interestingly, in some cases, the contribution of attributional style also remained significant, indicating that attributional style predicted variance that was separate from the variance accounted for by self-esteem.

Carver, Ganellen, and Behar-Mitrani (1985) showed that the tendency to overgeneralize following failure was related to higher levels of depression. In the current sample, this also proved to be the case, $r = .54$, $p < .01$. Furthermore, both low self-esteem and unstable self-esteem were uniquely related ($ps < .01$) to greater tendencies to overgeneralize, although the interaction effect was nonsignificant, $p > .20$. Given the significance and direction of the main effects, however, it seemed possible that overgeneralization could serve as a partial mediator. This proved not to be the case, as the Level × Stability interaction remained virtually unchanged in all instances (even though the contribution of overgeneralization remained significant).

Certainly there may be other factors that mediate the relationship between self-esteem and depression. Given the absence of effects for attributional style and overgeneralization in the analyses we conducted, such factors may not be of the cognitive variety. Perhaps measures of more general coping styles of affective regulation and reactivity (for example, the Affect Intensity Measure; Larsen, 1984) would fare better.

Finally, Whisenhunt, Waschull, and Greenier (1993) reported the results of a study using the same design and measures as Kernis, Waschull, Greenier, Whisenhunt, and Berry (1994), but with a substantially smaller sample. Here, instability related to greater depression among both low and high SEs (i.e., main effect for stability but not for level and no interaction).

In sum, the findings from all four studies revealed that among high SEs, instability related to greater depressive symptomatology (although the generality of the effect varied across studies). In light of unstable high SEs' tendencies to engage in various self-enhancement and self-protection strategies, this may seem surprising. It makes sense, however, if one recognizes that such strategies are not necessarily successful. In fact, we would argue that, among unstable high SEs, the dependence upon such strategies reflects a basic weakness in the foundation of their positive self-feelings. This weakness, accompanied by a heightened tendency to invest their self-worth in everyday activities, is what makes unstable high SEs more prone to depressive symptoms than stable high SEs.

Two studies reviewed in this section showed that among low SEs, self-esteem instability was related to greater vulnerability to depressive symptomatology (Kernis, Waschull, Greenier, Whisenhunt, & Berry, 1994; Whisenhunt et al., 1993), whereas two others suggested just the opposite (Kernis et al., 1991; Roberts & Monroe, 1992). Thus, we are confronted again with the question of what role self-esteem instability plays among low SEs. Before dealing with this issue at some length, we present additional data that lend further credence to the view that unstable low SEs may be less well-off than their stable low SE counterparts. Parenthetically, these data also support our contention that unstable high SEs are especially invested in maintaining positive self-views.

V. Domain-Specific Evaluations, Pride, and the "Big Five"

We recently administered Harter's Self-Perception Profile for College Students and the NEO Five-Factor Inventory (Costa & McCrae, 1989) to a sample of approximately 100 undergraduate students. The Self-Perception Profile assesses self-evaluations in 12 domains: scholastic competence; intellectual ability; creativity; job competence; athletic competence; physical appearance; peer acceptance; close friendships; romantic relationships; relationships with parents; morality; and sense of humor. Regression analyses revealed significant Level × Stability interactions for job competence, scholastic competence, relationships with parents, close friendships, and intelligence, and marginal interactions ($p <$ .08) for peer acceptance, physical appearance, and morality (Kernis, Cornell, & Berry, 1993). Although the effects were typically not very large, predicted values (displayed in Table VIII) yielded highly consistent patterns across the various subscales: Among high SEs, instability tended to relate to more positive self-evaluations, whereas among low SEs, instability tended to relate to more negative evaluations. Thus, across a wide range of dimensions, unstable low SEs

TABLE VIII
PREDICTED VALUES FOR DOMAIN-SPECIFIC
SELF-EVALUATIONS AS A FUNCTION OF LEVEL
AND STABILITY OF SELF-ESTEEM[a]

Stability	Low SE[b]	High SE
	Job competence	
Stable	12.57	13.78
Unstable	11.35	14.81
	Scholastic competence	
Stable	11.79	11.86
Unstable	10.38	13.15
	Peer acceptance	
Stable	12.05	12.94
Unstable	11.19	14.48
	Physical appearance	
Stable	9.51	10.71
Unstable	7.80	11.60
	Relationships with parents	
Stable	14.82	15.02
Unstable	12.21	15.45
	Close relationships	
Stable	13.29	14.25
Unstable	11.99	15.84
	Intellectual ability	
Stable	12.58	13.31
Unstable	11.47	14.59
	Morality	
Stable	13.19	14.08
Unstable	10.73	13.97

[a]Higher numbers reflect more positive self-evaluations. From Kernis, Cornell, and Berry (1993).
[b]SE, Self-esteem level.

tended to evaluate themselves quite negatively, which could contribute to increased vulnerability to depressive symptoms.[3]

---

[3]Examination of the items that constituted the peer acceptance subscale revealed that they tapped self-judgments of social skills as well as how well respondents thought they were liked by others.

It is interesting that among high SEs, instability tends to be related to more favorable self-judgments along particular dimensions. Again, we believe that rather than reflecting solidly based self-judgments that stem from a well-developed sense of self-worth, they reflect motivated efforts to shore-up fragile self-feelings through positive self-evaluations.

A. PRIDE

Consistent with the findings just discussed for unstable high SEs, we have found that among high SEs, instability is related to both extreme pride in oneself as a person and pride in one's behavior, as measured by the Test of Self-Conscious Affect (TOSCA; Tangney, Wagner, & Gramzow, 1989).[4] Pride in self (alpha pride) and pride in behavior (beta pride) are assessed in terms of the favorability of reactions to hypothetical positive events. An example of an event is shown in Table IX. Consistent with our framework, it was unstable high SEs who reacted in the most self-enhancing manner by embracing positive events as indicative of favorable self-qualities. That is, significant Stability × Level interactions revealed that among high SEs, instability was related to greater pride. Instability had no effect among low SEs, and there were no overall self-esteem level differences.

B. THE BIG FIVE

The Five-Factor Inventory is an abbreviated version of the NEO-PI (Costa & McCrae, 1989), which is designed to measure five broad facets of personality: neuroticism; extraversion; agreeableness; conscientiousness; and openness to experience. Berry, Kernis, and Cornell (1993) reported the results of analyses in

---

Thus the pattern of self-ratings that emerged for this dimension may have implications for interpreting the pattern of results that emerged for reactions to positive and negative interpersonal feedback that were presented earlier (Kernis, Cornell, Sun, Berry, & Harlow, 1993, Study 1). Specifically, unstable low SEs may have viewed negative feedback regarding their social confidence as especially accurate because it matched their self-views. Likewise, unstable high SEs may have responded especially favorably to positive feedback because it matched their self-views. This suggests that, at least in part, cognitive factors (i.e., comparison of feedback with one's self-concept) may underlie the pattern we observed (cf. Blaine & Crocker, 1993). It seems unlikely, however, that cognitive factors can completely account for our findings. Specifically, given that self-esteem instability was correlated with self-esteem uncertainty in this sample (Kernis et al., 1993, Study 1), it seems that, at least for high SEs, attempts to bolster fragile self-feelings were at least partially responsible for the effects that emerged for self-esteem instability.

[4]We thank June Price Tangney for suggesting that we incorporate this measure into our research and for providing us with the needed materials.

TABLE IX
SAMPLE ITEM FROM TEST OF SELF-CONSCIOUS AFFECT (TOSCA) USED TO ASSESS PRIDE IN BEHAVIOR AND PRIDE IN SELF[a]

You are out with friends one evening and you're feeling especially witty and attractive. Your best friend's spouse seems to particularly enjoy your company.
  a. You would think: I should have been aware of what my best friend is feeling.
  b. You would feel happy with your appearance and personality.
  c. You would feel pleased to have made such a good impression.
  d. You would think your best friend should pay attention to his or her spouse.
  e. You would probably avoid eye contact for a long time.

[a]Respondents are asked to read and imagine themselves in a series of scenarios (five are related to pride) and to indicate the extent to which they would respond in each of the ways that are described. In this scenario, reaction "b" taps into pride in self and reaction "c" taps into pride in behavior. Reprinted with permission of author.

which stability and level of self-esteem were used to predict scores on each of these facets. Main effects for level of self-esteem emerged for neuroticism and extraversion, indicating that high self-esteem (compared to low self-esteem) was related to lower neuroticism and greater extraversion. Also, a main effect for stability of self-esteem emerged for neuroticism, indicating that unstable self-esteem (compared to stable self-esteem) was related to greater neuroticism. Of particular interest here, stability and level of self-esteem interacted in predicting scores on neuroticism, agreeableness, and conscientiousness. Predicted values, displayed in Table X, indicate that among high SEs, instability was related to greater agreeableness and conscientiousness, but was not related to neuroticism. Among low SEs, instability was related to greater neuroticism, but to lower agreeableness and conscientiousness.

High scores on neuroticism are thought to be indicative of negative emotionality, insecurity, and excessive worry. On the other hand, high scores on agreeableness are thought to reflect good-naturedness, helpfulness, forgivingness, and straightforwardness, whereas low scores are associated with heightened suspiciousness, uncooperativeness, and irritability. Finally, high conscientiousness scores are associated with heightened tendencies to be organized, reliable, self-disciplined, neat, and persevering, whereas low scores are associated with being aimless, lazy, and careless (descriptions based on Costa & McCrae, 1989).

The picture that emerges suggests again that among low SEs, instability is related to emotional and behavioral difficulties that may be quite pervasive. On the other hand, the picture that emerges among high SEs suggests that instability is related to greater attempts to get along with others and to maintain control over

TABLE X
PREDICTED VALUES FOR NEUROTICISM,
AGREEABLENESS, AND CONSCIENTIOUSNESS
AS A FUNCTION OF LEVEL AND STABILITY
OF SELF-ESTEEM[a]

Stability	Low SE[b]	High SE
	Neuroticism	
Stable	36.08	30.93
Unstable	43.38	29.95
	Agreeableness	
Stable	44.67	44.81
Unstable	40.21	47.19
	Conscientiousness	
Stable	43.42	42.80
Unstable	38.42	48.18

[a]From Berry, Kernis, and Cornell (1993).
[b]SE, Self-esteem level.

the details of their lives. In so doing, they may be able to maximize the extent of goodwill they receive from others, as well as from themselves.

VI. Summary

A few years ago, we began a program of research that focused on the nature of stability of self-esteem and its role in psychological functioning because we were convinced that such research would lead to insights not afforded by an exclusive focus on level of self-esteem. We hope that readers of this chapter will also share this view. In this chapter, we reviewed evidence that suggested that one important factor associated with unstable self-esteem is a heightened tendency to be ego-involved in everyday activities. In other words, to the extent that people link their feelings of self-worth to specific outcomes or evaluative information, these feelings are likely to fluctuate. Another factor that may be important, but that has yet to be systematically examined, is the extent to which people's self-concepts are impoverished or well developed. Furthermore, we argued and presented evidence that individual differences in self-esteem instability have important implications for the essential nature of both high and low self-esteem.

A. HIGH SELF-ESTEEM

Earlier, we suggested that there are two broad perspectives on the essence of high self-esteem. One perspective holds that high SEs have a well-anchored sense of positive self-worth that is secure and that does not require constant validation. The other perspective holds that high self-esteem is a precious commodity that must be continually defended and promoted in order to survive. Consideration of the role of stability of self-esteem indicates that there is some truth to each of these perspectives. Specifically, evidence from a number of studies now indicates that among high SEs, self-esteem instability is related to especially favorable reactions to positive events, and to defensive reactions to negative events. Our findings suggest also that among high SEs, instability reflects fragility in positive self-feelings, which promotes externally directed self-protective (i.e., becoming angry, attacking the threat and its source) and self-enhancement strategies. Thus, for unstable high SEs, self-esteem does appear to be a precious commodity.

On the other hand, the more stable an individual's high self-esteem, the less reactive he or she will be to specific positive or negative self-relevant events. Rather, stable high self-esteem reflects a well-developed sense of one's self-worth that is characterized by genuine self-liking and self-acceptance. Stated differently, among stable high SEs, positive self-feelings do not require constant buffering or bolstering—such feelings are secure. Consequently, it makes little sense to place the locus of motivationally based tendencies to self-protect or self-enhance on the possession of high self-esteem per se. It is only when high self-esteem is accompanied by high ego-involvement, fragile, and susceptible to challenge (i.e., unstable) that such strategies predominate.[5]

---

[5] A reviewer of this chapter raised a question about the extent to which the distinction between stable and unstable high SEs is the same as an earlier distinction made in the literature between "true" and "defensive" high SEs. Defensive high SEs are identified by scoring high on a self-esteem measure and on a measure of social desirability, such as the Crowne-Marlowe (1964) Social Desirability Scale (e.g., Schneider & Turkat, 1975). Conceptually, these individuals are thought to harbor inner negative feelings of self-worth, but because of high approval needs, they report feeling positively about themselves. Research has shown that, compared to true high SEs, defensive high SEs are more likely to present themselves in positive ways and to have more adverse reactions to negative self-relevant events (e.g., Schneider & Turkat, 1975). Thus, there does seem to be overlap in the outcomes associated with unstable and defensive high self-esteem. However, for several reasons, we believe that unstable high SEs differ in important ways from their defensive high SE counterparts. First, unstable high SEs are not thought to harbor ill feelings toward themselves that they are unwilling to admit to. Rather, unstable high SEs are thought to have positive self-feelings that are fragile, and that require constant validation. Second, if in fact unstable high SEs are more defensive in the traditional sense, it is not clear why they would show fluctuations in their contextually based self-esteem. Rather, their ratings on these measures should be consistently positive. (We thank Keegan Greenier for offering this observation). Finally, self-esteem instability does not significantly correlate with scores on the Crowne-Marlow (1964) Social Desirability Scale (Kernis et al., 1992),

B. LOW SELF-ESTEEM

We also pointed out earlier that researchers and theorists differ in their views of what it means to have low self-esteem. Some view low self-esteem as reflecting pervasive psychological difficulties, whereas others take a more benign view. Here again, self-esteem instability may be important in reconciling these conflicting positions. Admittedly, at this point in time, the role of self-esteem instability among low SEs is less definitive. Some of our early research suggested that it related to internally directed self-protective strategies and possibly greater resiliency in the face of negative self-relevant events. For example, among low SEs, instability related to greater excuse making following subjectively based failure (Kernis, Cornell, Sun, Berry, & Harlow, 1992) and to lower levels of future depression (Kernis et al., 1991). Later research undermined this view, however, as a number of studies revealed that among low SEs, instability was related to less adaptive functioning. Specifically, among low SEs, instability was related to perceiving negative interpersonal feedback as more accurate (Kernis et al., 1993, Study 1), greater neuroticism (Berry et al., 1993), less positive self-evaluations along specific dimensions (Kernis, Cornell, & Berry, 1993), and to greater concurrent and subsequent depression especially when faced with numerous daily hassles (Kernis, Waschull, Greenier, Whisenhunt, & Berry, 1994).

Why should unstable low self-esteem be related to such adverse outcomes? Perhaps unstable low SEs may simply lack the necessary skills and resources to refute the validity of negative self-relevant events and to redirect their focus on to more positive self-aspects (see also Spencer, Josephs, & Steele, 1993). This lack of skills and resources may be particularly detrimental if they are highly ego-involved (and even less certain about their self-concepts than stable low SEs). Additionally, unstable low SEs may periodically experience a glimpse of positive self-feelings that are out of reach for them on a permanent basis. These elevations in self-feelings may tease unstable low SEs with a temporary experience of positive self-regard. Consequently, subsequent declines in self-feelings may be especially painful for them and thus be associated with various adverse outcomes. A third possibility is that unstable low SEs vacillate between adaptive functioning and poor self-regulation, perhaps depending upon whether they currently are experiencing predominantly positive or negative fluctuations in temporary self-esteem.

Given the disparity in findings across our studies, it seems premature to reach any definitive conclusions about the overall role of self-esteem instability among

---

nor do stability and level of self-esteem interact in the prediction of scores on that measure. Our view is that the constructs of self-esteem instability and defensive self-esteem each have valuable (though separate) contributions to make to our understanding of self-esteem. We thank the reviewer for raising this important issue.

low SEs. It may be that low SEs are not very consistent in their degree of instability over time.[6] This would help account for the fact that in some of our research unstable low SEs seem to fare better than stable low SEs, whereas in other research they seem to fare worse. Certainly an important agenda for future research (which we elaborate upon in the next section) is to better understand the implications of stable versus unstable low self-esteem. At the very least, our research to date does indicate that the role of self-esteem instability is different for low than for high SEs. Specifically, it is only among high SEs that unstable self-esteem is associated with greater tendencies to engage in direct self-enhancement. As we and others (e.g., Baumeister et al., 1989; Brown et al., 1988; Tice, 1991) have suggested, the absence of such tendencies may be due to low SEs' concerns about whether a positive identity can be defended (both to self and others).

VII. Future Directions

In closing, we would like to suggest several lines of research that seem especially important for sharpening our understanding of the construct of self-esteem stability and its role in psychological functioning. One line of research pertains to developmental factors that contribute to unstable self-esteem. Especially valuable would be longitudinal research with children in which the impact of parental styles and other contextual factors on stability of self-esteem is examined. Moreover, identification of factors that differentially promote self-esteem instability among low and high SEs is likely to be especially helpful in clarifying the role of self-esteem instability among low SEs. It may be, for example, that whereas parents of unstable high SEs are basically supportive and encouraging (though also providing controlling or noncontingent feedback), parents of unstable low SEs are particularly harsh and nonsupportive. In addition, systematic examination of children's attachment styles vis à vis their primary caretakers and how these styles relate to children's level and stability of self-esteem would be extremely valuable.[7]

A second line of research would be to focus systematically on the differential

---

[6]Again, we thank a reviewer for making this point.

[7]For the sake of completeness, we note that two studies have been conducted to examine how stability and level of self-esteem relate to attachment styles in college students (Waschull, Greenier, & Kernis, 1993; Waschull & Kernis, 1993). The results differed somewhat across the two studies, and they did not provide an entirely coherent picture, perhaps because different measures (based upon different theoretical frameworks) were used to assess attachment style. It is of interest, though, that unstable low SEs appeared to be especially likely to have attachment styles that involved either a negative self or other model. We emphasize, however, that more research is necessary, and that it is especially important to examine these relationships in children.

use of self-protective and self-enhancement strategies in response to various types of interpersonal and subjectively based evaluative events. Is it the case, for example, that unstable high SEs are not threatened by subjectively based failures? Do unstable low SEs routinely engage in adaptive self-protective strategies in response to subjectively based failures? Are unstable low SEs more likely to engage in "indirect" self-enhancement strategies than stable low SEs? In examining such issues, careful attention should be given to isolating motivational from cognitive factors (self-concept differences) that may underlie such strategies. Furthermore, future research should focus explicitly on how various self-protective and self-enhancement strategies relate to more global indices of psychological functioning (Tennen & Affleck, 1993).

Future research should also focus on the different patterns of short-term fluctuations that people exhibit. Are some patterns more deleterious than others? Are people consistent in the patterns of fluctuations they exhibit across time? Again, addressing such issues is likely to help clarify the role of self-esteem instability among low SEs. Finally, examination of the "psychological worlds" and life experiences associated with self-esteem instability would significantly enhance our understanding. Particularly important in this regard would be explorations of whether stability and level of self-esteem relate to life-task construals (Cantor & Kihlstrom, 1987), personal narratives (McAdams, 1989), personal strivings (Emmons, 1989), and personal projects (Little, 1989).

As this brief discussion of research directions indicates, there are many questions that remain to be answered with regard to the nature of self-esteem instability and its role in psychological functioning. Nevertheless, it seems to us that the time has come to move beyond the basic issue of how high SEs differ from low SEs, and to obtain a more comprehensive understanding of self-esteem processes through the systematic examination of both level and stability of self-esteem.

Acknowledgments

The authors thank Andrea Berry, Keegan Greenier, and Connie Whisenhunt for their many valuable contributions to the research and conceptualization reported in this chapter. We also thank Vicki Roberts for her valuable comments and suggestions regarding our conceptualization. Finally, we thank the two anonymous reviewers and Mark P. Zanna for their incisive comments on an earlier draft.

References

Alloy, L. B., & Abramson, L. Y. (1988). Depressive realism: Four theoretical perspectives. In L. B. Alloy (Ed.), *Cognitive processes in depression,* (pp. 223–265). New York: Guilford.

Anastasi, A., Cohen, N., & Spatz, D. (1948). A study of fear and anger in college students through the controlled diary method. *Journal of Genetic Psychology, 73,* 243–249.

Arkin, R. M., & Maruyama, G. M. (1981). Attribution, affect, and college exam performance. *Journal of Educational Psychology, 71,* 85–93.

Averill, J. R. (1982). *Anger and aggression: An essay on emotion.* New York: Springer-Verlag.

Bachman, J. G., O'Malley, P. M., & Johnson, J. J. (1978). *Youth in transition: Volume 6. Adolescence to adulthood: A study of change and stability in the lives of young men.* Ann Arbor, MI: Institute for Social Research.

Baron, R. M., & Kenny, D. A. (1986). The moderator-mediator distinction in social psychological research: Conceptual, strategic, and statistical considerations. *Journal of Personality and Social Psychology, 51,* 1173–1182.

Baumeister, R. F. (1993a). *Self-esteem: The puzzle of low self-regard.* New York: Plenum Press.

Baumeister, R. F. (1993b). Understanding the inner nature of low self-esteem: Uncertain, fragile, protected, and conflicted. In R. F. Baumeister (Ed.), *Self-esteem: The puzzle of low self-regard.* New York: Plenum Press.

Baumeister, R. F., Tice, D. M., & Hutton, D. G. (1989). Self-presentational motivations and personality differences in self-esteem. *Journal of Personality, 57,* 547–579.

Baumgardner, A. H. (1990). To know oneself is to like oneself: Self-certainty and self-affect. *Journal of Personality and Social Psychology, 58,* 1062–1072.

Baumgardner, A. H., Kaufman, C. M., & Levy, P. E. (1989). Regulating affect interpersonally: When low self-esteem leads to greater enhancement. *Journal of Personality and Social Psychology, 56,* 907–921.

Baumrind, D. (1971). Current patterns of parental authority. *Developmental Psychology Monographs, 4,* (1, pt. 2).

Beck, A. T. (1967). *Depression: Clinical, experimental, and theoretical aspects.* New York: Harper and Row.

Beck, A. T., Ward, C. H., Mendelson, M., Mock, J., & Erbaugh, J. (1961). An inventory for measuring depression. *Archives of General Psychiatry, 4,* 561–571.

Berglas, S. (1985). Self-handicapping and self-handicappers: A cognitive/attributional model of interpersonal self-protective behavior. In R. Hogan & W. H. Jones (Eds.), *Perspectives in personality* (Vol. 1, pp. 235–270). Greenwich, CT: JAI Press.

Berry, A. J., Kernis, M. H., & Cornell, D. P. (1993, March). *Examining the relationships between stability and level of self-esteem and the "Big Five" personality dimensions.* Presented at the annual convention of the Southeastern Psychological Association, Atlanta, GA.

Bibring, E. (1953). The mechanism of depression. In P. Greenacre (Ed.), *Affective disorders: Psychoanalytic contributions to their study* (pp. 13–48). New York: International Universities Press.

Blaine, B., & Crocker, J. (1993). Self-esteem and self-serving biases in reaction to positive and negative events: An integrative review. In R. F. Baumeister (Ed.), *Self-esteem: The puzzle of low self-regard* (pp. 55–86). New York: Plenum.

Bowlby, J. (1972). *Attachment and loss: Vol. 2 Separation.* New York: Basic Books.

Brockner, J., Wiesenfeld, B. M., & Raskas, D. F. (1993). Self-esteem and expectancy-value discrepancy: The effects of believing that you can (or can't) get what you want. In R. F. Baumeister (Ed.), *Self-esteem: The puzzle of low self-regard* (pp. 219–240). New York: Plenum.

Brown, J. D., Collins, R. L., & Schmidt, G. W. (1988). Self-esteem and direct versus indirect forms of self-enhancement. *Journal of Personality and Social Psychology, 55,* 445–453.

Buri, J. R., Louiselle, P. A., Misukanis, T. M., & Mueller, R. A. (1988). Effects of parental authoritarianism and authoritativeness on self-esteem. *Personality and Social Psychology Bulletin, 14,* 271–282.

Buss, A. H., & Durkee, A. (1957). An inventory for assessing different kinds of hostility. *Journal of Abnormal and Social Psychology, 21,* 343–349.

Campbell, J. D. (1990). Self-esteem and clarity of the self-concept. *Journal of Personality and Social Psychology, 59,* 281–294.

Campbell, J. D., Chew, B., & Scratchley, L. S. (1991). Cognitive and emotional reactions to daily events: The effects of self-esteem and self-complexity. *Journal of Personality, 59,* 473–506.

Cantor, N., & Kihlstrom, J. F. (1987). *Personality and social intelligence.* Englewood Cliffs, NJ: Prentice-Hall.

Carver, C. S., & Ganellen, R. J. (1983). Depression and components of self-punitiveness: High standards, self-criticism, and overgeneralization. *Journal of Abnormal Psychology, 92,* 330–337.

Carver, C. S., Ganellen, R. J., & Behar-Mitrani, V. (1985). Depression and cognitive style: Comparisons between measures. *Journal of Personality and Social Psychology, 49,* 722–747.

Cialdini, R. B., & Richardson, K. D. (1980). Two indirect tactics of image management: Basking and blasting. *Journal of Personality and Social Psychology, 39,* 406–415.

Chodoff, P. (1973). The depressive personality: A critical review. In R. J. Friedman & M. M. Katz (Eds.), *The Psychology of depression: Contemporary theory and research.* Washington, DC: V H Winston.

Coopersmith, S. (1967). *The antecedents of self-esteem.* San Francisco: W. H. Freeman and Company.

Costa, P. T. Jr., and McCrae, R. R. (1992). *Revised NEO Personality Inventory.* Odessa, FL: Psychological Assessment Resources, Inc.

Crocker, J., Thompson, L., McGraw, K., & Ingerman, C. (1987). Downward social comparison, prejudice, and evaluations of others: Effects of self-esteem and threat. *Journal of Social and Personality Psychology, 52,* 907–916.

Crowne, D. P., & Marlowe, D. (1964). *The approval motive: Studies in evaluative dependence.* New York: Wiley.

Darley, J. M., & Goethals, G. R. (1980). People's analyses of ability-linked performances. In L. Berkowitz (Ed.), *Advances in experimental social psychology* (Vol. 13, pp. 1–43). New York: Academic Press.

Deci, E. L., & Ryan, R. M. (1985). *Intrinsic motivation and self-determination in human behavior.* New York: Plenum Press.

Deci, E. L., & Ryan, R. M. (1987). The support of autonomy and the control of behavior. *Journal of Personality and Social Psychology, 53,* 1024–1037.

Deci, E. L., & Ryan, R. M. (in press). Human agency: The basis for true self-esteem. To appear in M. H. Kernis (Ed.), *Efficacy, agency, and self-esteem.* New York: Plenum.

De La Ronde, C., & Swann, W. B. (1993). Caught in the crossfire: Positivity and self-verification strivings among people with low self-esteem. In R. Baumeister (Ed.), *Low self-esteem: The puzzle of low self-regard* (pp. 147–166). New York: Plenum.

Demo, H. D., & Savin-Williams, R. C. (1983). Early adolescent self-esteem as a function of social class: Rosenberg and Pearlin revisited. *American Journal of Sociology, 88,* 763–774.

Dweck, C. S., & Leggett, E. L. (1988). A social-cognitive approach to motivation and personality. *Psychological Review, 95,* 256–273.

Emmons, R. A. (1989). The personal striving approach to personality. In L. A. Pervin (Ed.), *Goal concepts in personality and social psychology* (pp. 87–126). Hillsdale, NJ: Erlbaum.

Ewen, R. B. (1993). *An introduction to theories of personality* (4th Ed.). Hillsdale, NJ: Erlbaum.

Felson, R. B. (1985). Reflected appraisal and the development of self. *Social Psychology Quarterly, 48,* 71–77.

Fenichel, O. (1945). *The psychodynamic theory of neurosis.* New York: Norton.

Fitch, G. (1970). Effects of self-esteem, perceived performance, and choice on causal attributions. *Journal of Personality and Social Psychology, 16,* 311–315.

Franks, D. D., & Marolla, J. (1976). Efficacious action and social approval as interacting dimensions of self-esteem: A tentative formulation through construct validation. *Sociometry, 39,* 324–341.

Gates, G. S. (1926). An observational study of anger. *Journal of Experimental Psychology, 9,* 325–331.

Gecas, V., & Schwalbe, M. L. (1983). Beyond the look-glass self: Social structure and efficacy-based self-esteem. *Social Psychology Quarterly, 46,* 77–88.

Gecas, V., & Schwalbe, M. L. (1986). Parental behavior and adolescent self-esteem. *Journal of Marriage and the Family, 48,* 37–46.

Gibbons, F. X., & McCoy, S. B. (1991). Self-esteem, similarity, and reactions to active versus passive downward comparison. *Journal of Personality and Social Psychology, 60,* 414–424.

Grolnick, W. S., & Ryan, R. M. (1987). Autonomy in children's learning: An experimental and individual difference investigation. *Journal of Personality and Social Psychology, 52,* 890–898.

Grolnick, W. S., & Ryan, R. M. (1989). Parent styles associated with children's self-regulation and competence in school. *Journal of Educational Psychology, 81,* 143–154.

Harter, S. (1981). *A scale of intrinsic versus extrinsic orientation in the classroom.* Denver: University of Denver Press.

Harter, S. (1985). *Manual for the Self-Perception Profile for Children.* Denver: University of Denver Press.

Harter, S. (1993). Causes and consequences of low self-esteem in children and adolescents. In R. Baumeister (Ed.), *Self-esteem: The puzzle of low self-regard* (pp. 87–116). New York: Plenum.

Hazan, C., & Shaver, P. (1987). Conceptualizing romantic love as an attachment process. *Journal of Personality and Social Psychology, 52,* 511–524.

Hewitt, P. L., & Flett, G. L. (1991). Perfectionism in the self and social contexts: Conceptualization, assessment, and association with psychopathology. *Journal of Personality and Social Psychology, 60,* 895–910.

Jacobson, E. (1975). The regulation of self-esteem. In E. J. Anthony & T. Benedek (Eds.), *Depression and human existence.* Boston: Brown-Little.

Kanner, A. D., Coyne, J. C., Schaefer, C., & Lazarus, R. S. (1981). Comparison of two modes of stress measurement: Daily hassles and uplifts versus major life events. *Journal of Behavioral Medicine, 4,* 1–39.

Karniol, R., & Heiman, T. (1987). Situational antecedents of child's anger experiences and subsequent responses to adult versus peer provokers. *Aggressive Behavior, 13,* 109–118.

Kelley, H. H. (1972). Causal schemata and the attribution process. In E. E. Jones, D. E. Kanousa, H. H. Kelley, R. E. Nisbett, S. Valins, & B. Weiner (Eds.), *Attribution: Perceiving the causes of behavior.* Morristown, NJ: General Learning Press.

Kernis, M. H. (1993). The roles of stability and level of self-esteem in psychological functioning. In R. Baumeister (Ed.), *Self-esteem: The puzzle of low self-regard* (pp. 167–182). New York: Plenum.

Kernis, M. H., Brockner, J., & Frankel, B. S. (1989). Self-esteem and reactions to overgeneralization. *Journal of Personality and Social Psychology, 57,* 707–714.

Kernis, M. H., Cornell, D. P., & Berry, A. J. (1993). *Stability and level of self-esteem as predictors of specific self-evaluations.* Unpublished data, University of Georgia, Athens.

Kernis, M. H., Cornell, D. P., Sun, C. R., Berry, A. J., & Harlow, T. (1993). There's more to self-esteem than whether it is high or low: The importance of stability of self-esteem. *Journal of Personality and Social Psychology, 65,* 1190–1204.

Kernis, M. H., & Grannemann, B. D. (1990). Excuses in the making: A test and extension of Darley and Goethals' attributional model. *Journal of Experimental Social Psychology, 26,* 337–349.

Kernis, M. H., Grannemann, B. D., & Barclay, L. C. (1989). Stability and level of self-esteem as predictors of anger arousal and hostility. *Journal of Personality and Social Psychology, 56,* 1013–1023.

Kernis, M. H., Grannemann, B. D., & Barclay, L. C. (1992). Stability of self-esteem: Assessment, correlates, and excuse making. *Journal of Personality, 60,* 621–644.

Kernis, M. H., Grannemann, B. D., & Mathis, L. C. (1991). Stability of self-esteem as a moderator of the relation between level of self-esteem and depression. *Journal of Personality and Social Psychology, 61,* 80–84.

Kernis, M. H., Greenier, K., Whisenhunt, C., Waschull, S. B., & Berry, A. J. (1993, June). *Stability of self-esteem and ego-involvement: Initial considerations.* Paper presented at the Nags Head Self and Society Conference, Highland Beach, FL.

Kernis, M. H., & Johnson, E. K. (1990). Current and typical self-appraisals: Differential responsiveness to evaluative feedback and implications for emotions. *Journal of Research in Personality, 24,* 241–257.

Kernis, M. H., Waschull, S. B., Greenier, K., Whisenhunt, C., & Berry, A. (1994). *Self-esteem and vulnerability to depressive symptoms: Moderators and mediators.* Manuscript in preparation.

Larsen, R. J. (1984). Theory and measurement of affect intensity as an individual difference characteristic. *Dissertation Abstr. Acts International, 85,* 2297B (university microfilms, no. 84–22112).

Linville, P. (1985). Self-complexity and affective extremity: Don't put all of your eggs in one cognitive basket. *Social Cognition, 3,* 94–120.

Little, B. R. (1989). Personal projects analysis: Trivial pursuits, magnificent obsessions, and the search for coherence. In D. M. Buss & N. Cantor (Eds.), *Personality psychology: Recent trends and emerging directions* (pp. 15–31). New York: Springer-Verlag.

Marsh, H. W. (1986). Self-esteem: Its relation to specific aspects of the self-concept and their importance. *Journal of Personality and Social Psychology, 51,* 1224–1236.

Markus, H., & Kunda, Z. (1986). Stability and malleability of the self-concept. *Journal of Personality and Social Psychology, 51,* 858–866.

McAdams, D. P. (1989). The development of a narrative identity. In D. M. Buss & N. Cantor (Eds.), *Personality psychology: Recent trends and emerging directions* (pp. 160–174). New York: Springer-Verlag.

McCarthy, J. D., & Hoge, D. R. (1982). Analysis of age effects in longitudinal studies of adolescent self-esteem. *Developmental Psychology, 18,* 372–379.

Mead, G. H. (1934). *Mind, self, and society.* Chicago: University of Chicago Press.

Meltzer, H. (1933). Student's adjustments in anger. *Journal of Social Psychology, 4,* 285–309.

Novaco, R. W. (1975). *Anger control: The development and evaluation of an experimental treatment.* Lexington, MA: D.C. Heath.

O'Malley, P. M., & Bachman, J. G. (1983). Self-esteem: Change and stability between ages 13 and 23. *Developmental Psychology, 19,* 256–268.

Paulhus, D. L., & Martin, C. L. (1988). Functional flexibility: A new conceptualization of interpersonal flexibility. *Journal of Personality and Social Psychology, 55,* 88–101.

Paulhus, D. L., & Reid, D. B. (1991). Enhancement and denial in socially desirable responding. *Journal of Personality and Social Psychology, 60,* 307–327.

Pelham, B. W., & Swann, W. B., Jr. (1989). From self-conceptions to self-worth: On the sources and structure of global self-esteem. *Journal of Personality and Social Psychology, 57,* 672–680.

Peterson, C., Semmel, A., von Baeyer, C., Abramson, L. Y., Metalsky, G. I., & Seligman, M. E. P. (1982). The attributional style questionnaire. *Cognitive Therapy and Research, 6,* 297–300.

Plant, R. W., & Ryan, R. M. (1985). Intrinsic motivation and the effects of self-consciousness, self-awareness, and ego-involvement: An investigation of internally controlling styles. *Journal of Personality, 53,* 435–449.

Radloff, L. (1977). The CES-D scale: A self-report depression scale for research in the general population. *Applied Psychological Measurement, 1,* 384–401.

Roberts, J. E., & Monroe, S. M. (1992). Vulnerable self-esteem and depressive symptoms: Prospective findings comparing three alternative conceptualizations. *Journal of Personality and Social Psychology, 62,* 804–835.

Rogers, C. R. (1959). A theory of therapy, personality, and interpersonal relationships, as developed in the client-centered framework. In S. Koch (Ed.), *Psychology: A study of a science* (Vol. 3, pp. 184–256). New York: McGraw-Hill.

Rogers, C. R. (1961). *On becoming a person: A therapist's view of psychotherapy.* Boston: Houghton-Mifflin.

Rosenberg, M. (1965). *Society and the adolescent self-image.* Princeton, NJ: Princeton University Press.

Rosenberg, M. (1986). Self-concept from middle childhood through adolescence. In J. Suls & A. G. Greenwald (Eds.), *Psychological perspectives on the self* (Vol. 3). Hillsdale, NJ: Erlbaum.

Ryan, R. M. (1982). Control and information in the interpersonal sphere: An extension of cognitive evaluation theory. *Journal of Personality and Social Psychology, 43,* 450–461.

Ryan, R. M. (1993). Agency and organization: Intrinsic motivation, autonomy, and the self in psychological development. In J. Jacobs (Ed.), *Nebraska symposium on motivation: Developmental perspectives on motivation* (Vol. 40, pp. 1–56). Lincoln, NE: University of Nebraska Press.

Savin-Williams, R. C., & Demo, D. H. (1983). Situational and transituational determinants of adolescent self-feelings. *Journal of Personality and Social Psychology, 44,* 824–833.

Savin-Williams, R. C., & Demo, D. H. (1984). Developmental change and stability in adolescent self-concept. *Developmental Psychology, 20,* 1100–1110.

Schneider, D. J., & Turkat, D. (1975). Self-presentation following success or failure: Defensive self-esteem models. *Journal of Personality, 43,* 127–135.

Schlenker, B. R. (1980). *Impression management.* Belmont, CA: Wadsworth.

Shrauger, J. S. (1975). Responses to evaluation as a function of initial self-perceptions. *Psychological Bulletin, 82,* 581–596.

Snyder, C. R., & Higgins, R. L. (1988). Excuses: Their role in the negotiation of reality. *Psychological Bulletin, 104,* 23–35.

Solomon, S., Greenberg, J., & Pyszczynski, T. (1991). A terror management theory of social behavior: The psychological functions of self-esteem and cultural worldviews. In M. P. Zanna (Ed.), *Advances in experimental social psychology* (pp. 91–159). San Diego: Academic Press.

Spencer, S. J., Josephs, R. A., & Steele, C. M. (1993). Low self-esteem: The uphill struggle for self-integrity. In R. Baumeister (Ed.), *Self-esteem: The puzzle of low self-regard* (pp. 21–37). New York: Plenum.

Spielberger, C. D., Jacobs, G., Russell, S., & Crane, R. (1983). Assessment of anger: The state-trait anger scale. In J. N. Butcher & C. D. Spielberger (Eds.), *Advances in personality assessment,* (Vol. 2, pp. 159–187). Hillsdale, NJ: Erlbaum.

Swann, W. B., Jr., Griffin, J. J. Jr., Predmore, S. C., & Gaines, B. (1987). The cognitive-affective crossfire: When self-consistency confronts self-enhancement. *Journal of Personality and Social Psychology, 52,* 991–889.

Taylor, S. E., & Brown, J. D. (1988). Illusion and well-being: A social psychological perspective on health. *Psychological Bulletin, 103,* 193–210.

Tellegen, A. (1988). The analysis of consistency in personality assessment. *Journal of Personality, 56,* 621–663.

Tennen, H., & Affleck, G. (1993). The puzzles of self-esteem, a clinical perspective. In R. F. Baumeister (Ed.), *Self-esteem: The puzzle of low self-regard.* New York: Plenum.

Tesser, A. (1988). Toward a self-evaluation maintenance model of social behavior. In L. Berkowitz (Ed.), *Advances in experimental social psychology* (Vol. 21, pp. 181–227). San Diego: Academic Press.

Tice, D. M. (1991). Esteem protection or enhancement? Self-handicapping motives and attributions differ by trait self-esteem. *Journal of Personality and Social Psychology, 60,* 711–725.

Waschull, S. B., Greenier, K. D., & Kernis, M. H. (1993, March). *Unstable self-esteem: Familial antecedents and adult relationships.* Presented at the annual convention of the Southeastern Psychological Association, Atlanta, GA.

Waschull, S. B., & Kernis, M. H. (in press). Level and stability of self-esteem as predictors of children's intrinsic motivation and reasons for anger. *Personality and Social Psychology Bulletin*.

Waschull, S. B., & Kernis, M. H. (1993, April). *Unstable self-esteem: Familial influences and relationship effects*. Paper presented at the convention of the Midwestern Psychological Association, Chicago, IL.

Watson, D., & Clark, L. A. (1984). Negative affectivity: The disposition to experience aversive motivational states. *Psychological Bulletin, 96,* 469–490.

Whisenhunt, C., Waschull, S. B., & Greenier, K. D. (1993, March). *Role of self-esteem stability in the relationship between self-esteem and depression*. Presented at the annual convention of the Southeastern Psychological Association, Atlanta, GA.

Wills, T. A. (1981). Downward comparison principles in social psychology. *Psychological Bulletin, 90,* 245–271.

GENDER DIFFERENCES IN PERCEIVING INTERNAL STATE: TOWARD A HIS-AND-HERS MODEL OF PERCEPTUAL CUE USE

Tomi-Ann Roberts
James W. Pennebaker

I. Introduction

The perception of physical symptoms and sensations can be based on both internal physiological cues as well as external situational factors. Research on the accuracy with which people can detect physiological indices, as well as on self-reports of symptoms, emotions, and physical exertion suggests that women and men use internal and external cues differently in perceiving and defining bodily states. Relative to women, men detect physiological changes quite accurately without relying on external contextual cues, and appear to make relatively greater use of internal physiological data in determining how they feel. Women, compared to men, make greater use of external situational cues in defining their internal state. Because internal physiological and external contextual sources of information are typically redundant, men and women are usually equally adept at perceiving internal state in the natural environment. Speculations are made concerning possible mechanisms for such a gender difference in cue use, which focus on social dominance, specific biological factors such as hemispheric lateralization, and socialization based on bodily experiences. Implications of our theory for other gender differences research are discussed. Finally, we propose that competing psychological theories of emotion may be gender-linked, with women perceiving emotions in ways more congruent with cognitive appraisal theories and men doing so consistent with James's peripheralist theory.

II. Gender Differences in Perceiving Internal State: Toward a His-and-Hers Model of Perceptual Cue Use

A central issue in psychology concerns how individuals come to know their bodily states. For example, how do people know that their hearts are racing, or that they are fatigued, or hungry? As with the naturalistic perception of visual, auditory, or other stimuli, people make judgments about internal sensations[1] by relying on a variety of information sources, some of which originate within the body, whereas others are gleaned from external contextual sources. Consider, for example, how we "know" that we have a racing heart. To some degree, this percept is based on our awareness of a pounding in the chest (often due to increased stroke volume) and, to some extent, on our true heart rate. We also assume that our hearts are racing by processing relevant situational cues— hearing a loud, unexpected noise burst, seeing a person with whom we are infatuated, or looking out over a hostile audience of peers.

One of the core tenets of J. J. Gibson's (1979) ecological approach to perception is that most perceptions are based on multiple sources of information. Typically, information for any percept is plentiful, multimodal, and, fortunately, redundant. We perceive that we are hungry, for example, by noting stomach sensations or feelings of dizziness or trembling (internally based hunger cues) as well as by referring to the time since our last meal or seeing other people eating (external, situationally based hunger cues). Both internal and external types of information typically co-occur, are available to the perceiver, and serve as important sources of information for defining hunger, and, ultimately, eating.

Of particular import is that both internal and external cues may provide information regarding bodily sensations. That is, information that serves as the bases of percepts is highly redundant. If one information source is ambiguous or nonexistent, the perceiver may compensate by relying on the remaining information sources. For example, quadraplegics, who receive little if any sensory of proprioceptive feedback, report a normal emotional life, presumably because of their reliance on situational cues (Chwalisz, Diener, & Gallagher, 1988). Similarly, reports of emotion, pain, and other internal states can be influenced by physiologically arousing drugs or naturally occurring hormonal or metabolic disturbances (Rickels, 1968; Watson & Pennebaker, 1980; Wolf & Goodell, 1968).

A variety of literatures are converging to suggest that men and women may rely on internal and external cues differently in determining their bodily and

---

[1] By "internal sensation" we mean a *perception* that may or may not be directly correlated with its physiological referent. Similarly, a "physical symptom", although often used to define a pathological state, here is used interchangeably with "physical sensation" (cf. Pennebaker, 1982).

perhaps even their feeling states. Although women and men both report similar sensations of racing hearts, for example, growing evidence suggests that the bases of these bodily percepts may differ. The purpose of this chapter is to explore this gender difference in cue use. We first review several studies from the interoception literature suggesting that men and women use internal versus external cues differently when defining their bodily and feeling states. Then we discuss other areas of research that show that self-reports of various psychological states correspond more directly with physiological changes in men than in women. Next we review two literatures suggesting gender differences in cue use when both internal and external cues are available and competing. The final two sections are devoted to exploring why these gender effects occur and to pointing to several important implications of our "his-and-hers" model of bodily perception.

A. GENDER DIFFERENCES IN INTEROCEPTIVE ACCURACY

Since the mid-1970s, researchers have been devising paradigms to measure the degree to which healthy individuals can accurately detect or estimate subtle physiological changes in their bodies. Two general and complementary approaches to interoceptive accuracy[2] have examined detection abilities in highly controlled laboratory settings as well as in more naturalistic situations. The first approach, which has been heavily influenced by work in psychophysics, attempts to tape "pure" perceptions of physiological activity, by controlling for all external environmental biases in the perceptual process. For example, this approach might attempt to determine subjects' accuracy in detecting their own heartbeats, via signal-detection methodology. To do so, subjects are placed in sound-attenuated chambers and tested on their ability to identify the correct pattern of their heartbeats over repeated trials. In addition to heartbeat perception, other studies have examined the detection of blood pressure, blood glucose, respiratory resistance, stomach contraction, and finger temperature (Barr, Pennebaker, & Watson, 1988; Harver, Katkin, & Bloch, 1993; Pennebaker, 1982; Pennebaker & Epstein, 1983; Pennebaker, Gonder-Frederick, Cox, & Hoover, 1985; Pennebaker & Watson, 1988; Whitehead & Drescher, 1980). The second approach, which is more naturalistic, acknowledges that environmental cues are an inherent component of real-world interoception, and therefore is less concerned with control and more with ecological validity. For example, this approach might require subjects to estimate heart rate after engaging in a variety of physical or

---

[2]Within the psychophysiology literature, "interoception" is usually referred to as "visceral perception" or "visceral detection."

emotional tasks in a laboratory, or to estimate their heart rate repeatedly over a period of days in their own home or work environments.

Given the evolution of these two approaches, we can evaluate the degree to which individuals differ in their normal perceptual styles of relying on internal versus external cues in defining internal state. Interestingly, a number of studies using both approaches have failed to find any reliable personality scales that predict accuracy at perceiving physiological cues (see Pennebaker, 1982, for review). However, one individual difference factor has consistently been linked to interoceptive accuracy in controlled laboratory settings: gender. As we discuss below, males are more accurate at detecting heartbeats, stomach contraction, blood glucose levels, and other biological changes than are females in controlled experiments. In naturalistic studies, however, in which subjects estimate their internal states with a variety of cues available, no gender differences have been found.

B. CONTROLLED LABORATORY APPROACHES

A number of laboratory paradigms have been developed for the study of interoceptive accuracy. We will focus on two in particular, signal detection and self-report methods. These techniques can be construed as representing two ends of a continuum of experimental control. Signal-detection methods typically exclude most external situational and irrelevant internal sensory information in an attempt to focus subjects solely on the physiological index of interest. These techniques were developed in order to tap pure sensory discrimination of physiological indices as opposed to more cognitively determined estimation of such indices in the real world. Self-report techniques, on the other hand, attempt to simulate naturally occurring interoception processes, by allowing subjects to estimate their indices with access to *both* internal and external sources of information. Despite their differences in control, both laboratory approaches have found consistent gender effects.

1. Signal-Detection Methods

Brener and his colleagues (Brener & Jones, 1974; Brener, 1977) pioneered one of the earliest signal-detection methods for investigating heartbeat perception. The Brener and Jones method (or BJ technique) requires subjects to indicate whether or not each of a series of stimuli are associated with their heartbeats. On half of the trials, subjects receive stimulus trains (e.g., vibrations to the wrist or brief tones) triggered by the successive R-waves of their electrocardiogram (EKG) (which correspond to the contraction of the heart muscle). On these trials, then, each stimulus is dependent on the occurrence of a heartbeat. On the other half of the trials, the stimuli are triggered by a clock pulse generator, which approximates the frequency of the subject's heartbeats. Consequently, on these trials, heartbeat and signaling stimuli occur independently. At the end of each 10-sec trial, subjects must indicate whether the preceding train was either dependent or independent of their heartbeats.

Whitehead and his colleagues (Whitehead, Drescher, Heiman, & Blackwell, 1977; Whitehead & Drescher, 1980) developed a slightly different paradigm for investigations of heartbeat perception. In theirs, subjects are asked to discriminate between two sets of stimuli, presented at different time delays, with respect to their heartbeats. On half the trials, subjects see a light that flashes 128 ms after each R-wave of the EKG (i.e., immediate feedback). On the other half, the light flashes 384 ms after each R-wave (i.e., delayed feedback). The subject's task is to judge whether immediate or delayed feedback occurred. Finally, Katkin and his colleagues (Katkin, Morell, Goldband, Bernstein, & Wise, 1982; Katkin, 1985) have modified the Whitehead technique. With their method, subjects do not discriminate between immediate and delayed stimuli, but rather between stimuli that are presented either at a fixed or a variable time interval after the heartbeat.

The Whitehead, BJ, and Katkin techniques are particularly powerful in controlling for any external cues in subjects' attempts at detecting heartbeats. In virtually all studies, subjects sit quietly in sound-attenuated chambers while performing the signal-detection tasks. Furthermore, they are given explicit instructions not to manipulate their breathing, muscle tension, or other actions in an attempt to perceive heartbeat sensations.

Across the various heartbeat-detection paradigms, which typically require hundreds of trials per subject, untrained subjects perform at rates significantly better than chance (e.g., $d' = .40$ or within-subjects $r = .16$). Furthermore, one individual difference that reliably predicts heartbeat detection accuracy is gender. Across the different heartbeat detection paradigms, males consistently demonstrate significantly more accurate resting heartbeat detection than females (Blascovich et al., 1992; Harver, Katkin, & Bloch, 1993; Jones & Hollandsworth, 1981; Jones, Jones, Rouse, Scott, & Caldwell, 1987; Jones, O'Leary, & Pipkin, 1984; Katkin, 1985; Katkin, Blascovich, & Goldband, 1981; Pennebaker & Hoover, 1984; Whitehead & Drescher, 1980; Whitehead et al., 1977). These effects, although small, are highly significant. Averaging across the studies for which we were able to transform heartbeat-detection accuracy scores to within-subject correlations, the mean accuracy correlation for men is .29, whereas for women it is .13 (in a weighted regression, the beta-weight for gender $= .191, p < .001$). Given very low variability, these effects are highly stable and reliable.

This finding holds for the limited number of signal-detection studies on indices other than heartbeat as well. Whitehead and Drescher (1980), for example, found a gender difference in detecting stomach contractions. In their study, stomach contraction was continually monitored. The subjects' task was to judge whether a light signal was presented at the peak of a stomach contraction, or 12–15 s following the contraction. Males were significantly better able to detect their stomach contractions than females (Mean $d' = .54$ versus .29, $p < .05$, effect size $= .40$). In addition, Harver et al. (1993) found a gender difference in the ability to detect respiratory resistance. Subjects in their study breathed through external devices that manipulated the rate of airflow, and judged whether, at the presentation of a signal, their inspiration involved resistance or not. In this study the dependent variable was simply the number of correct responses. Again, males made a significantly greater number of correct responses on this task than females (Mean $= 65.83$ versus 57.00, $p < .05$, effect size $= .48$).

In sum, although the various signal-detection methods tap different aspects of interoception, most reliably demonstrate that males are better than females at detecting various physiological indices at rest in highly controlled lab settings. The combined overall mean effect size for the gender difference across the signal-detection paradigms on the various physiological indices is $r = .45$.

2. Self-Report Methods

Self-reports have been used in a variety of ways in an attempt to learn how accurate individuals are at perceiving physiological state.[3] Unlike the signal-detection methods, the self-repot methods do not control for subjects' perceptual and inferential biases. Because these "biases" naturally occur in the real world, however, self-report methods are more externally valid in that they allow subjects to use all the information normally available to them in judging bodily state. In addition, unlike the signal-detection paradigms, which all measure subjects' interoceptive accuracy in a resting state, such studies normally involve a variety of arousing tasks.

In within-subject self-report studies, subjects typically report on specific physiological indices 20 to several hundred times during a laboratory session. Usu-

---

[3]Self-reports have been used in both between-subjects and within-subjects paradigms. Typically, between-subjects paradigms require large groups of subjects to rate the degree to which they perceive a particular autonomic index, such as a fast pulse where, for example 1 = no fast pulse and 7 = fast pulse. At the same time, the actual physiological readings of that index are also collected. Most between-subjects studies indicate correlations between autonomic indices (e.g. heart rate, breathing rate, blood pressure) and their self-report referents averaging between .20 and .30 (Pennebaker, 1982). Across all of these between-subjects studies, no accuracy differences have been found between males and females. However, because between-subjects methods do not control for differences in physiological baselines among subjects, and because most of the previously discussed signal detection studies were done on a within-subjects basis, we will be focusing solely on within-subjects self-report studies.

ally, to ensure some degree of variability in both self-reports and physiological levels, various aspects of the subjects' environments or physiological states are manipulated. For example, subjects might be asked to walk in place, view frightening scenes, or blow up balloons until they pop. These techniques have been shown to manipulate physiological state as well as self-reports. Accuracy of perception is then determined by a correlation between subjects' own estimates of a particular index and its actual physiological determinant. For example, subjects' self-reports of perceived fast pulse at various points during the laboratory session would be correlated with concurrent measurements of their actual heart rate, for a measurement of the accuracy of their perceptions of heartbeat. Across several within-subject self-report laboratory studies, subjects are only moderately good at estimating the following indices: heartbeats = .22 (Pennebaker, 1982; Pennebaker & Epstein, 1983; Pennebaker & Watson, 1988), breathing rate = .22 (Pennebaker & Epstein, 1983), finger temperature = .10 (Pennebaker, 1982; Pennebaker & Epstein, 1983), blood pressure = .24 (Pennebaker & Watson, 1988; Barr et al., 1988), and blood glucose = .31 (Pennebaker et al., 1985).

The overall magnitudes of the accuracy relationships are slightly higher for self-report studies than for signal-detection methods. As with the signal-detection methods, there is a tendency for males to have higher accuracy correlations than females in these studies. However, in terms of heartbeat perception, the findings from the self-report studies show a less consistent pattern. Pennebaker (1982) found a significant difference, with males significantly more accurate in self-reported heartbeat perception than females ($r = .26$, versus $r = .13$). However, both Pennebaker and Hoover (1984) and Pennebaker and Watson (1988) found no significant relationship between gender and accuracy.

On other indices, consistent and statistically significant gender effects have been found in some self-report studies. The magnitude of these gender differences in accuracy is smaller, however, than in the signal-detection studies of interoception. The gender effect has also been shown for self-report studies of blood pressure estimation, where the mean accuracy r for men is .33, versus .22 for women (Pennebaker & Watson, 1988), finger temperature estimation, where the accuracy r for men is .23, versus .10 for women (Pennebaker, 1982), and, as will be discussed further in the next section, blood glucose level estimation, where the mean r for men is .42, versus .13 for women (Cox et al., 1985). Combining the effect sizes for gender differences in self-report lab studies yields a mean effect size of $r = .24$.

3. Summary

Comparing the two effect sizes of .45 for the signal-detection studies and .24 for the self-report lab studies yields a Z of 1.60, $p = .05$, indicating that the two effect sizes differ significantly. This simple meta-analysis reveals that the magnitude of the gender differences in self-report lab studies is smaller than the magnitude of the gender differences found in the signal-detection paradigms.

In general, then, subjects are slightly better at perceiving physiological cues in self-report studies than in signal-detection paradigms. Furthermore, the gender effects are not as robust in the self-report experiments. Interestingly, these differences may be understood, according to our theory, in terms of the different types of cues available to subjects. That is, in the signal-detection studies, subjects are only able to use internal physiological sources of information to define body state. In such studies, subjects are typically placed in completely darkened rooms and asked to attend to a single blinking light or sound, and judge its correspondence to their heartbeats. In the self-report experiments, on the other hand, subjects can use both internal physiological cues as well as external contextual information, because they typically engage in varied activities, such as jogging in place, placing a foot in cold water, blowing up a balloon until it pops, or viewing frightening scenes. These activities provide the subjects with cues that are multisensory.

Given that both types of information are available in the self-report studies, it would follow that subjects would be somewhat more accurate at perceiving physiological changes as long as external and internal cues were somewhat redundant or trustworthy. The weaker gender effect in the laboratory studies seems to reflect an improvement in women's performance rather than a decrement in men's (the average accuracy correlation for men in signal-detection studies is $r = .29$, versus .30 in the self-report lab studies, whereas the average accuracy correlation for women in the signal-detection studies is $r = .09$, versus .16 in the self-report studies). This pattern is consistent with the idea that women rely less heavily on internal, physiological cues than men, and perhaps more heavily on external, situational cues in determining their bodily state.

The differential gender effect in the two kinds of studies is also consistent with the fact that signal-detection paradigms tend to measure interoceptive accuracy in a resting state, whereas self-report studies normally involve a variety of arousing tasks. We would argue that if either internal cues (as would be the case in a laboratory where subjects exercise and thus increase their heart rates significantly above baseline) or external cues (as would be the case, for example, in an earthquake or any extremely traumatic event) are *highly salient,* gender differences in interoceptive accuracy ought to be minimal if they occur at all. In either of these cases one cue-source essentially obscures the other, providing perceivers with all the data they need. Indeed one signal-detection study assessed gender differences in interoceptive accuracy in a resting state and an aroused state (Blascovich et al., 1992), and found no gender differences in heartbeat-detection accuracy when subjects were aroused during moderate exercise.

C. NATURALISTIC FIELD STUDIES

Unfortunately, very few investigations have focused on interoceptive processes among people in their natural environments. One technique that has been employed is the self-cuing method, which requires subjects to measure specific physiological levels and complete self-reports at specified intervals, ranging from once every 20 min to 2–4 times per day. Self-cuing relies on subjects' memories and good intentions in order to collect self-report and physiological data. These studies indicate that subjects are relatively good at estimating physiological indices. As discussed in greater detail in the next section, two studies have found within-subject correlations of .37 between estimated and actual systolic blood pressure (Smith, 1986), and .62 between estimated and actual blood glucose levels (Cox et al., 1985). Notably, no consistent gender effects have emerged in these studies.

Another method of naturalistic data collection requires subjects to give multiple self-reports and physiological readings at a scheduled time, in a designated location, over an extended time period. In one such study (Baumann & Leventhal, 1985), subjects made multiple estimations of their blood pressure levels within their work environment. They made their estimations and had their actual blood pressure measured twice a day in a quiet room, over a two-week period. Results of this study revealed that subjects were, on the whole, not particularly accurate in predicting their blood pressure levels ($r = .14$). However, this mean r was significantly different from zero. The researchers divided the subjects into thirds, representing good, fair, and poor blood pressure predictors, based on their within-subject correlations. As with the other naturalistic investigations of interoceptive accuracy, based on this analysis, gender did not correlate with predictive accuracy.

D. STUDIES COMPARING LABORATORY WITH NATURALISTIC METHODS

To our knowledge, only two studies have directly compared interoceptive abilities in the laboratory with those in the real world using the same subjects. The first focused on insulin-dependent diabetics' abilities to estimate blood glucose levels in the lab versus the natural environment. The second examined subjects' abilities at estimating blood pressure fluctuations with adult normotensive and hypertensive subjects.

The first project, conducted by Cox et al. (1985), required 19 insulin-dependent diabetics to estimate their blood glucose levels 40–50 times just before measurement of actual blood glucose over a 9-hr period. The subjects participated in this procedure under two conditions. In the *hospital condition*, they were connected to an insulin–glucose infusion system that artificially manipulated blood glucose. This laboratorylike condition essentially eliminated any external cues to blood glucose levels, leaving subjects with only physiological cues as information sources. In other words, subjects were given something of a blood glucose roller coaster ride, during which they were prompted every 10 min to enter their own blood glucose estimation into a computer. After they made their estimate, a nurse, blind to the subjects' estimates, entered their actual blood glucose levels. In the *home condition,* subjects simply estimated their blood glucose prior to four actual blood glucose measurements, over a 10-day period. In this condition, subjects had access to both internal physiological as well as external cues such as food, exercise, and insulin.

Results indicated that, overall, subjects were significantly better at estimating their blood glucose levels in the home condition than in the hospital condition (hospital $r = .22$ versus home $r = .62$, $p < .001$). Furthermore, the accuracy correlation for men (.42) was significantly higher than that for women (.13) in the hospital condition only. No sex differences in accuracy were found in the home condition (male $r = .58$, female $r = .69$). In other words, men were more accurate at estimating blood glucose levels only when external cues were not available. When both internal and external cues were available, both men and women were equally good at estimating their levels.

The second project studied 55 adult subjects' abilities to estimate systolic blood pressure in the laboratory and at home. The laboratory phase, which was originally reported by Pennebaker and Watson (1988), required subjects to participate in a series of 45 tasks and intervening baselines. The tasks were occasionally arousing (e.g., walking in place, counting backwards by 7s), relaxing (e.g., viewing peaceful scenes), and neutral (touching various fabrics). During each task and baseline period, subjects estimated their blood pressure level while actual blood pressure was measured. Subjects never received feedback about their actual blood pressure levels. The second phase of the experiment, which took place 2–6 months after the laboratory study, required subjects to carry a portable blood pressure sphygmanomometer and questionnaire booklet with them during their daily activities for a 2-wk period. At least once per hour during their waking day, subjects first estimated their blood pressure and then measured actual blood pressure (Smith, 1986). For both phases of the study, within-subject correlations between actual and estimated systolic blood pressure were computed.

Results indicated that subjects were better at estimating their blood pressure at home, where they had access to a variety of real-world situational cues relevant to blood pressure levels, than in the laboratory, where these cues were minimized (laboratory $r = .28$ versus home $r = .37$, $p = .06$). Within-subject correlations from the laboratory indicated a significant gender difference in accuracy, with men being significantly more accurate in estimating blood pressure than women ($r = .39$ versus $r = .23$, $p = .01$). However, in the home condition there was no gender difference in accuracy (men's $r = .42$ versus women's $r = .35$, ns).

E. POSSIBLE EXPERIMENTAL CONFOUNDS IN INTEROCEPTIVE ACCURACY STUDIES

A number of experimental confounds could conceivably account for the findings we have presented thus far. However, there is ample evidence to rule out several. For example, anxiety could play a role in undermining women's accuracy on interoceptive tasks in laboratory as compared to natural settings. However, no consistent correlations between self-reported anxiety and interoceptive accuracy have been found in any investigation (Pennebaker, 1982), so it is highly unlikely that anxiety can account for the gender difference in accuracy in the laboratory.

A second possible confound of particular relevance to the laboratory signal-detection paradigms might be that males simply show higher ability on signal-detection tasks in general. Indeed, Weisz, Balazs, Lang, and Adam (1990) postulated that differences in time perception or sustained attention (skills required in any signal-detection task) could account for individual differences in heartbeat-detection tasks. One study tested this possibility directly with respect to gender. Harver et al. (1993) included a nonphysiological detection task (detecting light tones) in their study of heartbeat and respiratory resistance discrimination. They found that although males and females demonstrated significantly different accuracy levels in the detection of heartbeats and respiration, their performance on the light-tone detection task was identical.

Body fat has been offered as yet another potential explanation for the gender differences in the signal-detection paradigms particularly. For example, Rouse, Jones, and Jones (1988) postulated that females' greater ratio of body fat may reduce their accuracy compared to men. Indeed, Rouse et al. (1988) found that when percent of body fat was controlled, lean subjects demonstrated greater heartbeat-detection accuracy than the nonlean, regardless of gender. While a potentially provocative explanation for the gender difference in heartbeat-detection accuracy, the fact that interoceptive accuracy gender differences have been found on other physiological indices, such as respiratory resistance and gastric contraction, calls the body fat explanation into question, if one accepts the idea that body fat operates as a kind of muffler of the "signal" in the signal-detection paradigms. However, because body fat is highly correlated with dieting, then it could be that experience with restrained eating among those with higher body fat accounts for their lower interoceptive accuracy (cf. Heatherton, Polivy, & Herman, 1989). We will discuss the possibility that women's greater experience with restrained eating and dieting may contribute to poorer interoceptive awareness in a later section.

Another possible confound in the studies discussed is that females or males may cheat, or in some way distort their self-reports or physiological data when they are unsupervised under naturalistic field conditions. Although this may be possible, subjects in such studies are under treatment for high blood pressure or diabetes, and therefore are highly motivated to determine whether or not they can, in fact, reliably estimate their glucose or blood pressure levels for future treatment. Thus, cheating would not be in their best interest. In one attempt to check for "cheating," Gonder-Frederick, Julian, Cox, Clarke, and Carter (1988) installed monitoring devices on blood glucose apparati to independently check their diabetics' reports. Overall, subjects' diaries did show inaccuracies. However, these errors did *not* represent attempts to present a more positive clinical profile of the subjects' accuracy. Both positive and negative diary entries were equally likely. Furthermore, and most important for our argument, gender was not correlated with any measures of diary accuracy.

A final, related possibility is that males and females are equivalent in accuracy in the field studies because of the feedback they receive concerning their physiological state. Two findings argue against this, however. First, in one signal-detection study, which employed performance feedback in order to learn the degree to which interoception can be improved, men improved with feedback whereas women did not (Katkin et al., 1981). Second, internal analyses of both the naturalistic phases of the blood pressure and blood glucose projects failed to find an improvement in interoceptive abilities over the course of the studies.

In sum, although some potential confounds such as the relationship between body fat and accuracy in the controlled lab settings or possible cheating in naturalistic settings, may not be ruled out entirely, the studies of interoceptive accuracy do seem to indicate that men are more accurate than women at discriminating a variety of internal visceral sensations in highly controlled laboratory settings, in which only internal physiological cues are made available. In more naturalistic settings, however, where external contextual cues are also available, women's and men's accuracy at estimating a variety of internal indices does not differ.

III. Gender Differences in Self-Reports of Symptoms, Emotions, and Physical Exertion

To this point, we have summarized several interoception studies that have directly tapped females' and males' *accuracy* at estimating specific physiological indices. Three additional lines of research show fascinating gender differences in the areas of symptom-reporting, emotion-reporting, and perceptions of athletic effort. In these studies subjects do not make estimates about particular physiological indices per se, nor are they measured in terms of their "accuracy." Rather, they are simply asked to make self-reports of symptoms, emotional arousal, or athletic exertion in situations where corresponding physiological indices are also tapped. Results show that such self-reports covary with physiological changes to a higher degree in males than in females, suggesting that men make relatively greater use of internal, physiological data in determining how they feel.

For example, one laboratory study of self-reports of blood pressure symptoms involved subjects who completed a general "symptom checklist" just prior to the actual physiological measurement of their blood pressure (Pennebaker, Gonder-Frederick, Stewart, Elfman, & Skelton, 1982, Study I). Within-subject correlations revealed higher blood pressure symptom correspondence for males than for females (R-squared = .58 versus .41, p = .01). In other words, men's reports of blood pressure-related symptoms corresponded more directly with actual blood pressure changes than did women's.

In another laboratory study involving married couples' discussions of conflicts, husbands' self-reported emotional negativity was significantly correlated with several physiological indices (Levenson, Carstensen, & Gottman, 1994). In contrast, wives showed no significant correlations between physiology and affect self-ratings. This gender difference in the relationship between physiology and affect ratings was found despite no clear pattern of gender differences in mean levels of physiological reactivity to the conflict discussion.

A third area of correlational research that suggests men's and women's differential reliance on internal versus external cues is that of perceived athletic exertion. These studies have generally demonstrated a higher relationship between perceived effort and cardiovascular change in men than in women engaged in comparably strenuous exercise. For example, Koltyn, O'Connor, and Morgan (1991) fond that overall ratings of perceived exertion during a swimming task, which was paced at 90% maximum velocity, were found to be significantly lower for women than for men. The male and female swimmers in their study were matched for fitness level, and therefore had similar resting heart rates. Interestingly, in contrast to the perceptual data, the researches found that heart rates were significantly *higher* for the female swimmers than for the male swimmers. In other words, women judged the exercise task to be less effortful than did the men, despite greater actual physiological strain as measured by heart rate.

These results can be interpreted with the help of the previously discussed interoceptive accuracy studies, and fit in well with our theory of men's and women's differential cue-use in determining bodily state. That is, males' greater awareness of changes in heart rate may contribute to an inflation of their perceptions of athletic exertion. Women, perhaps paying attention as well to other competing cues and therefore less attuned to their heart rate increases, rate their workout as less physically exhausting.

The studies of perception of athletic effort and the previously mentioned study of couples' emotional reactivity to conflict also illustrate an important aspect of our argument regarding gender and cue use, in that they provide evidence against the possibility that gender differences in awareness of internal, physiological indices can be explained by greater physiological surges in men than in women. In other words, it does not seem to be the case that men simply have more internal data to use in determining their internal state. Indeed, several studies of perceived exertion comparing subjects at the same relative exercise intensity have shown that female subjects rate perceived exertion lower than males, despite higher overall exercise heart rates (e.g., Eynde & Ostyn, 1986; Winborn, Meyers, & Mulling, 1988). As well, the Levenson et al. (1994) study reported no significant differences between men's and women's actual physiological responsiveness to the conflict discussion.

A. SUMMARY

The studies we have reviewed show a clear pattern of gender effects. That is, in highly controlled laboratory studies of interoceptive accuracy, men are more accurate than women in judging their internal state. Laboratory approaches that are less controlled, and that require subjects to participate in various tasks, also result in higher accuracy correlations for men than for women. However, in these studies the gender difference is less pronounced. In naturalistic field studies of interoceptive accuracy, on the other hand, men and women are equally accurate in judging internal state. The primary difference between controlled laboratory approaches and naturalistic approaches to interoception is that in naturalistic settings, subjects have greater access to external contextual cues, such as food intake, exercise, and time of day, in judging their internal states. All such cues are removed from the subjects' perceptual field in the controlled lab situations, leaving them with only their internal physiological sensations on which to base their judgments. Additional research evidence shows a gender difference in perceptions of symptoms, emotional arousal, and physical exertion, reflecting a greater correspondence between men's self-reports and their physiological indices.

IV. Gender Differences in the Use of Internal and External Cues

All of the sources of data we have reviewed thus far would suggest that whereas men use internal physiological cues, women make more use of external situational cues in defining their internal states. However, none of the studies provided an actual controlled test; our theory was, to this point, merely deduced from a variety of sources of evidence. In this section we elaborate on two areas of research that provide a much more direct test of the idea that men and women make differential use of internal and external cues in situations where both are available.

A. SPATIAL NAVIGATION

One fascinating area of research that has revealed gender differences in the use of internal and external cues, when both are made available in controlled settings, is that of spatial navigation. Studies investigating the cognitive components of mental maps have shown that there are two ways to "get there from here." That is, there are two kinds of abstract representations, each emphasizing different aspects of spatial knowledge (Bever, 1992). The first is episodic knowledge of individual landmarks and how they appear in relation to some home base, whereas the second is configurational knowledge of the spatial relationship between landmarks.

Both folklore and research have demonstrated that men are more adept than women at reading conventional maps (Bever, 1992). However, this difference does not seem to influence men's and women's ability to negotiate their way through novel or familiar neighborhoods efficiently. Interestingly, women recognize photographs of areas in their home neighborhoods better than men (Colledge, 1988). Recent research efforts into the question of gender and spatial learning have revealed that these differences may reflect a more broadly based difference in the ways men and women organize spatial knowledge. The idea is that females have richer access to landmarks, and make greater use of them in spatial learning. Males, on the other hand, evidence more of the configurational style of spatial learning, relying less on landmarks, and more on "dead reckoning," or a vector strategy, in getting there from here (Bever, 1992).

Both animal and human studies have been conducted on mental maps, and both have revealed provocative differences between males and females in navigational learning. For example, Williams and Meck (1991) showed that male and female rats differ in the kinds of cues they use in spatial navigation. In their studies of maze learning, they found that female rats referred to nearby external cues, or landmarks, in the experimental room to learn the maze. When these landmarks were moved around, the female rats became confused, but the male rats' performance was undisturbed. In contrast, the male rats seemed to rely more on "kinesic" memory, or dead reckoning in learning the maze. Their performance was disrupted by altering the geometry of the room containing the maze, whereas the female rats were unaffected by this kind of change.

Extending this work to humans, Bever and colleagues have found remarkably similar differences between men's and women's navigational styles (see Bever, 1992, for a detailed review of the following studies). In their first study, involving the learning of several routes in a "maze" of corridors, they found that men were significantly better at choosing the correct configurational representation of the corridor arrangement after wandering through it. However, overall running performance on the corridor task was the same for males and females.

In another series of studies, Bever (1992) had subjects run mazes either one way only, or two ways. Here he found that women relied more on landmarks and performed better on mazes with landmarks. In running the maze one way only, women were able to quickly memorize one set of landmarks. But in running the maze two ways, requiring the more complex task of learning landmarks in opposite directions, their performance was negatively affected. Men, in contrast, performed better than women in mazes without landmarks. Men were also better at running the maze in the two-way condition, presumably by using a vector strategy. Their performance deteriorated, however, when the maze geometry was altered. Furthermore, when simply shown photographs of various intersections in the university's tunnel system, men could not identify them as easily as women, because they were not actually moving through the tunnels.

Yet another study in the area of spatial learning examined how changes in travel paths through a city influenced men's and women's cognitive maps (Antes, McBride, & Collins, 1988). Subjects were asked to judge the distance between selected points in the city both before and after the construction of a new overpass. Women's distance estimates were influenced, whereas men's were not, by the new overpass. The researchers concluded that women made their judgments based on inferences from travel paths, whereas men approached the task in a way that reflected more of a configurational spatial representation of the city.

These studies all provide provocative evidence, under controlled conditions, for a gender difference in internal versus external cue use. Women seem to make greater use of external local cues or landmarks. Men, in contrast, seem to use more of a vector strategy, which requires knowledge of what direction one is pointing and how far one has traveled, and in this way represents more of an "internal distance clock" based on bodily, kinesic knowledge. Although both genders get from point A to point B just as efficiently, and neither is more likely to get lost, this research strongly suggests that males and females may be using different cognitive styles, each relying on different cues, in their spatial learning. Popular lore has it that men do not ask for directions as often as women. According to this analysis, this may be because men do not "feel" as lost as women in novel environments without familiar landmarks. Furthermore, women's lesser ability at reading maps may not reflect a cognitive deficiency so much as a bias in the way conventional maps have always been drawn, emphasizing configurational space rather than landmarks.

B. FIELD DEPENDENCE AND INDEPENDENCE

A second, somewhat controversial area of research that demonstrates that men and women seem to rely differently on internal and external cues is that of field dependence or independence. This research examines whether people can judge if a visual stimulus, such as a line or rod, is vertical in situations where there is conflicting external, visual information. In the most popular version of this test, subjects are shown a glowing rod within a frame, projected in a completely darkened room (Witkin & Goodenough, 1977). Their task is to adjust the rod to an upright position. To do so successfully requires that the subject "extract" the rod from the tilted frame through reference to their body position. On some trials, subjects sit erect and on others they are tilted in a chair. Another version requires subjects to adjust a tilting chair (in which they are sitting) to upright when the room around them is tilted (Witkin & Goodenough, 1977). Field-independent subjects are able to make these adjustments quite accurately, ignoring the contradictory framing information, and basing their judgments instead on bodily sensations and internal vestibular information. Field-dependent subjects, on the other hand, do not adjust the rod or their chair adequately, and hence remain strongly oriented toward the tilt of the frame.

Many studies have found that men and women perform differently on these tests. Specifically, women are consistently found to be more field dependent than men (e.g., Bauermeister, Wapner, & Weiner, 1963; Bennett, 1956; Vaught, 1965; Witkin, 1949). In other words, women make use of the external field information provided by the frame or the room in making their verticality estimates. They do not make their judgments based on perceptions of their bodies. Men, on the other hand, tend to make judgments by relying more on internal bodily information, presumably from the vestibular system, and therefore are not as influenced by the conflicting contextual information. In further extensions of this work Witkin and colleagues have found that field-dependent people are more attentive to external cues of a social nature as well, whereas field-independent people are less sensitive to such cues (Witkin & Goodenough, 1977).

C. SUMMARY

In sum, then, both the research on spatial navigation and on field dependence or independence provide confirmatory evidence that the genders rely differently on internal versus external cues. These two areas of study are the only ones of which we are aware that offer direct tests of the use of these sorts of cues under controlled conditions in which both are present, and, in a sense, competing. The results suggest that the genders may indeed differ on a fairly global level with respect to cognitive abduction strategies (cf. Bever, 1992). The studies also point to the need for more highly controlled tests of the gender–cue use hypothesis in the area of bodily and self-perception. Studies that focus on subjects' perceptions of their own symptoms, emotions, or physical sensations in controlled situations that offer relevant but competing internal and external cues are clearly needed to test the gender and cue-use hypothesis directly.

V. Why Women and Men Might Rely on Different Sources of Information in Judging Their Internal States

The question of mechanisms for such a gender difference in cue use is certainly a provocative one. In this section, we review possible mechanisms driving the gender difference in attention to and skill at incorporating internal and external cues in judging bodily state, addressing both differential attention to and use of external social cues to the behavioral consequences of women's lower status in our society. Then we will look at one particular biological explanation, differences in brain hemispheric lateralization between men and women, and the implications for this on their differential attention to and skill at incorporating internal and external cues in determining bodily state. Finally, we will address the idea that socialization around the body and bodily learning experiences shape the way the genders attend to and employ internal and external cues in determining how their bodies feel.

A. SOCIAL STATUS

Males generally enjoy higher status than females in human society (Mead, 1935; Rosaldo & Lamphere, 1974). Indeed, several studies have documented that gender functions as a status cue in social perception, such that men are generally perceived by both genders as higher in social status than women (e.g., Eagly & Wood, 1982; Wood & Karten, 1986). One explanation for gender differences in internal versus external cue use assumes that individuals who exercise a lower degree of social power become more attentive to, and skilled at understanding, the social environment around them than individuals higher in social status (English, 1972; Frieze & Ramsey, 1976; Henley, 1977). More specifically, by being alert to subtle changes in the social environment, females, as the less dominant members of society, devote more attention to the behavior of the more powerful societal members. Males, on the other hand, being the dominant members of society, are freer to act on the basis of their own desires, and hence have less of a need for highly developed social-environmental cue reading skills. Thus, women's tendency to use external cues in interpreting their physiological state may be a by-product of their greater attention to such cues by virtue of their lower status.

Research in the area of nonverbal communication reveals sex differences both in attention to and accuracy at reading cues delivered through nonverbal channels. DePaulo, Jordan, Irvine, and Laser (1982) have shown that females generally pay more attention to facial and situational cues than males. Girls and women have been shown to gaze at others' faces (see Hall, 1984, for a summary of the gazing literature), and to prefer gazing at *social* stimuli in particular (Lewis, Kagan, & Kalafat, 1966) more than males, and they are also better *decoders* of nonverbal expressions than men (see Hall, 1978, for a thorough review of the relevant research). Furthermore, beyond simply paying more attention to such social-situational cues, Roberts (1991) has argued that women are more likely than men to approach and use social situations to gain information about themselves and their abilities. For example, in her studies she found that women rated others' evaluations as more informative in making determinations of their own abilities than did men, and were more influenced by such evaluations.

Very little research has actually tested the notion that less dominant individuals are more vigilant with regard to the social environment than more dominant individuals. However, there are a few interesting studies that do support the status argument. For example, Anderson and Willis (1976) found that less dominant children in a group spend more time glancing at others in the group than do more dominant children. Also, several studies have shown that more dominant members of a group *receive* more gazes than less dominant members (e.g., Efran, 1968; Exline, 1972). One interesting study showed that among college students who interacted in leader-subordinate dyads, subordinates were found to be more attentive to and concerned with the leaders' feelings and behaviors than vice versa, regardless of gender (Snodgrass, 1985). Interestingly, the role effect of being subordinate was strongest for women when their partner was a man.

The work on nonverbal cues lends some support to the notion that differences in the social status of men and women play a role in their differential attentiveness to cues in the social environment. However, the question of whether greater attention to and processing of social environmental information undermines the accurate processing of internal physiological cues remains to be studied. One criticism of the research on nonverbal gender differences is that it has tended to focus solely on differences in attention to social cues, and in accuracy of reading such cues in noninteractive, nonpersonally relevant lab settings. Indeed, more recent studies have shown no gender differences in empathic accuracy in contexts in which male and female subjects rate others' emotions displayed in more realistic, dyadic interactions (e.g., Ickes, Stinson, Bissonnette, & Garcia, 1990; Levenson & Reuf, 1992).

Because of these as yet unexplained contradictions in the nonverbal research and the many remaining questions, the status argument falls short of an adequate explanation of women's greater use of external cues in making judgments of bodily state. Important future research in this area would test directly whether manipulations of subordinate or dominant status in social situations predicts attention to and use of internal versus external cues in making determinations about bodily and feeling states.

B. BIOLOGICAL DIFFERENCES: HEMISPHERIC LATERALIZATION

Biological influences may also play a role in gender differences in cue use. Indeed, the studies showing remarkably similar animal and human sex differences in spatial navigation suggest biological contributors. Of particular relevance to internal and external cue use may be cerebral hemispheric lateralization. The two hemispheres of the brain show specialized functions. Specifically, the right hemisphere has been shown to be particularly involved in the processing of spatial and emotional stimuli (McGee, 1979; Safer, 1981). The left hemisphere, on the other hand, is usually associated with most language functions (McGee, 1979). Findings in the area of hemispheric lateralization are of relevance to our hypothesis about women's greater use of external and men's greater use of internal cues in judging bodily state. A number of studies have found that males show a greater degree of lateral asymmetry than females on a wide variety of both verbal and nonverbal tasks (Bryden, 1982; Lake & Bryden, 1976; McGee, 1979; McGlone, 1980). Furthermore, there is evidence that females are less lateralized in general than males (De La Coste-Utamsing & Holloway, 1982; Springer & Deutsch, 1989).

These hemispheric specialization differences map interestingly onto a number of interoception studies, which have found that right-hemisphere activation and preference is correlated with higher levels of heartbeat-detection accuracy (regardless of gender) using signal-detection paradigms (Davidson, Horowitz, Schwartz, & Goodman, 1981; Hantas, Katkin, & Reed, 1984; Katkin, Cestaro, & Weitkunat, 1991; Katkin & Reed, 1988; Weisz et al., 1990). These studies point to the interesting possibility that the sex difference in interoceptive accuracy in highly controlled laboratory studies may be driven by differences in hemispheric laterality. Perhaps men's greater hemispheric specialization is the key to their advantage in a setting in which strictly internal perceptions are required.

Hemispheric laterality has also been shown to play a role in the gender differences in nonverbal cue reading accuracy. For example, one study tested the role of hemispheric laterality in men's and women's judgments of facial expressions

(Safer, 1981). Males showed greater right-hemisphere involvement than females during a task of identifying various facial expressions of emotion. However, males were worse (as they have consistently been found to be) at the task of accurately identifying this nonverbal information. Safer argues that nonverbal judgment tasks require processing in *both* hemispheres, the right for recognition of emotions and the left for labeling those emotions. Therefore, it is females' greater bilaterality, and hence their greater integration of verbal *and* nonverbal information such as emotion, that leads to their greater nonverbal reading skills. Males' greater laterality, in contrast, impedes them in such situations where integration is required.

Further studies are clearly needed in order to clarify the extent to which there are important gender differences in hemispheric laterality, and also whether this is in fact a primary mechanism behind the gender differences in interoception. At this point, however, the findings in this area certainly provide a provocative explanation for what may be driving men's and women's differential attention to, and skill at incorporating, internal and external cues in judging bodily state.

C. SOCIALIZATION AND LEARNING BASED ON BODILY EXPERIENCES

Males and females undergo quite different learning experiences in understanding and interpreting their bodies' signals. One of the first ways girls and boys differ in bodily experience is at the time of menarche. Adolescent girls must learn to live with the bodily disruptiveness of menstruation. Numerous studies have shown that the culture perceives menstruation as aversive, unpredictable, and ambiguous. In one study of seventh- and eighth-grade boys and girls, for example, Brooks-Gunn and Ruble (1983) reported that the majority believed that menstruation is accompanied by physical discomfort, increased emotionality, and a disruption of activities. In another survey, with over 1000 respondents, Milow (1983) found that one-third believed that menstruation affects a women's ability to think, and more than one-fourth believed that women cannot function properly at work while menstruating. In other words, our culture focuses far more on the disruptive, aversive aspects of the menstrual cycle than on its potential as a source for important bodily information. Our culture's further emphasis on the shamefulness of menstrual events adds powerful socialization that may encourage young women to turn away from and mistrust their bodies' physiological cues (Steiner-Adair, 1990).

Ironically, having one's period may come to act itself as a powerful situational cue for women. Indeed, one study (Ruble, 1977) showed that women who *believed* that they were closer to the onset of their period than they actually were reported more pain and water retention than another group who believed they were intermenstrual. This result was despite no actual differences between the groups on their cycle phases. Numerous studies have shown that, when answering questions raised in the context of menstruation, women report more negative moods and physical discomfort during premenstrual and menstrual days than during intermenstrual days (e.g., Golub & Harrington, 1981; Swandby, 1979). However, when women report on moods and physical sensations over a period of time, with no mention of menstruation, such reports are *not* related to objective menstrual phase (e.g., Golub & Harrington, 1981; Parlee, 1982; Swandby, 1979). In other words, cultural prescriptions about menstruation may lead women not only to mistrust their own physiological cues as indicators of bodily state, but also may serve as a powerful situational cue in itself, providing women with an explanation for emotional and physical experiences that may or may not be menstrually linked.

A second area of bodily socialization experience for girls is that of dieting and restrained eating. Weight concerns among adolescent girls and women in our country are practically universal and considered normative (Rodin, Silverstein, & Striegel-Moore, 1984). Far more women than men within normal weight ranges wish they were thinner and have been on diets (Dornbusch, Gross, Duncan, & Ritter, 1987; Thornberry, Wilson, & Golden, 1986). Slimness norms are much stronger for women than for men, and dieting is more narrowly targeted toward women (cf. Unger & Crawford, 1992). Furthermore, Herman and Polivy (1980) have shown that compliance with these norms requires suppression of internal cues of hunger and satiety, suggesting that girls' experiences with restrained eating may teach them to actively avoid attending to physiological cues. Indeed, for dieters, unresponsiveness to hunger signals may become habitual, and may generalize to related physical cues, making restrained eaters particularly insensitive to internal cues (Heatherton et al., 1989). Garner, Olmstead, and Polivy's Eating Disorders Inventory (1983) includes a subscale assessing "interoceptive awareness," and studies show that eating-disordered individuals, the overwhelming majority of whom are female, score higher than noneatingdisorderd individuals on poor interoceptive awareness (e.g., Leon, Fulkerson, Perry, & Cudek, 1993). Furthermore, other studies have shown that those with eating disorders also demonstrate severely distorted perceptions of their body's shape and size, and have high external loci of control (cf. Polivy, Herman, & Pliner, 1990).

As the onset of puberty undermines females' trust in their physiological cues, the hormonal changes in males during this period may actually enhance their attentiveness to an use of their bodies' signals. Specifically, the salience and clarity of sexual arousal is quite different for males and females. Morokoff (1988), for example, has pointed out that the actual physiological cues of sexual arousal for females are more ambiguous compared to males. In one study of responsiveness to erotic materials, in which the vasocongestion of subjects' genitals was measured, Heiman (1975) found that when physiologically aroused, half the women failed to self-report their arousal, whereas no physically aroused males ever made errors in their self-reports (and, furthermore, the subjects who volunteered for this study were unlikely to have been shy about reporting their sexual arousal).

Females may also be socialized to restrict knowledge of their genitals, and to be more ashamed of their genitalia than males. Our culture regards the sexuality of boys and men in general as more important, cleaner, and less embarrassing than the sexuality of girls and women (Lott, 1987). Fine (1988) argues that sex education in schools restricts information particularly about female sexual desire and agency, imbuing discussions of female sexuality with mystery and fear. Studies have, in fact, shown that girls receive less clear information about how to refer to their genitals than boys. For example, Gartrell and Mosbacher (1984) found that girls are far less likely than boys to have learned the correct anatomical names for their genitalia from their parents, and that both boys and girls learn the word "penis" significantly earlier than they learn any correct term for female genitals. In addition, the nonanatomical words taught for female genitals were found to be more euphemistic and pejorative than those for male genitals.

Perhaps women's experiences of being bodily and emotionally influenced by menstrual fluctuations, and their relative lack of *direct* sensory contact with such physiological cues as sexual arousal, contribute to a general belief that variations in their bodily state are uncontrollable, ambiguous, and unreliable indicators of such things as arousal, exertion, or illness. In addition, they suffer the culture's emphasis on the disruptiveness and shamefulness of their hormonal fluctuations and sexuality. As a consequence, they actively avoid attending to bodily sensations. Instead, they focus on the more predictable and less threatening external environment for information about how their bodies feel. Dieting and restrained eating may further contribute to the interruption of internal cue use for women.

Men, on the other hand, may simply have more experience with bodily changes that are directly connected to their own feelings and actions. They also enjoy the culture's acceptance of the importance and nonshamefulness of their bodies' signals as indices of their strength and sexuality. Hence, they may learn to count on the reliability of physiological sources of information in making judgments of their bodily state.

Of the three proposed mechanisms we have presented, the ideas presented in this section are admittedly the most speculative. The theory that men's and women's different socialization with respect to bodily experiences in puberty could influence their relative use of internal and external cues in judging bodily states has only been deduced from indirect evidence, and could be open to a variety of alternative interpretations. However, we feel that these ideas go beyond the simple "nature versus nurture" explanations that are so often invoked for gender differences and invite research on the interplay between biological events in puberty and sociocultural perspectives on these bodily experiences. Some feminist scholars, particularly, have called for social science to begin to take such a social-constructionist perspective on developmental events (e.g., Gergen, 1988). The links that we have made have yet to be directly tested, but research in this area certainly could provide important developmental information about attentiveness to internal physiological versus external contextual cues in determining how one feels.

C. SUMMARY

It is likely that social roles, hemispheric laterality, and socialization all contribute somewhat to the gender differences in the attention to and use of internal and external cues in judging bodily state. We believe that a promising approach to the study of interoception in general, and to gender differences in particular, would focus on the biological bases of perception that can be shaped through socialization and cultural roles. It may be, for example, that differences in hemispheric laterality are responsible for the gender differences in the use of internal versus external cues in judging bodily state. However, the direction of causality could be the reverse. Socialization or cultural roles may shape men's and women's differential attention to and use of such cues in determining how their bodies feel, and such training and experience could shape the way the hemispheres process information. We believe that taking such a "biopsychosocial" approach will help to promote a more ecologically based understanding of human perception.

VI. Discussion

Drawing on several lines of research, there appears to be sufficient evidence to suggest that males and females rely on different sources of information to define and understand internal state. Whereas males tend to use internal physiological cues, women tend to rely on external situational sources of information. This conclusion about gender and differential cue use has been based on inference rather than direct experimental test, although two lines of research, in the areas of spatial navigation and field dependence or independence, provide supportive evidence.

Of particular importance is that males and females appear to be equally good at knowing their physiological state in the natural environment. Unlike controlled laboratory settings, only in the real world are both internal sensory and external situational cues abundant. As Gibson (1979) has suggested in other domains, the natural environment provides internal and external cues that are usually redundant in offering similar information to the organism. The net result is that males and females are normally equally adept at regulating their behaviors based on their perceptions of internal state in the real world.

A. INCREASING OUR UNDERSTANDING OF EXISTING GENDER DIFFERENCES

Our theory has implications for a number of other literatures, and may offer alternative explanations for a variety of previously documented gender differences. For example, our theory suggests that the research on gender differences in spatial reasoning may be gender biased. Linn and Petersen (1985, 1986) have argued that the spatial tasks used in studies of spatial reasoning can be divided into three categories: spatial perception tasks, such as the rod-and-frame test; mental rotation tasks; and spatial visualization tasks, such as embedded figures. Their analysis of the gender effects found in each of these three sorts of spatial tasks revealed that males show superior performance on tasks of spatial perception and mental rotation. However, spatial visualization studies do not typically result in gender differences. These tasks require complex analyses of the relationship *between* different spatial representations.

An alternative explanation for this pattern of gender effects in spatial reasoning studies, then, may be that spatial perception and mental rotation tasks emphasize more internal cue use, whereas spatial visualization tasks allow for the relevance of the external, surrounding context in making spatial judgments. In other words, there may be a gender bias built into the majority of tasks used in studies of spatial reasoning. Devising and including more spatial tests that involve relevant external, contextual cues may therefore minimize the currently accepted magnitude of the gender difference in spatial reasoning.

Feminist poets and essayists (e.g., Rich, 1979; Young, 1990) have argued that the self-consciousness that results from the cultural objectification of women results in women's alienation and distancing from their own bodies. In discussing women's sexual experience in particular, Lerner (1993) argues that when women are taught that their bodies are not for themselves, but rather are for others, they stop attending to internal bodily cues that signal sexual desires and rhythms. This has been called "spectatoring," and it is thought to play a substantial role in female sexual dysfunction (Heiman & Verhulst, 1982; Tevlin & Lieblum, 1983). Indeed such theorizing fits well within our framework of gender differences in the use of internal and external cues in determining bodily state. That is, at least part of the answer to why there is far greater incidence of sexual dysfunction in women than men (Frank, Anderson, & Rubenstein, 1978) may lie in their differential attention to and accurate detection of internal, physiological cues of sexual arousal.

Yet another area of research for which our theory may offer a valuable framework is that of gender differences in approaches to interpersonal conflicts. Studies of heterosexual couples show that men are more likely to withdraw from conflict-filled interactions and adopt an interpersonal style of conflict avoidance (e.g., Carstensen, Morrow, & Roberts, 1992). Based on their finding that males become more physiologically aroused during interpersonal conflict than do females, Levenson and Gottman (1985) argue that the negative emotion associated with interpersonal conflict is more aversive for men than women. Furthermore, recent research indicates greater awareness on the part of men of this heightened physiological arousal (Levenson et al., 1994). According to our theory, then, the perceived aversiveness of conflicts for men may be partly a consequence of men's greater *focus* on their physiological arousal. For women, on the other hand, being less aware of physiological changes during conflicts, and perhaps attending to other external cues as well, may contribute to their perception of conflict arousal as less overwhelming and aversive.

B. DISCOVERING NEW GENDER DIFFERENCES

In addition to offering a potentially informative explanation for known gender differences, our theory of gendered approaches to internal and external cue use may offer some fascinating predictions for as yet unknown gender differences. For example, our model has implications for investigations into facial and bodily feedback (e.g., Ekman, Levenson, & Friesen, 1983; Stepper & Strack, 1993; Strack, Martin, & Stepper, 1988), and suggests that fascinating gender differences may emerge in further studies of this kind. That is, we would predict that facial and bodily feedback manipulations might produce more robust effects in men than in women in situations where contextual cues to emotional state are minimal.

One might also predict from our model that motion sickness and zero-gravity situations would cause more performance disruption and feelings of illness in men than in women, given that such situations induce vestibular activation. Extrapolating directly from the field dependence and independence literature, if women are better able to remain oriented to the surrounding context (and remain relatively less aware of the bodily vestibular disturbance induced), then one might predict that illness sensations would be mediated for them in such situations more than for men.

Our theory might further predict that women and men have different reasons for using drugs and alcohol: men more for the changes in physical state that they induce, and women more for altering their perceptual field. Furthermore, our theory implies that placebo manipulations might produce, on average, more robust effects in women than in men.

It should be noted that all of these suggestions about possible gender differences remain to be tested, and are meant as invitations to researchers in the areas mentioned not as definitive conclusions. Furthermore, this short list of ideas is in no way exhaustive. Numerous fascinating predictions based on our proposed model for gender differences in a variety of literatures undoubtedly exist.

C. TOWARD HIS-AND-HERS THEORIES OF EMOTION

Elsewhere, we have proposed "his-and-hers" emotion theories, arguing that peripheralist theories may describe men's emotion perception more accurately, whereas women's emotion perception may correspond more closely to cognitive appraisal theories (Pennebaker & Roberts, 1992). As we have summarized here, men appear to be better at directly perceiving physiological changes than women, a prerequisite for James's (1950) theory of emotion. Women may be particularly sensitive to reading and using contextual cues, a central aspect of the Schachter and Singer (1962) cognitive labeling theory.

Indeed, investigations into the relationship between arousal and emotion have revealed that *both* the perception of arousal (not simply the manifestation of arousal) and external cues determine affect intensity (Blascovich, 1990). Furthermore, males and females have been shown to differ on the dispositional construct of affect intensity (Larsen & Diener, 1987), with females scoring higher on such measures. Interestingly, and congruent with the cue-use theory we have presented, Blascovich et al. (1992) found that affect intensity, although unrelated to actual arousal levels, was negatively correlated with interoceptive accuracy. The authors postulate that those subjects (predominantly women) without accurate perception of their own physiological indices of arousal must rely on external, contextual cues to interpret their affect, and are therefore biased toward reporting heightened negative emotional intensity. Thus, preliminary evidence exists to support the notion that females and males rely differently on internal and external cues for emotional experience.

All things being equal, the theory we have advanced in this chapter would predict that men may be more aware of, and therefore may tend to focus more, on their perception of a racing heart or sweaty palms in determining feelings of anger, for example. In contrast, women may tend to focus more on their perception of relevant anger-eliciting cues in the surrounding context. However, although there may be a tendency for males and females to use different sources of information in defining emotional states, we must emphasize that gender undoubtedly accounts for only a small portion of the variance in our understanding of emotional experience. Of course it is not the case that all men experience emotion one way, and all women another way. Therefore, given the current lack of evidence, it is clearly premature to posit his-and-her theories of emotion.

However, we would emphasize that researchers appreciate the different sources of information that people can use to define their bodily and feeling states.

We must also emphasize that our purpose in this chapter has been to encourage new theory and research in these areas, and in this way it is meant to be provocative rather than definitive. Furthermore, our intention has not been simply to focus on gender differences, but rather on social and bodily perceptual style differences. Numerous sources of evidence suggest that men tend to use one style, and women another. The value of our gender differences argument has been to isolate the two perceptual styles, and hence encourage researchers to study these styles. The gender–cue use hypothesis holds great promise in our understanding of how men and women come to perceive, label, and act on a variety of internal states—ranging from specific physical sensations to emotions. Although two people may report similar levels of emotion, exertion, or hunger in exactly the same situation, they may be relying on different types of information in making their determinations. Because most real-word situations provide a host of relevant internal and external cues, men and women, despite their differential reliance on these cues, are equally accurate in determining how they feel. As we have summarized in this chapter, our understanding of gender effects may provide a better understanding of perceptual processes and vice versa.

Acknowledgments

We gratefully acknowledge Jim Blascovich and C. Peter Herman for their constructive and insightful comments on this chapter, as well as Fletcher Blanchard for a number of discussions that contributed indirectly, but nevertheless invaluably, to its quality. Preparation of this chapter was made possible, in part, by grants to James W. Pennebaker from the National Science Foundation, BNS90-21518 and SBR94-11674.

References

Anderson, F. J., & Willis, F. N. (1976). Glancing at others in preschool children in relation to dominance. *Psychological Record, 26,* 467–472.

Antes, J. R., McBride, R. B., & Collins, J. D. (1988). The effect of a new city traffic route on the cognitive maps of its residents. *Environment and Behavior, 20,* 75–91.

Barr, M., Pennebaker, J. W., & Watson, D. (1988). Improving blood pressure estimation through internal environmental feedback. *Psychosomatic Medicine, 50,* 37–45.

Bauermeister, M., Wapner, S., & Weiner, H. (1963). Sex differences in the perception of apparent verticality and apparent body position under conditions of body tilt. *Journal of Personality, 31,* 394–407.

Baumann, L. J., & Leventhal, H. (1985). "I can tell when my blood pressure is up, can't I?" *Health Psychology, 4,* 203–218.

Bennett, D. H. (1956). Perception of the upright in relation to body image. *Journal of Mental Science, 102*, 478–506.

Bever, T. (1992). The logical and extrinsic sources of modularity. In M. Gunnar and M. Maratsos (Eds.), *Modularity and constraints in language and cognition, Volume 25 of the Minnesota Symposia on Child Psychology* (pp. 179–212). Hillsdale, NJ: Erlbaum.

Blascovich, J. (1990). Individual differences in physiological arousal and perception of arousal: Missing links in Jamesian notions of arousal-based behaviors. *Personality and Social Psychology Bulletin, 16*, 665–675.

Blascovich, J., Brennan, K., Tomaka, J., Kelsey, R. M., Hughes, P., Coad, M. L., Adlin, R. (1992). Affect intensity and cardiac arousal. *Journal of Personality and Social Psychology, 63*, 164–174.

Brener, J., & Jones, J. M. (1974). Interoceptive discrimination in intact humans: Detection of cardiac activity. *Physiology and Behavior, 13*, 763–767.

Brener, J. (1977). Sensory and perceptual determinants of voluntary visceral control. In G. Schwartz, & J. Beatty (Eds.), *Biofeedback theory and research* (pp. 29–66). New York: Academic Press.

Brooks-Gunn, J., & Ruble, D. (1983). Dysmenorrhea in adolescence. In S. Golub (Ed.), *Menarche* (pp. 251–261). Boston: Lexington Books.

Bryden, M. P. (1982). *Laterality: Functional asymmetry in the intact brain*. New York: Academic Press.

Carstensen, L. L., Morrow, J., & Roberts, T. (1992). *Gender, conflict and emotion*. Unpublished manuscript, Stanford University, Palo Alto, CA.

Chwalisz, K., Diener, E., & Gallagher, D. (1988). Autonomic arousal feedback and emotional experience: Evidence from the spinal cord injured. *Journal of Personality and Social Psychology, 54*, 820–828.

Colledge, R. G. (1988). *Integrating spatial knowledge*. Santa Barbara: Geographical Press.

Cox, D. J., Clarke, W. L., Gonder-Frederick, L., Pohl, S., Hoover, C., Snyder, A., Zimbelman, L., Carter, W. R., Bobbitt, S., & Pennebaker, J. (1985). Accuracy of perceiving blood glucose in IDDM. *Diabetes Care, 8*, 529–535.

Davidson, R. J., Horowitz, M. E., Schwartz, G. E., & Goodman, D. M. (1981). Lateral differences in the latency between finger tapping and the heart beat. *Psychophysiology, 18*, 36–41.

De La Coste-Utamsing, C., & Holloway, R. L. (1982). Sexual dimorphism in the human corpus callosum. *Science, 216*, 1431–1432.

DePaulo, B. M., Jordan, A., Irvine, A., & Laser, P. S. (1982). Age changes in the detection of deception. *Child Development, 53*, 701–709.

Dornbusch, S. M., Gross, R. T., Duncan, P. D., & Ritter, P. L. (1987). Stanford studies of adolescence using the national health examination survey. In R. M. Lerner & T. T. Foch (Eds.), *Biological-psychosocial interactions in early adolescence* (pp. 189–205). Hillsdale, NJ: Erlbaum.

Eagly, A. H., & Wood, W. (1982). Inferred sex differences in status as a determinant of gender stereotypes about social influence. *Journal of Personality and Social Psychology, 43*, 915–928.

Efran, J. S. (1968). Looking for approval: Effects on visual behavior of approbation from persons differing in importance. *Journal of Personality and Social Psychology, 10*, 21–25.

Ekman, P., Levenson, R. W., & Friesen, W. V. (1983). Autonomic nervous system activity distinguishes among emotions. *Science, 221*, 1208–1210.

English, P. W. (1972). *Behavioral concomitants of dependent and subservient roles*. Unpublished Manuscript, Harvard University.

Exline, R. V. (1972). Visual interaction: The glances of power and preference. In J. K. Cole (Ed.), *Nebraska Symposium on Motivation, 1971*. Lincoln: University of Nebraska Press.

Eynde, B. V., & Ostyn, M. (1986). Rate of perceived exertion and its relationship with cardiorespiratory response to submaximal and maximal muscular exercise. In G. Borg and D. Ottoson (Eds.), *The perception of exertion in physical work* (pp. 327–335). London: McMillan Press.

Fine, M. (1988). Sexuality, schooling, and adolescent females: The missing discourse of desire. *Harvard Educational Review, 58,* 29–53.

Frank, E., Anderson, A., & Rubenstein, D. (1978). Frequency of sexual dysfunction in "normal" couples. *New England Journal of Medicine, 299,* 111–115.

Frieze, I. H., & Ramsey, S. J. (1976). Nonverbal maintenance of traditional sex roles. *Journal of Social Issues, 32,* 133–141.

Garner, D. M., Olmstead, M. P., & Polivy, J. (1983). Development and validation of a multidimensional eating disorder inventory for anorexia nervosa and bulimia. *International Journal of Eating Disorders, 2,* 15–34.

Gartrell, N., & Mosbacher, D. (1984). Sex differences in the naming of children's genitalia. *Sex Roles, 10,* 867–876.

Gergen, M. M. (1988). Toward a feminist metatheory and methodology in the social sciences. In M. M. Gergen (Ed.), *Feminist thought and the structure of knowledge* (pp. 87–104). New York: New York University Press.

Gibson, J. J. (1979). *The ecological approach to visual perception.* Boston: Houghton-Mifflin.

Golub, S., & Harrington, D. M. (1981). Premenstrual and menstrual mood changes in adolescent women. *Journal of Personality and Social Psychology, 41,* 961–965.

Gonder-Frederick, L., Julian, D. M., Cox, D. J., Clarke, W. L., & Carter, W. R. (1988). Self-measurement of blood glucose: Accuracy of self-reported data and adherence to recommended regimen. *Diabetes Care, 11,* 579–585.

Hall, J. A. (1978). Gender effects in decoding nonverbal cues. *Psychological Bulletin, 85,* 845–857.

Hall, J. A. (1984). *Nonverbal sex differences.* Baltimore: Johns Hopkins University Press.

Hantas, M. N., Katkin, E. S., & Reed, S. D. (1984). Cerebral lateralization and heartbeat discrimination. *Psychophysiology, 21,* 274–278.

Harver, A., Katkin, E. S., & Bloch, E. (1993). Signal-detection outcomes on heartbeat and respiratory resistance detection tasks in male and female subjects. *Psychophysiology, 30,* 223–230.

Heatherton, T. F., Polivy, J., & Herman, C. P. (1989). Restraint and internal responsiveness: Effects of placebo manipulations of hunger on eating. *Journal of Abnormal Psychology, 98,* 89–92.

Heiman, J. (1975). The physiology of erotica: Women's sexual arousal. *Psychology Today, 8,* 90–94.

Heiman, J., & Verhulst, J. (1982). Gender and sexual functioning. In I. Al-Issa (Ed.), *Gender and psychopathology* (pp. 305–320). New York: Academic Press.

Henley, N. M. (1977). *Body politics: Power, sex and nonverbal communication.* Englewood Cliffs: Prentice-Hall.

Herman, C. P., & Polivy, J. (1980). Restrained eating. In A. J. Stunkard (Ed.), *Obesity* (pp. 208–225). Philadelphia, PA: Saunders.

Ickes, W., Stinson, L., Bissonnette, V., & Garcia, S. (1990). Naturalistic social cognition: Empathic accuracy in mixed-sex dyads. *Journal of Personality and Social Psychology, 59,* 730–742.

James, W. (1950). *The principles of psychology.* New York: Dover. (originally published in 1890)

Jones, G. E., & Hollandsworth, J. G. (1981). Heart rate discrimination before and after exercise-induced augmented cardiac activity. *Psychophysiology, 18,* 252–257.

Jones, G. E., O'Leary, R. T., & Pipkin, B. L. (1984). Comparison of the Brener-Jones and Whitehead procedures for assessing cardiac awareness. *Psychophysiology, 21,* 143–148.

Jones, G. E., Jones, K. R., Rouse, C. H., Scott, D. M., & Caldwell, J. A. (1987). The effect of body position on the perception of cardiac sensations: An experiment and theoretical implications. *Psychophysiology, 24,* 300–311.

Katkin, E. S., Blascovich, J., & Goldband, S. (1981). Empirical assessment of visceral self-perception: Individual and sex differences in the acquisition of heartbeat discrimination. *Journal of Personality and Social Psychology, 40,* 1095–1101.

Katkin, E. S., Morell, M. A., Goldband, S., Bernstein, G. L., & Wise, J. A. (1982). Individual differences in heartbeat discrimination. *Psychophysiology, 19,* 160–166.

Katkin, E. S. (1985). Blood, sweat and tears: Individual differences in autonomic self-perception. *Psychophysiology, 22*, 125–137.
Katkin, E. S., & Reed, S. D. (1988). Cardiovascular asymmetries and cardiac perception. *International Journal of Neuroscience, 39*, 45–52.
Katkin, E. S., Cestaro, V. L., & Weitkunat, R. (1991). Individual differences in cortical evoked potentials as a function of heartbeat detection ability. *International Journal of Neuroscience, 61*, 269–276.
Koltyn, K. F., O'Connor, P. J., & Morgan, W. P. (1991). Perception of effort in female and male competitive swimmers. *International Journal of Sports Medicine, 12*, 427–429.
Lake, D. A., & Bryden, M. P. (1976). Handedness and sex differences in hemispheric asymmetry. *Brain and Language, 3*, 266–282.
Larsen, R. J., & Diener, E. (1987). Affect intensity as an individual difference characteristic: A review. *Journal of Research in Personality, 21*, 1–39.
Leon, G. R., Fulkerson, J. A., Perry, C. L., & Cudeck, R. (1993). Personality and behavioral vulnerabilities associated with risk status for eating disorders in adolescent girls. *Journal of Abnormal Psychology, 102*, 438–444.
Lerner, H. G. (1993). *The dance of deception: Pretending and truth-telling in women's lives.* New York: Harper Collins.
Levenson, R. W., & Gottman, J. M. (1985). Physiological and affective predictors of change in relationship satisfaction. *Journal of Personality and Social Psychology, 49*, 85–94.
Levenson, R. W., Carstensen, L. L., & Gottman, J. M. (1992). Marital interaction in old and middle aged long-term marriages: Physiology, affect and their interrelations. Unpublished manuscript, University of California at Berkeley.
Levenson, R. W., & Reuf, A. M. (1992). Empathy: A physiological substrate. *Journal of Personality and Social Psychology, 63*, 234–246.
Levenson, R. W., Carstensen, L. L., & Gottman, J. M. (1994). The influence of age and gender on affect, physiology, and their interrelations: A study of long-term marriage. *Journal of Personality and Social Psychology, 67*, 56–68.
Lewis, M., Kagan, J., & Kalafat, J. (1966). Patterns of fixation in the young infant. *Child Development, 37*, 331–341.
Linn, M. C., & Petersen, A. C. (1985). Emergence and characterization of sex differences in spatial ability: A meta-analysis. *Child Development, 56*, 1479–1498.
Linn, M. C., & Petersen, A. C. (1986). A meta-analysis of gender differences in spatial ability: Implications for mathematics and science achievement. In J. S. Hyde & M. C. Linn (Eds.), *The psychology of gender: Advances through meta-analysis* (pp. 67–101). Baltimore: Johns Hopkins.
Lott, B. (1987). *Women's lives: Themes and variations in gender learning.* Belmont, CA: Wadsworth, Inc.
McGee, M. G. (1979). Human spatial abilities: Psychometric studies and environmental, genetic, hormonal, and neurological influences. *Psychological Bulletin, 86*, 889–918.
McGlone, J. (1980). Sex differences in human brain asymmetry: A critical survey. *Behavioral and Brain Sciences, 3*, 215–263.
Mead, M. (1935). *Sex and temperament in three primitive societies.* New York: Morrow.
Milow, V. J. (1983). Menstrual education: Past, present, and future. In S. Golub (Ed.), *Menarche* (pp. 127–132). Boston: Lexington Books.
Morokoff, P. (1988). *Self awareness of sexual arousal in women.* Paper presented at the American Psychological Association, Atlanta, GA.
Parlee, M. B. (1982). Changes in moods and activation levels during the menstrual cycle in experimentally naive subjects. *Psychology of Women Quarterly, 7*, 119–131.
Pennebaker, J. W. (1982). *The psychology of physical symptoms.* New York: Springer-Verlag.
Pennebaker, J. W., Gonder-Frederick, L., Stewart, H., Elfman, L., & Skelton, J. A. (1982). Physical symptoms associated with blood pressure. *Psychophysiology, 19*, 201–210.

Pennebaker, J. W., & Epstein, D. (1983). Implicit psychophysiology: Effects of common beliefs and idiosyncratic physiological responses on symptom reporting. *Journal of Personality, 51,* 468–496.

Pennebaker, J. W., & Hoover, C. W. (1984). Visceral perception versus visceral detection: Disentangling methods and assumptions. *Biofeedback and Self-Regulation, 9,* 339–352.

Pennebaker, J. W., Gonder-Frederick, L., Cox, D. J., & Hoover, C. W. (1985). The perception of general versus specific visceral activity and the regulation of health-related behavior. *Advances in Behavioral Medicine, 1,* 165–198.

Pennebaker, J. W., & Watson, D. (1988). Blood pressure estimation and beliefs among normotensives and hypertensives. *Health Psychology, 7,* 309–332.

Pennebaker, J. W., & Roberts, T. (1992). Toward a his and hers theory of emotion: Gender differences in visceral perception. *Journal of Social and Clinical Psychology, 11,* 199–212.

Polivy, J., Herman, C. P., & Pliner, P. (1990). Perception and evaluation of body image: The meaning of body shape and size. In J. M. Olson & M. P. Zanna (Eds.), *Self-Inference Processes: The Ontario Symposium, 6,* (pp. 87–114). Hillsdale, NJ: Erlbaum.

Rich, A. (1979). *On lies, secrets, and silence: Selected prose 1966–1978.* New York: Norton.

Rickels, K. (1968). *Non-specific factors in drug therapy.* Springfield, IL: Thomas.

Roberts, T. (1991). Gender and the influence of evaluations on self-assessments in achievement settings. *Psychological Bulletin, 109,* 297–308.

Rodin, J., Silverstein, L. R., & Striegel-Moore, R. H. (1984). Women and weight: A normative discontent. In T. B. Sonderegger (Ed.), *Psychology and gender: Nebraska symposium on motivation, 1984* (pp. 267–307). Lincoln, NE: University of Nebraska Press.

Rosaldo, M. Z., & Lamphere, L. (Eds.) (1974). *Women, culture and society.* Stanford, CA: Stanford University Press.

Rouse, C. H., Jones, G. E., & Jones, K. R. (1988). The effect of body composition and gender on cardiac awareness. *Psychophysiology, 25,* 400–407.

Ruble, D. N. (1977). Premenstrual symptoms: A reinterpretation. *Science, 197,* 291–292.

Safer, M. A. (1981). Sex and hemisphere differences in access to codes for processing emotional expressions and faces. *Journal of Experimental Psychology: General, 110,* 86–100.

Schachter, S., & Singer, J. (1962). Cognitive, social and physiological determinants of emotional state. *Psychological Review, 69,* 379–399.

Smith, V. C. (1986). *Perception and estimation of blood pressure fluctuations in natural settings.* Unpublished master's thesis, Southern Methodist University, Dallas, Texas.

Snodgrass, S. E. (1985). Women's intuition: The effect of subordinate role on interpersonal sensitivity. *Journal of Personality and Social Psychology, 49,* 146–155.

Springer, S. P., & Deutsch, G. (1989). *Left brain, right brain: Third Edition.* New York: W.H. Freeman and Company.

Steiner-Adair, C. (1990). The body politic: Normal female adolescent development and the development of eating disorders. In C. Gilligan, N. P. Lyons, and T. J. Hanmer (Eds.), *Making connections: The relational worlds of adolescent girls at Emma Willard School* (pp. 162–182). Cambridge, MA: Harvard University Press.

Stepper, S., & Strack, F. (1993). Proprioceptive determinants of emotional and nonemotional feelings. *Journal of Personality and Social Psychology, 64,* 211–220.

Strack, F., Martin, L., & Stepper, S. (1988). Inhibiting and facilitating conditions of the human smile: A nonobtrusive test of the facial feedback hypothesis. *Journal of Personality and Social Psychology, 54,* 768–777.

Swandby, J. R. (1979). *Daily and retrospective mood and physical symptom self-reports and their relationship to the menstrual cycle.* Unpublished Master's Thesis, University of Wisconsin, Milwaukee.

Tevlin, H. E., & Leiblum, S. R. (1983). Sex-role stereotypes and female sexual dysfunction. In

V. Franks & E. D. Rothblum (Eds.), *The stereotyping of women: Its effects on mental health* (pp. 129–150). New York: Springer-Verlag.

Thornberry, O. T., Wilson, R. W., & Golden, P. (1986). Health promotion and disease prevention provisional data from the National Health Interview Survey: United States, January–June, 1985. *Vital and Health Statistics of the National Center for Health Statistics, 119,* 1–16.

Unger, R., & Crawford, M. (1992). *Women and gender: A feminist psychology.* New York: McGraw Hill, Inc.

Vaught, G. M. (1965). The relationship of role identification and ego strength to sex differences in the rod and frame test. *Journal of Personality, 33,* 271–283.

Watson, D., & Pennebaker, J. W. (1989). Health complaints, stress, and distress: Exploring the central role of negative affectivity. *Psychological Review, 96,* 234–254.

Weisz, J., Balazs, L., Lang, E., & Adam, G. (1990). The effect of lateral visual fixation and the direction of eye movements on heartbeat discrimination. *Psychophysiology, 27,* 523–527.

Whitehead, W. E., & Drescher, V. M. (1980). Perception of gastric contractions and self-control of gastric motility. *Psychophysiology, 17,* 552–558.

Whitehead, W. E., Drescher, V. M., Heiman, P., & Blackwell, B. (1977). Relation of heart rate control to heartbeat perception. *Biofeedback and Self-Regulation, 2,* 371–392.

Williams, C. L., & Meck, W. H. (1991). The organizational effects of gonadal steroids on sexually dimorphic spatial ability. *Psychoneuroendocrinology, 16,* 155–176.

Winborn, M. D., Meyers, A. W., & Mulling, C. (1988). The effects of gender and experience on perceived exertion. *Journal of Sports and Exercise Psychology, 10,* 22–31.

Witkin, H. A. (1949). Sex differences in perception. *Transactions of the New York Academy of Science, 12,* 25.

Witkin, H. A., & Goodenough, D. R. (1977). Field dependence and interpersonal behavior. *Psychological Bulletin, 84,* 661–689.

Wolf, S., & Goodell, H. (1968). *Harold G. Wolff's stress and disease.* Springfield, IL: Charles C. Thomas.

Wood, W., & Karten, S. J. (1986). Sex differences in interaction style as a product of perceived sex differences in competence. *Journal of Personality and Social Psychology, 50,* 341–347.

Young, I. M. (1990). *Throwing like a girl and other essays on feminist philosophy and social theory.* Bloomington, IN: Indiana University Press.

ON THE ROLE OF ENCODING PROCESSES IN STEREOTYPE MAINTENANCE

William von Hippel
Denise Sekaquaptewa
Patrick Vargas

I. Introduction

"When you see a Black man in this neighborhood with his arms full of stereo equipment, you know damn good and well what he's doing. We called the police right away." The Gillmans have just caught Andrew Sterling, noted African-American author and playwright, setting up a stereo in his new home in a wealthy, all-White community. When the police arrive, they mistake Andrew's auto alarm remote control for a handgun, and start firing. So begins a series of misunderstandings that prompt Andrew eventually to ask, "Don't you think I should be able to set up a stereo in my own home without being mistaken for a thief?"

The interpretive mistake that the Gillmans made at the beginning of the movie *Amos & Andrew* is typically not made thoughtfully or slowly. Nor is it usually arrived at while reflecting back on the day's activities. Rather, it is made immediately, at the time of the event, and is not experienced as an interpretation so much as a perception. The Gillmans thought they *saw* Andrew stealing a stereo out of a nice home. The police thought they *saw* a pistol in his hand. Such interpretive mistakes occur all too often outside the theater as well. The beating of Rodney King, for example, probably stemmed in part from stereotypic misperceptions on the part of the police officers. Had Rodney King been a tweed-clad and bespectacled academic, it seems unlikely that the police would have interpreted his repeated efforts to stand up as evidence of his intent to do them harm. Such is the role of encoding in stereotype maintenance.

In this chapter, we explore the impact that stereotypes have on encoding processes, and the role that encoding processes play, in turn, on stereotype maintenance. Our goal is not to advance a new theory of stereotyping, but rather to promote a certain perspective. It is our belief that nearly all of the effects of stereotyping on perception, judgment, and memory take place at encoding. We propose, and attempt to document, that stereotypes selectively influence the amount and nature of the information that the individual encodes in such a way as to promote their own survival. Importantly, we believe that this influence of stereotypes takes place almost entirely at the front end of the system, at encoding, and not later while the information is stored or when it is retrieved.

Certainly, many researchers would accept the proposition that stereotypes lead to biases primarily in the encoding of information, but this perspective has received little systematic attention in the literature. We believe that an examination of stereotyping from this perspective sheds light not only on the processes by which stereotypes sustain themselves in the absence of supporting evidence, but also on the ways that stereotypes relate to, and translate into, prejudice. Thus, it is our hope that by highlighting the role of encoding processes in stereotype maintenance, we might focus attention on potentially critical aspects of stereotyping. Before beginning this review, we devote a brief discussion to how we are defining prejudice and stereotyping and how we are treating the relevant literature. We then spend a moment describing what is meant by encoding before we turn to the empirical literature relevant to stereotype processes and encoding.

A. STEREOTYPES

Along with many social psychologists, we hold the view that a stereotype is a consensual belief held by members of one group concerning the characteristics of members of another group. A stereotype is more than just this, however, in that it is also a *theory* about how members of another group look, think, and act, and how and why these attributes are linked together (Wittenbrink, Guest, & Hilton, 1993). This theory need not be consciously expressed, or even consciously expressible, but it nevertheless guides behavior and judgment (see Banaji & Greenwald, 1993; Greenwald & Banaji, in press). Furthermore, this theory may be represented in a variety of fashions: as a social category, a schema, a base rate, a distribution, an expectancy, a prototype, an exemplar, an associative network, or even perhaps a vast collection of instances (see Andersen & Klatzky, 1987; Brooks, 1978; Gaertner & McLaughlin, 1983; Hamilton, 1979; Hilton & Fein, 1989; Locksley, Borgida, Brekke, & Hepburn, 1980; Manis, Nelson, & Shedler, 1988; Smith & Zarate, 1990, 1992; Stangor & Lange, 1994). In all likelihood, stereotypes are represented in most or all of these ways, as a function of how they are learned and the amount and type of experience that the perceiver has with group members (cf. Park & Hastie, 1987).[1] Consequently, for the purposes of this review, we are going to borrow considerably from research on social schemas, categories, and other cognitive representations.

B. PREJUDICE

Prejudice has been defined in various ways, with early definitions focusing more on a tendency toward prejudgment, and later definitions focusing more on the negative content of attitudes concerning out-group members (for excellent discussions of prejudice, see Brewer, 1993; Esses, Haddock, & Zanna, 1993). For example, in his highly influential book, *The Nature of Prejudice,* Allport (1954, p. 9) wrote, "Ethnic prejudice is an antipathy based on a faulty and inflexible generalization. It may be felt or expressed. It may be directed toward a group as a whole, or toward an individual because he is a member of that group." Recently, Haddock, Zanna, and Esses (1993) extended this definition by demonstrating that prejudice is to differing degrees based on symbolic beliefs, affective associates, and past experiences, as well as stereotypes concerning members of the out-group. In the first two sections of this review, we follow Allport (1954) and Haddock et al. (1993), and tacitly define prejudice as negative attitudes toward members of an out-group that are based somewhat loosely on stereotypes, beliefs, and so forth, concerning that out-group. Thus, high- and low-prejudice individuals are differentiated on personality scales that focus not so much on endorsement of group stereotypes, but rather on the degree to which individuals report negative feelings toward out-groups (e.g., the Modern Racism Scale; McConahay, Hardee, & Batts, 1981). In the third section of this review, we propose and examine a new definition of prejudice that is in many ways a modern incarnation of early views of prejudice as a tendency toward prejudgment. We will provide a reinterpretation of prejudice in that section.

---

[1] Although we know of very little data on this point, it seems likely that stereotypes will vary in the nature of their representation as a function of how they are learned. For example, a person who has little experience with members of a stereotyped group, but has learned the stereotype from others, may represent the stereotypes in some abstract format such as a schema. A person who has more experience with the group may represent the stereotype in the form of one or more highly available exemplars. A person who has a great deal of experience with the group may represent the stereotype as a large collection of instances that are probably strongly linked to one another in memory. Furthermore, it seems likely that the more experience an individual gains with the stereotype, and with members of the stereotyped group, the more likely it will be that the stereotype will be multiply represented in a variety of these formats. Different judgment tasks, as well as different contexts and retrieval cues, are likely to draw to mind alternative representations of the stereotype depending on the similarity and usefulness of the particular representation to the task at hand.

C. ENCODING

Encoding begins as the environment impinges on our five senses. From here the information is translated (or encoded) into mental representations that are stored in a variety of formats (e.g., see Cohen & Squire, 1980; Jacoby, 1983; Tulving, 1972). At the broadest level, the encoding process varies in the degree to which it is perceptual or conceptual in nature. For example, if an event is stared at intently but not given much thought, then the encoding and resulting representations will be largely perceptual. If an event is perceived only briefly but given considerable thought, then the encoding and resulting representations will be largely conceptual. Both perceptual and conceptual encoding processes are highly sensitive to perceivers' goals and beliefs, and both can lead to biases in the type and amount of information that is processed and retained. Consider, for example, possible encoding strategies that might be adopted while witnessing a young girl struggle with a difficult math problem. One perceiver might focus on the expression of doubt on the child's face, another might be surprised at her correct response and marvel at her teacher, whereas still another might notice that this child seems a bit like a "tomboy" (cf. Cohen, 1981; Pettigrew, 1979; Weber & Crocker, 1983). Such variable encoding strategies lead to a very different type, amount, and accessibility of information in memory, with far-reaching implications for how that information is later used (see Craik & Lockhart, 1972; Hastie, 1984; Kolers, 1976; Morris, Bransford, & Franks, 1977).

Encoding is itself often divided into different stages or types of processes, beginning with preattentive analysis and ending with elaborative processing. Although all of the research that we will be discussing can be subsumed by one or more of the various stages of encoding, this sort of typology is not very useful in the current context, as social psychological research is only rarely conducted in a manner that would allow one to determine at what point in the encoding process the effects take place. Additionally, not all of the information that is encoded is processed through all of the encoding stages, and the importance of the different stages or processes varies with perceiver goals and task demands (for useful discussions of encoding, see Anderson, 1990; Fiske & Taylor, 1991; Medin & Ross, 1992). For these reasons, our discussion of the literature on encoding and stereotyping is organized around the broader brush strokes of perceptual and conceptual processes.

We begin this chapter with a discussion of perceptual processes. Here we discuss how stereotypes might change what is actually perceived from the world. We then discuss our research on the roles played by stereotypes and schemas in perceptual encoding processes, and how these processes can strengthen the original stereotypes. Next we turn to various conceptual encoding processes, including elaborative processes, attributional processes, contrast and assimilative processes, attentional processes, and automatic versus controlled processes. Our research on these issues focuses on the ways that these processes influence the conceptual encoding of information and thereby contribute to a stereotypic view of the world. We then examine how our perspective concerning stereotyping and encoding might change the way that we view prejudice and its relationship to stereotypes. Finally, we conclude with a discussion of how our perspective might lead to new hypotheses and methodologies.

II. Perceptual Processes

Before beginning this discussion it is worth noting that any evidence that perceptual processes influence and are influenced by stereotypes and prejudice would have profound implications. People view their senses as documentary devices that faithfully translate the environment into understandable and manageable units. Although people may occasionally be swayed or persuaded by argumentation and reason, they *accept* what they see and hear. For this reason, Bem (1970) has referred to perceptions as "zero-order beliefs," in that they are accepted automatically with no concern about their accuracy (see also McGuire, 1981). Yet despite their potential importance to stereotyping (and a variety of other social phenomena), perceptual processes are relatively underresearched and discussed in social psychology. The evidence that does exist speaks both to the credence that people place in their perceptual processes, and to the potential for these processes to influence stereotyping and prejudice in a variety of ways.

Of necessity, perception is a mixture of bottom-up and top-down processes. Although arguments have been made to the contrary (e.g., see Gibson, 1979), most researchers in perception accept the proposition that the perceptual system must rely on at least some assumptions, expectancies, and biases to perceive an inherently ambiguous world. As Medin and Ross (1992) explain,

> one of the central problems in perception is that two-dimensional image arrays on the retina underdetermine possible percepts. That is to say, retinal information is consistent with an infinite number of interpretations. Yet our experience of the world reveals nothing of this ambiguity. It appears that the perceptual system makes assumptions about the nature of the world and these assumptions, coupled with the input, allow for an unambiguous output or interpretation. (pp. 109–110)

Although some of the assumptions made by the perceptual system are inborn, others are learned through experience (see Spelke, 1990). Consequently, because our knowledge of the world guides what we see and hear, stereotypes have a great deal of potential to influence perception. Furthermore, because perceptual processes underlie many stereotypes (e.g., see Allport, 1954; Berry & McArthur, 1986; Friedman & Zebrowitz, 1992; McArthur, 1982), any potential influence of stereotyping on perceptual processes becomes all the more important, as it leads to the possibility that stereotypes may self-perpetuate in a circular fashion through their influence on perception.

A. STEREOTYPES GUIDE SOCIAL PERCEPTION

Similar to the way that our perceptual system interprets ambiguous information about distance, size, or motion as if it were unambiguous, we also tend to unknowingly disambiguate social information. A person who is crying is seen as unambiguously sad to a perceiver who believes the person has lost a loved one, and unambiguously happy to a perceiver who believes the person has won the lottery (Trope, 1986). Under such circumstances, there is no phenomenological experience of interpreting an ambiguous stimulus. Rather, the perceiver is unaware of the extent to which prior knowledge and context facilitated the identification of such behaviors, believing that the evidence of happiness or sadness was inherent to the person perceived. Thus, at a fundamental level, expectancies, biases, stereotypes, and prejudices can change our view of the world in a way that is completely outside of awareness (see Heider, 1958).

Expectancies also play an important role when we are aware of the ambiguity inherent in the perceptual world. For example, merely by generating theories about ambiguous perceptual information, people can construe that information in such a way that interferes with alternative construals later, even when the information becomes less ambiguous. Wyatt and Campbell (1951) demonstrated this phenomenon by presenting subjects with a series of blurred pictures and asking them to generate hypotheses about what the pictures might be. They found that the act of generating hypotheses about the picture inhibited subjects' ability to identify them correctly as they were brought into focus. Bruner and Potter (1964) demonstrated that such expectancies interfere with perception even when people are not explicitly required to generate them. In their experiment subjects were shown a series of slides, some of which were first shown at an extremely poor level of focus before being brought to a level of moderate focus, and some of which were simply shown at a moderate level of focus. Bruner and Potter found that perception of the slides at a very poor level of focus inhibited subjects' ability to identify them later when they were presented at a moderate level of focus. It seems that subjects were spontaneously generating theories about the slides when they were initially presented, and those who were shown slides at a very poor level of focus were more likely to generate false theories. As a consequence, when the slide was brought into focus subjects attempted to construe the data as consistent with their theories, rather than abandon their theories, and this theory-driven processing interfered with perceptual identification (for a connectionist account of this effect, see Snodgrass & Hirshman, 1991).

These experiments demonstrate that people often rely on their stereotypes, expectancies, or social schemas to interpret ambiguous information. Sometimes this interpretation and the consequent disambiguation takes place outside of awareness (as in Trope's experiments), and sometimes people are aware of their attempts to interpret ambiguous information (as in Wyatt and Campbell's and Bruner and Potter's experiments). Under either circumstance, prior theories, expectancies, and stereotypes play an important role in how the perceptual world is construed. Nevertheless, these phenomena do not provide direct evidence that identification processes change what is actually *perceived* rather than what is simply *interpreted* from the world.

B. HOW STEREOTYPES CHANGE PERCEPTUAL PROCESSING

There is suggestive evidence from two different lines of research that stereotypes may change the nature of what is actually perceived. The most dramatic evidence comes from research on minority and majority influence, and although it does not speak directly to stereotyping, the implications are intriguing. In order to determine whether a consistent minority could actually change the way a stimulus is perceived, Moscovici and Personnaz (1980; see also Moscovici and Personnaz, 1991) presented subjects with a series of blue slides in an Asch-like paradigm. For half of the subjects a majority consistently reported that the slides were green, while for the other half of the subjects a minority consistently reported that the slides were green. Subjects were then shown another series of blue slides interspersed with presentations of a blank screen, and were asked to report the color of the blank screen (in reality their own chromatic afterimage). When a consistent minority had labeled the blue slides as green, subjects reported a more red afterimage than in the control condition or when a consistent majority had labeled the blue slides as green (a red afterimage is associated with prior perception of green). Because chromatic afterimages are thought to be a consequence of peripheral (low level) sensory activity (e.g., Padgham & Saunders, 1975), this finding suggests that subjects in the minority condition were actually being influenced by the minority in their *visual perception* of the color. The Moscovici and Personnaz (1980) experiment has not always replicated (see Doms & Van Avermaet, 1980), but the change in chromatic afterimages found by Moscovici and Personnaz has now been demonstrated many times (see Moscovici and Personnaz, 1991).

Although these results seem quite remarkable, in that they propose that higher order cognition can influence low-level (or peripheral) perceptual activity, experiments in cognitive psychology have yielded results that hint at a mechanism for the Moscovici and Personnaz effect. Research on mental imagery has revealed that people cannot generate appropriate chromatic afterimages by imagining a color in the absence of any color presentation (see Finke, 1980). Nevertheless, people can change the nature of the chromatic afterimages that are formed by imagining visual stimuli while being presented with a color display (Finke & Schmidt, 1977, 1978). In order to explain these phenomena, a brief digression is necessary.

As noted above, people perceive chromatic afterimages following the viewing of a retinal-stationary color for an extended period of time. These afterimages are the complement of the color that was earlier perceived. McCollough (1965) demonstrated that under certain conditions, these chromatic afterimages can become orientation-contingent. Specifically, McCollough found that if she presented horizontal black bars superimposed on a background of one color alternating with vertical black bars superimposed on a background of another color, subjects would perceive different chromatic afterimages when later presented with horizontal or vertical black bars in the absence of any color. When later presented with horizontal bars, subjects perceived the complementary afterimage of the color that had been presented with horizontal bars; when later presented with vertical bars, subjects perceived the complementary afterimage of the color that had been presented with vertical bars. Thus, subjects in McCollough's experiment perceived the appropriate chromatic afterimage from an earlier color presentation only when the context matched that of the earlier presentation. The mechanism of this effect is still not well understood, but it is generally accepted that it results from the interaction between higher order pattern processing and lower order color processing (see Skowbo, Timney, Gentry, & Morant, 1975).

Importantly, some aspects of the McCollough effect replicate under imagery conditions and some do not. When subjects perceive alternating colors but only imagine the superimposed black bars, they experience a similar, albeit weakened version of the McCollough effect. When subjects perceive the alternating vertical and horizontal bars and only imagine the color fields, the McCollough effect does not emerge (Finke & Schmidt, 1977, 1978). These imagery experiments suggest that people cannot intentionally cause their peripheral sensory system to perceive color in the absence of color, but they can cause their peripheral sensory system to perceive forms that interact with the real image of color in the absence of such forms. Thus, it seems possible that when subjects in the Moscovici and Personnaz experiment considered the responses of the minority source, they might have imagined that the blue slide contained some green tones. Such a conjunction of imagery and perception may have led subjects to perceive a blue slide as containing overtones of green, and thereby to experience a chromatic afterimage that contains the complementary color for green. This mechanism would suggest that imaging and perceiving interacted in the Moscovici and Personnaz experiment to produce an appropriate chromatic image and afterimage.[2]

The possibility that people can generate mental images that change the nature of their chromatic afterimages suggests that the mind and the eye can work together, interactively and constructively, to produce what we commonly regard as perception. Although such a possibility seems surprising under a model of perception and cognition as distinct and separable processes, it is less surprising under the predominate model that perception and imagery are mediated by the same brain mechanisms (e.g., see Farah, 1988; Kosslyn, 1990). With such an interactive model for perception and imagery, it seems more plausible that higher order cognitions, including expectations and beliefs, have the potential to influence perception. Thus, prejudiced perceivers may actually *see* African-Americans behave in a hostile manner, or women behave in an emotional manner, even if that perception is not consistent with the distal stimulus. It awaits future research, however, to determine whether stereotypes can change the way we perceive the world.

It is important to note that evidence for top-down influences on perception is not limited to visual phenomena. A substantial body of evidence suggests that cognitive processes play an equally important role in auditory phenomena. For example, people are relatively unable to detect a missing phoneme in human speech when it is masked by a sound such as a cough or a burst of white noise. Instead, it sounds to the listener as if the cough or white noise occurred along with the phoneme that was actually removed (Samuel, 1981). This effect also emerges in the perception of other types of sounds, such as music, where the replacement of appropriate chords with white noise is also often impossible for subjects to detect. Importantly, the inability to detect missing sounds such as scales or chords is exacerbated when the scales and chords are expected on the basis of prior keys (DeWitt & Samuel, 1990). These findings suggest that higher order knowledge about context, even the type of complex and elaborate context that is abstracted from musical melodies, allows people to mentally replace missing sounds in such a way that the sounds actually seem to be heard. Even more striking, McGurk and McDonald (1976) have shown that auditory perception can be highly determined by accompanying visual information. In their experiment they played a videotape of a speaker mouthing the sound, "pa-pa," while the soundtrack played the sound, "na-na." In integrating these two pieces of information, subjects reported hearing, "ma-ma," which is the closest sound

---

[2]Whether such a conjunction of imagery and perception would lead to modification of the chromatic afterimage is not currently known, but is at least feasible in the context of previous research. Furthermore, research in neuroanatomy has revealed the potential for top-down influences on sensory perception in the presence of *descending* fibers in the neural pathways for both vision and audition (Martin, 1989; Van Essen, 1988).

that would be appropriate for the accompanying visual image (for evidence of this phenomenon with real words, see Dekle, Fowler, & Funnell, 1992).

Although there is currently no research examining the role of stereotypes in auditory perception, experiments like those of McGurk and McDonald and DeWitt and Samuel suggest that stereotypes might influence the nature of what we actually hear. Because changing a single phoneme in many words can lead to dramatic alteration in the meaning of the word (for example, most four letter words have a variety of similar sounding and more innocent alternatives), it would seem that stereotypes have considerable potential to determine auditory perception. Thus, our knowledge that an African-American or a woman or an elderly person or a rabbi is speaking might lead us to misperceive a variety of words in stereotype-congruent ways.

Summary

- Stereotypes have the potential to influence the way that we encode the behaviors of others by changing what we actually see and hear. Although there are no data that directly address this possibility, suggestive research from cognitive and social psychology speak to the power that expectancies and beliefs have to change the input we receive from our perceptual system.

C. HOW STEREOTYPES INHIBIT PERCEPTUAL PROCESSING

Less dramatic, but equally important, our research indicates that stereotypes have the potential to influence the amount of perceptual information that is encoded. Because stereotypes provide perceivers with a wealth of background information about individual targets, perceivers do not pay as much attention to individuals when they can rely on a social schema or stereotype as when they cannot (Belmore, 1987; Fiske, Neuberg, Beattie, & Milberg, 1987; Macrae, Milne & Bodenhausen, 1994).[3] Although the relationship between attention and perceptual encoding is complex (e.g., see Hawley & Johnston, 1991; Kintsch & Keenan, 1973; Neill, Beck, Bottalico, & Molloy, 1990), overall decreases in looking time tend to be associated with poorer perceptual encoding (von Hippel & Hawkins, 1994). In conjunction with the fact that stereotypic processing is associated with decreased attention, this finding suggests that perceivers may

---

[3]It is important to note that this finding emerges only when the stereotype is strong (Sekaquaptewa & von Hippel, 1994; Stangor & McMillan, 1992) or when the information is ambiguous or stereotype-congruent. When the stereotype is of moderate strength and the information is stereotype-incongruent, perceivers tend to pay more attention to such information when they are relying on a stereotype or social schema than when they are not (e.g., Srull, 1981; Stern, Marrs, Millar, & Cole, 1984).

encode less perceptual information when they are relying on a stereotype than when they are not.

Numerous experiments have demonstrated that schematic perceivers engage in greater conceptual processing than aschematic perceivers (for reviews, see Fiske & Taylor, 1991; Markus & Zajonc, 1985; see also McCann, Ostrom, Tyner, & Mitchell, 1985), yet none of this research has examined perceptual processing and consequent perceptual memory. Because aschematic perceivers do not have prior theories to facilitate their ongoing perception, von Hippel, Jonides, Hilton, and Narayan (1993) proposed that aschematic perceivers would engage in greater perceptual processing than schematic perceivers. In order to test this possibility, they presented subjects with various types of information under conditions in which subjects could rely on a schema or stereotype to facilitate processing or could not rely on a schema.

In Experiment 1 schematicity was manipulated as in Bransford and Johnson (1973), such that subjects read an ambiguous paragraph that was either preceded by a thematic title ("Washing Clothes") or was not preceded by such a title. Perceptual encoding of information from the paragraph was then assessed via word-stem completion, a procedure in which subjects are presented with the first three letters of a word, and are asked to complete the word stem with the first English word that comes to mind. Encoding is indicated in this task by the extent to which subjects are more likely to solve these puzzles with words they have just seen rather than with words they have not encountered in the experiment. This measure has been shown to be highly sensitive to prior perceptual processing, but rather insensitive to prior conceptual processing (Graf & Mandler, 1984; Graf, Shimamura, & Squire, 1985). In contrast to Bransford and Johnson's (1973) results with recall (which is highly sensitive to prior conceptual processing but rather insensitive to prior perceptual processing; see Roediger, 1990), von Hippel et al. (1993) found greater perceptual encoding when subjects did not receive a thematic title to the paragraph than when they did.

Experiment 2 replicated this finding relying on a more social manipulation of schemata. In this experiment, subjects were presented with a series of behaviors from two different sources, such that one source exhibited primarily intelligent behaviors and the other source exhibited primarily unintelligent behaviors. In order to manipulate the presence versus absence of a schema, for some subjects the sources of the behaviors were two different individuals and for other subjects the sources of the behaviors were two meaningless groups (specifically, people grouped together on the basis of the first letter of their last name). Srull (1981) has demonstrated that when a source is psychologically meaningful, such as a single individual or a group of people who share important qualities, perceivers expect the source to behave in a consistent fashion. Furthermore, when the source does behave consistently, people abstract this information and rely on it as a schema to facilitate their processing of further information (see also Srull,

Lichtenstein, & Rothbart, 1985; Stern, Marrs, Millar, & Cole, 1984). When a source is not psychologically meaningful, however, perceivers do not expect the source to behave in a consistent fashion, indeed they may not even notice such consistency if it does exist, and thus cannot rely on it as a schema to guide information processing. As in Experiment 1, and in contrast to Srull's (1981) findings with the conceptual measure of recall, this experiment revealed greater perceptual encoding when subjects read behaviors from meaningless groups rather than single individuals.

Experiment 3 replicated this finding through the use of self-schemata. Specifically, subjects in this experiment were presented with a series of trait words and were asked to make judgments about whether the trait words were self-descriptive, as in Markus (1977). Some of the trait words were from domains on which subjects were self-schematic, and some of the trait words were from domains on which subjects were aschematic. After completing this "me/not me" task, subjects were presented with either conceptual or perceptual memory measures to tap their conceptual versus perceptual encoding of the trait words. In order to measure conceptual encoding, subjects were given either a recall or a recognition task. In order to measure perceptual encoding, subjects were given either a word-fragment completion task or a perceptual identification task. Word-fragment completion is similar to word-stem completion, but rather than removing all of the letters after the first three, select letters are removed throughout the word. Encoding is indicated in this task by the extent to which subjects are more likely to complete the word fragments with words that they have previously encountered in the experiment, rather than with words they have not encountered in the experiment. Perceptual identification is a task in which subjects are presented with a brief exposure of a word (in this case, 33 ms) and are asked to identify it. Encoding is indicated in this task by the extent to which subjects are more able to identify words that they have encountered in the experiment than words they have not encountered in the experiment. Word-fragment completion and perceptual identification have been shown to be primarily sensitive to prior perceptual rather than conceptual processing (e.g., see Blaxton, 1989; Jacoby, 1983; Roediger & Blaxton, 1987). As can be seen in Figure 1, subjects showed greater conceptual memory when they encoded the trait words with a schema, and greater perceptual memory when they encoded the trait words without a schema.

1. The Role of Perceptual Memory in Impression Revision

Despite the fact that the consequences of decreased conceptual processing are well documented (i.e., decreased understanding, decreased ability to retrieve information, etc.), the consequences of decreased perceptual processing have received relatively little attention in social psychology. The research that has been conducted suggests that perceptual processing may be critical to the ability to reinterpret or revise initial impressions. For example, Massad, Hubbard, and

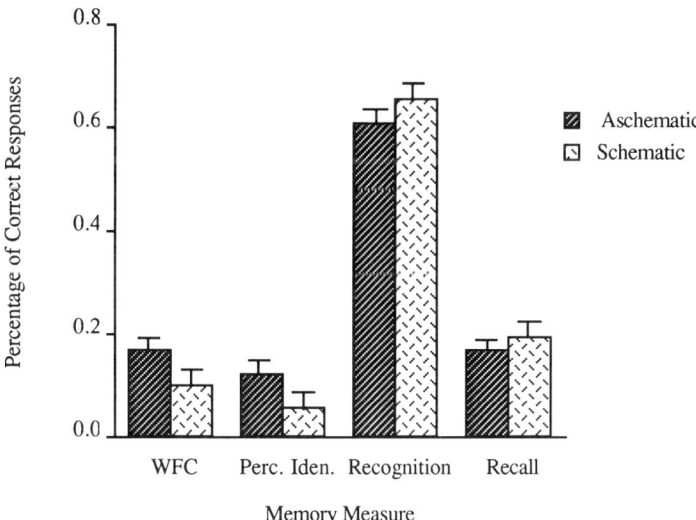

Fig. 1. A representation of the effect of schematic processing on conceptual and perceptual encoding. WFC, word fragment completion, Perc. Iden., perceptual identification. (From von Hippel, Jonides, Hilton, and Narayan, 1993.)

Newtson (1979) presented subjects with Heider and Simmel's (1944) classic film of moving shapes. Consistent with earlier research, Massad et al. found that subjects could easily interpret the film under one of two alternative anthropomorphic explanations for the events. When subjects were provided with the alternative explanation after viewing the film, however, they were unable to reinterpret it and adjust their impressions according to the new schema unless they were allowed to view it again. Thus, it seems that as a result of their prior schematic processing, the perceptual information that subjects encoded was tagged to certain meanings or interpretations, and was no longer available for reinterpretation. Had subjects recognized at encoding that multiple interpretations were possible, current evidence suggests that they would have been quite capable of integrating information provided later to reinterpret the original event (Fein, 1991; Langer & Piper, 1987). Because stereotypes tend to provide a single explanation for behaviors, however, stereotypic processing tends to be associated with poor perceptual memory and a low likelihood of reinterpretation.

Research from cognitive psychology also provides evidence of the importance of perceptual encoding in the ability to reinterpret information. In their research on perception and imagery, Chambers and Reisberg (1985) presented subjects with Figure 2. When subjects were only allowed to view the figure for five seconds, they all arrived at the interpretation that it was the head of a duck. The image was then removed from sight and subjects were asked if they could reinterpret it from memory. At this point, none of them were able to do so. When

Fig. 2. Ambiguous figure. (From Chambers and Reisberg, 1985.)

subjects were told to draw the image from memory and then reinterpret the picture that now lay before them, most subjects were able to conclude that it could also be the head of a rabbit. Thus it seems that even though subjects had all the perceptual information in memory that was necessary to enable reinterpretation, they could not do so from memory, but only from their actual perception of the event.

Does this finding mean that people can never go back and reinterpret prior perceptual events in memory? To the contrary, the eyewitness literature is replete with evidence that people can be led to reinterpret earlier events, even in ways that are outside of awareness (e.g., Loftus & Palmer, 1973). It seems that the crucial factor in determining whether events can be reinterpreted from memory is the role played by the schema or stereotype at encoding. When schemas are necessary for comprehension people seem unable to reinterpret information that has been schematically encoded. When the schema or stereotype plays little role in comprehension or interpretation, and simply provides one perspective in favor of another, people seem quite capable of reinterpreting earlier information.

By way of explanation, consider some classic experiments on the role played by schemas in interpretation and memory. In Bransford and Johnson's (1973) experiment, subjects were presented with an ambiguous paragraph that could not be interpreted without a thematic title. It began, "The procedure is actually quite simple. First you arrange things into different groups. Of course, one pile may be sufficient depending on how much there is to do." If subjects were not given the thematic title, "Washing Clothes," before reading this paragraph, it was uninterpretable and thereby relatively impossible to recall. Importantly, if subjects were given the title after they had read the paragraph, they still could not interpret it, nor could they remember the information from it. This experiment provides a classic example of the role played by schemas in encoding otherwise ambiguous information. Here, as in Chambers and Reisberg (1985) and Massad et al. (1979), the schema is absolutely necessary for interpretation; the information has no meaning in the absence of the schema. For this reason, the information cannot be reinterpreted once it has been tagged to a certain meaning through the schematic encoding process.

When events are comprehensible but the schema provides one interpretation in favor of another, the schema can determine which information will be available to later retrieval, if not to reinterpretation. For example, Rothbart, Evans, and Fulero (1979) found that subjects who expected a group to be friendly had better memory for friendly than intelligent behaviors, whereas those who expected intelligence had better memory for intelligent than friendly behaviors. Furthermore, this effect only emerged when the expectation about the group was provided before the behaviors were encoded (see also Zadny & Gerard, 1974). Similarly, Howard and Rothbart (1980) demonstrated that a positivity bias exists in memory for in-group information only when people are aware of their group membership before they encode the behaviors of others. Under such circumstances, it seems that the schema facilitates selective attention to a sufficient degree that some information becomes irretrievable later on.

In contrast to these examples, Pichert and Anderson (1977) provide a different portrayal of the role played by schemas in interpretation and memory. In their experiment subjects read a story about a house. Some were told to take the perspective of a potential home buyer, and some were told to take the perspective of a burglar. Consistent with other schema research, Pichert and Anderson found that subjects tended to remember information that was relevant to the schema they adopted. For example, subjects who played the role of a home buyer tended to remember that one room was newly painted and another had a leaky roof. Subjects who played the role of a burglar, on the other hand, tended to remember that the garage door was unlocked and furs were stored in a bedroom closet. In a follow-up experiment, when subjects were told after reading the paragraph from one perspective to adopt an alternative perspective for retrieval, they were perfectly capable of retrieving previously irretrievable information that was relevant to the alternative schema (Anderson & Pichert, 1978). The difference between this experiment and experiments of Bransford and Johnson (1973) and Howard and Rothbart (1980), however, is that here the schema was not critical to comprehension or interpretation of the paragraph (see also, Hirt, 1990). Whether subjects were given a burglar schema, a home-buyer schema, or no schema at all, they interpreted the paragraph in the same way and were perfectly capable of understanding and remembering the information. In this case, the schema seemed to play little role beyond that of a retrieval cue.

Thus, it seems from this research that whether information can later be reinterpreted or retrieved from memory depends on the role played by the schema or stereotype at encoding. When a particular behavior is ambiguous and/or its interpretation is heavily dependent on the schema instantiated at encoding that behavior will be less amenable to reinterpretation later on. When the behavior is equally comprehensible and similarly interpreted in the presence or absence of a particular schema, or in the presence of multiple schemas, it will be relatively amenable to reinterpretation or retrieval upon the provision of an alternate schema. We know of no experiments that have directly tested this hypothesis, but such a manipulation of the role played by the schema or stereotype at encoding should lead to predictable differences in the potential for reinterpretation and retrieval from memory.

Summary

- Stereotypes inhibit encoding of perceptual information.
- By inhibiting perceptual encoding, and thereby reducing the amount of perceptual information in memory, stereotypes can inhibit perceivers' ability to reinterpret information from memory.
- Thus, inhibition of perceptual encoding may be an important factor contributing to the resiliency of stereotypes and the low probability of stereotype revision.

D. HOW STEREOTYPES FACILITATE PERCEPTUAL PROCESSING

Not only do stereotypes have the potential to limit perceptual encoding, but recent research suggests that they may have the seemingly contradictory ability to facilitate it as well. When stereotype-relevant information is fleeting, incomplete, or degraded, stereotypes and social schemas may facilitate the ability to arrive at an accurate perception of the event by virtue of the perceptual experience that they provide. In order to test this possibility, von Hippel, Hawkins, and Narayan (in press) presented subjects with a series of trait words at very brief exposure durations (33 ms). Some of the trait words were relevant to subjects' self-schemas and some were not. Additionally, some of the trait words were presented in a format designed to match prior perceptual experience (i.e., the first letter was capitalized and the rest of the letters were in lower case), and some of the trait words were presented in a format designed to be inconsistent with prior perceptual experience (i.e., the second and last letters were capitalized and the rest of the letters were in lower case). Finally, half of the subjects were preselected to be moderately depressed, and thus were hypothesized to be schematic only for negative information, and half of the subjects were preselected to be nondepressed, and thus were hypothesized to be schematic only for positive information. Consistent with the notion that schemas facilitate accurate perception by providing extensive prior perceptual experience, subjects were facilitated in their ability to identify schematic information only when it was in a valence appropriate to their (presumably) chronic levels of depression, and when the capitalization matched everyday experience (see Fig. 3).

In a second experiment, von Hippel et al. presented anorexic and nonanorexic

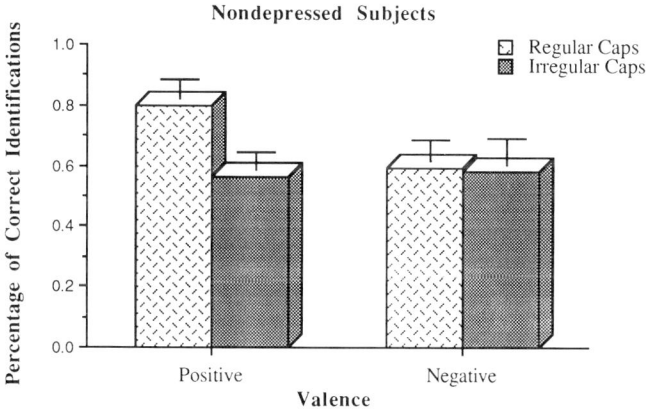

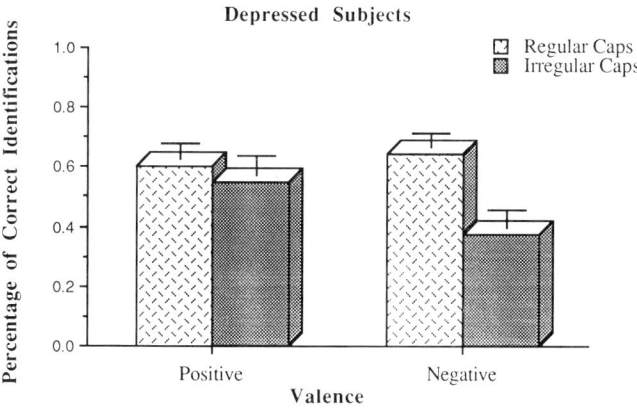

Fig. 3. Percentages of correct identifications of positive and negative schematic trait words as a function of depression and word regularity. (From von Hippel, Hawkins, and Narayan, in press.)

subjects with brief exposures of food words. Disruption of capitalization again provided a manipulation of consistency with prior perceptual experience. In order to assess schematicity, subjects indicated which foods they thought about most often. Consistent with the results of the first experiment, anorexic subjects were more able to identify schematic food words than nonanorexic subjects, but only when letter capitalization matched prior perceptual experience. This effect only emerged with foods for which subjects were schematic.

These experiments suggest that by virtue of their chronic attention to information in a particular domain, people can gain perceptual expertise in that domain[4] (see also Anthony, Copper, & Mullen, 1992; Malpass & Kravitz, 1969; Pettigrew, Allport, & Barnett, 1958; for evidence of increased visual accuracy at intraracial face recognition). Importantly, this perceptual expertise only emerges for information that is congruent with the perceiver's schema or stereotype. Thus, it is possible that a prejudiced perceiver might become adept at actually perceiving African-Americans behaving in a hostile manner, but not at perceiving African-Americans behaving in a friendly manner. This possibility suggests that stereotypes have the potential to lead to an increase in discriminability of stereotype-congruent information, in addition to an increase in the tendency to incorrectly judge that stereotype-congruent information was presented (e.g., Duncan, 1976; see also Macrae, Stangor, & Milne, 1994; Powell & Fazio, 1993). That is, prejudiced people may become more likely to perceive stereotype-congruency when it does exist, as well as more likely to guess that they perceived it when it does not exist. As a consequence, prejudiced people may perceive a much greater prevalence of stereotype-confirming information than is perceived by nonprejudiced people.

At first it might seem that these findings and observations are inconsistent with the earlier-presented evidence that stereotypes inhibit encoding of perceptual information. However, it is more likely that these two seemingly discrepant phenomena are actually causally linked. Specifically, it seems that stereotypes and social schemas facilitate rapid initial identification of congruent information. Once this initial identification is complete, however, the stereotypes themselves allow the perceiver to "go beyond the information given" (Bruner, 1957), so additional attention to a particular person or event is no longer necessary. As a consequence, stereotypes lead to a lower perceptual threshold in relevant domains (von Hippel et al., in press) and yet decreased perceptual encoding in both relevant and irrelevant domains (von Hippel et al., 1993). Thus, the stereotyping perceiver is quick to identify congruent information, but then ceases to attend further and thus can only remember (or infer) stereotypic attributes.

Consistent with this reasoning, Markus, Smith, and Moreland (1985) demonstrated that perceivers who rely on a social schema unitize incoming information into larger chunks than aschematic perceivers, as they encode information in more global and abstract terms. Yet, when required to do so, schematic perceivers can also unitize incoming information into smaller chunks than aschematic perceivers, as schematic perceivers are able to perceive finer distinctions in the flow of incoming information. Thus, Markus et al.'s data suggest that social

---

[4]Research in motion perception (Ball & Sekuler, 1982, 1987) has also provided evidence that through repeated exposure to particular stimuli, people can gain visual expertise for those specific stimuli. This expertise seems to emerge at the level of visual functioning, in that it does not translate to different domains and does not even depend on sensorimotor responding (Kosnik, Fikre, & Sekuler, 1985).

schemas have the potential to lead to both greater perceptual sensitivity and to encoding at a more abstract level. Importantly, Markus et al.'s data demonstrate that although schematic perceivers have the necessary expertise to encode information in a more fine-grained fashion, their natural inclination is to encode in more global terms. Again, this inclination toward a more global encoding strategy arises because the schema itself can be relied upon to fill in the missing details if that ever becomes necessary (e.g., see Sulin & Dooling, 1974).

Summary

• Stereotypes promote perceptual expertise for stereotype-congruent information, thereby causing perceivers to encode a greater preponderance of stereotype-congruent behavior than is encoded by perceivers not relying on a stereotype.

III. Conceptual Processes

Clearly stereotypes are maintained by a variety of conceptual processes. The literature has tended to focus on the ways that stereotypes serve as a crutch, allowing people to get through their day with a minimum of cognitive activity (for a review, see Fiske & Taylor, 1991). For example, Bodenhausen (1990) has demonstrated that people rely on stereotypes more when they are off-cycle of their circadian rhythm: nocturnals stereotype more in the morning and diurnals stereotype more at night. Similarly, Kruglanski and Freund (1983) showed that people are more likely to rely on their stereotypes when they are under time pressure, and Bechtold, Naccarato, and Zanna (1986) showed that males and traditional females are more likely to discriminate against women, and liberal females are more likely to discriminate against men, when they are under time pressure. Finally, Macrae, Hewstone, and Griffiths (1993) found that people are more likely to stereotype when they are under conditions of information overload (see also Pratto & Bargh, 1991).

Stereotypes are not just maintained as a path of least resistance, however. They are also maintained at the expense of cognitive effort. In this section we will review some of the ways that perceivers engage in additional cognitive activity at encoding, sometimes even mental gymnastics, in order to maintain their stereotypic views of the world. We will begin with a discussion of elaborative processes, attributional processes, and assimilation effects. We are not proposing that these processes are inherently illogical or nonnormative, but rather that they are used much more often in service of stereotype maintenance than in efforts toward stereotype accommodation. Following this discussion of the role of effortful processes in stereotype maintenance, we will discuss some of the ways that stereotypes are maintained precisely because people do not engage in effortful encoding strategies. This discussion will focus on attentional processes and the automatic activation of stereotypes.

A. ELABORATIVE PROCESSES

Despite the fact, or perhaps because of the fact, that stereotypes and social schemas facilitate information processing, perceivers go to great efforts to maintain their stereotypes and schemas when they are challenged. Sometimes the types of processes in which people engage are apparent, and other times the processes are invisible and only the outcome is evident. Additionally, sometimes the motivation for stereotype maintenance is evident, and sometimes the stereotype seems only to serve a cognitive function. Nevertheless, perceivers show a surprising tenacity in defending the integrity of even meaningless or unimportant categorizations. For example, Krueger, Rothbart, and Sriram (1989) presented subjects with an induction series of two different categories of numbers that were nonoverlapping but that directly abutted one another. After being exposed to the induction series, subjects were asked to estimate the means of the two categories and were found to be quite accurate in their estimation. Subjects were then presented with additional numbers that were identified as members of the induction categories. For some subjects the additional numbers shifted the mean of the target category closer to the context category, whereas for other subjects the additional numbers shifted the mean of the target category away from the context category.

Krueger et al. found that when the distance between the target and context categories was increased by the presence of the additional numbers, subjects were adept at adjusting their perception of the target category to reflect these additional numbers. When the distance between the categories was attenuated by the presence of the additional numbers, however, subjects did not sufficiently adjust their perception of the target category. Subsequent experiments revealed that this inability or unwillingness to perceive the categories as overlapping only emerged when the categories were initially distinct. Subjects were perfectly capable of perceiving overlapping categories if they were initially encoded in such a fashion. Thus, it seems that even in a case in which there is no motivational reason to preserve category uniqueness, people nevertheless attempt to maintain differentiation (see also Ford & Stangor, 1992; Wilder, 1981). Although the mechanism by which people accomplish this goal is not clear from this experiment, it seems that they must somehow ignore or insufficiently integrate numbers that would attenuate category differences.

In contrast to the Krueger et al. study, in which failure to integrate information facilitated category differentiation, people also maintain their stereotypes by integrating information that should be kept distinct from the category. In a clever demonstration of the role of imagination and integration in stereotype maintenance, Slusher and Anderson (1987) presented subjects with members of different social categories such as priests and lawyers. Subjects were then presented with information that confirmed stereotypes about these groups, and information that was stereotype-irrelevant. Additionally, subjects were asked to imagine members of these different groups in a variety of vaguely defined scenarios (e.g., "Picture person X standing in front of his home"). Slusher and Anderson found that subjects' imagined scenarios tended to be stereotype-congruent; lawyers were imagined in front of expensive homes and priests were imagined in front of modest homes. Importantly, subjects then integrated these imagined events sufficiently with the actual events they had encoded that they were unable to differentiate them from each other (a failure in "reality monitoring," Johnson & Raye, 1981). Consequently, subjects tended to overestimate the extent to which they had been presented with stereotype-confirming information (see also, Sulin & Dooling, 1974). As Slusher and Anderson note, such an integration of imagination with actual events could play an important role in stereotype maintenance, as people often ponder possible scenarios when they encode stereotype-relevant information from secondary sources such as a friend or the media.

The Krueger et al. and Slusher and Anderson experiments provide provocative examples of how and when people rely on integrative encoding strategies to maintain social stereotypes, but there is not yet much research on these types of strategies. In contrast to these cases, the "memory incongruency effect"—which results from attempts to maintain expectancies and stereotypes in the face of incongruency—has become one of the most heavily researched consequences of conceptual encoding strategies. The memory incongruency effect is the oft-displayed tendency to have better recall for information that is incongruent with an expectancy than for information that is congruent with an expectancy (for reviews, see Rojahn & Pettigrew, 1992; Srull & Wyer, 1989; Stangor & McMillan, 1992).

1. Encoding Incongruent Information

The memory incongruency effect was first documented by Hastie and Kumar (1979), who proposed that the incongruency effect emerged because people engage in attributional processing in order to make sense of the incongruency. This attributional processing might conceivably result in a change of meaning of the incongruent behavior (see Asch, 1946), or perhaps discounting of the incongruent behavior. Either way, because attributional processing involves considering incongruent behaviors in relation to semantic and episodic information stored in long-term memory, this sort of processing is considered "elaborative" (Craik & Lockhart, 1972; Klein & Loftus, 1990). Hastie and Kumar (1979) went on to propose that as a result of this elaborative encoding, the perceiver forms links in memory between incongruent and congruent behaviors. This process of forming links or associations between pieces of information in working memory is considered "organizational" or "associative" (Anderson & Bower, 1973; Klein & Loftus, 1990). Thus, Hastie and Kumar's proposal was a hybrid model containing components of an associative network explanation and an elaborative processing explanation.

Two years later, Srull (1981) published a substantial extension of Hastie and Kumar's model, outlining a number of phenomena that provided support for an associative network explanation of the incongruency effect. For example, Srull demonstrated that congruent information tends to be followed by incongruent information in recall output (see also O'Sullivan & Durso, 1984). According to an associative network model, this order effect emerges as a consequence of the associative links that people form between incongruent and congruent pieces of information as they try to resolve the incongruency. With the discovery of such phenomena, research on the incongruency effect became increasingly directed toward uncovering consequences of, and evidence for, an associative network explanation. Although Hastie (e.g., Hastie, 1984) continued to promote a hybrid model, whereby incongruency led to attributional (or elaborative) processing, which in turn led to interbehavior associations (or organization), he and others proposed that the memorial consequences of incongruency resulted from increased associations between incongruent and congruent information.

At one level, it does not matter whether the incongruency effect is attributed to increased organizational or elaborative processing, as both processes are conceptual encoding strategies that lead to facilitation in memory (e.g., Jenkins, Mink, & Russell, 1958; Klein & Loftus, 1990). The type of processing that underlies the incongruency effect does play an important role, however, in determining why social schemas and expectancies lead to incongruency in memory and yet congruency in evaluations. An associative network model cannot explain this dissociation between memory and judgment, whereas an elaborative processing model can.[5]

According to an elaborative account, incongruent information leads to explanatory, attributional processing, which in turn causes information to be more memorable through the establishment of "longer lasting and stronger traces" (Craik & Lockhart, 1972, p. 675). It is the elaboration itself that facilitates memory, not a subsequent organizational process, and it is also the elaboration that causes the incongruent information to no longer be incongruent. That is, to the extent that a perceiver engages in cognitive effort to explain away a seeming inconsistency, the perceiver is both more likely to be successful in discounting or reinterpreting the information, and more likely to remember the (no longer) incongruent information as a consequence of the extensive cognitive processing.

---

[5]Hastie and Park's (1986) research on memory-based versus on-line processing does provide an explanation for the memory-judgment dissociation based on an associative memory model. In the case of on-line processes, however, their research simply states that memory and judgment will not necessarily be related.

According to this perspective, the dissociation between memory and judgment that seems to exist among subjects who show better memory for incongruent information, but nevertheless continue to endorse congruent evaluations, is really not a dissociation at all. Rather, these people are remembering information because they thought about it a lot in order to make sense of it, and because they thought about it a lot they are also more likely to make sense of it (i.e., reinterpret it in the light of the original expectancy).

In order to test such a possibility, it is necessary to rely on measures of memory that are sensitive to elaborative processing but insensitive to organizational processing. Recall and recognition are insufficient for this task, because they are sensitive to both elaborative and associative processing. That is, increases in both types of processing lead to consequent increases in recall and recognition (e.g., see Anderson & Bower, 1973; Bower, 1970, 1972; Bower & Karlin, 1974; Craik & Lockhart, 1972; Craik & Tulving, 1975). Conceptually driven implicit memory measures, on the other hand, are ideal for the task because they are sensitive to elaborative processing (Blaxton, 1989; Hammann, 1990) but many of them are insensitive to organizational processing (MacLeod & Bassili, 1989).

Implicit memory measures are procedures that allow subjects to demonstrate memory for information without requiring explicit retrieval of an episode (for reviews, see Richardson-Klavehn & Bjork, 1988; Roediger, 1990; Schacter, 1987). A major advantage of implicit memory measures is that they allow a more direct examination of encoding processes than is provided by explicit memory measures, as implicit measures are not influenced by conscious retrieval strategies. For example, if a person were able to read a paragraph more rapidly on the second presentation than on the first, this would be evidence of implicit memory for the paragraph, even though the person was not asked if (s)he could recall reading the paragraph (Kolers, 1976). Because implicit memory measures do not rely on conscious retrieval of information, they are *in*sensitive to organizational processes that facilitate intentional retrieval of information by providing associative links between items. The subject does not travel down associative pathways to retrieve information when tested for memory implicitly, so the presence of those pathways does not interact with memory performance.[6] Rather, the strength of the trace is critical in determining whether it will influence behavior or judgment in an implicit memory task: Strong traces are likely to influence behavior or judgment, and weak traces are unlikely to influence behavior or judgment. Consistent with the notions of transfer-appropriate processing and encoding specificity (Morris et al., 1977; Tulving & Thomson, 1973), factors

---

[6]This statement only applies to implicit memory measures such as general knowledge or category accessibility that request subjects to provide a single response to each item (von Hippel & Baker, 1994). When subjects are allowed to generate multiple responses to each item, as in category exemplar generation, potential responses that are associated with one another *are* more likely to be generated (Rappold & Hashtroudi, 1991).

that determine the strength of a trace for implicit memory measures differ with different types of measures. As noted above, for conceptually driven implicit measures the strength of the trace is determined by prior elaborative processing (Blaxton, 1989; Hammann, 1990; Smith & Branscombe, 1988).

If elaborative processing can account for the memory incongruency effect, then people should show the incongruency effect with implicit as well as explicit memory measures. Furthermore, if elaborative processing leads to both reinterpretation or discounting *and* better memory, then implicit memory for incongruent information should be associated with *congruent* evaluations. In order to test this possibility, von Hippel and Baker (1993) presented subjects with a series of positive, negative, and neutral trait words that were said to describe a man named Hans, who was supposedly either a Nazi or a Peace Corps worker. Positive traits were incongruent with a Nazi (but congruent with a Peace Corps worker), and negative traits were incongruent with a Peace Corps worker (but congruent with a Nazi). In order to measure implicit memory for the trait words, subjects were given the category accessibility task from Smith and Branscombe (1988). In this task, subjects are presented with a series of behaviors that could be described by a variety of traits, and are asked to provide trait words that they think are the best descriptors of each behavior. For example, subjects are presented with, "ran across the pond before the ice had completely frozen," which could be described by traits such as foolish, courageous, and so on. Implicit memory in this task is measured as the extent to which subjects are more likely to provide trait descriptors that had been presented earlier in the experiment rather than trait descriptors that they had not earlier encountered.

Consistent with predictions, von Hippel and Baker (1993) found that subjects had better implicit memory for positive traits when they were used to describe a Nazi, and better implicit memory for negative traits when they were used to describe a Peace Corps worker. An index of the valence of subjects' implicit memory was then computed by dividing the number of negative traits that subjects provided on the memory task from the sum of the number of positive and negative traits that subjects provided on the memory task. When this measure was regressed simultaneously with the nature of the source (either Nazi or Peace Corps worker) on subjects' final impressions of Hans, a significant negative beta weight emerged for the implicit memory measure, indicating that implicit memory for incongruent information was significantly associated with congruent evaluations. Thus, independent of the nature of the source, the more negative information about Hans that subjects remembered, the more they liked him.

These results suggest that people engage in increased elaborative processing when they encounter incongruent information. These results further suggest that it is not necessary to postulate an associative consequence of elaboration in order to explain increased memory for incongruent information. Rather, elaborative processing itself seems sufficient to cause increased memory for incongruent information. Furthermore, because elaborative processing also leads to change of meaning or discounting of incongruent information, a (seemingly) negative relationship arises between memory and judgment. To the perceiver, enhanced memory for incongruent information is actually enhanced memory for information that once seemed incongruent, but upon reflection revealed itself to be either irrelevant or congruent with the original expectancy. Because so many social behaviors are inherently ambiguous (Trope, 1986, 1989), this sort of change of meaning process and the resultant pseudodissociation between memory and judgment are likely to be quite common.

2. Encoding Incongruent Information That Is Extreme or Unambiguous

The question remains, however, as to what happens when perceivers encounter incongruent information that is sufficiently extreme to be unambiguous and relatively unavailable to reinterpretation. One line of research by Maass and her colleagues (Maass, Salvi, Arcuri, & Semin, 1989, described below) suggests that people simply fail to make abstractions from information when it is clearly incongruent with their stereotypes or expectancies. Such a finding is important because it suggests that people would tend to have poor memory for clearly incongruent information, by virtue of their failure to engage in elaborative encoding strategies. In order to examine the impact of such a possibility on people's memory for incongruent information, Sekaquaptewa and von Hippel (1994) presented subjects with what appeared to be newspaper articles describing events that were either stereotype-congruent or stereotype-incongruent. Specifically, subjects read about either an African-American or Caucasian male (manipulated via an attached picture) who won a spelling bee or a track meet. The spelling bee winner was planning to attend M.I.T. to become a physicist, and the track star was described as one of the best natural athletes in the state. In this way, the behaviors were designed to be sufficiently extreme so that they could not be reinterpreted as evidence of stupidity or poor athletic ability, nor could they be discounted. Furthermore, because the events were presented as newspaper articles that appeared legitimate, subjects could not explain away the incongruent events as unrealistic or hypothetical.

In order to measure cognitive processing on-line, subjects attempted to tap a regular pace on a keypad attached to a timer box while they read the bogus newspaper articles. To the extent that subjects were devoting a lot of cognitive activity to the encoding of the articles, they should show disruptions in this secondary task performance. That is, their tapping rates should become slowed or irregular when they were devoting considerable attention to the articles (Kahneman, 1973; Michon, 1966; see also, Macrae et al., 1994). When subjects finished reading the articles, they attempted to recall the information, and were given the Modern Racism Scale in order to assess level of prejudice.

Consistent with predictions, Sekaquaptewa and von Hippel (1994) found a three-way interaction on the recall measure between level of prejudice, type of story, and race of target (see Fig. 4). This three-way interaction was composed of a mild memory incongruency effect among low-prejudice subjects, and a strong memory congruency among high-prejudice subjects. An interaction also emerged between level of prejudice and race of target, such that low-prejudice subjects tended to have better recall for the behaviors of the African-American target, and high-prejudice subjects tended to have better recall for the behaviors of the Caucasian target. Finally, low-prejudice subjects' tapping speeds were predictive of their memory scores, in that slowed tapping was associated with

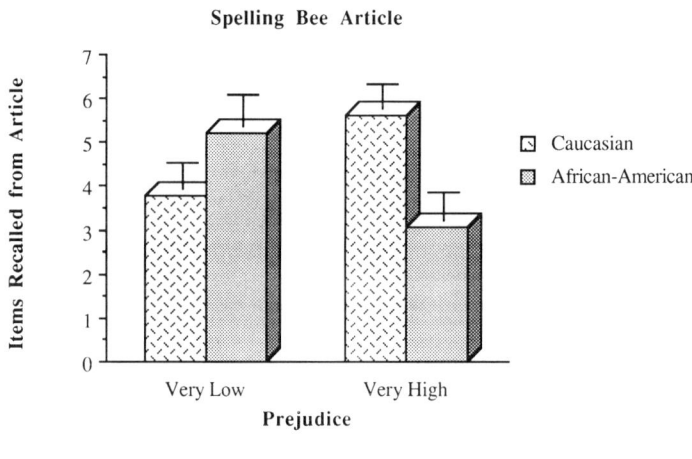

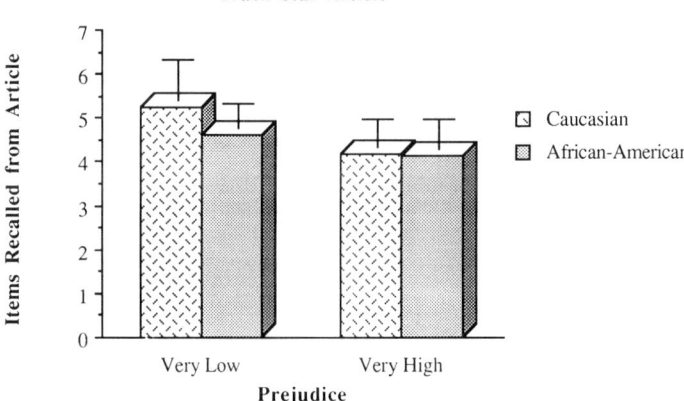

Fig. 4. Recall for information from the "spelling bee" story and the "track star" story as a function of level of prejudice. (From Sekaquaptewa and von Hippel, 1994.)

better recall, whereas high-prejudice subjects' tapping speeds were unassociated with their recall.

These results suggest that high- and low-prejudice individuals respond very differently to unambiguous stereotype-incongruent information. Low-prejudice individuals seemed to integrate incongruent information in an effortful fashion, as they showed better memory for incongruent information and their on-line measure of cognitive load predicted their memorial performance. High-prejudice individuals, on the other hand, seemed simply to ignore incongruent information. In fact, they seemed to ignore a substantial portion of the information that was presented about African-Americans, whether it was congruent or incongruent with their stereotypes. These results suggest divergent patterns of responding to incongruency on the part of low- and high-prejudice individuals, with different consequences for memory or judgment. If one conceives of level of prejudice as a personality variable that is stable over time, it seems likely that the strategies that high-prejudice individuals adopted reflect long-term individual differences in the way that they encode and evaluate out-group members.

Summary

• Perceivers selectively encode information about group members in a way that highlights those factors that best differentiate members of one group from members of another. This selective encoding is facilitated by an elaborative encoding process, whereby perceivers mentally generate stereotype-congruent images as they attempt to understand stereotype-relevant behaviors. These images are then sufficiently integrated with the images that were actually perceived so that the perceiver can no longer differentiate between the two.

• When perceivers encounter information that is moderately incongruent with their stereotypes, they encode this information effortfully in order to reinterpret it in a stereotype-congruent manner. This effortful encoding leads to facilitation in memory of the (erstwhile) incongruent information.

• When prejudiced perceivers encounter information that is unambiguously incongruent with their stereotypes, they encode this information in such a fashion as to make it less memorable than it is for nonprejudiced perceivers.

B. ATTRIBUTIONAL PROCESSES

Attributional processes are relatively effortless or automatic components of the way that people encode information about each other (e.g., Carlston & Skowronski, 1994; Newman & Uleman, 1989; Winter & Uleman, 1984; Winter, Uleman, & Cuniff, 1985). Attributions can also be effortful, however, as when people encounter target persons who behave in a manner that is inconsistent with their prior expectancies (e.g., Hastie, 1984; Pyszczynski & Greenberg, 1981). Such processes are initiated at encoding by the incongruency, and are an important determinant of impressions that are formed. Furthermore, these effortful attributional processes tend to be highly sophisticated, in which a variety of processes converge to bias the attributional outcome in stereotype-congruent ways.

Perceivers can respond in a variety of ways when a person's behavior violates their expectancies or preferences. At the most basic level, perceivers can simply refuse to make any inferences at all when confronted with incongruency. For example, in Maass et al.'s (1989) experiment, subjects from rival neighborhoods in a small Italian village were presented with cartoons depicting in-group and out-group members engaging in unambiguous socially desirable and undesirable behaviors. Subjects were asked to describe the behavior that the in-group or out-group member was engaging in. Maass et al. found that positive behaviors of in-group members and negative behaviors of out-group members were described more abstractly than negative behaviors of in-group members and positive behaviors of out-group members. That is, subjects tended to describe stereotype-congruent (or perhaps preference-congruent) events in terms of relevant trait concepts (e.g., "Person A is violent"), but stereotype-incongruent events in terms of the actual behaviors, which might conceivably imply a variety of traits (e.g., "Person A hit Person B"). Thus, subjects made no inferences from behaviors that were contrary to their expectations (or preferences), but made and communicated inferences from behaviors that were congruent with their expectations.[7]

This proclivity to make abstractions only when encoding behaviors that are stereotype-congruent is important for two reasons. First, when making memory-based judgments people tend to remember and rely on their abstractions in place of the original behaviors that led to the abstractions (see Reder, 1982; Srull & Wyer, 1989). Because abstractions do not contain the details of the original information, it becomes difficult if not impossible for perceivers later to reinterpret the behaviors that led to the abstractions. Second, and somewhat relatedly, abstractly encoded information tends to be more resistant to disconfirmation and more stable over time than information that is encoded at a specific level (Semin & Fiedler, 1988). Because abstractions play these important roles in memory and judgment, the Maass et al. findings suggest that perceivers are more likely to remember, believe, rely on, and communicate stereotype-congruent

---

[7] A partial mechanism for this finding may lie in the research of Fein, Hilton, and Miller (1990), who demonstrated that people are unwilling to make dispositional inferences when they are suspicious of a target's motives. To the extent that subjects in the Maass et al. experiments might have been suspicious of the motives of out-group members who were engaged in seemingly positive acts, they would be relatively unwilling to infer anything from these behaviors. In support of this logic, Crocker, Voekl, Testa, and Major (1991) have demonstrated that African-Americans tend to be suspicious of their interactions with Caucasians, and thus unlikely to accept at face-value negative *or* positive feedback from Caucasians.

information than stereotype-incongruent information. In this regard, the Maass et al. (1989) findings also provide a possible attributional mechanism for Sekaquaptewa and von Hippel's (1994) finding that high-prejudice individuals show poorer memory than low-prejudice individuals for events that are incongruent with their stereotypes.

It is critical to the Maass et al. experiments that subjects were not asked why the target individuals behaved as they did. In many situations, people are asked why a behavior occurred. Additionally, people often ponder this issue themselves when they encounter incongruency that is somewhat ambiguous in nature (Hastie, 1984; Pyszczynski & Greenberg, 1981). When the situation does induce attributional processing, people make very different types of inferences from stereotype-congruent versus stereotype-incongruent information. For example, people are more likely to infer dispositional causes for stereotype-congruent than incongruent behaviors (Deaux & Emswiller, 1974; Feldman-Summers & Kiesler, 1974; Yee & Eccles, 1988), even when congruent behaviors are normative for the situation (Kulik, 1983). Because the stereotype provides an available explanation for stereotype-congruent events, it can block people's ability to encode covariation between stereotype-irrelevant factors and the stereotype-congruent event (Sanbonmatsu, Akimoto, & Gibson, 1994).

Relatedly, and consistent with the Maass et al. findings, people are also more likely to infer dispositional causes for negative out-group and positive in-group behaviors than for positive out-group and negative in-group behaviors (Hewstone & Jaspars, 1984; Taylor & Jaggi, 1974). Pettigrew (1979) has labeled this tendency the "ultimate attribution error," and has proposed that it underlies a variety of in-group biases. In a test of this hypothesis, Chatman and von Hippel (1993) presented African-American and Caucasian subjects with a résumé of an African-American or Caucasian woman who had either been fired for absenteeism or laid off. Subjects were asked why they thought she had been fired or laid off, and whether the reason that they generated was caused by something about her personality or her situation. Subjects were then asked how willing they would be to hire her for a new position. An interaction emerged between subject race and applicant race on subjects' attributions, such that they generated situational attributions for the applicant's unemployment when she was an in-group member and dispositional attributions when she was an out-group member. An interaction also emerged for subjects' willingness to hire the applicant, such that subjects showed a hiring preference for members of their own race.[8] In order to

---

[8]In a prior experiment subjects were simply asked whether they would be willing to hire the applicant for a new position, and were not asked to generate reasons for her unemployment. This experiment revealed an in-group bias of approximately the same magnitude as that of the current experiment, suggesting that the act of generating reasons for her situation did not change subjects' responses to her.

assess the mediation of this preference, a path analysis was conducted in which the interaction between subject race and target race was regressed, along with subjects' attributional inferences, on their hiring preferences. Consistent with Pettigrew's (1979) theorizing about the ultimate attribution error, the path analyses revealed that subjects' increased willingness to hire in-group members was mediated by the type of attributions they made for her being fired or laid off (see Fig. 5).

As can be seen in Figure 5, when subjects' attributions were not included in the path analysis, a significant relationship emerged between the interaction of subject race and target race and willingness to hire the applicant. When subjects' attributions were included as a mediating variable in the analysis, however, the direct path between the interaction variable and willingness to hire the applicant was reduced by almost 50%, and was no longer significant (see Baron & Kenny, 1986). Thus, these analyses suggest that subjects' attributional patterns were mediating the extent to which they showed in-group biases in their hiring decisions.

3. Identification and Inferential Processes

Although the picture portrayed by this research on attributional biases seems relatively straightforward, Trope's (1986) research suggests that it is substantially more complex. According to Trope's model, attribution is a two-stage process, in which behaviors are first automatically identified, and then dispositional inferences are drawn (see also, Gilbert, Pelham, & Krull, 1988). Trope has argued that priors (expectancies, stereotypes, etc.) play a role not only in determining whether dispositional or situational attributions will be inferred from specific behaviors, but in determining the actual meaning of ambiguous behaviors as well. Because perceivers are unaware of the impact that their priors have on this behavioral identification stage, they are unable to sufficiently discount or augment their resultant inferences. For example, at a logical level it would seem that a perceiver who witnesses a person shove somebody when provoked would infer less dispositional hostility than a perceiver who witnesses a person shove somebody without provocation. According to Trope's model, however, the perceiver who witnesses the aggression in the presence of provocation will perceive the shove as more powerful than the perceiver who witnesses the aggression in the absence of provocation. Consequently, even if the perceiver attempts to discount for the provocation when making a dispositional inference, to the extent that the original behavior was perceived more extremely as a function of the context, the discounting is likely to be insufficient. For this reason, a person who shoves somebody in return may be seen as more aggressive than a person who shoves somebody without provocation.

A number of studies have provided support for just such a pattern of disposi-

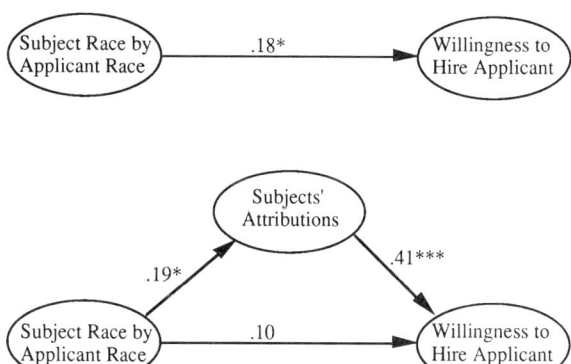

Fig. 5 Path analyses depicting the mediating role of attributions in subjects' in-group biases. *p < .05; *** p < .001. (From Chatman and von Hippel, 1993.)

tional inferences (e.g., Kruglanski, 1970; Trope, 1986; Trope, Cohen, & Alfieri, 1991). For example, Snyder and Frankel (1976) presented subjects with silent videotapes of two women being interviewed. Subjects were told that one interview concerned sexual topics and the other concerned political topics. Subjects who thought an interview was about sex perceived the woman as behaving more nervously on the tape, and importantly, inferred greater dispositional nervousness on her part than subjects who thought the interview was about politics. It seems that the same behavior (e.g., shifting of weight or failure to make eye contact) that was interpreted as evidence of nervousness by "sex" subjects was interpreted as evidence of boredom by "politics" subjects. Then, when evaluating how dispositionally nervous the woman was, subjects seemed unaware that they had interpreted the original behaviors differently as a function of context, and thus did not discount sufficiently for their prior knowledge of the discussion topic.

Importantly, this influence of context on identification and inferences only emerged when subjects were aware of the discussion topics prior to viewing the videotapes. When subjects were told of the topics after viewing the tapes they showed the opposite pattern, judging the woman to be less dispositionally nervous when she discussed sex than when she discussed politics. This finding suggests that when "priors" are not available at encoding, they cannot influence the (largely unconscious) identification process, but they still have an impact on the (largely conscious) process by which people infer dispositions from behaviors. Thus, it seems that as a consequence of the role played by expectancies and stereotypes in behavioral identification, the attributions that people make on-line as they encode the information are fundamentally different from those made at retrieval.

If priors can influence behavioral identification, and if identification of one interactant's behaviors can influence the identification of others, Trope's model (1986) provides a unique method for studying implicit stereotyping (see Greenwald & Banaji, in press). The model allows one to make predictions about how the identification of the behavior of one member of an interaction should influence the identification of the behaviors of others. In a test of this possibility, Vargas and von Hippel (1993) presented high- and low-prejudice subjects (measured via the Modern Racism Scale) with a videotape of a confrontation between two men, in which one man demands money from the other and the other complies. Half of the subjects witnessed an African-American male make this demand, and half witnessed a Caucasian male make this demand. The videotaped segment of the person giving the money was always an identical clip, interleaved with the other, of a Caucasian male reaching into his pocket and handing over an unidentifiable amount of cash. Vargas and von Hippel asked subjects how threatening the man was when he demanded the money and how meek the other man was when he complied.

Due to the reactive nature of this question concerning threat, it seemed unlikely that high-prejudice subjects would indicate that they perceived the African-American as more threatening than he was perceived by low-prejudice subjects. In contrast to the transparent nature of this question, however, subjects are unlikely to have noticed the importance of their answer to the question concerning the meekness of the man who provided the money. To the extent that high-prejudice subjects relied on their stereotypes to identify the behavior of the African-American as threatening, they should be likely to perceive the person who provided the money as *not particularly meek*. In this regard, responses to the meekness question provide an implicit measure of stereotyping.

By way of explanation, consider a person who gives his money to a stranger wielding a gun in a dark alley. This person would be considered a lot less meek than a person who gives his money to an unintimidating individual standing in the middle of a well-lit street. After all, any thinking person would give his money to a gun-wielding requester, so one would discount this behavior, and it would not seem particularly meek (Kelley, 1972). Many people would refuse to give their money to an unarmed requester, however, so this behavior would be likely to seem relatively meek. To the extent that high-prejudice subjects perceive African-American males as inherently threatening and dangerous, they should view giving money to an African-American as synonymous to giving money to an armed assailant—any thinking individual would do so and thus it is not indicative of meekness.

Consistent with this logic, high-prejudice subjects reported that the behavior of the African-American requester was no more threatening than it was perceived by low-prejudice subjects. Nevertheless, high-prejudice subjects reported that the man who provided the money to the African-American, but not to the Caucasian, was less meek than he was perceived by low-prejudice subjects (see Fig. 6).

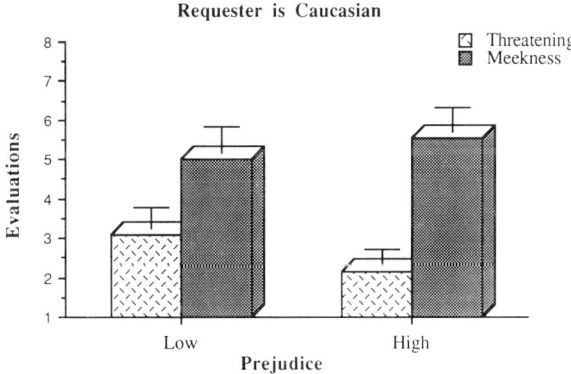

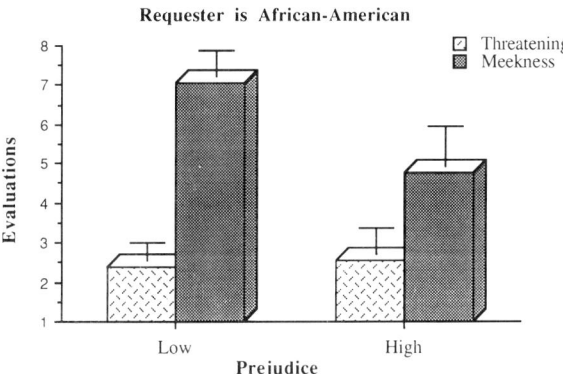

Fig. 6. Ratings of how threatening the man was who requested the money and how meek the man was who gave the money. (From Vargas and von Hippel, 1993.)

This finding suggests that high-prejudice subjects perceived the African-American as more threatening than he was perceived by low-prejudice subjects. There are two implications of this finding that are noteworthy in this context: First, it suggests that as a group, individuals who indicate little or no racial prejudice on personality scale ratings really do perceive African-Americans differently from those who indicate substantial prejudice on such scales. Thus, it is not simply a response bias or differential willingness to report negative attitudes toward African-Americans that leads people to score differently on such scales. Rather, the responses of at least some of the people on such scales seem to underlie actual differences in beliefs.

Second, these findings provide a mechanism by which people can reinstantiate their stereotypic interpretations of an individual, even if those interpretations have long been forgotten. Specifically, as Trope (1986) proposes, "the results of the identification process serve as input for dispositional inference processes wherein causal schemas guide backward inference of personal dispositions" (p. 253). Thus, when people retrieve from memory an interracial interaction such as the one described above, if they remember that the person who gave over the money was not particularly meek, they may reinfer that the person who requested the money must have been relatively dangerous. This inference would serve to maintain the original stereotype, but because it is made on the basis of the Caucasian's and not the African-American's behavior, it would seem like a justified conclusion and not a racist reaction. It awaits future research to determine whether people make such backward inferences from one individual to another based on their behavioral identifications, and whether these interindividual inferences serve to justify prejudiced responses or reflections.

Summary

• Perceivers encode information that is unambiguously incongruent with their stereotypes in a less abstract fashion than information that is congruent with their stereotypes. These encoding strategies may provide a mechanism for the finding that prejudiced perceivers show poorer memory than nonprejudiced perceivers for unambiguously stereotype-incongruent information.

• Perceivers encode stereotype-congruent behaviors in dispositional terms and stereotype-incongruent behaviors in situational terms. This attributional tendency seems to underlie in-group bias.

• The way that perceivers encode stereotype-relevant behaviors of one person in an interaction can influence the way that perceivers identify behaviors of other members of the interaction. Assessment of these identifications can provide an unobtrusive measure of stereotypic processing.

C. PREFERENCE, BIAS, AND ASSIMILATION EFFECTS

Perceivers assimilate their perceptions of individuals and behaviors to prior conceptions and stereotypes for both cognitive and affective reasons, but typically through cognitive mechanisms. It is the rare individual who can decide that the world is as it should be in the absence of any supporting evidence. Rather, people engage in various cognitive strategies in order to find or generate support for their preferred worldview. Sometimes people are relatively skeptical of incongruent evidence but relatively accepting of congruent evidence (Lord, Ross, & Lepper, 1979). Other times people dismiss incongruent information as situationally determined but accept congruent information as dispositionally diagnostic (Chatman & von Hippel, 1993). Still other times people simply continue to seek additional evidence in an effort to find some support for their desired beliefs (Ditto & Lopez, 1993). Thus, although it is clear that preferences have a biasing impact on evaluations, the mechanism of this bias tends to be a cognitive one.

Furthermore, our research indicates that locus of this bias is at encoding rather than retrieval. For example, in an experiment by Vargas, von Hippel, Fein, and Darr (1994) subjects were presented with a partner who evaluated them either negatively or positively. Half of the subjects learned of their partner's evaluation before receiving background information about him, and half did not learn of his evaluation until after receiving this background information. Vargas et al. found an interaction between type and timing of feedback, such that subjects rated their partner more extremely when they were aware of his evaluation before learning about his background than when they were unaware of his evaluation until after they had learned about his background. Subjects who received positive feedback liked their partner slightly more when they knew about this feedback prior to encoding his background information, and subjects who received negative feedback liked their partner significantly less when they knew about this feedback prior to encoding his background information.

It appears from such experiments that preferences and affect exert an influence on judgment by changing the nature of people's encoding strategies. For example, once affect is aroused perceivers are more likely to form category-based rather than individuated impressions, seemingly as a consequence of accompanying decrements in attentional resources (Wilder & Shapiro, 1989; see also Holmes, Zanna, & Whitehead, 1986). Additionally, perceivers who form affect-based impressions of others are more likely to change their impressions when presented with affectively rather than cognitively incongruent information (Edwards & von Hippel, in press). Often, as in these examples, affect is explicit to the situation. Other times, it is merely presumed to underlie cognitive processing in the form of a motivation to maintain existing beliefs or perceive consistency in the environment. It is this sort of presumed affect that probably underlies most of the encoding strategies described in this chapter, as well as many of the assimilation effects that are commonly found in research on stereotyping.

1. Assimilation and Contrast

Similar to the way that an eight-pound weight is judged to weigh more than eight pounds in the context of a ten-pound weight, but less than eight pounds in the context of a six-pound weight, individuals typically seem more similar to their reference group than they really are. For example, an African-American seen shoving someone is perceived to be more hostile than a Caucasian engaging in the same behavior (Duncan, 1976; Sagar & Schofield, 1980). Although a relatively articulate African-American is judged more positively than a similar Caucasian, a relatively inarticulate African-American is judged more negatively than a similar Caucasian (Linville & Jones, 1980; see also Jussim, Coleman, & Lerch, 1987). Similarly, a poor child who answers a few questions incorrectly is perceived as less intelligent than a wealthy child who misses the same questions (Darley & Gross, 1983). Such findings point to the power that stereotypes have to influence encoding in stereotype-consistent ways, but because the stereotypes existed before subjects arrived at the laboratory, it is difficult to know the absolute extent of the assimilation effects that emerged. For example, such studies typically do not (nor were they intended to) indicate whether individuals are assimilated to stereotypes even when their behavior is completely outside the range of the stereotype.

In order to answer such questions, and develop a more fine-grained analysis of contrast and assimilation effects, some researchers have turned to generating artificial stereotypes in the laboratory. Because such stereotypes are formed entirely from new information with a known distribution, laboratory-based stereotypes can provide more precise estimates of the preconditions that lead to contrast and assimilation effects. Manis and his colleagues have developed a substantial research program directed toward delimiting assimilation and contrast effects through the use of laboratory-generated stereotypes (e.g., see Manis et al., 1988; Manis & Paskewitz, 1984a, 1984b; Manis, Paskewitz, & Cotler, 1986). In a prototypical example of such experiments, Manis et al. (1988) presented subjects with a series of word definitions that were said to originate from two different hospitals. For some subjects the definitions from one hospital were all high in pathology, whereas the definitions from the other hospital were all low in pathology; this induction series led to nonoverlapping stereotypes of the two hospitals. For other subjects the definitions from one hospital ranged from high to midrange in pathology, whereas the definitions from the other hospital ranged from normal to midrange in pathology; this induction series led to overlapping stereotypes of the two hospitals (see Table I for high-, midrange-, and low-pathology definitions). Subjects were then presented with pairs of midrange definitions, one from each of the two hospitals, and were asked which of the two definitions was more pathological.

Manis et al. found that when subjects had induced nonoverlapping stereotypes, they contrasted the midrange items away from the associated hospital label. In terms of their methodology, this meant that subjects rated the midrange item associated with the pathological hospital as less pathological than the midrange item associated with the normal hospital. When subjects had induced overlapping stereotypes, however, the opposite pattern emerged, as they assimilated the midrange items to the associated hospital label (for related findings, see also Herr, 1986; Herr, Sherman, & Fazio, 1983; Wilder & Thompson, 1988). Because Manis et al. relied on a paired-comparison method to determine how

TABLE I
High, Midrange, and Low Pathology Definitions[a]

Word	Definition
	High pathology
Fable	Trade good sheep to hide in the beginning.
Mosaic	A stone place to put people, death.
Cushion	To sleep on a pillow of God's sheep.
	Middle pathology
Seclude	To hide, remove from probing eyes.
Spangle	Means of bright like star spangles.
Pewter	Something that don't smell so good.
	Low pathology
Cushion	A padded item used for comfort.
Gamble	Take a chance, a risk.
Bacon	Product of a pig.

[a]From Manis, Nelson, and Shedler (1988).

pathological the midrange items were perceived to be, it seems likely that the contrast and assimilation effects that emerged were at the level of subjects' representations of the items, and not simply in their use of labels or scales at the response stage (see Biernat & Manis, 1994; Biernat, Manis, & Nelson, 1991).

Although this research from the Manis laboratory indicates that stereotypes lead to contrast of behaviors that are outside the distribution of the stereotype, Hilton and von Hippel (1990) proposed that these results may be moderated by the nature of the stereotype. Hilton and von Hippel argued that stereotypes concerning hospital members might be associated with a rather low expectation of internal consistency. As proposed by Srull (1981) and others (e.g., Stern et al., 1984), Hilton and von Hippel suggested that people expect relatively little internal consistency from such loosely knit groups as hospitals because there is no reason to believe that all members should be psychologically alike. In contrast to this situation, the hallmark of most real stereotypes is that people perceive outgroup members as relatively homogeneous (see Linville & Jones, 1980; Ostrom & Sedikides, 1992; Judd & Park, 1988; Quattrone, 1986; Quattrone & Jones, 1980). Consequently, people feel some pressure to perceive the behaviors of outgroup members as similar to one another, because the psychological disposition underlying the behaviors is thought to be relatively homogeneous across the group. For this reason, it seemed that subjects would experience less pressure in the Manis paradigm to assimilate individual behaviors to their associated stereotypes than might be experienced with real stereotypes. Thus, behaviors that were outside the distribution of expected behaviors from a particular hospital were contrasted away from that hospital rather than assimilated to it, even though assimilation might have emerged had such discrepant behaviors been associated with real stereotypes.

In order to test this hypothesis, Hilton and von Hippel (1990) ran a pair of experiments in which stereotypes were created in the laboratory. In the first experiment, subjects were presented with the identical behaviors and hospital labels that were used by Manis et al. (1988). As in Manis et al.'s experiment, subjects were led to induce either overlapping or nonoverlapping distributions of the two hospitals by presenting them with either pathological items from one hospital and normal items from the other (nonoverlapping), or pathological and midrange items from one hospital and normal and midrange items from the other (overlapping). Subjects were then presented with midrange items associated with one of the two hospital labels and were asked to rate these items. In a replication of Manis et al., assimilation of the midrange items emerged with overlapping distributions and contrast of the midrange items emerged with nonoverlapping distributions. In this experiment, however, subjects had also been asked whether the label might have been incorrectly assigned; that is, whether the patient labeled as coming from one hospital might really have come from the other. When the distributions were overlapping, subjects tended to accept both hospital labels for patients who produced behaviors at a moderate level of pathology. When the distributions were nonoverlapping, however, subjects tended to reject both hospital labels for patients at a moderate level of pathology. Furthermore, subjects' acceptance or rejection of the labels mediated the extent to which they assimilated or contrasted the midrange definitions. Midrange items associated with accepted labels were assimilated to the category label, and midrange items associated with rejected labels were contrasted away from the category label.

These results suggest that perceptions of discrepancy with the category label determined whether the individual items were contrasted away or assimilated to the category. The goal of the second experiment was to manipulate such perceptions of discrepancy by varying subjects' expectations of internal consistency from the source of the behaviors. Hilton and von Hippel (1990) reasoned that when subjects expected high levels of consistency from a source, they would attempt to minimize any discrepancy that appeared between the individual items and the category labels. When subjects expected low levels of consistency from a source, however, they would be unlikely to minimize or dismiss such discrepancy. In order to test this possibility, some subjects were told that the sources were two different groups of individuals who happened to have last names that begin with letters in the same half of the alphabet (low expectation of internal consistency), some subjects were told that the sources were two different extended families (moderate expectation of internal consistency), and some subjects were told that the sources were two different individuals (high expectation of internal consistency). In the stereotype-induction phase, subjects were presented with pathological items from one source and normal items from the other, inducing nonoverlapping distributions. In the test phase, subjects were presented with items at a moderate level of pathology, and were asked to rate the items.

Consistent with the first experiment, subjects contrasted midrange items away from the label when the sources were described as two alphabet groups. When the sources were described as two families, however, subjects neither contrasted nor assimilated the midrange items, and when the sources were two individuals, subjects assimilated the midrange items to the individuals with whom they were associated (see Fig. 7). Thus, this experiment suggests that when expectations of internal consistency are raised to a sufficiently high level, relatively incongruent behaviors will no longer be perceived as discrepant and will be assimilated to the source with whom they are associated.

Natural groups are likely to vary in the extent to which consistency is expected from group members. Very large and heterogeneous groups (such as females or African-Americans) are likely to be associated with lower expectations of internal consistency than smaller and more homogeneous groups (such as tax accountants or football players). Importantly, by virtue of their seeming homogeneity, out-groups will tend to be associated with higher levels of perceived internal consistency than in-groups. Thus, there should be a greater tendency to assimilate incongruent behaviors to out-group members than to in-group members. Given that factors such as expected competition with an out-group can increase the magnitude of the out-group homogeneity effect (Judd & Park, 1988), it seems likely that differences in the tendency to perceive internal consistency emerge as a function of factors that influence overall impressions of out-groups. Thus, individual differences in perceptions of internal consistency are probably

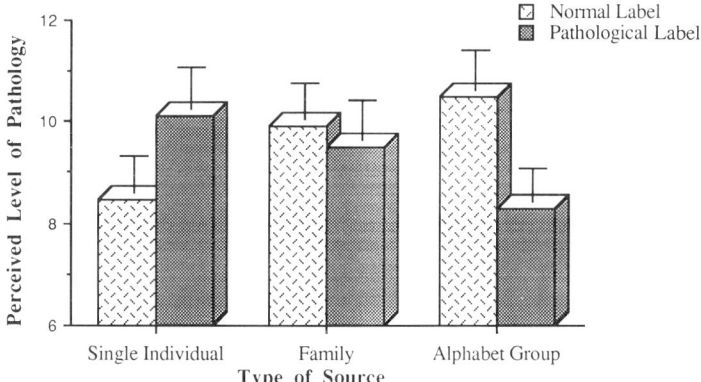

Fig. 7. Ratings of pathology of midrange definitions associated with either a single individual, a family, or an alphabet group. (From Hilton and von Hippel, 1990.)

associated with level of prejudice (cf. Judd & Park, 1988; Park & Rothbart, 1982), experience with the source (Linville, Salovey, & Fischer, 1986), and so forth. Extending the findings of Hilton and von Hippel (1990), one could then infer that prejudiced individuals would be more likely to assimilate incongruent behaviors to their stereotypes than nonprejudiced individuals, and people who have little experience with out-group members would be more likely to assimilate incongruent behaviors to their stereotypes than those who have a lot of experience with out-group members.

Summary

• By selectively encoding information, perceivers increase their chances of arriving at a preference-consistent impression of others.

• As perceivers expect greater internal consistency from group members, they increase their tendency to assimilate incongruent behaviors to the group norm. This process enables people to encode moderately incongruent behaviors as congruent with the group stereotype, while simultaneously maintaining their perceptions of internal consistency within the group.

D. ATTENTIONAL PROCESSES

By definition, attention is selective. Because we are continually bombarded by the environment, we select information that seems worth encoding and we ignore the rest. The environment can impinge upon attention uninvited (if one were to sit on a tack), and attention can draw out a bland environment (if one were to concentrate on a body part, such as a shoulder blade, that is not otherwise transmitting any sensation), but most of the time the perceiver and the environment interact to determine what is attended to and what is ignored (see James, 1890).[9] For example, novel objects tend to receive more perceptual and conceptual processing than familiar objects (e.g., Friedman, 1979), whereas familiar objects tend to be more difficult *not* to process than novel objects (Bargh, 1982; Johnston, 1978). Of course, both familiarity and novelty result from an interaction between perceiver and environment.

Characteristics of objects that draw attention (e.g., intensity, movement, complexity, and novelty, see Berlyne, 1958; Jeffrey, 1968) also play a role in person perception. For example, individuals under a bright spotlight, rocking in a rocking chair, or wearing a boldly patterned shirt draw more attention than control

---

[9]Although information that impinges upon the senses is still encoded even when it does not receive conscious attention (see Greenwald, 1992; Johnston & Dark, 1986), conscious attention makes encoded information much more available to intentional identification and retrieval (e.g., Rock & Guttman, 1981).

persons (McArthur & Post, 1977). More germane to stereotyping, people who are in the minority in their immediate social surroundings, by virtue of race, gender, or some other physical marker, attract more attention than their majority group counterparts (Taylor & Fiske, 1978). Furthermore, because it is minority group membership that attracts attention, people tend to perceive the behaviors of minority group members as being caused by their minority status (cf. Arkin & Duval, 1975). As a consequence, minority group members tend to be perceived in a stereotypic fashion (e.g., Heilman, 1980; Taylor, Fiske, Etcoff, & Ruderman, 1978). For example, S. Taylor et al. (1978) found that as the ratio of women to men in a discussion group decreased, female speakers were rated as more stereotypically female, whereas as the ratio of men to women in a discussion group decreased, male speakers were rated as more stereotypically male (see also, Nesdale & Dharmalingam, 1986; Nesdale, Dharmalingam, & Kerr, 1987).

Research on the perception of covariation has revealed results that are conceptually similar to the S. Taylor et al. findings concerning the salience of minority group members. Because minority group members are definitionally more distinct than majority group members, their behavior is inherently more noticeable at encoding (e.g., Hamilton & Gifford, 1976; S. Taylor et al., 1978). Additionally, negative behaviors are perceived as more distinct than positive behaviors, and consequently are more noticeable as well (e.g., Fiske, 1980; Kanouse & Hanson, 1972; Pratto & John, 1991; Skowronski & Carlston, 1987, 1989). In conjunction, the increased distinctiveness at encoding of both minority group members and negative behaviors leads to the illusory perception of a correlation between the two. Indeed, such illusory correlations emerge any time distinctive events co-occur, as well as whenever people have *a priori* beliefs that events should be related (see Chapman & Chapman, 1967; Hamilton & Rose, 1980).

Although additional attention to minority group members can underlie stereotype formation (as in Hamilton & Gifford, 1976; S. Taylor et al., 1978), once the stereotype is formed this process tends to be reversed. That is, when the perceiver is already relying on a stereotype, additional (unbiased) attention typically leads to individuating processes, whereas reduction in attention is associated with category-based evaluations (Fiske & Neuberg, 1990). For example, Hilton, Klein, and von Hippel (1991) presented subjects with a pair of dossiers about two fifth-grade boys whom they were to evaluate. The description of one of the boys (hereafter referred to as the control child) was held constant across conditions, and he seemed a rather typical child although very little information was provided about him. For half of the subjects, the other boy (the experimental child) was depicted as an upper-middle-class child; his parents were well educated and employed, and a videotape showed him playing basketball in a well-appointed backyard. For the other half of the subjects, the experimental child was presented as coming from a rather impoverished background; his father was absent, his mother was a seamstress, and a videotape showed him playing basketball in a dirt yard in front of a burned-out van and a dilapidated trailer home.

Subjects were told that they would be hearing the two children's responses to a scholastic test played over a set of headphones. The performance of one child was played in one ear, and the performance of the other child was played in the other ear. Subjects' task in this experiment was to evaluate the performance of the two children. In order to determine which child they were attending to, they were told to indicate by pressing keys on a computer keyboard whether the child on the right or the left had answered a question correctly or not. This task provided an on-line measure of subjects' attention to the experimental child.

Orthogonal to the manipulation of social class, half of the subjects heard a test performance from the experimental child that began well but ended poorly, and half heard a test performance that began poorly but ended well. Because the high-socioeconomic status (SES) child would be expected to perform well and the low-SES child would be expected to perform poorly (Darley & Gross, 1983), this manipulation of test performance caused half of the subjects to be presented with a target who initially performed as expected and half to be presented with a target who initially performed contrary to expectations. Hilton et al. found that subjects paid more attention to the target when his initial performance was inconsistent with expectations than when his initial performance was consistent with expectations. Furthermore, the extremity of their final evaluations of the child was mediated by their attention to his performance—the more attention they paid him, the more moderate and complex were their evaluations.

Hilton et al.'s experiment provides evidence that not only do stereotypes inhibit attention to targets who behave in a stereotype-consistent manner (see also Belmore, 1987; White & Carlston, 1983), but also that decreased attention leads to assimilation to the stereotype, whereas increased attention leads to accommodation to the target. It is important to note that the attentional patterns of the subjects in this experiment were not necessarily biased or motivated by a desire to maintain expectancies. Rather, subjects were simply coping to the best of their ability with an attentionally demanding environment. Because subjects could not possibly attend simultaneously to both children, at some point they had to shift their attention from the one child to the other. Given the prior expectancy that a poor child will perform poorly (or a wealthy child will perform well), a logical integration between expectancy and performance would suggest that once the child has confirmed the expectancy, information of greater diagnosticity is likely to be gathered elsewhere. If the child initially disconfirms the expectancy, however, then the contradiction between expectancy and behavior would demand that additional information be gathered before a judgment can be made.

The consequence of this reasonable integration of individual behavior and prior information is that stereotypes lead to attentional patterns that are stereotype-confirming. As a function of whether the target child initially confirmed or disconfirmed their expectancies, subjects in Hilton et al. perceived the test performance differently. Path analyses confirmed that the identical performance was perceived differently across conditions as a consequence of the attentional strategies that subjects adopted. Because subjects failed to pay much attention when the wealthy child began well or the poor child began poorly, they perceived these two cases somewhat extremely. Because they paid rather close attention when the wealthy child began poorly or the poor child began well, they perceived these two cases more moderately. Given that most children perform at an average level, these results suggest that those who are expected to perform well will be perceived as performing from moderately to well, whereas those who are expected to perform poorly will be perceived as performing from moderately to poorly. Furthermore, this difference in perception will emerge even when performance is unambiguous, simply by virtue of the attentional strategies adopted by stereotyping perceivers.

It should be noted that these results have only been shown to emerge when the environment is attentionally demanding. As many researchers have argued, however, attentionally demanding environments are likely to be the norm in social situations (e.g., see Gilbert, Pelham, & Krull, 1988). Additionally, a cognitively lazy (miserly) perceiver would be likely to show such attentional effects even when the environment does not induce an information overload. Thus, a perceiver low in Need for Cognition (Cacioppo & Petty, 1982) or relatively unconcerned with accuracy, for example, would be likely to show the attentional patterns described above even when (s)he had sufficient attentional resources to attend fully to all of the targets in the social situation.

Summary

• Minority group members attract attention. Because it is their minority group membership that is perceptually salient, their behavior tends to be attributed to their minority status. This effect should be particularly strong with negative behaviors, which are more noticeable than positive behaviors. In this way, attentional patterns can facilitate the formation and maintenance of stereotypes.

• Once the stereotype is in place, perceivers pay less attention to group members who initially confirm the stereotype than group members who initially disconfirm the stereotype. As a consequence of these attentional patterns, perceivers can confirm their stereotypes even when members of different groups behave identically.

E. AUTOMATIC VERSUS CONTROLLED PROCESSES

Under the right circumstances, information processing becomes automatic, or relatively effortless, with extensive practice (Posner & Snyder, 1975; Schneider & Shiffrin, 1977; Shiffrin & Schneider, 1977). Whereas a great deal of effort and attention is required in the early stages of learning to drive, for example, after many years of practice people can often drive a familiar route without conscious attention to traffic signals, other automobiles, or even brake and clutch. Recently a number of theorists have proposed that automaticity develops in the activation and application of social stereotypes just as it does with the visual search and motor control tasks that underlie driving a car. Thus, it has been proposed that whenever people encounter one another, they automatically encode each other's membership in various social categories (e.g., see Brewer, 1988), and may thereby activate associated stereotypes.

Of the various models proposing automatic activation of stereotypes, Devine's (1989) is perhaps the most provocative and well known. In brief, Devine proposed that because our culture is suffused with information pertaining to the stereotype of African-Americans, activation of this stereotype becomes automatized at a young age for most Americans. Importantly, however, as people grow older and begin to evaluate and reflect on their beliefs, those who are not prejudiced learn to suppress or replace the automatically activated stereotypic thoughts in favor of more egalitarian ones. This suppression or replacement of stereotypic cognition is proposed to be an effortful, controlled process that requires conscious cognitive resources from the perceiver (but possibly becomes automatized itself as people get older and more practiced at it, thereby effectively negating any automatic activation that may or may not still take place).

Devine's theory is important both as a process model of stereotype activation and application, and for the implications that it has for stereotype use under a variety of circumstances. If group membership and the accompanying stereotypic information is automatically encoded whenever a member of a social category is encountered, the potential for that stereotype to influence later encoding and behavior is manifestly increased. Even if the perceiver is generally successful at inhibiting the stereotypic information that is activated, there will be a variety of predictable circumstances that will enable activation but not inhibition of the stereotype. Any time the perceiver's cognitive resources are sapped by heavy or multiple demands, the ability to suppress the stereotype will be hindered while the ability to activate it will continue relatively unimpeded. Thus, a busy teacher in the classroom will be likely to rely on race and gender stereotypes even if (s)he is not a racist or sexist person. Similarly, a person under the influence of alcohol will be likely to behave in a racist or sexist manner, even if such behaviors are completely discordant with his or her beliefs, simply by virtue of the cognitive deficits caused by alcohol in intentional but not automatic processing (von Hippel, Hawkins, & Fu, 1994).

1. Are Stereotypes Activated Automatically?

Although there is currently not much research concerning the automatic activation and subsequent suppression of stereotyping, the evidence that does exist seems to be largely supportive of Devine's theory. On the question of whether stereotypes can be activated automatically, the answer seems to be "yes." For example, conscious presentation of race-related words induces semantic priming of stereotypic traits (Dovidio, Evans, & Tyler, 1986; Gaertner & McLaughlin, 1983), and conscious presentation of occupational titles evokes visual imagery of stereotypic faces (Klatzky, Martin, & Kane, 1982). Because the stimulus onset asynchrony (SOA; the time elapsed from the beginning of the first presentation to the beginning of the second) was as rapid as 350 ms in Klatzky et al., and because the presentation of prime and target was simultaneous in Gaertner and McLaughlin (1983), the facilitation effects in these experiments seem to be under automatic rather than intentional control (see Neely, 1977).

More convincingly, it has been demonstrated that *nonconscious* presentation of age (Perdue & Gurtman, 1990) and gender (Klinger & Beall, 1992) information activates associated stereotypes. Furthermore, nonconscious priming of the category leads to equivalent activation of the stereotype among people who consciously endorse it and people who do not. Conscious priming of the category, on the other hand, leads to differential activation among people who express different attitudes toward the stereotyped group. For example, in the Klinger and Beall (1992) experiment, nonconscious priming of evaluatively neutral but gender-related words such as "female" and "woman" led to equivalent levels of stereotype activation among high- and low-sexism subjects, whereas conscious priming of "female" led to differential activation among high- and low-sexism subjects. Such findings are consistent with Devine's (1989, p. 6) proposal that "unintentional activation of the stereotype is equally strong and equally inescapable for high- and low-prejudice persons," at least at an aggregate level.

Despite the evidence that stereotypes are activated automatically, a recent paper has suggested that they may not be. In a clever pair of experiments, Gilbert and Hixon (1991) demonstrated that although cognitive busyness facilitates stereotype application (as proposed by Devine, 1989), it inhibits stereotype activation. This finding suggests that stereotypes require conscious attention and effort to be activated, and thus are not automatic. There are two important caveats, however, that must be considered with regard to the Gilbert and Hixon (1991) experiments.

First, Gilbert and Hixon were studying stereotypes concerning Asian-Americans, which are likely to be substantially different in automaticity from stereotypes concerning African-Americans and women studied by Devine (1989) and Klinger and Beall (1992). Recall that Devine proposed that stereotypes concerning African-Americans become automatic by virtue of their cultural ubiquity (the same can clearly be said for gender stereotypes). In support of this notion, children between the ages of five and seven have been shown to endorse stereotypes concerning African-Americans (see Allport, 1954; Katz, 1976, 1983; Porter, 1971; Proshansky, 1966), and to endorse gender stereotypes as early as age five (Biernat, 1991; Katz, 1983; Ruble & Stangor, 1986; Stangor & Ruble,

1987). Although different parts of the country are likely to be exposed to different amounts of information concerning the Asian-American stereotype, students at the University of Texas are not likely to have learned about such stereotypes until adolescence or perhaps even college. Furthermore, they probably have not been exposed to the Asian-American stereotype with anywhere near the regularity that stereotypic information is presented about African-Americans or women. Thus, it seems likely that whereas stereotypes toward African-Americans and women may be activated automatically among nearly all Americans, stereotypes toward other racial, ethnic, or religious groups will vary in their automaticity as a function of the amount, type, and duration of experience that people have had with the stereotype.

Second, in Gilbert and Hixon's experiments, subjects had no particular reason to engage in stereotypic processing. They were simply presented with a "research assistant," in a very tangential fashion, who was either Asian-American or Caucasian. In an effort to determine whether cognitively busy subjects in Gilbert and Hixon's experiments *could* have activated their stereotypes had they been more motivated to do so, Spencer and Fein (1994) relied on Gilbert and Hixon's paradigm and stimulus materials, but added a manipulation of threat to self-esteem (negative feedback on an intelligence test). Because motivation to stereotype is enhanced when people experience a threat to their self-esteem (Crocker & Luhtanen, 1990; Crocker, Thompson, & McGraw, 1987; Fein & Spencer, 1993; Lemyre & Smith, 1985; Wills, 1981), Spencer and Fein (1994) hypothesized that even cognitively busy subjects would activate their stereotype when they had been threatened. Consistent with this prediction, they found that although cognitively busy subjects who had not been threatened did not show any evidence of stereotype activation, cognitively busy subjects who had experienced a threat to their self-esteem did show evidence of activation of the Asian-American stereotype. Thus it seems that activation of stereotypes, even stereotypes of relatively low environmental prevalence, is accomplished with minimal cognitive resources by persons who are motivated to search for a basis of negative evaluation.

What can we conclude then from these seemingly disparate data? On the one hand, there is evidence that perception of gender and age information leads to stereotype activation even when that information is presented nonconsciously. On the other hand, perception of an Asian-American does not lead to stereotype activation when people are cognitively busy unless they have strong motivation to engage in downward social comparison. The solution to this seeming discrepancy lies in the complex, conditional nature of automaticity. As Bargh (1989) has pointed out, automaticity is not a unitary construct (see also Logan, 1988, 1990). Rather, there are different types of automaticity that require different levels of processing on the part of the perceiver. It seems likely that stereotypes concerning African-Americans, women, and older persons are at the level of *pre-*

conscious automaticity, in that conscious awareness of this information is not necessary to activate the stereotype. Stereotypes that are less prevalent, such as those toward Asian-Americans, seem likely to be at the level of *goal-dependent* automaticity, in that the perceiver must have a specific goal (e.g., denigration) for the stereotype to be activated automatically. Thus, it seems likely that stereotypes become increasingly automatic as the perceiver gains experience with them. Some stereotypes do not require conscious awareness of a target person to be activated, others probably require at least minimal awareness, and still others require a specific cognitive or motivational goal.

2. Do Nonprejudiced Individuals Inhibit Stereotype Activation?

To the question of whether nonprejudiced people suppress or replace their stereotypic thoughts once they are activated, the answer is "probably." First of all, prejudiced and nonprejudiced people report very different attitudes about African-Americans when directly asked about their beliefs (Devine, 1989; Kinder & Sears, 1981; McConahay, Hardee, & Batts, 1981; McConahay & Hough, 1976; Taylor, Sheatsley, & Greeley, 1978). Such evidence, however, is open to criticisms concerning social desirability and response biases (Brigham, 1971; Gaertner, 1976; Sigall & Page, 1971). That is, it is possible that nonprejudiced people in these experiments did not suppress or replace their stereotypic cognitions, but rather simply chose not to report them. For this reason, more convincing evidence for the question concerning the suppression or replacement of stereotypic cognitions comes from research in which stereotyping is assessed indirectly. To the extent that differences emerge between high- and low-prejudice subjects when their stereotypes are assessed indirectly, such differences indicate that at least some percentage of low-prejudice subjects are indeed suppressing or replacing their automatically activated stereotypic cognitions.

Two studies described in earlier sections of this chapter bear directly on this issue. Recall that Vargas and von Hippel (1993) found that high- and low-prejudice subjects responded similarly when they were directly asked how threatening an African-American male was. When their evaluations were assessed indirectly, however, by asking for their opinions about another member of the interaction, low-prejudice subjects' responses indicated that they felt the African-American male was less threatening than he was perceived by high-prejudice subjects. Because subjects are unlikely to have known that their evaluations of one member of an interaction were indicative of their feelings toward the other, this experiment indicates that high- and low-prejudice people really do view African-Americans differently.

In a slightly different vein, Sekaquaptewa and von Hippel (1994) found that a memory incongruency effect (i.e., better memory for stereotype-incongruent information) emerged among low-prejudice subjects, but a memory congruency effect emerged among high-prejudice subjects. Because people show better memory for incongruent information when they have weak to moderate expectancies, and better memory for congruent information when they have strong expectancies (for a meta-analytic review, see Stangor & McMillan, 1992), this finding suggests that racial stereotypes are held more tenuously by low-prejudice than high-prejudice individuals. Thus, it seems that the egalitarian responses provided by low-prejudice individuals on surveys and personality scales really do reflect a difference, on the whole, between their beliefs and those of high-prejudice individuals. In conjunction with the data concerning automatic activation of stereotypes among high-prejudice and low-prejudice individuals, these findings suggest that people who are not prejudiced must indeed be suppressing or replacing their stereotypic cognitions.

Summary

• Stereotypes can be automatically activated when perceivers encounter members of stereotyped groups. When the stereotype is automatically activated at encoding, it has a much greater chance of influencing perceptions and interpretations of out-group members.

• Not all stereotypes have an equal probability of being automatically activated at encoding. Rather, those stereotypes with which people have greater familiarity are more likely to be activated automatically. Stereotypes with which people do not have much familiarity seem not to be activated automatically unless the perceiver has a goal that can be fulfilled by stereotyping.

• Nonprejudiced perceivers differ from their prejudiced counterparts in that they suppress or replace their automatically activated stereotypes.

IV. Prejudice as Encoding Processes

The viewpoint that stereotypes exert their influence at encoding has important implications for the way we view the nature of prejudice. Currently, prejudice is conceived as evaluative content: high- and low-prejudice individuals are differentiated on the basis of their valenced beliefs concerning members of a particular out-group. These beliefs tend to be assessed on self-report personality scales, which have the advantage of being easy to administer, but the disadvantage of being transparent to many individuals, and hence subject to social desirability pressures. Indeed, racism and sexism scales that result in a useful range at some universities provide only floor effects at many others (e.g., Etling, 1993; LeCount, Marayuma, Peterson, Petersen-Lane, & Thomsen, 1992). Additionally, it is not clear what percentage of the people who endorse "sexist" or "racist" responses on such scales are indeed sexist or racist individuals, rather than simply traditional or politically conservative (see Sniderman, Piazza, Tetlock, & Kendrick, 1991; Sniderman & Tetlock, 1986). Furthermore, it seems likely that there are differences in the tendency to apply stereotypes even among people who hold identically prejudiced attitudes toward members of a particular group. For example, although two people might hold equally negative attitudes toward Jews, one person might assimilate every Jew she meets to her stereotype, whereas the other abandons the stereotype at the slightest hint of incongruency. Consequently, rather than operationalizing prejudice in terms of evaluative content, or the type of attitudes an individual is willing and able to report, prejudice might be reconceptualized in terms of encoding processes, *or the proclivity of an individual to encode information in stereotype-congruent ways.*

Naturally, the suggestion that prejudice might be reconceptualized as process rather than evaluative content leads to the question of how this goal might be accomplished. We believe that a number of the studies reviewed in this chapter provide methodologies that could be adapted to enable the measurement of prejudice as encoding processes. For example, Maass et al.'s (1989) procedure could easily be adapted into such a measure of prejudice. Recall that in their experiments subjects were asked to describe drawings of unambiguous positive and negative behaviors performed by in-group and out-group members. Their results indicated that people describe positive in-group and negative out-group behaviors in more abstract terms than negative in-group and positive out-group behaviors. It seems likely that this tendency would be strongest among those who are most prejudiced, so one would simply need to present such drawings to individuals (perhaps depicting the behaviors of males and females, or African-Americans and Caucasians) and ask them to choose a description at the most appropriate level of abstraction (as in Maass et al., 1989, Experiment 1). One would want to include several drawings that were stereotype-irrelevant as well, in order to get baseline measures of each person's tendency to choose descriptions at various levels of abstraction.

Another possible method of measuring prejudice as process would be to rely on Hastie's (1984) sentence-continuation procedure, in which a person is presented with the first half of a sentence describing a relatively ambiguous behavior and is asked to provide an appropriate continuation. As Hastie has demonstrated, when the behavior is incongruent with expectancies people are more likely to provide a continuation that is an explanation than when the behavior is congruent with expectancies. Once again, the tendency to engage in this sort of elaborative encoding may be a function of the degree of inconsistency between the behavior and the expectancy or stereotype (although the behaviors used for this sort of a task could not be too extreme or they would be likely to inhibit attributional processing and simply be discounted; see Maass et al., 1989). Consequently, if behaviors that are slightly stereotype-incongruent were presented to people, those who are highest in prejudice should perceive the greatest incongruency, and thus should be most likely to generate explanatory sentence continuations. As noted above, one would again want to present sentences that were stereotype-irrelevant to get a baseline measure of the tendency to provide explanatory or attributional completions.

In order to begin to examine the plausibility of assessing prejudice as process, we (von Hippel, Vargas, & Sekaquaptewa, 1994) ran a series of experiments in which we borrowed Hastie's and Maass et al.'s procedures, and attempted to assess (a) the relationship between prejudice as process and prejudice as content, and (b) the extent to which prejudice as process versus prejudice as content predicts evaluations of stereotypic and counterstereotypic individuals.

A. THE RELATIONSHIP BETWEEN CONTENT AND PROCESS PREJUDICE

Experiment 1 examined prejudice toward women, and relied on an extension of methods used by Hastie (1984). The goal of this experiment was simply to determine whether prejudice as process correlates with prejudice as content. In order to accomplish this goal, we presented male subjects with sentence beginnings that were mildly congruent or incongruent with gender stereotypes. Subjects read sentence beginnings such as, "Jane drove the pickup truck," and, "Fred baby-sat the neighbor's kids," and were asked to provide a continuation for each sentence. If prejudice as process correlates at all with prejudice as content, high-sexism subjects should be more likely than low-sexism subjects to perceive these sentence beginnings as incongruent and in need of explanation. They should thus engage in elaborative encoding of the incongruent sentences, thereby explaining them away (see Hastie, 1984).

Consistent with this prediction, males who were identified as high in sexism on the Attitudes Toward Women Scale (Spence, Helmreich, & Stapp, 1973) were significantly more likely than low-sexism males to provide an explanation when females engaged in male behaviors. This effect did not emerge when males engaged in female behaviors, but the means suggested a greater tendency toward explanations among high- rather than low-sexism subjects. Such a tendency to explain females who engage in male behaviors but not males who engage in female behaviors may result from out-group homogeneity effects (e.g., Judd & Park, 1988)—perceptions that it is more appropriate for in-group members to engage in out-group behaviors than vice-versa, or possible differences in the extent to which the male and female behaviors were gender incongruent. Without female subjects, such a question cannot be definitively answered. Nevertheless, Experiment 1 suggests that there is indeed some degree of overlap between assessments of prejudice as process and prejudice as content. Importantly, however, this overlap is far from complete, as the effect for level of sexism was rather small. Thus, results from this study suggest that the two measures may tap different components of prejudice.

Experiment 2 examined prejudice toward African-Americans, and relied on an extension of Maass et al. (1989). In this experiment, subjects were presented with seven stories that were formatted like newspaper articles. Three of these articles were fillers, and four were stereotype-relevant. One of the stereotype-relevant articles was from Sekaquaptewa and von Hippel (1994), and described a person who had won a spelling bee and was planning to attend M.I.T. to become a physicist. A second article described a person who was an accountant at a major firm and had been arrested for embezzlement. The third article described a jewelry thief who had been arrested by the police on a tip from his ex-girlfriend whom he had allegedly battered. Finally, the fourth article described the winner of a basketball slam-dunk contest. Each article was paired with a picture of either an African-American or Caucasian male. After reading the packet of articles, subjects were presented with four different descriptors of each article that varied in the extent to which they provided specific versus abstract portrayals of the articles (as in Maass et al., 1989). Subjects were asked to evaluate the extent to which each of the four statements provided a good description of the article. Subjects were then given the Modern Racism Scale (MRS).

Prejudice as process measures were computed for both the stereotype-congruent and stereotype-incongruent articles. In order to compute a process prejudice score for the stereotype-congruent articles (jewelry thief and slam dunk), subjects' rating of the abstract description of the article paired with a Caucasian photograph were subtracted from their rating of the abstract description of the article paired with an African-American photograph. Thus, positive numbers on this measure indicate a greater preference for the abstract description when the target is African-American rather than Caucasian. For the stereotype-incongruent articles (spelling bee and embezzlement), subjects' rating of the abstract description of the article paired with an African-American were subtracted from their rating of the abstract description of the article paired with a Caucasian. Thus, positive numbers on this measure indicate a greater preference for the abstract description when the target was Caucasian rather than African-American. These two measures of prejudice as process were then correlated with each other and with subjects' scores on the MRS. The stereotype-incongruent measure did not correlate with the either the stereotype-congruent measure or the MRS. In contrast, the stereotype-congruent measure of process prejudice did correlate moderately with the MRS ($r = .209$, $p = .05$).

B. THE EFFECT OF PROCESS PREJUDICE ON EVALUATIONS

In combination, the first two experiments examining prejudice as process indicate small but reliable relationships between prejudice as process and prejudice as content. In Experiment 1 this effect only emerged when subjects were evaluating out-group rather than in-group members, and in Experiment 2 this effect only emerged when subjects were evaluating stereotype-congruent rather than stereotype-incongruent articles. Nevertheless, in both cases correlations emerged between process measures of prejudice and content measures. The goals of the next three experiments were twofold. First, we wanted to assess whether the stereotype-congruent measure is a reliably better indicator of process prejudice than the stereotype-incongruent measure. Second, we wanted to determine whether the process measure of prejudice would predict subjects' evaluations of in-group and out-group members. If the process measure of prejudice does successfully predict evaluations, the question then remained whether it would serve as an equivalent, better, or worse predictor than the content measure of prejudice.

Similar to Experiment 2, Experiment 3 examined prejudice toward African-Americans by relying on an extension of Maass et al.'s (1989) procedures. In this experiment, subjects were presented with four stories that were again formatted like newspaper articles. Two of these articles were fillers, and two were stereotype-relevant. One of the stereotype-relevant articles was about the person who won a spelling bee, and the other was about the jewelry thief. The articles were again paired with either a picture of an African-American or Caucasian male.

When subjects finished reading the articles they were asked to give their overall impression of the protagonist, and were asked to evaluate the extent to which the specific and abstract statements provided good descriptions of the articles. Subjects were then given the MRS. Prejudice as content was computed through a median split on subjects' scores on the MRS. Prejudice as process was operationalized as subjects' preference for the abstract description over the specific description of the stereotype-congruent and stereotype-incongruent articles. Subjects were classified as high in process prejudice for the stereotype-congruent (jewelry thief) article if they preferred the abstract description to the specific description when the target was African-American, or showed the opposite pattern of preferences when the target was Caucasian. Subjects were classified as high in process prejudice for the stereotype-incongruent (spelling bee) article if they preferred the abstract description to the specific description when the target was Caucasian, or showed the opposite pattern of preferences when the target was African-American. Unlike Experiment 2, neither of these measures of process prejudice were significantly correlated with the MRS.

Subjects' overall evaluations of the target of each article were then submitted to three-way analyses of variance, in which race of the target, subjects' content prejudice, and subjects' process prejudice were predictor variables. For the stereotype-incongruent article (spelling bee), two-way interactions emerged between target race and content prejudice and target race and process prejudice. As can be seen in the Figure 8a, both of these interactions were such that low-prejudice subjects showed a stronger preference for the African-American target over the Caucasian target than did high-prejudice subjects. For the stereotype-congruent article (jewelry thief), a two-way interaction emerged between target race and process prejudice, but not between target race and content prejudice. As can be seen in Figure 8b, the interaction between target race and process prejudice was such that low-prejudice subjects showed a slight preference for the African-American target, and high-prejudice subjects showed a preference for the Caucasian target. No three-way interaction emerged between target race, process prejudice, and content prejudice for either of these articles.

Although Experiment 3 was promising in that it demonstrated that process prejudice can predict subjects' evaluations of Caucasian and African-American targets, sometimes even when content prejudice cannot, there are important limitations to this finding. First of all, the process prejudice measure seemed to be more effective when it was assessed on a stereotype-congruent article than when it was assessed on a stereotype-incongruent article. This finding is consistent with Experiment 2, which demonstrated a relationship between the process and content measures of prejudice only when process prejudice was measured via the stereotype-congruent articles. Second, and more importantly, the process prejudice measures in this experiment were only being used to predict evaluations that were made about the same target from which the process measures were computed. For this reason, it is not too surprising that the process measures worked as expected. It would be a more impressive demonstration of the utility of process measures of prejudice if they could predict evaluations of a target who was unassociated with the target from whom the measure was computed. Third, the method of computing process prejudice in this experiment is limited somewhat by the use of only one congruent and one incongruent article. The fact that the process and content measures of prejudice were not correlated using this procedure suggests that the measure of process prejudice from Experiment 2 (in which subjects' evaluations of abstract descriptions of African-American targets were compared with their evaluations of abstract descriptions of Caucasian targets) may be superior to the procedure used in this experiment.

Experiment 4 was conducted to examine these three issues. In Experiment 4 subjects were first presented with the videotape from Vargas and von Hippel (1993) that depicted either an African-American or a Caucasian demanding money from a Caucasian passerby. After watching this tape, subjects rated how threatening the person was who demanded the money. Subjects were then pre-

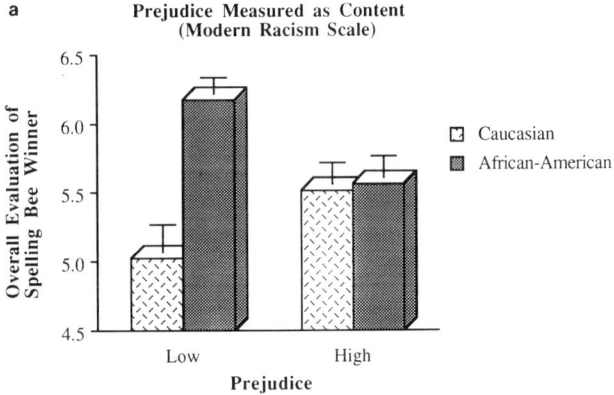

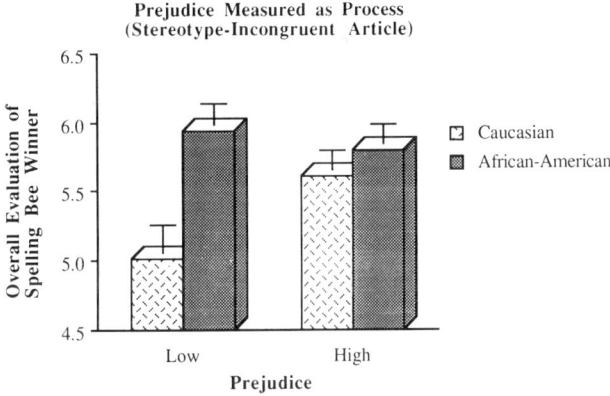

Fig. 8a. The ability of prejudice as process versus prejudice as content to predict evaluations. (From Experiment 3, von Hippel, Vargas, and Sekaquaptewa, 1994.)

sented with the seven bogus newspaper articles from Experiment 2. As in Experiment 2, subjects were asked to indicate for each article how well they thought the abstract descriptions portrayed the main point of the article. Subjects were then given the MRS as a measure of content prejudice, and process prejudice measures for the stereotype-congruent and incongruent articles were computed as in Experiment 2. Somewhat surprisingly, but consistent with the results of Experiment 3, both measures of process prejudice were uncorrelated with the MRS.

Subjects' evaluation of the person who demanded the money on the videotape were then submitted to a three-way analysis of variance, with race of the person demanding the money, process prejudice, and content prejudice as predictor variables. No interaction emerged between target race and the content measure of

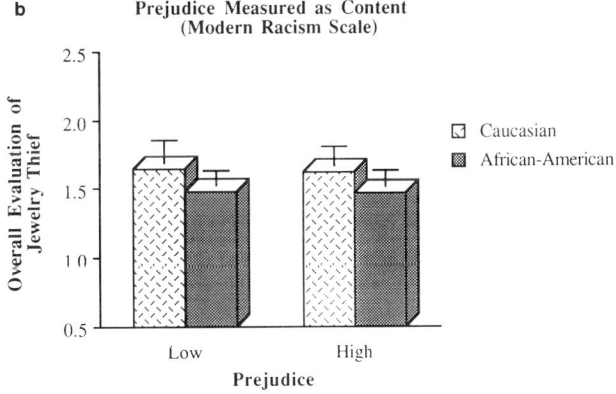

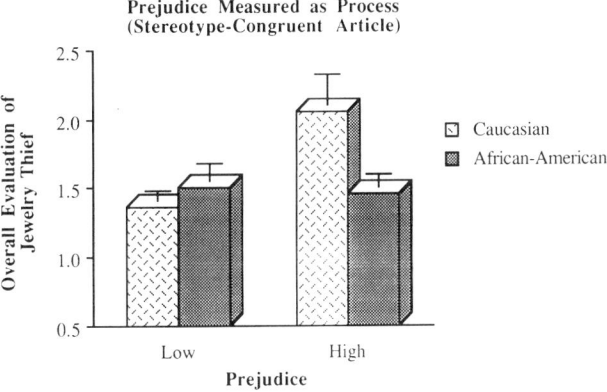

Fig. 8b. The ability of prejudice as process versus prejudice as content to predict evaluations. (From Experiment 3, von Hippel, Vargas, and Sekaquaptewa, 1994.)

prejudice (see panel A of Figure 9). With the process measures generated from stereotype-incongruent articles (spelling bee and embezzler), no interactions emerged between target race and process prejudice (see panel B of Figure 9). With the process measures generated from stereotype-congruent articles (slam-dunk contest and jewelry thief), however, an interaction emerged between target race and process prejudice. As can be seen in panel C of Figure 9, this interaction was such that low-prejudice subjects rated the Caucasian target as more threatening, whereas high-prejudice subjects rated the African-American target as slightly more threatening. No three-way interaction emerged between target race, process prejudice, and content prejudice. Thus, as in Experiment 3, the process measure generated from stereotype-congruent events had greater predictive pow-

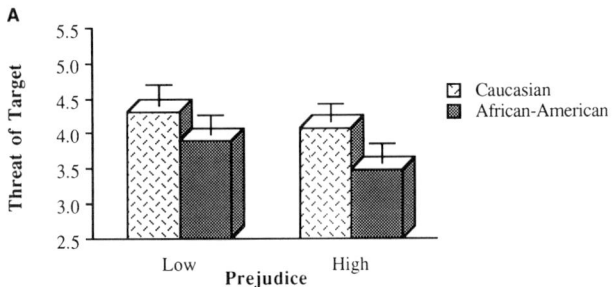
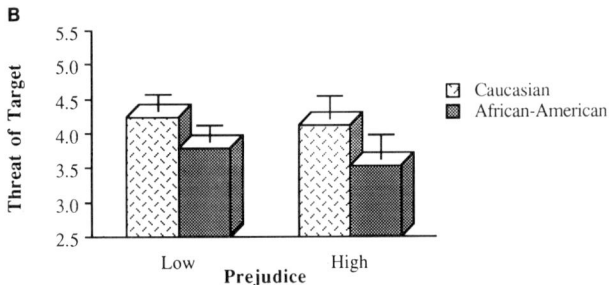
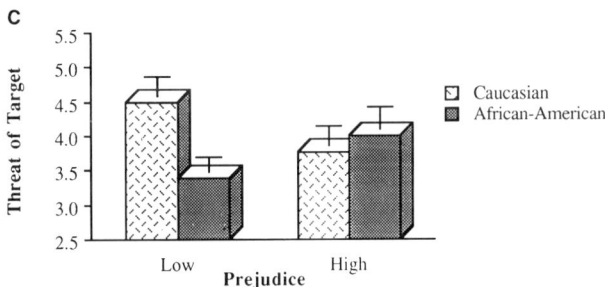

Fig. 9. The ability of prejudice as process versus prejudice as content to predict evaluations. a, Prejudice as content, MRS; b, Prejudice as process, stereotype-incongruent articles; c, Prejudice as process, stereotype-congruent articles. (From Experiment 4, von Hippel, Vargas, and Sekaquaptewa, 1994.)

er than the process measure generated from stereotype-incongruent events. Also as in Experiment 3, the process measure was more able than the content measure to predict subjects' evaluations.

The only finding from Experiment 4 that seems somewhat puzzling is the fact that low process prejudice subjects rated the Caucasian target as more threatening than the African-American target, whereas high process prejudice subjects did not differentiate between the Caucasian and African-American targets. It seems likely, however, that this asymmetrical finding was caused by the direct nature of the question subjects were asked about the target. That is, the question assessing how threatening subjects perceived the target to be was probably sensitive to social desirability pressures that caused subjects to evaluate the African-American as less threatening than they really perceived him. In order to address this possibility, a conceptual replication of Experiment 4 was conducted, with the only difference being that subjects were asked if they could recall whether the person who demanded the money stepped into the path of the other person and whether he touched the other person when he asked for the money. Subjects' responses to these questions were combined, along with their associated confidence scores, into an aggregate "harassment" variable which was analyzed as a function of content and process prejudice. Consistent with Experiment 4, no interaction emerged between target race and content prejudice (see panel A of Figure 10), or between target race and process prejudice assessed with the stereotype-incongruent articles (see panel B of Figure 10). With the process prejudice score assessed from the stereotype congruent articles, however, an interaction emerged such that low-prejudice subjects recalled the Caucasian and African-American as equally harassing, whereas high-prejudice subjects recalled the African-American as more harassing than the Caucasian (see panel C of Figure 10). Thus, this experiment replicated Experiment 4, and also demonstrated that high-prejudice subjects will show differential evaluations of African-American and Caucasian targets when the ratings they make are relatively insensitive to social desirability concerns.

The results from these experiments on process prejudice are clearly just the beginning of an endeavor to reconceive of prejudice as process rather than content. They demonstrate that process prejudice can predict evaluations when content prejudice fails to do so, but they also demonstrate that the relationship between the two phenomena is a complex one. Whereas Experiments 1 and 2 found a relationship between process and content prejudice, Experiments 3, 4, and 5 did not. This discrepancy between experiments may be a function of the fact that the relationship between process and content prejudice is a small one, and thus may simply be difficult to replicate. This discrepancy between experiments may also be a function of the *type* of prejudice that is measured, however, as social desirability may play a differentially important role in content prejudice toward women as compared to content prejudice toward African-Americans. Thus, it seems that although content and process measures of prejudice may be modestly correlated latent variables, the same measurement issues that cloud the accurate assessment of content prejudice may weaken the relationship between these constructs.

We are aware of one other experiment that might be conceived of as a study of prejudice as process rather than evaluative content. In order to develop an unobtrusive measure of racial attitudes, Fazio and Jackson (1994) conducted a very

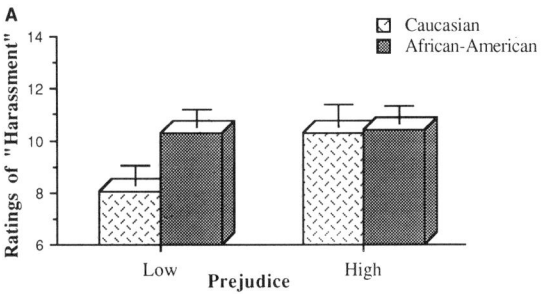

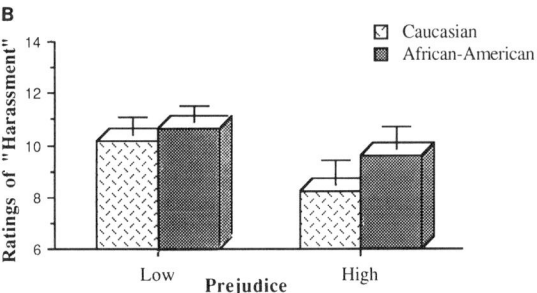

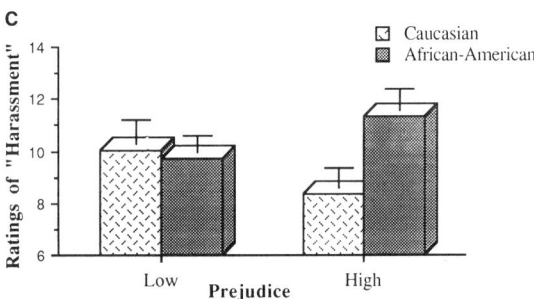

Fig. 10. See legend to Figure 9.

clever study that can be conceived under the rubric of prejudice as process. In this experiment, subjects were told that they would be conducting several tasks. In the first phase of the experiment, they were exposed to a series of trait adjectives, to which they made *good* or *bad* judgments as rapidly as possible. These judgments served as baseline evaluation latencies for the various traits. In the second phase of the experiment subjects were exposed to a series of photographs of faces, and their task was to remember the faces so that they could identify them later. Fazio and Jackson then told subjects that they were interested in determining whether they could conduct these two tasks simultaneously, that is, whether subjects could learn the faces while they were evaluating the words.

This ruse allowed them to present African-American and Caucasian faces that were followed directly (450 ms later) by positive and negative trait words. Fazio and Jackson could then measure subjects' decision latencies when they were evaluating positive and negative words that were paired with African-American or Caucasian faces.

By measuring the extent to which subjects made faster decisions about negative traits and slower decisions about positive traits when they were paired with African-American rather than Caucasian faces, Fazio and Jackson then computed what we would call a process prejudice measure for each subject. Subjects had also been given the MRS earlier in the semester, and thus Fazio and Jackson had a measure of content prejudice as well. After completing the process prejudice measure, subjects were asked to indicate how appropriate and justified they believed the Rodney King verdict was, and whether the riots that followed the verdict were primarily the responsibility of African-Americans or Caucasians. Subjects were then debriefed by an African-American woman who was blind to their scores on the MRS and the newly developed process prejudice measure. The debriefer scored each subject on the degree to which they were friendly and interactive with her during the session. When Fazio and Jackson correlated the two measures of prejudice with the debriefer's evaluation, they found that the process prejudice measure was significantly correlated with her evaluation, such that people higher in process prejudice were rated as being less friendly during debriefing. The MRS, on the other hand, showed no relationship to her evaluations of the debriefing session. In contrast to these results, the MRS *was* correlated with subjects' opinions about the Rodney King verdict and the riots that followed, whereas the process prejudice measure correlated with subjects' opinions about the riots that followed the verdict, but not the verdict itself. Finally, as in Experiments 3, 4, and 5 of von Hippel, Vargas, and Sekaquaptewa (1994), the process prejudice measure was uncorrelated with the MRS.

C. PROCESS/CONTENT DISCREPANCIES

Although this experiment and the experiments by von Hippel et al. (1994) are just initial efforts at conceiving of prejudice as process, they provide results that strongly suggest that the process component of prejudice might provide important information in addition to the content component. It seems likely that conceiving of prejudice as process might provide a different picture of just who is prejudiced, how these prejudices influence judgment, and when these prejudices are likely to emerge. Does this mean that prejudice should be measured only as process and no longer as content? Clearly not. The content measure predicted attitudes in the Fazio and Jackson (1994) study when the process measure did not, and the content measure also predicted evaluations in Experiment 2 of von Hippel et al. (1994). Thus, it seems likely that by conceptualizing prejudice as process in addition to content, a more complete picture of the prejudiced perceiver might emerge. In combination, the Fazio and Jackson and von Hippel et al. results suggest that process measures of prejudice are likely to predict some types of responses, and content measures are likely to predict others. At this point it is too early to determine what types of responses will be predicted by the two types of measures. Nevertheless, it seems likely that process measures are going to *tend* to be better at predicting other processes (i.e., other types of encoding biases, such as assimilation effects, etc.), whereas content measures are going to *tend* to be better at predicting other beliefs (i.e., the content of related prejudices, stereotypes, etc.).

Because content and process measures of prejudice are relatively uncorrelated, or show only modest correlations, there are likely to be a large number of people whose content and process measures of prejudice indicate inconsistencies. That is, there will be people who show high content prejudice but low process prejudice, and people who show low content prejudice but high process prejudice. One explanation for these discrepancies would be that those who are high in content prejudice but low in process prejudice hold negative beliefs about an outgroup but are unlikely to apply those beliefs to individual out-group members, whereas people who are low in content prejudice but high in process prejudice are in reality high in both types of prejudice but are responding to social desirability pressures in their responses on content measures. Another possibility is that people low in content but high in process prejudice may simply be less aware of the stereotypes and prejudices that they hold (cf. Snyder, Kleck, Strenta, & Mentzer, 1979); for such people stereotypes and prejudice may operate automatically and largely outside of conscious awareness.

Although such explanations might hold true for a proportion of the people who show content–process discrepancies, it seems likely that discrepant individuals may actually differ in more substantive ways from nondiscrepant individuals. One possibility is that discrepant individuals may be higher than nondiscrepant individuals in their feelings of ambivalence toward out-group members (see I. Katz & Hass, 1988). If this is the case, then one would expect the judgments and evaluations of discrepant individuals to be more easily influenced by situational priming of different components of their value structure than the judgments and evaluations of nondiscrepant individuals. Currently this remains an untested hypothesis.

The point of this proposal is that it seems that prejudice is probably not a uniform or monolithic construct, but rather is more likely to be a flexible response strategy that is invoked in some situations and not others. Consequently, rather than measuring prejudice simply in terms of some sort of evaluative content or ideation, it might be more profitable to measure prejudice in terms of a complex interrelation of processes, proclivities, and content (for example, much the same way that IQ is currently measured). Indeed, such a conception of prejudice has the potential to recapture early notions of prejudice as a tendency toward prejudgment. Clearly considerable work would have to go into the design, validation, and implementation of procedures in which prejudice is operationalized as encoding processes in addition to content, but the potential theoretical and empirical payoff are likely to be substantial as well.

Summary

• If, as is argued in this chapter, stereotypes exert their impact at encoding, then prejudice might be reconceptualized as a proclivity to display stereotypic encoding biases. That is, prejudice might be conceived as encoding processes rather than the evaluative content of a perceiver's beliefs about an out-group. Prejudice as process can easily be measured, simply by extending previous research on the role of stereotypes in encoding processes.

• Prejudice as process predicts evaluations under circumstances when prejudice as content does not. On the other hand, prejudice as content seems occasionally to predict opinions when prejudice as process does not. Additionally, prejudice as process correlates only irregularly with prejudice as content. These results suggest that process and content measures of prejudice should be combined to create a more complete picture of the prejudiced perceiver.

V. Conclusions

The goal of this chapter has been to show that across a wide variety of experimental contexts, stereotypes, expectancies, and social schemas play a critical role in encoding. Throughout this review we have attempted to highlight research that clearly implicates encoding processes in judgmental and memorial effects. We began with perceptual processes, which are critical at the front end of any encoding operation. We then turned to a variety of conceptual processes which (other than attention and assimilation effects) are as likely to play a role at encoding as at any other stage of information processing. Additionally, these processes are likely to be associated or unassociated with stereotyping. For these reasons, we limited our discussion of these processes to research that was directly concerned with encoding phenomena and their role in stereotype maintenance.

A. ENCODING VERSUS RETRIEVAL

It should be noted before closing this review that there is a small body of research that has directly manipulated the presence of a stereotype at encoding versus retrieval in order to determine the locus of stereotypic processes. This research has been uniform in its conclusions: Only when stereotypes and social schemas are activated at encoding do they exert an impact on memory and judgment. For example, although a Hispanic defendant is more likely to be judged guilty of a crime than a Caucasian defendant when his ethnicity is known before the evidence is evaluated, no effect emerges when his ethnicity is not learned until after the evidence has already been considered (Bodenhausen, 1988). Similarly, although positive behaviors of in-group members are more memorable than negative behaviors, this effect only emerges when group membership is known before the behaviors are encountered (Howard & Rothbart, 1980). As a rule, such research has shown that only when stereotypes are activated prior to encoding do they facilitate memory (Cohen, 1981; Ostrom, Lingle, Pryor, & Geva, 1980; Pyszczynski, Laprelle, & Greenberg, 1988; Rothbart et al., 1979; Zadny & Gerard, 1974), and influence interpretation (Massad et al., 1979; Snyder & Frankel, 1976; Srull & Wyer, 1980; see also, Darley & Gross, 1983; Park & Hastie, 1987).

The only notable exception to this rule is the finding of Snyder and Uranowitz (1978) that a stereotypic label provided after behaviors have been encountered can make stereotype-congruent behaviors more memorable. As Bellezza and Bower (1981) demonstrated through a signal-detection analysis, however, this finding was entirely driven by stereotype-congruent guessing effects, and was not associated with any increase in the actual memorability of schema-congruent information. Specifically, in Bellezza and Bower's experiment, subjects were presented with similar behaviors to those of Snyder and Uranowitz, and were then provided with a stereotypic label after reading the passage. One week later subjects completed a recognition task, which included an equal proportion of items that had been presented (targets) and items that had not been presented (foils). Additionally, half of the foils were designed to be stereotype-consistent and half were designed to be stereotype-inconsistent. Bellezza and Bower found that subjects were no more accurate in their ability to detect stereotype-consistent targets as a function of the label that was provided, although they were more likely to guess that stereotype-consistent targets *and* foils had been presented. Had Snyder and Uranowitz provided a stereotypic label before subjects read the passage, this information would probably have had an impact on their memory. Nevertheless, providing such a label after the behaviors were encountered had little if any effect.

Thus, it seems that for motivational and cognitive reasons, perceivers simplify and interpret their world as they encounter it. These simplifications and interpretations then become more important in storage and retrieval than the original information, and thereby serve as both the cause and the effect, as well as the justification, of the original stereotypes. Consequently, although stereotyping is not made inevitable, avoiding stereotypic processing can be a lot more effortful than succumbing to it (Devine & Monteith, 1993; Monteith, 1993).

B. STEREOTYPE ACCURACY

We should also note before closing this review that we have purposely avoided the thorny issue of stereotype accuracy. Although stereotype accuracy is an important concern that is receiving considerable attention (e.g., Jussim, 1991; Judd & Park, 1992; Stangor & Lange, 1994), the information-processing perspective is theoretically neutral on this issue. This is because the same factors that lead to biases in perception when the stereotype is inaccurate often lead to accuracy in perception when the stereotype is accurate. Indeed, the obvious reason why perceivers rely on social and object schemas to facilitate perception is that schemas dramatically facilitate the ease and accuracy of information processing. As was discussed above, visual and auditory perception would be nearly impossible if the perceiver could not rely on prior knowledge to disambiguate the stimulus (Medin & Ross, 1992).

Nevertheless, it is our belief that stereotypes that are based on immutable features of the target (e.g., race or gender) are likely to be rife with error. Although many treatments of this topic have reported considerable accuracy in social stereotypes (e.g., Jussim, 1991; Swim, 1994), these treatments examine accuracy in only one block of time, and thus fail to consider the powerful role that the stereotypes themselves may have played in creating the social reality that is being assessed (see Merton, 1948; Rosenthal & Jacobson, 1968). For example, consider the case of a racial group that is stereotyped oppositely in two different societies: People of African descent are stereotyped as being lazier than Caucasians in the United States (e.g., Devine, 1989), but as less lazy than Caucasians in the Dominican Republic (where they are also stereotyped as being stronger, more honest, more responsible, less attractive, and less intelligent than Caucasians; Silvestre, 1994). Because of the extensive interaction that exists between the people who hold these stereotypes and the people who are the targets of these stereotypes, it is quite possible that research on stereotype accuracy would find that there is an equivalent degree of truth to both stereotypes. Does that mean that the opposite stereotypes should be labeled as accurate in the two societies? We think not. Rather, it seems that the notion of stereotype accuracy has lost all meaning.

To further illustrate this point, compare these cases to a more blatant example of stereotyping based on self-fulfilling prophecies. The following remark was made in 1989 by a Caucasian woman from South Africa who was being questioned by an American reporter from the "CBS Evening News." In defense of apartheid, she stated, "Blacks in South Africa are not like Blacks in America. They're animals—they're uneducated and they sleep in the streets." Although the "accuracy" of her stereotype is more obviously a product of self-fulfilling prophecies than is the "accuracy" of stereotypes about laziness in the United States or the Dominican Republic, in all of these cases the same social factors are at work creating whatever group differences do exist. Whether in South Africa or the United States, the extent to which such stereotypes are true seems to be the result of self-fulfilling prophecies and the consequent social construction of reality (e.g., see Snyder & Swann, 1978). For this reason, the objective assessment of stereotype accuracy may be a largely impossible endeavor whenever the perceiver who holds the stereotype has the opportunity to interact with the target of that stereotype.

C. IMPLICATIONS OF THE CURRENT PERSPECTIVE

Beyond what this review tells us about process, and how it might change our view of prejudice (as discussed above), the viewpoint that stereotypes exert their impact at encoding has three important implications. First, it provides yet another reason why social stereotypes are so tenacious. By way of example, consider a rather strained metaphor of the human as a computer. In this example, our senses are the computer operator—the person who is typing information into the system. If, rather than faithfully transcribing the external world, the computer operator were biased to such a degree that sometimes (s)he would completely fail to enter important information, and other times (s)he would enter a rather inaccurate version of what took place, then our human-as-computer would be faced with a real dilemma. Under such circumstances, there would be no way that the human-as-computer could ever correct the errors made by the computer operator. Because complete and accurate information was never entered in the first place, it would be impossible to put an original picture of the events back together. Had the locus of the bias been at retrieval, on the other hand, the bias would not pose such a serious setback. Under this scenario one might simply hope that some environmental or internal cue would eventually remind the human-as-computer of the original events, causing the bias to disappear. But, if the bias is there from the very beginning, from encoding, there is little hope that the system could ever become aware of it, much less do anything about it.

Second, our perspective suggests that individuals who are members of multiple social categories will tend to be evaluated only as a function of the categories that are activated at encoding. For example, an African-American woman who is an art collector, a lawyer, and a feminist, is likely to be evaluated very differently as a function of which of these social categories is activated at encoding. Such activation could be a function of social context, suggesting that she would be perceived differently depending on whether she were encountered in the kitchen, in the courtroom, in the inner city, in an art gallery, or at a rally. Such activation could also be a function of an earlier priming experience, suggesting that she would be perceived differently depending on whether the concepts of hostility, passivity, extroversion, creativity, or righteousness had recently been considered by the perceiver (see Banaji, Hardin, & Rothman, 1993). Importantly, activation of one category in favor of another is likely to determine not only how she is evaluated at the initial encounter, but also how she is remembered later on, and perhaps how she will be evaluated during subsequent encounters as well (see Smith, Stewart, & Buttram, 1992). According to the analysis proposed in this chapter, later retrieval of other social categories that might have described her is unlikely to influence memory or interpretation of her behaviors. Rather, the social category instantiated at encoding is likely to play a primary role in her evaluation.

As noted above, her gender and race should be activated automatically, but whether the presence of other social categories could override and thereby attenuate the impact of these automatic categories is an empirical question. Research suggests that such an attenuation of even automatically activated social categories is possible (Zarate & Smith, 1990). Zarate and Smith presented subjects with slides of African-American and Caucasian males and females, and asked them to indicate either the gender or the race of the target individuals. Zarate and Smith found that race judgments were made more slowly when the target was female, and gender (and race) judgments were made more slowly when the target was African-American. Furthermore, speed of race categorization predicted the extent to which target persons were described in race-stereotypic terms (suggesting that this may serve as another measure of prejudice as process). Thus, it seems that race and gender information interfered with each other in selective ways, attenuating or at least slowing the activation of alternative information. Because nearly everyone is a member of multiple social categories, the possibility that some categories can inhibit the activation of others suggests that seemingly trivial factors like social context might have a larger impact on stereotyping than has previously been considered.

Finally, the viewpoint that stereotypes exert their influence at encoding would suggest that a much greater research emphasis be placed on how people initially perceive the targets of their stereotypes. Currently very little work addresses this issue, in part because perceptual processing is difficult to measure. Nevertheless, there are methodologies available that enable the assessment of various perceptual processes. For example, subjects might be presented with slides depicting interactions between African-Americans and Caucasians, or between males and females. To the extent that stereotypes influence the way that such information is encoded, recordings of eye movements should reveal that prejudiced perceivers spend more time visually processing stereotype-congruent information than stereotype-incongruent information.[10] Furthermore, such recordings of eye movements should be associated with, and indeed may partially mediate, prejudiced and nonprejudiced subjects' differential evaluations of the interactants (for a discussion of eye movements and information processing, see Just & Carpenter, 1980).

---

[10]Such a finding is likely to be moderated by the ambiguity of the behavior. Specifically, it seems likely that prejudiced perceivers would actually spend more time visually processing ambiguously incongruent behaviors than ambiguously congruent behaviors, in their attempt to reconstrue such behaviors as congruent with their stereotypes.

Another possible procedure would be to present subjects with drawings depicting ambiguous interracial or intergender interactions that could be perceived as stereotype-congruent by those high in prejudice. Subjects could then be presented later with similar drawings that differ only in the extent to which they more or less closely approximate stereotypic interpretations of the earlier drawings. By degrading these second presentations (e.g., by blurring them or presenting them very rapidly) and then requiring subjects to identify the drawings, this procedure would allow one to examine the nature of the stored image that subjects have retained in memory. To the extent that the initial picture was perceived in a stereotype-congruent fashion, subjects should be more able to identify the degraded drawing that is more, rather than less, congruent with the stereotype. A strong test of the hypothesis that subjects actually perceived the initial drawing as consistent with their stereotypes would be to ascertain whether subjects are more able to identify the degraded pictures when they have been made slightly more stereotypical than when they are presented in their original format. Such a finding would demonstrate that the original perceptual encoding was biased in the direction of the stereotype, and hence the perceptual information in memory is more stereotype-congruent than the original event. Essentially, the procedure proposed in this example relies on an implicit memory measure (ability to identify a degraded image) to provide information about the nature of subjects' original encodings. Such an examination of perceptual encoding might be an atypical endeavor for social psychology, but it has the potential to provide a great deal of information about how stereotypes influence the way we see, and thereby experience and create, our social world.

Acknowledgments

We would like to thank Marilynn Brewer, John Cacioppo, Kari Edwards, Tony Greenwald, James Hilton, John Jonides, Lee Jussim, Jon Krosnick, Tom Ostrom and the Social Cognition Research Group, Richard Petty, David Sanbonmatsu, John Skowronski, Chuck Stangor, and especially Steve Fein for their helpful comments on earlier drafts of this manuscript. We would also like to thank Mark Zanna and two anonymous reviewers for their thoughtful advice. This chapter is dedicated to our colleague and mentor, and our close friend, Tom Ostrom.

References

Allport G. (1954). *The nature of prejudice.* Cambridge, MA: Addison-Wesley.
Andersen, S. M., & Klatzky, R. L. (1987). Traits and social stereotypes: Levels of categorization in person perception. *Journal of Personality and Social Psychology, 53,* 235–246.
Anderson, J. R. (1990). *Cognitive psychology and its implications.* (3rd ed.). New York: Freeman.
Anderson, J. R., & Bower, G. H. (1973). *Human associative memory.* Hillsdale, NJ: Erlbaum.

Anderson, R. C., & Pichert, J. W. (1978). Recall of previously unrecallable information following a shift in perspective. *Journal of Verbal Learning and Verbal Behavior, 17*, 1–12.

Anthony, T., Copper, C., & Mullen, B. (1992). Cross-racial facial identification: A social cognitive integration. *Personality and Social Psychology Bulletin, 18*, 296–301.

Arkin, R. M., & Duval, S. (1975). Focus of attention and causal attributions of actors and observers. *Journal of Personality and Social Psychology, 11*, 427–438.

Asch, S. (1946). Forming impressions of personality. *Journal of Abnormal and Social Psychology, 410*, 258–290.

Ball, K., & Sekuler, R. (1982). A specific and enduring improvement in visual motion discrimination. *Science, 218*, 697–698.

Ball, K., & Sekuler, R. (1987). Direction-specific improvement in motion discrimination. *Vision Research, 27*, 953–965.

Banaji, M. R., & Greenwald, A. G. (1993). Implicit stereotyping and prejudice. In M. P. Zanna & J. M. Olson, (Eds.), *Psychology of prejudice: The Ontario Symposium* (Vol. 7, pp. 55–76). Hillsdale, NJ: Erlbaum.

Banaji, M. R., Hardin, C., & Rothman, A. J. (1993). Implicit stereotyping in person judgment. *Journal of Personality and Social Psychology, 65*, 272–281.

Bargh, J. A. (1982). Attention and automaticity in the processing of self-relevant information. *Journal of Personality and Social Psychology, 43*, 425–436.

Bargh, J. A. (1989). Conditional automaticity: Varieties of automatic influence in social perception and cognition. In J. S. Uleman & J. A. Bargh (Eds.), *Unintended thought*. New York: Guilford Press.

Baron, R. M., & Kenny, D. A. (1986). The moderator-mediator variable distinction in social psychological research: Conceptual, strategic, and statistical considerations. *Journal of Personality and Social Psychology, 51*, 1173–1182.

Bechtold, A., Naccarato, M. E., & Zanna, M. P. (1986). *Need for structure and the prejudice-discrimination link*. Paper presented at the annual meeting of the Canadian Psychological Association, Toronto.

Bellezza, F. S., & Bower, G. H. (1981). Person stereotypes and memory for people. *Journal of Personality and Social Psychology, 41*, 856–865.

Belmore, S. M. (1987). Determinants of attention during impression formation. *Journal of Experimental Psychology: Learning, Memory, and Cognition, 13*, 480–489.

Bem, D. J. (1970). *Beliefs, attitudes, and human affairs*. Belmont, CA: Brooks-Cole.

Berlyne, D. W. (1958). The influence of complexity and novelty in visual figures on orienting responses. *Journal of Experimental Psychology, 55*, 289–296.

Berry, D. S., & McArthur, L. Z. (1986). Perceiving character in faces: The impact of age-related craniofacial changes on social perception. *Psychological Bulletin, 100*, 3–18.

Biernat, M. (1991). Gender stereotypes and the relationship between masculinity and femininity: A developmental analysis. *Journal of Personality and Social Psychology, 61*, 351–365.

Biernat, M., & Manis, M. (1994). Shifting standards and stereotype-based judgments. *Journal of Personality and Social Psychology, 66*, 5–20.

Biernat, M., Manis, M., & Nelson, T. E. (1991). Stereotypes and standards of judgment. *Journal of Personality and Social Psychology, 60*, 485–499.

Blaxton, T. A. (1989). Investigating dissociations among memory measures: Support for a transfer appropriate processing framework. *Journal of Experimental Psychology: Learning, Memory and Cognition, 15*, 657–668.

Bodenhausen, G. V. (1988). Stereotypic biases in social decision making and memory: Testing process models of stereotype use. *Journal of Personality and Social Psychology, 55*, 726–737.

Bodenhausen, G. V. (1990). Stereotypes as judgmental heuristics: Evidence of circadian variations in discrimination. *Psychological Science, 1*, 319–322.

Bower, G. H. (1970). Organizational factors in memory. *Cognitive Psychology, 1*, 18–46.

Bower, G. H. (1972). A selective review of organizational factors in memory. In E. Tulving & W. Donaldson (Eds.), *Organization of Memory.* New York: Academic Press.

Bower, G. H., & Karlin, M. B. (1974). Depth of processing pictures of faces and recognition memory. *Journal of Experimental Psychology, 103,* 751–757.

Bransford, J. D., & Johnson, M. K. (1973). Considerations of some problems of comprehension. In W. G. Chase (Ed.), *Visual information processing.* New York: Academic Press.

Brewer, M. B. (1988). A dual process model of impression formation. In R. S. Wyer, Jr., & T. K. Srull (Eds.), *Handbook of social cognition.* (Vol. 1, pp. 1–36). Hillsdale, NJ: Erlbaum.

Brewer, M. B. (1993). The social psychology of prejudice: Getting it all together. In M. P. Zanna & J. M. Olson, (Eds.), *Psychology of prejudice: The Ontario Symposium,* (Vol. 7, pp. 315–329). Hillsdale, NJ: Erlbaum.

Brigham, J. C. (1971). Ethnic stereotypes. *Psychological Bulletin, 76,* 15–38.

Brooks, L. R. (1978). Non-analytic concept formation and memory for instances. In E. Rosch & B. Lloyd (Eds.), *Cognition and categorization.* Hillsdale, NJ: Erlbaum.

Bruner, J. S. (1957). Going beyond the information given. In J. S. Bruner, E. Brunswik, L. Festinger, F. Heider, K. F. Muenzinger, C. E. Osgood, & D. Rapaport, (Eds.), *Contemporary approaches to cognition: The Colorado symposium* (pp. 41–69). Cambridge, MA: Harvard University Press.

Bruner, J. S., & Potter, M. C. (1964). Interference in visual recognition. *Science, 144,* 424–425.

Cacioppo, J. T., & Petty, R. E. (1982). The need for cognition. *Journal of Personality and Social Psychology, 42,* 116–131.

Carlston, D. E., & Skowronski, J. J. (1994). Savings in relearning of trait information as evidence for spontaneous trait inference generation. *Journal of Personality and Social Psychology, 66,* 840–856.

Chambers, D., & Reisberg, D. (1985). Can mental images be ambiguous? *Journal of Experimental Psychology: Human Perception and Performance, 11,* 317–328.

Chapman, L. J., & Chapman, J. P. (1967). Genesis of popular but erroneous psychodiagnostic observations. *Journal of Abnormal Psychology, 72,* 193–204.

Chatman, C., & von Hippel, W. (1993, May). *In-group biases among Blacks and Whites: Evidence for the ultimate attribution error.* Paper presented at the 65th Annual Meeting of the Midwestern Psychological Association, Chicago, IL.

Cohen, C. E. (1981). Person categories and social perception: Testing some boundaries of the processing effects of prior knowledge. *Journal of Personality and Social Psychology, 40,* 441–452.

Cohen, N. J., & Squire, L. R. (1980). Preserved learning and retention of pattern-analyzing skill in amnesia: Dissociation of knowing how and knowing that. *Science, 210,* 207–210.

Craik, F. I. M., & Lockhart, R. S. (1972). Levels of processing: A framework for memory research. *Journal of Verbal Learning and Verbal Behavior, 11,* 671–684.

Craik, F. I. M., & Tulving, E. (1975). Depth of processing and the retention of words in episodic memory. *Journal of Experimental Psychology: General, 104,* 268–294.

Crocker, J., & Luhtanen, R. (1990). Collective self-esteem and ingroup bias. *Journal of Personality and Social Psychology, 58,* 60–67.

Crocker, J., Thompson, L. L., & McGraw, K. M. (1987). Downward comparison, prejudice, and evaluations of others: Effects of self-esteem and threat. *Journal of Personality and Social Psychology, 52,* 907–916.

Crocker, J., Voelkl, K., Testa, M., & Major, B. (1991). Social stigma: The affective consequences of attributional ambiguity. *Journal of Personality and Social Psychology, 60,* 218–228.

Darley, J. M., & Gross, P. H. (1983). A hypothesis-confirming bias in labeling effects. *Journal of Personality and Social Psychology, 44,* 20–33.

Deaux, K., & Emswiller, T. (1974). Explanations of successful performance on sex-linked tasks: What is skill for the male is luck for the female. *Journal of Personality and Social Psychology, 29,* 80–85.

Dekle, D. J., Fowler, C. A., & Funnell, M. G. (1992). Audiovisual integration in perception of real words. *Perception and Psychophysics, 51,* 355–362.

Devine, P. G. (1989). Stereotypes and prejudice: Their automatic and controlled components. *Journal of Personality and Social Psychology, 56,* 5–18.

Devine, P. G., & Monteith, M. J. (1993). The role of discrepancy-associated affect in prejudice reduction. In D. M. Mackie & D. L. Hamilton (Eds.), *Affect, cognition, and stereotyping: Interactive processes in group perception.* (pp. 317–344). San Diego: Academic Press.

DeWitt, L. A., & Samuel, A. G. (1990). The role of knowledge-based expectations in music perception: Evidence from musical restoration. *Journal of Experimental Psychology: General, 119,* 123–144.

Ditto, P. H., & Lopez, D. A. (1993). Motivated skepticism: Use of differential decision criteria for preferred and nonpreferred conclusions. *Journal of Personality and Social Psychology, 63,* 568–584.

Doms, M., & Van Avermaet, E. (1980). Majority influence, minority influence and conversion behavior: A replication. *Journal of Experimental Social Psychology, 16,* 283–292.

Dovidio, J. F., Evans, N., & Tyler, R. B. (1986). Racial stereotypes: The content of their cognitive representations. *Journal of Experimental Social Psychology, 22,* 22–37.

Duncan, B. (1976). Differential social perception and attribution of intergroup violence: Testing the lower limits of stereotyping of blacks. *Journal of Personality and Social Psychology, 34,* 590–598.

Edwards, K., & von Hippel, W. (in press). Hearts and minds: The priority of affective versus cognitive factors in person perception. *Personality and Social Psychology Bulletin.*

Esses, V. M., Haddock, G., & Zanna, M. P. (1993). Values, stereotypes, and emotions as determinants of intergroup attitudes. In D. M. Mackie & D. L. Hamilton (Eds.), *Affect, cognition, and stereotyping: Interactive processes in group perception* (pp. 137–166). San Diego: Academic Press.

Etling, K. (1993). *Stereotyping of African-American business people: The effects of cognitive load, target race, performance level, and racism level.* Unpublished master's thesis, University of Virginia, Charlottesville, VA.

Farah, M. J. (1988). Is visual imagery really visual? Overlooked evidence from neuropsychology. *Psychological Review, 95,* 307–317.

Fazio, R. H., & Jackson, J. (1994, January). *An unobtrusive measure of racial attitudes.* Paper presented at the Social Psychology Winter Conference, Park City, UT.

Fein, S. (1991). *The suspicious mind.* Unpublished doctoral dissertation, University of Michigan, Ann Arbor, MI.

Fein, S., Hilton, J. L., & Miller, D. T. (1990). Suspicion of ulterior motivation and the correspondence bias. *Journal of Personality and Social Psychology, 58,* 753–764.

Fein, S., & Spencer, S. J. (1993, August). *Self-esteem and stereotype-based downward social comparison.* Paper presented at the 101st Annual Meeting of the American Psychological Association, Toronto, Canada.

Feldman-Summers, S., & Kiesler, S. B. (1974). Those who are number two try harder: The effect of sex on attribution of causality. *Journal of Personality and Social Psychology, 30,* 846–854.

Finke, R. A. (1980). Levels of equivalence in imagery and perception. *Psychological Review, 87,* 113–132.

Finke, R. A., & Schmidt, M. J. (1977). Orientation-specific color after-effects following imagination. *Journal of Experimental Psychology: Human Perception and Performance, 13,* 599–606.

Finke, R. A., & Schmidt, M. J. (1978). The quantitative measure of pattern representation in images using orientation-specific color aftereffects. *Perception & Psychophysics, 23,* 515–520.

Fiske, S. T. (1980). Attention and weight in person perception: The impact of negative and extreme behavior. *Journal of Personality and Social Psychology, 38,* 889–906.

Fiske, S. T., & Neuberg, S. L. (1990). A continuum model of impression formation from category-based to individuating processes: Influences of information and motivation on attention and interpretation. In M. P. Zanna (Ed.), *Advances in Experimental Social Psychology*, (Vol. 23, pp. 1–74). San Diego: Academic Press.

Fiske, S. T., Neuberg, S. L., Beattie, A. E., & Milberg, S. J. (1987). Category-based and attribute-based reactions to others: Some informational conditions of stereotyping and individuating processes. *Journal of Experimental Social Psychology, 23,* 399–427.

Fiske, S. T., & Taylor, S. E. (1991). *Social cognition.* New York: McGraw Hill.

Ford, T. E., & Stangor, C. (1992). The role of diagnosticity in stereotype formation: Perceiving group means and variances. *Journal of Personality and Social Psychology, 63,* 356–367.

Friedman, A. (1979). Framing pictures: The role of knowledge in automatised encoding and memory for gist. *Journal of Experimental Psychology: General, 108,* 316–355.

Friedman, H., & Zebrowitz, L. A. (1992). The contribution of typical sex differences in facial maturity to sex role stereotypes. *Personality and Social Psychology Bulletin, 18,* 430–438.

Gaertner, S. L. (1976). Nonreactive measures in racial attitudes research: A focus on "Liberals." In P. A. Katz (Ed.), *Towards the elimination of racism* (pp. 183–212). New York: Pergamon.

Gaertner, S. L., & McLaughlin, J. P. (1983). Racial stereotypes: Associations and ascriptions of positive and negative characteristics. *Social Psychology Quarterly, 46,* 23–40.

Gibson, J. J. (1979). *The ecological approach to visual perception.* Boston: Houghton Mifflin.

Gilbert, D. T., & Hixon, J. G. (1991). The trouble of thinking: Activation and application of stereotypic beliefs. *Journal of Personality and Social Psychology, 60,* 509–517.

Gilbert, D. T., Pelham, B. W., & Krull, D. S. (1988). On cognitive busyness: When person perceivers meet persons perceived. *Journal of Personality and Social Psychology, 54,* 733–740.

Graf, P., & Mandler, G. (1984). Activation makes words more accessible but not necessarily more retrievable. *Journal of Verbal Learning and Verbal Behavior, 23,* 553–568.

Graf, P., Shimamura, A. P., & Squire, L. R. (1985). Priming across modalities and priming across category levels: Extending the domain of preserved function in amnesia. *Journal of Experimental Psychology: Learning, Memory, and Cognition, 11,* 385–395.

Greenwald, A. G., & Banaji, M. R. (in press). Implicit social cognition: Attitudes, self-esteem, and stereotypes. *Psychological Review.*

Greenwald, A. G. (1992). New Look 3: Unconscious cognition reclaimed. *American Psychologist, 47,* 766–779.

Haddock, G., Zanna, M. P., & Esses, V. M. (1993). Assessing the structure of prejudicial attitudes: The case of attitudes toward homosexuals. *Journal of Personality and Social Psychology, 65,* 1105–1118.

Hamilton, D. L. (1979). A cognitive-attributional analysis of stereotyping. In L. Berkowitz (Ed.), *Advances in Experimental Social Psychology,* (Vol. 12, pp. 53–81). New York: Academic Press.

Hamilton, D. L., & Gifford, R. K. (1976). Illusory correlation in interpersonal perception: A cognitive basis of stereotypic judgments. *Journal of Experimental Social Psychology, 12,* 392–407.

Hamilton, D. L., & Rose, T. L. (1980). Illusory correlation and the maintenance of stereotypic beliefs. *Journal of Personality and Social Psychology, 39,* 832–845.

Hammann, S. B. (1990). Level-of-processing effects in conceptually driven implicit tasks. *Journal of Experimental Psychology: Learning, Memory, and Cognition, 16,* 970–977.

Hastie, R. (1984). Causes and effects of causal attribution. *Journal of Personality and Social Psychology, 46,* 44–56.

Hastie, R., & Kumar, P. A. (1979). Person memory: Personality traits as organizing principles in memory for behaviors. *Journal of Personality and Social Psychology, 37,* 25–38.

Hastie, R., & Park, B. (1986). The relationship between memory and judgment depends on whether the judgment task is memory-based or on-line. *Psychological Review, 93,* 258–268.

Hawley, K. J., & Johnston, W. A. (1991). Long-term perceptual memory for briefly exposed words as a function of awareness and attention. *Journal of Experimental Psychology: Human Perception and Performance, 17,* 807–815.

Heider, F. (1958). *The psychology of interpersonal relations.* New York: Wiley.

Heider, F., & Simmel, M. (1944). An experimental study of apparent behavior. *American Journal of Psychology, 57,* 243–259.

Heilman, M. E. (1980). The impact of situational factors on personnel decisions concerning women: Varying the sex composition of the applicant pool. *Organizational Behavior and Human Performance, 26,* 386–395.

Herr, P. M. (1986). Consequences of priming: Judgment and behavior. *Journal of Personality and Social Psychology, 51,* 1106–1115.

Herr, P. M., Sherman, S. J., & Fazio, R. H. (1983). On the consequences of priming: Assimilation and contrast effects. *Journal of Experimental Social Psychology, 19,* 323–340.

Hewstone, M., & Jaspars, J. M. F. (1984). Social dimensions of attribution. In H. Tajfel (Ed.), *The social dimension: European developments in social psychology* (Vol. 2, pp. 379–404). Cambridge, England: Cambridge University Press.

Hilton, J. L., & Fein, S. (1989). The role of typical diagnosticity in stereotype-based judgments. *Journal of Personality and Social Psychology, 57,* 201–211.

Hilton, J. L., Klein, J. G., & von Hippel, W. (1991). Attention allocation and impression formation. *Personality and Social Psychology Bulletin, 17,* 548–559.

Hilton, J. L., & von Hippel, W. (1990). The role of consistency in the judgment of stereotype-relevant behaviors. *Personality and Social Psychology Bulletin, 16,* 430–448.

Hirt, E. R. (1990). Do I see only what I expect? Evidence for an expectancy-guided retrieval model. *Journal of Personality and Social Psychology, 58,* 937–951.

Holmes, J. G., Zanna, M. P., & Whitehead, L. A. (1986). Stress and social perception. Described in Jamieson, D. W., & Zanna, M. P. (1989). Need for structure in attitude formation and expression. In A. R. Pratkanis, S. J. Breckler & A. G. Greenwald (Eds.), *Attitude structure and function.* Hillsdale, NJ: Erlbaum.

Howard, J. W., & Rothbart, M. (1980). Social categorization and memory for ingroup and outgroup behavior. *Journal of Personality and Social Psychology, 38,* 301–310.

Jacoby, L. L. (1983). Remembering the data: Analyzing interactive processes in reading. *Journal of Verbal Learning and Verbal Behavior, 22,* 485–508.

James, W. (1890). *The principles of psychology.* New York: Dover.

Jeffrey, W. E. (1968). The orienting reflex and attention in cognitive development. *Psychological Review, 75,* 323–334.

Jenkins, J. J., Mink, W. D., & Russell, W. A. (1958). Associative clustering as a function of verbal associative strength. *Psychological Reports, 4,* 127–136.

Johnson, M. K., & Raye, C. L. (1981). Reality monitoring. *Psychological Review, 88,* 67–85.

Johnston, W. A. (1978). The intrusiveness of familiar nontarget information. *Memory and Cognition, 6,* 38–42.

Johnston, W. A., & Dark, V. J. (1986). Selective attention. *Annual Review of Psychology, 37,* 43–75.

Judd, C. M., & Park, B. (1988). Outgroup homogeneity: Judgments of variability at the individual and group levels. *Journal of Personality and Social Psychology, 54,* 778–788.

Judd, C. M., & Park, B. (1992). Definition and assessment of accuracy in social stereotypes. *Psychological Review, 100,* 109–128.

Jussim, L. (1991). Social perception and social reality: A reflection-construction model. *Psychological Review, 98,* 54–73.

Jussim, L., Coleman, L. M., & Lerch, L. (1987). The nature of stereotypes: A comparison and integration of three theories. *Journal of Personality and Social Psychology, 52,* 536–546.

Just, M. A., & Carpenter, P. A. (1980). A theory of reading: From eye movements to comprehension. *Psychological Review, 87,* 329–354.

Kahneman, D. (1973). *Attention and effort.* Englewood Cliffs: Prentice-Hall.

Kanouse, D. E., & Hanson, L. R. (1972). Negativity in evaluations. In E. E. Jones, D. E. Kanouse, H. H. Kelley, R. E. Nisbett, S. Valins, and B. Weiner (Eds.), *Attribution: Perceiving the causes of behavior* (pp. 47–62). Morristown, NJ: General Learning Press.

Katz, I., & Hass, R. G. (1988). Racial ambivalence and American value conflict: Correlational and priming studies of dual cognitive structures. *Journal of Personality and Social Psychology, 55,* 893–905.

Katz, P. A. (1976). The acquisition of racial attitudes in children. In P. A. Katz (Ed.), *Towards the elimination of racism* (pp. 125–154). New York: Pergamon Press.

Katz, P. A. (1983). Developmental foundations of gender and racial attitudes. In R. L. Leahy (Ed.), *The child's construction of social inequality* (pp. 41–78). New York: Academic Press.

Kelley, H. H. (1972). Attribution in social interaction. In E. E. Jones, D. E. Kanouse, H. H. Kelley, R. E. Nisbett, S. Valins, & B. Weiner (Eds.), *Attribution: Perceiving the causes of behavior* (pp. 1–26). Morristown, NJ: General Learning Press.

Kinder, D. R., & Sears, D. O. (1981). Prejudice and politics: Symbolic racial threats to the good life. *Journal of Personality and Social Psychology, 40,* 414–431.

Kintsch, W., & Keenan, J. (1973). Reading rate and retention as a function of the number of propositions in the base structures of sentences. *Cognitive Psychology, 5,* 257–274.

Klatzky, R. L., Martin, G. L., & Kane, R. A. (1982). Influence of social-category activation on processing of visual information. *Social Cognition, 1,* 95–109.

Klein, S. B., & Loftus, J. (1990). Rethinking the role of organization in person memory: An independent trace storage model. *Journal of Personality and Social Psychology, 59,* 400–410.

Klinger, M. R., & Beall, P. M. (1992, May). *Conscious and unconscious effects of stereotype activation.* Paper presented at the 64th Annual Meeting of the Midwestern Psychological Association, Chicago, IL.

Kolers, P. A. (1976). Reading a year later. *Journal of Experimental Psychology: Human Learning and Memory, 2,* 554–565.

Kosnik, W., Fikre, J., & Sekuler, R. (1985). Improvement in direction discrimination: No role for eye movements. *Perception and Psychophysics, 38,* 554–558.

Kosslyn, S. M. (1990). Mental imagery. In D. N. Osherson and S. M. Kosslyn (Eds.), *Visual cognition and action: An invitation to cognitive science,* Vol. 2. Cambridge, MA: MIT Press.

Krueger, J., Rothbart, M., & Sriram, N. (1989). Category learning and change: Differences in sensitivity to information that enhances or reduces inter-category distinctions. *Journal of Personality and Social Psychology, 56,* 866–875.

Kruglanski, A. W. (1970). Attributing trustworthiness in supervisors' worker relations. *Journal of Experimental Social Psychology, 6,* 214–232.

Kruglanski, A. W., & Freund, T. (1983). The freezing and unfreezing of lay inferences: Effects on impressional primacy, ethnic stereotyping, and numerical anchoring. *Journal of Experimental Social Psychology, 19,* 448–468.

Kulik, J. A. (1983). Confirmatory attribution and the perpetuation of social beliefs. *Journal of Personality and Social Psychology, 44,* 1171–1181.

Langer, E. J., & Piper, A. I. (1987). The prevention of mindlessness. *Journal of Personality and Social Psychology, 53,* 280–287.

LeCount, J., Maruyama, G., Peterson, R. S., Petersen-Lane, R. P., & Thomsen, C. J. (1992, August). *How reactive are measures of modern racism?* Paper presented at the 100th Annual Meeting of the American Psychological Association, Washington, DC.

Lemyre, L., & Smith, P. M. (1985). Intergroup discrimination and self-esteem in the minimal intergroup paradigm. *Journal of Personality and Social Psychology, 49,* 660–670.

Linville, P. W., & Jones, E. E. (1980). Polarized appraisals of outgroup members. *Journal of Personality and Social Psychology, 38,* 689–703.

Linville, P. W., Salovey, P., & Fischer, G. W. (1986). Stereotyping and perceived distributions of social characteristics: An application to ingroup-outgroup perception. In J. Dovidio & S. L. Gaertner (Eds.), *Prejudice, discrimination, and racism* (pp. 165–208). New York: Academic Press.

Locksley, A., Borgida, E., Brekke, N., & Hepburn, C. (1980). Sex stereotypes and social judgment. *Journal of Personality and Social Psychology, 39,* 821–831.

Loftus, E. F., & Palmer, J. C. (1973). Reconstruction of automobile destruction: An example of the interaction between language and memory. *Journal of Verbal Learning and Verbal Behavior, 13,* 585–589.

Logan, G. D. (1988). Toward an instance theory of automatization. *Psychological Review, 95,* 492–527.

Logan, G. D. (1990). Repetition priming and automaticity: Common underlying mechanisms? *Cognitive Psychology, 22,* 1–35.

Lord, C. G., Ross, L., & Lepper, M. (1979). Biased assimilation and attitude polarization: The effects of prior theories on subsequently considered evidence. *Journal of Personality and Social Psychology, 37,* 2098–2109.

Maass, A., Salvi, D., Arcuri, L., & Semin, G. (1989). Language use in intergroup contexts: The linguistic intergroup bias. *Journal of Personality and Social Psychology, 57,* 981–993.

MacLeod, C. M., & Bassili, J. N. (1989). Are implicit and explicit tests differentially sensitive to item-specific versus relational information? In S. Lewandowsky, J. C. Dunn, & K. Kirsner (Eds.), *Implicit Memory: Theoretical Issues* (pp. 159–172). Hillsdale, NJ: Erlbaum.

Macrae, C. N., Hewstone, M., & Griffiths, R. J. (1993). Processing load and memory for stereotype-based information. *European Journal of Social Psychology, 23,* 76–87.

Macrae, C. N., Milne, A. B., & Bodenhausen, G. V. (1994). Stereotypes as energy-saving devices: A peek inside the cognitive toolbox. *Journal of Personality and Social Psychology, 66,* 37–47.

Macrae, C. N., Stangor, C., & Milne, A. B. (1994). Activating social stereotypes: A functional analysis. *Journal of Experimental Social Psychology, 30,* 370–389.

Malpass, R. S., & Kravitz, J. (1969). Recognition of faces of own and other race. *Journal of Personality and Social Psychology, 13,* 330–334.

Manis, M., Nelson, T. E., & Shedler, J. (1988). Stereotypes and social judgment: Extremity, assimilation, and contrast. *Journal of Personality and Social Psychology, 55,* 28–36.

Manis, M., & Paskewitz, J. (1984a). Specificity and contrast effects: Judgments of psychopathology. *Journal of Experimental Social Psychology, 20,* 217–230.

Manis, M., & Paskewitz, J. (1984b). Judging psychopathology: Expectation and contrast. *Journal of Experimental Social Psychology, 20,* 363–381.

Manis, M., Paskewitz, J., & Cotler, S. (1986). Stereotypes and social judgments. *Journal of Personality and Social Psychology, 50,* 461–473.

Markus, H. (1977). Self-schemas and processing information about the self. *Journal of Personality and Social Psychology, 35,* 63–78.

Markus, H., Smith, J., & Moreland, R. L. (1985). Role of the self-concept in the perception of others. *Journal of Personality and Social Psychology, 49,* 1494–1512.

Markus, H., & Zajonc, R. B. (1985). The cognitive perspective in social psychology. In G. Lindzey & E. Aronson (Eds.), *Handbook of Social Psychology, 3.* Hillsdale, NJ: Erlbaum.

Martin, J. H. (1989). *Neuroanatomy.* New York: Elsevier.

Massad, C. M., Hubbard, M., & Newtson, D. (1979). Selective perception of events. *Journal of Experimental Social Psychology, 15,* 513–532.

McArthur, L. Z. (1982). Judging a book by its cover: A cognitive analysis of the relationship between physical appearance and stereotyping. In A. Hastorf & A. Isen (Eds.), *Cognitive social psychology* (pp. 149–211). New York: Elsevier.

McArthur, L. Z., & Post, D. L. (1977). Figural emphasis and person perception. *Journal of Experimental Social Psychology, 13,* 520–535.

McCann, C. D., Ostrom, T. M., Tyner, L. K., & Mitchell, M. L. (1985). Person perception in heterogeneous groups. *Journal of Personality and Social Psychology, 49,* 1449–1459.

McCollough, C. (1965). Color adaptation of edge-detectors in the human visual system. *Science, 149,* 1115–1116.
McConahay, J. B., Hardee, B. B., & Batts, V. (1981). Has racism declined? It depends upon who's asking and what is asked. *Journal of Conflict Resolution, 25,* 563–579.
McConahay, J. B., & Hough, J. C. (1976). Symbolic racism. *Journal of Social Issues, 32,* 23–45.
McGuire, W. (1981). The probabological model of cognitive structure and attitude change. In R. E. Petty, T. M. Ostrom, & T. C. Brock (Eds.), *Cognitive responses in persuasion* (pp. 291–308). Hillsdale, NJ: Erlbaum.
McGurk, H., & McDonald, J. (1976). Hearing lips and seeing voices. *Nature, 264,* 746–748.
Medin, D. L., & Ross, B. H. (1992). *Cognitive Psychology.* Fort Worth, TX: Harcourt Brace.
Merton, R. K. (1948). The self-fulfilling prophecy. *Antioch Review, 8,* 193–210.
Michon, J. A. (1966). Tapping regularity as a measure of perceptual motor load. *Ergonomics, 9,* 401–412.
Monteith, M. (1993). Self-regulation of prejudiced responses: Implications for progress in prejudice-reduction efforts. *Journal of Personality and Social Psychology, 65,* 469–485.
Morris, C. D., Bransford, J. D., & Franks, J. J. (1977). Levels of processing versus transfer appropriate processing. *Journal of Verbal Learning and Verbal Behavior, 16,* 519–533.
Moscovici, S., & Personnaz, B. (1980). Studies in social influence: V. Minority influence and conversion behavior in a perceptual task. *Journal of Experimental Social Psychology, 16,* 270–282.
Moscovici, S., & Personnaz, B. (1991). Studies in social influence: VI. Is Lenin orange or red? Imagery and social influence. *European Journal of Social Psychology, 21,* 101–118.
Neely, J. H. (1977). Semantic priming and retrieval from lexical memory: Role of inhibitionless spreading activation and limited-capacity attention. *Journal of Experimental Psychology: General, 106,* 226–254.
Neill, W. T., Beck, J. L., Bottalico, K. S., & Molloy, R. D. (1990). Effects of intentional versus incidental learning on explicit and implicit tests of memory. *Journal of Experimental Psychology: Learning, Memory, & Cognition, 16,* 457–463.
Nesdale, A. R., & Darmalingham, S. (1986). Category salience, stereotyping, and person memory. *Australian Journal of Psychology, 38,* 145–151.
Nesdale, A. R., & Darmalingham, S., & Kerr, G. K. (1987). Effect of subgroup ratio on stereotyping. *European Journal of Social Psychology, 17,* 353–356.
Newman, L. S., & Uleman, J. S. (1989). Spontaneous trait inferences. In J. S. Uleman & J. A. Bargh (Eds.), *Unintended thought* (pp. 155–188). New York: Guilford Press.
O'Sullivan, C. S., & Durso, F. T. (1984). Effect of schema-incongruent information on memory for stereotypical attributes. *Journal of Personality and Social Psychology, 47,* 55–70.
Ostrom, T. M., Lingle, J. H., Pryor, J., & Geva, N. (1980). Cognitive organization of person impressions. In R. Hastie, T. M. Ostrom, D. L. Hamilton, R. S. Wyer, E. Ebbesen, & D. Carlston (Eds.), *Person memory: The cognitive basis of social perception.* Hillsdale, NJ: Erlbaum.
Ostrom, T. M., & Sedikides, C. (1992). Out-group homogeneity effects in natural and minimal groups. *Psychological Bulletin, 112,* 536–552.
Padgham, C. A., & Saunders, J. E. (1975). *The perception of light and color.* London: Bell.
Park, B., & Hastie, R. (1987). Perception of variability in category development: Instance- versus abstraction-based stereotypes. *Journal of Personality and Social Psychology, 53,* 621–635.
Park, B., & Rothbart, M. (1982). Perception of out-group homogeneity and levels of social categorization: Memory for the subordinate attributes of in-group and out-group members. *Journal of Personality and Social Psychology, 42,* 1051–1068.
Perdue, C. W., & Gurtman, M. B. (1990). Evidence for the automaticity of ageism. *Journal of Experimental Social Psychology, 26,* 199–216.
Pettigrew, T. F. (1979). The ultimate attribution error: Extending Allport's cognitive analysis of prejudice. *Personality and Social Psychology Bulletin, 5,* 461–476.

Pettigrew, T. F., Allport, G. W., & Barnett, E. O. (1958). Binocular resolution and perception of race in South Africa. *British Journal of Psychology, 40,* 265–278.

Pichert, J. W., & Anderson, R. C. (1977). Taking different perspectives on a story. *Journal of Educational Psychology, 69,* 309–315.

Porter, J. D. R. (1971). *Black child, white child: The development of racial attitudes.* Cambridge, MA: Harvard University Press.

Posner, M. I., & Snyder, C. R. R. (1975). Attention and cognitive control. In R. L. Solso (Ed.), *Information processing and cognition: The Loyola symposium.* Hillsdale, NJ: Erlbaum.

Powell, M. C., & Fazio, R. H. (1993). Unpublished raw data reported in Fazio, R. H., Roskos-Ewoldson, D. R., & Powell, M. C. (1994). Attitudes, perception, and attention. In P. M. Niedenthal & S. Kitayama (Eds.), *The heart's eye: Emotional influences in perception and attention* (pp. 197–216). San Diego: Academic Press.

Pratto, F., & Bargh, J. A. (1991). Stereotyping based on apparently individuating information: Trait and global components of sex stereotypes under attention overload. *Journal of Experimental Social Psychology, 27,* 26–47.

Pratto, F., & John, (1991). Automatic vigilance: The attention-grabbing power of negative social information. *Journal of Personality and Social Psychology, 61,* 380–391.

Proshansky, H. M. (1966). The development of intergroup attitudes. In L. W. Hoffman & M. L. Hoffman (Eds.), *Review of child development research* (Vol. 2, pp. 311–371). New York: Russell Sage Foundation.

Pyszczynski, T. A., & Greenberg, J. (1981). Role of disconfirmed expectancies in the instigation of attributional processing. *Journal of Personality and Social Psychology, 40,* 31–38.

Pyszczynski, T. A., Laprelle, J., & Greenberg, J. (1987). Encoding and retrieval effects of general person characterizations on memory for incongruent and congruent information. *Personality and Social Psychology Bulletin, 13,* 556–567.

Quattrone, G. A. (1986). On the perception of a group's variability. In S. Worchel & W. Austin (Eds.), *Psychology of intergroup relations* (pp. 25–48). Chicago: Nelson Hall.

Quattrone, G. A., & Jones, E. E. (1980). The perception of variability within in-groups and out-groups: Implications for the law of small numbers. *Journal of Personality and Social Psychology, 38,* 141–152.

Rappold, V. A., & Hashtroudi, S. (1991). Does organization improve priming? *Journal of Experimental Psychology: Learning, Memory, & Cognition, 17,* 103–114.

Reder, L. M. (1982). Plausibility judgments versus fact retrieval: Alternative strategies for sentence verification. *Psychological Review, 89,* 250–280.

Richardson-Klavehn, A., & Bjork, R. A. (1988). Measures of memory. *Annual Review of Psychology, 39,* 475–543.

Rock, I., & Guttman, D. (1981). The effect of inattention on form perception. *Journal of Experimental Psychology: Human Perception and Performance, 7,* 275–285.

Roediger, H. L. III (1990). Implicit memory: Retention without remembering. *American Psychologist, 45,* 1043–1056.

Roediger, H. L. III, & Blaxton, T. A. (1987). Effects of varying modality, surface features and retention interval on priming in word-fragment completion. *Memory & Cognition, 15,* 379–388.

Rojahn, K., & Pettigrew, T. F. (1992). Memory for schema-relevant information: A meta-analytic resolution. *British Journal of Social Psychology, 31,* 81–109.

Rosenthal, R., & Jacobson, L. (1968). *Pygmalion effects in the classroom.* New York: Holt, Rinehart, & Winston.

Rothbart, M., Evans, M., & Fulero, S. (1979). Recall for confirming events: Memory processes and the maintenance of social stereotypes. *Journal of Experimental Social Psychology, 15,* 343–355.

Ruble, D. N., & Stangor, C. (1986). Stalking the elusive schema: Insights from developmental and social psychological analyses of gender schemas. *Social Cognition, 4,* 227–261.

Sagar, H. A., & Schofield, J. W. (1980). Racial and behavioral cues in black and white children's perceptions of ambiguously aggressive acts. *Journal of Personality and Social Psychology, 56,* 698–708.

Samuel, A. G. (1981). Phonemic restoration: Insights from a new methodology. *Journal of Experimental Psychology: General, 110,* 474–494.

Sanbonmatsu, D. M., Akimoto, S. A., & Gibson, B. D. (1994). Stereotype-based blocking in social explanation. *Personality and Social Psychology Bulletin, 20,* 71–81.

Schacter, D. (1987). Implicit memory: History and current status. *Journal of Experimental Psychology: Learning, Memory, and Cognition, 13,* 501–518.

Schneider, W., & Shiffrin, R. M. (1977). Controlled and automatic human information processing: I. Detection, search, and attention. *Psychological Review, 84,* 1–66.

Sekaquaptewa, D., & von Hippel, W. (1994, May). *The role of prejudice in encoding and memory of stereotype-relevant behaviors.* Paper presented at the 66th Annual Meeting of the Midwestern Psychological Association, Chicago, IL.

Semin, G. R., & Fiedler, K. (1988). The cognitive functions of linguistic categories in describing persons: Social cognition and language. *Journal of Personality and Social Psychology, 54,* 558–568.

Shiffrin, R. M., & Schneider, W. (1977). Controlled and automatic human information processing: II. Perceptual learning, automatic attending, and a general theory. *Psychological Review, 84,* 127–190.

Sigall, H., & Page, R. (1971). Current stereotypes: A little fading, a little faking. *Journal of Personality and Social Psychology, 18,* 247–255.

Silvestre, E. (1994). *Cultural identity and racial self-prejudice.* Visiting Lecture Series in Comparative Studies, Ohio State University, Columbus, OH.

Skowbo, D., Timney, B., Gentry, T., & Morant, R. B. (1975). McCollough effects: Experimental findings and theoretical accounts. *Psychological Bulletin, 82,* 497–510.

Skowronski, J. J., & Carlston, D. E. (1987). Social judgment and social memory: The role of cue diagnosticity in negativity, positivity, and extremity biases. *Journal of Personality and Social Psychology, 52,* 689–699.

Skowronski, J. J., & Carlston, D. E. (1989). Negativity and extremity biases in impression formation: A review of explanations. *Psychological Bulletin, 105,* 131–142.

Slusher, M. P., & Anderson, C. A. (1987). When reality monitoring fails: The role of imagination in stereotype maintenance. *Journal of Personality and Social Psychology, 52,* 653–662.

Smith, E. R., & Branscombe, N. R. (1988). Category accessibility as implicit memory. *Journal of Experimental Social Psychology, 24,* 490–504.

Smith, E. R., & Zarate, M. A. (1990). Exemplar and prototype use in social categorization. *Social Cognition, 8,* 243–262.

Smith, E. R., & Zarate, M. A. (1992). Exemplar-based model of social judgment. *Psychological Review, 99,* 3–21.

Smith, E. R., Stewart, T. L., & Buttram, R. T. (1992). Inferring a trait from a behavior has long-term, highly specific effects. *Journal of Personality and Social Psychology, 62,* 753–759.

Sniderman, P. M., Piazza, T., Tetlock, P. E., & Kendrick, A. (1991). The new racism. *American Journal of Political Science, 35,* 423–447.

Sniderman, P. M., & Tetlock, P. E. (1986). Symbolic racism: Problems of political motive attribution. *Journal of Social Issues, 42,* 129–150.

Snodgrass, J. G., & Hirshman, E. (1991). Theoretical explorations of the Bruner-Potter (1964) interference effect. *Journal of Memory and Language, 30,* 273–293.

Snyder, M., & Uranowitz, S. W. (1978). Reconstructing the past: Some cognitive consequences of person perception. *Journal of Personality and Social Psychology, 36,* 941–950.

Snyder, M., & Swann, W. B., Jr. (1978). Behavioral confirmation in social interaction: From social perception to social reality. *Journal of Experimental Social Psychology, 14,* 148–162.

Snyder, M. L., & Frankel, A. (1976). Observer bias: A stringent test of behavior engulfing the field. *Journal of Personality and Social Psychology, 34,* 857–864.

Snyder, M. L., Kleck, R. E., Strenta, A., & Mentzer, S. J. (1979). Avoidance of the handicapped:

An attributional ambiguity analysis. *Journal of Personality and Social Psychology, 37,* 2297–2306.
Spelke, E. S. (1990). Principles of object perception. *Cognitive Science, 14,* 29–56.
Spence, J., Helmreich, R., & Stapp, J. (1973). A short version of the Attitudes Toward Women Scale. *Bulletin of the Psychonomic Society, 2,* 219–220.
Spencer, S. J., & Fein, S. (1994, May). *The effect of self-image threats on stereotyping.* Paper presented at the 65th Annual Meeting of the Eastern Psychological Association, Providence, RI.
Srull, T. K. (1981). Person memory: Some tests of associative storage and retrieval models. *Journal of Experimental Psychology: Human Learning and Memory, 7,* 440–463.
Srull, T. K., Lichtenstein, M., & Rothbart, M. (1985). Associative storage and retrieval processes in person memory. *Journal of Experimental Psychology: Learning, Memory, and Cognition, 11,* 316–345.
Srull, T. K., & Wyer, R. S. (1980). Category accessibility and social perception: Some implications for the study of person memory and interpersonal judgments. *Journal of Personality and Social Psychology, 38,* 841–856.
Srull, T. K., & Wyer, R. S. (1989). Person memory and judgment. *Psychological Review, 96,* 58–83.
Stangor, C., & Lange, J. (1994). Mental representations of social groups: Advances in understanding stereotypes and stereotyping. In M. Zanna (Ed.), *Advances in experimental social psychology,* (Vol. 26, pp. 357–416). San Diego: Academic Press.
Stangor, C., & McMillan, D. (1992). Memory for expectancy-congruent and expectancy-incongruent information: A review of the social and social developmental literatures. *Psychological Bulletin, 111,* 42–61.
Stangor, C., & Ruble, D. (1987). Development of gender role knowledge and gender constancy. In W. Damon (Ed.), *Children's gender schemata: New directions for child development* (Vol. 38, pp. 5–22). San Francisco: Jossey-Bass, Inc.
Stern, L. D., Marrs, S., Millar, M. G., & Cole, E. (1984). Processing time and the recall of inconsistent and consistent behaviors of individuals and groups. *Journal of Personality and Social Psychology, 47,* 253–262.
Sulin, R. A., & Dooling, D. J. (1974). Intrusion of a thematic idea in retention of prose. *Journal of Experimental Psychology, 103,* 255–262.
Swim, J. K. (1994). Perceived versus meta-analytic effect sizes: An assessment of the accuracy of gender stereotypes. *Journal of Personality and Social Psychology, 66,* 21–36.
Taylor, D. G., Sheatsley, P. B., & Greeley, A. M. (1978). Attitudes toward racial integration. *Scientific American, 238,* 42–49.
Taylor, D. M., & Jaggi, V. (1974). Ethnocentrism and causal attribution in a South Indian context. *Journal of Cross-Cultural Psychology, 5,* 162–171.
Taylor, S. E., & Fiske, S. T. (1978). Salience, attention, and attribution: Top of the head phenomena. In L. Berkowitz (Ed.), *Advances in experimental social psychology* (Vol. 11, pp. 249–288). New York: Academic Press.
Taylor, S. E., Fiske, S. T., Etcoff, N., & Ruderman, A. (1978). The categorical and contextual bases of person memory and stereotyping. *Journal of Personality and Social Psychology, 36,* 778–793.
Trope, Y. (1986). Identification and inferential processes in dispositional attribution. *Psychological Review, 93,* 239–257.
Trope, Y. (1989). Stereotypes and dispositional judgments. In D. Bar-Tal, C. F. Graumann, A. W. Kruglanski, & W. Stroebe (Eds.), *Stereotypes and prejudice: Changing conceptions* (pp. 133–149). New York: Springer-Verlag.
Trope, Y., Cohen, O., Alfieri, T. (1991). Behavior identification as a mediator of dispositional inference. *Journal of Personality and Social Psychology, 61,* 873–883.
Tulving, E. (1972). Episodic and semantic memory. In E. Tulving & W. Donaldson (Eds.), *Organization of memory* (pp. 381–403). New York: Academic Press.
Tulving, E., & Thomson, D. M. (1973). Encoding specificity and retrieval processes in episodic memory. *Psychological Review, 80,* 352–373.

Van Essen, D. C. (1988). Extrastriate visual cortex. In R. Held (Ed.) *Sensory systems I: Vision and visual systems.* Birkhauser: Cambridge, MA.

Vargas, P., & von Hippel, W. (1993, June). *The role of stereotypes and prejudice in behavioral identification.* Paper presented at the 5th Annual Meeting of the American Psychological Society, Chicago, IL.

Vargas, P., von Hippel, W., Fein, S., & Darr, K. (1994, May). *The role of encoding processes in motivated elevations.* Paper presented at the 66th Annual Meeting of the Midwestern Psychological Association, Chicago, IL.

von Hippel, W., & Baker, S. (1993). *Implicit memory for incongruent information: The role of effortful encoding in stereotype maintenance.* Unpublished manuscript, Ohio State University, Columbus, OH.

von Hippel, W., & Baker, S. (1994). *Unpublished raw data.* Ohio State University, Columbus, OH.

von Hippel, W., & Hawkins, C. (1994). Stimulus exposure time and perceptual memory. *Perception and Psychophysics, 56,* 525–535.

von Hippel, W., Hawkins, C., & Fu, V. (1994, August). *The effect of alcohol intoxication on intentional and automatic processes.* Paper presented as part of the symposium, Alcohol intoxication and social behavior, at the 102nd Annual Convention of the American Psychological Association, Los Angeles, CA.

von Hippel, W., Hawkins, C., & Narayan, S. (in press). Personality and perceptual expertise: Individual differences in perceptual identification. *Psychological Science.*

von Hippel, W., Jonides, J., Hilton, J. L., & Narayan, S. (1993). Inhibitory effect of schematic processing on perceptual encoding. *Journal of Personality and Social Psychology, 64,* 921–935.

von Hippel, W., Vargas, P., & Sekaquaptewa, D. (1994). *Prejudice as process.* Unpublished manuscript. Ohio State University, Columbus, OH.

Weber, R., & Crocker, J. (1983). Cognitive processes in the revision of stereotypic beliefs. *Journal of Personality and Social Psychology, 45,* 961–977.

White, J. D., & Carlston, D. E. (1983). Consequences of schemata for attention, impressions, and recall in complex social interactions. *Journal of Personality and Social Psychology, 45,* 538–549.

Wilder, D. A. (1981). Perceiving persons as a group: Categorization and intergroup relations. In D. L. Hamilton (Ed.), *Cognitive processes in stereotyping and intergroup behavior* (pp. 213–257). Hillsdale, NJ: Erlbaum.

Wilder, D. A., & Shapiro, P. (1989). Effects of anxiety on impression formation in a group context: An anxiety-assimilation hypothesis. *Journal of Experimental Social Psychology, 25,* 481–499.

Wilder, D. A., & Thompson, J. E. (1988). Assimilation and contrast effects in the judgments of groups. *Journal of Personality and Social Psychology, 54,* 62–73.

Wills, T. A. (1981). Downward comparison principles in social psychology. *Psychological Bulletin, 90,* 245–271.

Winter, L., & Uleman, J. S. (1984). When are social judgments made? Evidence for the spontaneousness of trait inferences. *Journal of Personality and Social Psychology, 47,* 237–252.

Winter, L., Uleman, J. S., & Cuniff, C. (1985). How automatic are social judgments? *Journal of Personality and Social Psychology, 49,* 904–917.

Wittenbrink, B., Guest, P., & Hilton, J. L. (1993, June). *Turning base metal into gold: Stereotypes as explanatory frameworks.* Paper presented at the 3rd Annual Meeting of the Society for Personality and Social Psychology, Chicago, IL.

Wyatt, D. F., & Campbell, D. T. (1951). On the liability of stereotype or hypothesis. *Journal of Abnormal and Social Psychology, 46,* 496–500.

Yee, D. K., & Eccles, J. S. (1988). Parent perceptions and attributions for children's math achievement. *Sex Roles, 19,* 317–333.

Zadny, J., & Gerard, H. B. (1974). Attributed intentions and informational selectivity. *Journal of Experimental Social Psychology, 10,* 34–52.

Zarate, M. A., & Smith, E. R. (1990). Person categorization and stereotyping. *Social Cognition, 8,* 161–185.

PSYCHOLOGICAL BARRIERS TO DISPUTE RESOLUTION

Lee Ross
Andrew Ward

Yet, there remains another wall. This wall constitutes a psychological barrier between us, a barrier of suspicion, a barrier of rejection; a barrier of fear, of deception, a barrier of hallucination without any action, deed or decision.
A barrier of distorted and eroded interpretation of every event and statement. . . .
Today, through my visit to you, I ask why don't we stretch out our hands with faith and sincerity so that together we might destroy this barrier?

—President Anwar al-Sadat,
Statement before the Israeli Knesset,
Jerusalem, November 29, 1977

I. Introduction

Why do labor and management endure long and costly strikes? Why do plaintiffs and defendants waste time and money in endless litigation? And, of course, why do nations so often squander their resources and the lives of their citizenry in ruinous military ventures before coming to the negotiation table? Why, in short, do deadly conflicts and debilitating stalemates persist in the face of potential settlements that plainly would serve the interests of both sides?

The barriers of special concern in this chapter,[1] as our opening quote from the late Egyptian leader suggests, are psychological. We explore cognitive and motivational processes that impede mutually beneficial exchanges of concessions and render seemingly tractable conflicts refractory to negotiated resolution. In such cases, we argue, the failure to achieve significant progress represents a kind of "market inefficiency," in much the same sense that there is a failure or ineffi-

---

[1]The content and organization of this chapter draw heavily upon two earlier overviews: Ross and Stillinger (1991) and Mnookin and Ross (in press).

ciency when a motivated buyer and seller are unable to consummate a deal under conditions where the buyer's maximum purchase price exceeds the seller's minimum selling price.

We shall begin by distinguishing psychological barriers from two other kinds of impediments—those that are essentially products of strategic calculation and those that arise from "impersonal" organizational, institutional, or structural factors having little to do either with calculation or with the psychological biases exhibited by individual actors. We shall then proceed to a more detailed examination of five particular psychological barriers that have figured heavily in our own research and that of our fellow investigators at the Stanford Center on Conflict and Negotiation (SCCN). Next, we shall examine three broader theoretical perspectives that speak to sources of resentment, misunderstanding, misattribution, and distrust in the negotiation process—once again with disproportionate, but not exclusive, emphasis on our own work and that of our SCCN colleagues (see Arrow, Mnookin, Ross, Tversky, & Wilson, in press). Finally, we shall explore some tentative implications for the theory and practice of dispute resolution, especially for those intrepid third-party facilitators, mediators, or peacemakers who confront what is surely one of the most important and difficult challenges in the whole broad spectrum of applied social psychology.

II. Types of Barriers

A. INSTITUTIONAL BARRIERS

One category of barriers relates to broad organizational, institutional, and other structural factors that impede settlements. These factors, outlined below, range from bureaucratic structures restricting the free flow of information to the political realities that make leaders reluctant to expose themselves to criticism and second-guessing.

1. Restricted Channels of Information and Communication

Sometimes channels of communication are nonexistent, or so heavily restricted that the parties cannot air their grievances or otherwise provide each other with information about priorities and interests that could allow them to frame mutually beneficial settlement proposals (see Arrow, in press; Wilson, in press). Restrictions to information transfer can be bureaucratic, reflecting divided or even conflicting responsibilities and areas of expertise (for example, the responsibilities of technical experts, financial officers, advisory boards, and elected officials). Such restrictions can even be mandated by laws or regulations. Lawyers, office-holders, entrepreneurs, and union officials all face restrictions on whom they can meet with, and what they can discuss privately. Restrictions in communication may even be the result of the very conflicts that need resolution. Countries that break off diplomatic relations may forbid all contact with the "enemy." And, of course, individuals can reach the point in a conflictual relationship where they simply refuse to communicate with their antagonists.

2. Problems of Intermediate Steps or Stages

Attempts to bridge the existing chasm between the parties to a conflict, or rather to bridge the gap between an unsatisfactory present relationship and a more salutary future one, may be thwarted by a structural problem involving intermediate steps or stages. That is, in order to reach a long-term resolution that is satisfactory to both parties, one or even both parties may be obliged to take a step backward—that is, to accept, at least temporarily, changes in the status quo that leave it poorer, weaker, or more vulnerable than before. Labor may have to make a temporary wage concession in order for management to increase the resources it subsequently will be able to bring to the table to satisfy labor's long-term needs for improved salary, benefits, or security. One side in a civil war may have to agree to give up some of its weapons, territory, or rhetoric before the other side will agree to participate in unification talks or take a meaningful step on the path to reconciliation. In so doing, however, the side taking the initial step or making the initially greater or more concrete concession leaves itself vulnerable. For the other side may find the new state of affairs to its liking—an improvement not only over the pre-existing status quo but also over the state of affairs envisioned as the longer term resolution. Accordingly, it may renege upon its promises to take further steps on the path to resolution, and leave the initial concession-maker worse off than before.

In part, of course, the problem of intermediate stages may be seen in psychological rather than structural terms, as a problem not of staging or temporary disadvantage but of trust. But even the most wary antagonists may find that they can take a step on the path to a happier future by utilizing or creating structures that depend neither on trust nor trustworthiness. Thus, third parties can be empowered from the outset of the dispute to adjudicate any disagreements that subsequently arise about timetables or compliance. They even can be given the means to enforce agreements—for example, by holding resources belonging to each party that will be forfeited if either party fails to take the subsequent steps to which it has committed itself. Conversely, distrustful antagonists unnecessarily may remain locked in a debilitating struggle because neither side dares to put itself at the mercy of the other, and no structures or institutions exist to prevent one side's temporary disadvantage or sacrifice from becoming permanent.

3. Multiple Interest Groups

A number of structural problems or barriers arise when disputes involve more than two parties or interest groups. Disputes about protection of the global environment, including matters such as utilization of natural resources or location of waste disposal sites, are a case in point (see Sebenius, in press; Susskind, 1994; Susskind, in press; Susskind & Cruikshank, 1987; and Zeckhauser & Parson, in press). Many different stakeholders (workers, politicians, tax payers, entrepreneurs, nature enthusiasts, home owners, etc.) who have many different types of interests and degrees of investment are likely to be involved. It is very difficult in such cases to ensure that all parties will be represented at the bargaining table and more difficult still to reach agreements that leave all the parties better off, or at least satisfied that their concerns have been given appropriate weight. Indeed, formal arguments have been offered (Arrow, 1951) to demonstrate the depth and elusiveness of this problem.[2]

The problem of multiple interest groups becomes particularly intractable when (as in many environmental negotiations) a small, well-defined group of actors (e.g., major investors in a utility company, land owners and developers, etc.) clearly stand to gain or lose a great deal of money, while a larger and less well-defined group of bystanders (e.g., local residents, occasional resource users, etc.) face prospective changes in "quality of life"—changes that are uncertain, subject to dispute, and impossible to quantify in purely financial terms. The institutions available for handling such disputes (i.e., courts and government agencies) generally are poorly equipped to weigh and resolve such competing interests. Moreover, existing institutions may even be prevented by legal, ethical, or political constraints from entertaining settlement plans and procedures of the sort that could increase the efficiency of agreements and the satisfaction of the contending parties (e.g., use of "side payments," or the creation of "markets" for exchanging costs and benefits). For example, in theory a sensible plan might call for governments to "hire" communities to accept undesirable projects—that is, to place waste disposal sites, power plants, halfway houses, and so forth in whichever communities would demand the least in the way of direct financial payments or other social benefits to local residents. But existing institutions of law and government generally make such "auctions" unfeasible or even illegal.

4. The Principal/Agent Problem

A third barrier to be discussed relates to transaction-cost economics, and is often called the principal/agent problem (Pratt & Zeckhauser, 1985; see also Gilson & Mnookin, in press; Mnookin & Wilson, 1989). The basic idea is familiar.

---

[2]What Arrow (1951) specifically demonstrated was the "impossibility" of satisfying simultaneously even a modest set of desirable conditions or requirements for aggregating individual preference orderings.

The personal interests of an agent who is serving as a negotiator (whether it be a lawyer, diplomat, labor leader, or corporate executive) may be quite different from the interests of the party that the agent represents, and this difference in interests may constitute a significant barrier to the efficient resolution of conflict.

Litigation is fraught with such principal/agent problems. In civil litigation, for example—particularly where the lawyers on both sides are being paid by the hour—there is very little incentive for the opposing lawyers to cooperate in reaching early, resource-conserving settlements. Indeed, the incentive structure of the situation may induce them to favor costly, adversarial litigation and avoid resolving otherwise "settleable" cases until they reach the courthouse steps (see Png, 1983). Alternatively, lawyers seeking to maintain a reputation for cooperativeness that will aid in their ongoing relationships with other litigators may sacrifice the interests of their clients by avoiding confrontation and aggressive bargaining (Gilson & Mnookin, in press).

Principal/agent problems may extend to areas beyond those involving the distribution of financial costs and benefits or the maintenance of personal reputations for toughness or cooperativeness. Agents may have ideological axes to grind, be constrained by institutional loyalties, or be seeking to curry favor with particular constituencies. They may feel that their clients do not know their own best interests. They may even create obstacles to settlement because they feel that their clients are negotiating deals that are immoral, unethical, or against the public interest. More generally, agents and other third parties inevitably bring their own mix of strategic concerns and psychological biases to the negotiation process—all of which can create barriers to efficient dispute resolution beyond those presented by the conflicting interests and aspirations of the principal parties.

5. Political Considerations

Negotiators, and those they serve, often are constrained by the political context within which their efforts and outcomes will be evaluated. This problem has been particularly acute in arms-control negotiations (see Panofsky, in press). Even when a proposed resolution or policy change would advance his or her side's overall interests, the negotiator's willingness to make particular concessions in achieving that resolution can be exploited by political opponents. Critics can always complain that the proposed deal is less advantageous or equitable than some *other* deal that might have been obtained through more resolute or skilled negotiation strategies. Often they even can point to specific predictions or promises suggesting that the price of settlement would be smaller or the gains of settlement larger. Critics will find receptive audiences when they insist that their side was entitled to, and should have insisted on, these more favorable terms. Indeed, such critics can rely on the fact that psychological processes and biases of the sort that we explore later in this chapter generally will make proposed terms of settlement, especially those involving exchanges of concessions, seem disappointingly unattractive and unfair.

In light of these political risks, maintenance of the status quo often proves to be an attractive option for individuals who currently hold favor or power. Those individuals have more to lose from a mistake (or even from the *charge* that they have made a mistake) than they have to gain from any "breakthrough." Indeed, it is all too easy to see the political advantages of foot-dragging (i.e., continuing to negotiate, but refusing to culminate specific, consequential agreements). Such a strategy permits political leaders to proclaim their commitment to the goal of conflict resolution, while at the same time demonstrating firmness of resolve in protecting the interests of their constituencies, without facing the disappointment and criticism that are bound to come when one settles for less than had been sought, anticipated, or even promised earlier in the political process.

B. STRATEGIC BARRIERS

Barriers of the second type we shall consider are products of calculation. Adversaries adopt negotiation strategies that they believe will increase their share of any gains achievable through trades of concessions; but in so doing, they preclude or diminish the possibility of efficient outcomes. Although there is nothing counternormative about the employment of such strategies, miscalculation or misinterpretation can lead those who employ them to compromise both their immediate interests and their long-term relationship (see Fisher, Ury, & Patton, 1991; Raiffa, 1982; Wilson, in press).

The relevant barriers to efficiency can be appreciated in most general terms by recognizing the "negotiator's dilemma" (see Lax & Sebenius, 1986; Mnookin, 1993; Rubin, 1994). In most bargaining sessions, negotiators are working to achieve simultaneously two very different objectives. First, they are trying to maximize the joint value of the ultimate settlement, that is, to increase the pool of benefits or, metaphorically, the size of the "pie" to be divided. At the same time, however, they are seeking to maximize their own side's share of the benefit pool, that is, the size and attractiveness of their particular "slice" of the pie. Therein lies the dilemma. Ploys that can be used by bargainers to increase their share of the pie tend to shrink the overall size of that pie. Conversely, strategies that help to maximize the size of the pie compromise the bargainer's ability to claim the largest possible slice for their own side.

1. The Practice of Secrecy or Deception

The negotiators' dilemma that we have described is particularly clear with respect to the problem of revealing versus concealing interests. On the one hand, accurate information about goals, priorities, preferences, resources, and opportunities is essential for negotiating parties to frame agreements that offer optimal "gains of trade"—that is, agreements tailored to take fullest advantage of asymmetries in the parties' objectives and interests (see Arrow, in press). Such information may even allow the parties to "create additional value" by taking advantage of their complementary needs (Follet, 1942) or by combining their resources synergistically in a way that creates previously unforeseen "win–win" opportunities (see Fisher, 1994; Fisher et al., 1991; Lax & Sebenius, 1986; Raiffa, 1982). Accordingly, the parties have a clear incentive to determine each other's interests, and perhaps even to reveal their own so that the other side, or some creative third party, can frame a deal to maximize joint advantage.

On the other hand, the parties also have a clear incentive to conceal their true interests and priorities, or even to mislead the other side about them. By feigning attachment to whatever resources they are ready to give up in trade, and by feigning relative indifference to whatever resources they seek to gain (while concealing opportunities and plans for utilization of those resources), each party seeks to win the best possible terms of trade for itself. In other words, total frankness and "full disclosure," or at least greater frankness and fuller disclosure than that practiced by the other side in a negotiation, leave one vulnerable in the distributive aspects of bargaining. Accordingly, the sharp bargainer is tempted, and may rationally deem it advantageous to practice secrecy and deception.

Such tactics, however, can lead to unnecessary deadlocks and costly delays or, more fundamentally, to failures to discover efficient trades or outcomes (see Raiffa, 1982; Wilson, in press). A simple example can illustrate the dilemma facing negotiators, and the barrier imposed by the strategic concealment or misrepresentation of information. Suppose that Andrew receives a Christmas gift of ten tickets to upcoming basketball games, whereas Lee receives a gift of ten bottles of a fine California chardonnay. Suppose further that, unbeknownst to Lee, Andrew loves wine and hates basketball, while Lee, unbeknownst to Andrew, values a basketball ticket and a bottle of chardonnay equally. Andrew, in service of his current resources and preferences, suggests to Lee that both of them might benefit from a trade.

Now, if Andrew discloses to Lee that he loves wine but has no interest in basketball, Lee might "strategically" but deceptively insist that he shares Andrew's preferences and, accordingly, propose that Andrew give him all ten basketball tickets (which he says have relatively little value to him but might interest his children) in exchange for one of his "very valuable" bottles of wine. Andrew might even agree, and thus sell his tickets more cheaply than he could have sold them if, concealing his taste for wine and distaste for basketball, he had suggested a trade of five tickets for five bottles of chardonnay (on the grounds that he would prefer some variety in his self-indulgences).

Note, however, that such an "even trade" (i.e., five tickets for five bottles of wine), although more equitable than the ten-for-one exchange proposed by Lee, would still be inefficient, because it fails to take full advantage of the differing tastes of the two parties. That is, a more efficient trade surely would have been accomplished if both Andrew and Lee had been candid about their preferences, either to each other or to some trusted broker. In the face of such mutual candor, Andrew would have ended up exchanging all or at least most of his basketball tickets for all or at least most of Lee's wine, perhaps with some "side payment" to sweeten the deal for Lee, or better still, with linkage of this exchange to some other equally efficient exchange in which it was Andrew, who, at little or no cost to himself, accommodated Lee's particular needs or tastes.

2. Intransigence and Other "Hard Ball" Tactics

Even when both parties in a negotiation know all the relevant information, and are fully aware of the potential gains available from a negotiated deal, strategic bargaining over how to "divide the pie" can still lead to deadlock (with no deal at all), or to protracted and expensive bargaining that essentially shrinks the pie. In particular, tough, intransigent bargaining tactics, which may be rational for self-interested parties concerned with maximizing the size of their own slice of the pie, can often lead to inefficient outcomes. Those subjected to such tactics often respond in kind, and the net result is likely, at best, to be the incurring of additional costs in the dispute-resolution process (frustration, fees to agents, and loss of opportunity arising from delay) and at worst the failure to consummate a mutually beneficial agreement (see Raiffa, 1982; Rubin, 1994; Rubin, Pruitt, & Kim, 1994).

The potential costs of intransigent bargaining strategies were nicely demonstrated in a study conducted a generation ago by Benton, Kelley, and Liebling (1972). Subjects bargained with a confederate over the division of a sum of money under experimental constraints that prohibited an "even split" of the cash, and provided that neither party would receive any money if the bargainers failed to reach an agreement by the end of the session. Depending on condition, the confederate adopted one of three negotiations strategies: (a) initially demanding the most self-serving division of the money possible and then maintaining that demand throughout the negotiation; (b) initially demanding a "minimum win" allocation (i.e., the most even distribution favoring the confederate) then maintaining that more modest demand throughout the negotiation; or (c) initially demanding the most self-serving division but, if the offer was not accepted, slowly reducing the demand to the more moderate minimum-win level.

The results were clear-cut. The strategy of making an extreme demand but then reducing it to a more moderate level when it proved necessary to do so yielded greater monetary gains than either intransigent strategy. Two factors accounted for this advantage. First, the flexible strategy produced many more agreements than the sustained demand for the most self-serving division (61%

vs. 36%)—indeed, almost as many as the sustained moderate demand (64%). Second, unlike the sustained moderate demand, the flexible strategy was able to take advantage of those few opportunities in which the subject agreed to an early demand for a more unequal division. Interestingly, Benton et al. also found that subjects faced with an opponent who was initially extreme in his demands but willing to compromise felt more responsible for the outcome, and more satisfied, than did those who faced an intransigent opponent—even one who was "moderate" from the outset.

Intransigent bargaining is particularly likely to occur when one or both parties believes that "time is on its side"—that it has greater patience or greater resources than its adversary, or that delay will exact greater costs from the other side than its own side, or, more generally, that the passage of time will weaken the other side's bargaining position relative to its own. Indeed, in the search for strategic advantage, the parties in a conflict or negotiation may threaten to escalate the costs of deadlock, and may carry out their threats (thereby shrinking the size of the pie and the prospect for an outcome satisfactory to both sides). Those experienced in the civil litigation process see this all too often. One or both parties threatens extensive and costly pretrial discovery as leverage to force the other side into agreeing to a more favorable settlement. It even makes its threat credible, by producing a great deal of "paper" for the other side to deal with—to which the other side responds in kind. And the net result, typically, is that both sides waste a great deal of time and money in the process.

C. PSYCHOLOGICAL BARRIERS

The final set of barriers to be considered are *psychological* in nature. Individually and collectively, they reflect the impact of cognitive and motivational processes, governing the way that human beings interpret information, evaluate risks, set priorities, and experience feelings of gain or loss. Five specific barriers are considered below, the last of which relates closely to our own recent work and will be discussed in some detail.

III. More Detailed Examination of Five Specific Psychological Barriers

A. DISSONANCE ARISING FROM THE PAST

One of the best known and most extensively researched psychological biases involves the individual's motivated effort to seek and preserve cognitive consistency, and conversely to avoid and reduce *dissonance* vis-à-vis his or her actions, values, feelings, or beliefs (Festinger, 1957). Upon reflection, however, it becomes clear that the changes in perception, beliefs, and priorities undertaken to reduce dissonance can create a stumbling block to dispute resolution. The implications of dissonance reduction become particularly troubling when a conflictual and costly status quo has been maintained for long periods of time, and possible resolutions offering apparent advantages over the status quo have, for one reason or another, been rejected in the past. Specifically, it becomes dissonant for the disputing parties to accept terms today that could have been achieved, without the ensuing costs associated with delay, at some earlier point in time. By the same token, past justifications for rejecting advantageous terms—justifications offered to oneself, as well as those offered to one's peers and critics—serve to increase the psychic and social costs of accepting those terms now. One obvious way to reduce dissonance of this sort, unfortunately, is to convince oneself, and others, that the rejected proposal was even *more* one-sided, insincere, or blocked by additional impediments than it had seemed, and therefore that even *better* terms will be required for any agreement to be reached in the future.

We should note that the problem of justifying one's immediate decision to settle involves questions not only about the past but about the future as well. Disputants may be reluctant to resolve a conflict, or move toward such resolution, unless there is an obvious reason—either a benefit to be obtained or a possible cost to be avoided—for doing so now rather than later. Specifically, the antagonists may each feel that by agreeing to an initiative today they are giving up the opportunity for more favorable terms tomorrow. Indeed, one side or both is likely to feel that by holding out it is guaranteed terms of settlement *at least as favorable* and perhaps *more* favorable than those under consideration. In the absence of factors that make immediate settlement more attractive, or the prospect of later settlement less attractive, continued intransigence by one or both parties will be the rule rather than the exception.

Although the implications of dissonance reduction may be bleak in the context of protracted and costly stalemates, there is one optimistic note worth sounding before we continue our account of the formidable barriers that stand in the way of bargaining efficiency and success. Once a settlement has been reached, the human penchant for reducing dissonance can play a rather constructive role—especially if the decision to settle has been freely reached, if effort has been expended or sacrifices made, and if public defense of the settlement has been demanded (Aronson, 1969; J. W. Brehm & Cohen, 1962). Thus, the process of dissonance reduction may compel leaders and followers alike to find and exaggerate positive features of the settlement, and to minimize or disregard negative ones. We saw such processes occur in dramatic fashion early in 1972 when Richard Nixon suddenly and unexpectedly reached detente with China. And we watch, hopefully, as Palestinians and Israelis, and South Africans of different races, face the aftermath of their own historic, but dissonance-producing agreements.

B. OPTIMISTIC OVERCONFIDENCE

Litigants deciding whether to go to trial rather than pursue an out-of-court settlement, heads-of-state deciding whether to undertake military initiatives rather than continue to pursue patient diplomacy, and labor leaders deciding whether or not to walk away from the negotiating table and call a strike, may all be subject to a judgmental bias that Kahneman and Tversky (in press) have termed "optimistic overconfidence." Such overconfidence, which is but one manifestation of the more general and much documented tendency for people to place unwarranted confidence in their assessments and predictions (Alpert & Raiffa, 1982; Dunning, Griffin, Milojkovic, & Ross, 1990; Fischhoff, Slovic, & Lichtenstein, 1977; Kahneman & Tversky, 1973; Oskamp, 1965b), is apparent in the tendency for disputants to overestimate the prospects for prevailing in the absence of a negotiated settlement (see Bazerman, 1990; Bazerman & Neale, in press).

A primary source of this overestimation is an obvious asymmetry in the availability of information. In a wide range of disputes, each side tends to have greater access to the factors that strengthen its position or would promote its success than to those factors that would weaken its position or promote its adversary's success. In particular, disputants know their own goals, assumptions, and plans better than they know those of their adversary; and they fail to make adequate inferential allowance for such gaps in their knowledge by lowering their subjective certainty of success. Essentially, they adopt an "insider's" rather than an "outsider's" perspective, one that focuses too much on what they know or assume about the particular case at hand, and too little on the type of base rate information or historical precedent that ought to alert them to the possibility of miscalculation and protracted costly struggle.

Experimental evidence for the role of asymmetric information in overconfidence comes from recent research on litigation predictions and preferences. In one study, for example, Brenner, Koehler, and Tversky (1993) investigated subjects' ability to predict jury verdicts from incomplete case summaries. Subjects were presented with the background details of several legal disputes and, in addition, were exposed to either the plaintiff's arguments, the defendant's arguments, or the arguments of both sides in the cases. They were then asked to predict the verdict (i.e., to estimate how many members of a twenty-person "jury" consisting of other subjects who were exposed to both sides' arguments would find for the defendant) and to assign a confidence level to their prediction.

Subjects who saw only one side of a case were aware that they had been arbitrarily assigned to that condition, and that there was nothing exceptional about the incomplete information they were exposed to. Similarly, the arguments for either side in these cases were quite predictable from the arguments offered for the other side. Nevertheless, the results showed that subjects who had been exposed to only one side's arguments were both more confident and less accurate in their predicted verdicts than were those subjects exposed to both sides. Research consistent with Brenner et al.'s findings suggests that such overconfident predictions of trial outcomes can contribute to litigants' reluctance to settle cases, and their unwillingness to undergo the uncertainties and additional costs associated with going to trial (see Rachlinski, 1994; also, Loewenstein, Issacharoff, Camerer, & Babcock, 1993).

Optimistic overconfidence obviously can lead disputants to forego attempts at settlement, believing that "time is on their side," and that complete, unilateral victory is "just around the corner." Indeed, a conflict may become "ripe" for attempts at negotiated resolution only when this barrier is overcome. That is, real progress through problem solving and mutually beneficial exchanges of compromises may become possible only when hard-won experience teaches the parties the full costs and uncertainties of protracted struggle, or when fears of sharply escalating future costs convince them that the possibility of eventually imposing their will on their adversary is simply not worth the gamble.

C. LOSS AVERSION

In an important series of studies, Kahneman and Tversky (1979, 1984) showed that decision makers tend to attach greater weight to prospective losses than to prospective gains of equivalent magnitude. Such "loss aversion" may make parties in a conflict reluctant to trade concessions—even when a dispassionate analysis of the parties' interests, and even of their expressed values and preferences, suggests that the relevant trade would be mutually advantageous (see Kahneman & Tversky, in press).

Consider, for example, a conflict between a company management determined to cut costs and a union determined to enhance and protect the interests of its workers (see Mnookin & Ross, in press). In principle, a third-party mediator should be able to serve both sides in the conflict by identifying benefits currently held by workers that have been highly costly to management but only moderately valuable to the workers (for example, a health insurance policy that calls for no copayment) and prerogatives currently held by management that have been highly costly to and highly resented by the workers, but only moderately valuable to management (for example, the freedom to dictate working hours rather than allow flexible working schedules). The phenomenon of loss aversion suggests that the obvious proposal by a mediator, that the union give up its benefit and that management give up its prerogative, may meet a cooler than expected reception from both sides—assuming, of course, that the two sides do, in fact, frame what they are ceding as "losses" and what they are receiving as "gains" (see Neale & Bazerman, 1991). A proposed trade of "land for peace," or a proposed reduction in conventional forces and weapons by one side in return for a reduction in nonconventional weapons by the other side, or a proposed scrapping of a particular missile system by one side in return for the scrapping of a particular antimissile system by the other may meet a similarly cool reception for a similar reason.

The phenomenon of loss aversion also manifests itself in the tendency for decision makers to risk large but uncertain losses rather than accept smaller but certain ones. President Lyndon Johnson's decision to escalate the Vietnam War, and his subsequent unwillingness to "cut his losses" by accepting the unfavorable terms that would have been available in any negotiated settlement, may have reflected precisely this bias. That is, contrary to popular lore, Johnson's folly may not have been due to his acceptance of overly optimistic reports and projections by military advisors promising him "light at the end of the tunnel." For, we are told, he actually treated such optimism with great skepticism. Nevertheless, he went forward in the hope that some new undertaking or unanticipated twist of fortune would salvage victory from the jaws of defeat, as it had done so often before in his own political career. Johnson, in short, was less a victim of his own or his advisors' optimistic overconfidence than of his willingness to undertake reckless gambles rather than accept the certain political and psychological consequences of conceding that his military objectives would not and could not be met.[3]

The tendency for decision makers to take unwise risks rather than accept certain losses also holds an obvious implication for civil litigation. The general tendency to litigate rather than settle out of court, which we noted earlier in our discussion of optimistic overconfidence, may be especially marked in the case of defendants, who thereby risk a large loss or award to the plaintiff rather than accept the certainty of a small one. Indeed, in experimental investigations of "prospect theory," Kahneman and Tversky (1979, 1984) showed that in the domain of losses, decision makers make "risk-seeking" choices, rejecting certain losses in favor of gambles with equal or even inferior expected values. In the domain of gains, on the other hand, decision makers tend to be "risk averse," preferring certain gains over gambles with equal or even greater expected values. Plaintiffs, then, may be expected to settle when their expected gain would actually be increased by undertaking the risks of litigation (i.e., accepting a modest but certain gain rather than gambling on the prospect of a potentially large but uncertain one).

Archival and experimental research conducted by Rachlinski (1994) found

---

[3]This unconventional but persuasive analysis was first offered by Daniel Ellsberg in a seminar sponsored by the Stanford Center on Conflict and Negotiation in 1987.

evidence for just such an asymmetry. Defendants, operating as they do in the domain of potential losses, tended to go to trial when they would have been better advised to settle. That is, rather than accept the moderate but certain loss entailed in accepting the plaintiff's settlement offers, they opted for the uncertainty of a trial (or, alternatively, they made settlement offers too low to win agreement from the plaintiff). As the subsequent jury awards made clear, they ended up, at least on average, paying dearly for having done so. Plaintiffs, by contrast, operating as they do in the domain of potential gains, proved risk averse. That is, they were inclined to accept the certain gain of a negotiated settlement even when they would have fared better, at least on average, by accepting the uncertainties associated with a verdict by judge or jury.

D. DIVERGENT CONSTRUAL

Opposing partisans exposed to the same objective information are apt to interpret those facts differently. As Bruner's (1957) oft-quoted title suggests, people are wont to go "beyond the information given." In the process of assimilating information, they fill in details of context and content, they infer linkages between events, and they adopt dynamic scripts or schemas to give events coherence and meaning (see Nisbett & Ross, 1980; also, Fiske & Taylor, 1991; Schank and Abelson, 1977). Accordingly, opposing partisans faced with the same objective facts, evidence, and history of events may both find additional support for their pre-existing views and become more polarized in their sentiments.

Early evidence for such polarization was provided in the classic Hastorf and Cantril (1954) study in which Dartmouth and Princeton football fans viewed the film of a particularly hard-fought game between their teams. Despite the fact that they were observing the very same stimulus, the two sets of partisan viewers seemingly "saw" two very different games. The Princeton fans saw a continuing saga of Dartmouth atrocities and occasional Princeton retaliations, whereas the Dartmouth fans saw a hard-hitting contest in which both sides contributed equally to the violence. Moreover, each side thought that the "truth" (i.e., what *they* saw) ought to be apparent to any objective observers of the same events.

Thirty-five years later, Lord, Ross, and Lepper (1979) demonstrated the existence of similar assimilation biases in the way partisans respond to social science data. As the investigators predicted, death penalty advocates and opponents alike were undaunted by contrived research reports that objectively offered as much support to the other side as to their own. Each side proceeded to accept uncritically the results of the study supporting their position and to identify obvious flaws in the study opposing their position—and thus, as predicted, to become increasingly polarized in their views as they "assimilated" the relevant findings.

The cognitive and motivational biases underlying such polarization phenomena obviously can exacerbate intergroup conflict. Disputants are apt to feel that they have acted more honorably in the past, have been more sinned against than sinning, and are seeking no more than that to which they are entitled. Each disputant, moreover, is apt to feel that its interests are the ones that most require protection in any future agreement—for example by avoiding ambiguities in language that could be used as a loophole by its adversary, while at the same time avoiding rigidities in formulation that could compromise its own legitimate need to guard itself against unforeseen future developments. And, when their adversaries make parallel claims, or when third parties offer relatively evenhanded summaries of the past or commentaries about the legitimacy of respective claims, they are apt to perceive bias in such efforts and to infer unreasonableness, hostility, or devious strategic intent on the part of that third party.

The disputants may show similarly divergent biases in the way they interpret prospective settlements of their conflict. Specifically, each side may interpret its potential concessions in a manner that maximizes their apparent significance and value but interpret the other side's potential concessions in a manner that minimizes their apparent significance and value. Thus, as Mnookin and Ross (in press) suggest, the prospect of an "impartial citizens board" to review alleged incidents of police brutality is apt to be interpreted very differently by the members of a poor, inner-city community ("a bunch of political appointees who don't understand our experiences and would take the word of the police over that of people like us") and by the police ("outsiders who wouldn't understand our problems and frustrations and would worry too much about politics"). Acceptance of such an "impartial" board, accordingly, would be seen as a far greater concession to the community by the police officers who would be subject to its review than by the community members whose grievances it would hear.

Often, differences in construal and resulting differences in evaluation of proposals for conflict resolution may reflect divergent perceptions of motives and intent (Thomas & Pondy, 1977). If each side in a business negotiation, for example, feels that its reputation is less blemished, its intentions more honorable, and its assurances more reliable than its competitor, then each side will feel that its promise of "future cooperation" or "good faith efforts" to achieve particular goals would represent a major concession indeed, while a similar promise by its competitor would be a concession of modest and uncertain value. When such differences in construal or evaluation are great enough, a conflict or negotiation deadlock that appears amenable to agreements offering mutual advancement of interests may nevertheless prove intractable. But even when such differences in perceptions and evaluations are not so great as to preclude a negotiated agreement, such differences may be sufficient to make the two sides disagree about which side would be making the larger concessions and, therefore, which would be entitled to receive more generous concessions in the future. The net result of these biases will be a tendency for the negotiating parties to characterize the overall valence or balance of a given proposal in terms that would strike an outside observer as biased and self-serving.

E. REACTIVE DEVALUATION

The final conflict-resolution barrier to be discussed here has been termed *reactive devaluation* (Ross, in press; Ross & Stillinger, 1991; Stillinger, Epelbaum, Keltner, & Ross, 1990). It refers to the fact that the very act of offering a particular proposal or concession may diminish its apparent value or attractiveness in the eyes of the recipient.

Newspaper articles that describe failed negotiations and prolonged deadlocks generally provide anecdotal evidence of the parties' negative characterizations of each other's proposals. Similarly, unilateral initiatives and pump-priming concessions designed to show good faith and induce reciprocation (of the sort advocated by Osgood, 1962, and others) all too often are received coolly or contemptuously dismissed as propaganda or public relations ploys. It is easy, however, to dismiss such uncharitable responses as mere tactical posturing. Labor has obvious incentives to denigrate the wage concessions that management proposes at the outset of contract negotiations. Parties involved in litigation have similar incentives to disparage each other's current settlement offers, as do nations involved in political, economic, or military disputes. Characterizing the other side's offers as ungenerous and inadequate demonstrates resoluteness to one's own constituency, bids for the sympathy of third parties, and may even help convince the other side to "up the ante." The theoretical question that remains unanswered, however, is whether such devaluation also occurs in the parties' private evaluations.

Ideally, one would like to answer this question by gaining access to the candid evaluations, or better still the changes in evaluation, that occur in the context of a broad sample of face-to-face "real-world" negotiations. As researchers, however, we rarely enjoy such access—certainly not under circumstances where suitable experimental procedures can be employed and where sample sizes are large enough to permit valid statistical inference. We have, however, been able to conduct a number of studies that examined the proposed reactive devaluation in contexts where the evaluators had no strategic reason to misrepresent their private sentiments.

The first study (Stillinger, Epelbaum, Keltner, & Ross, 1990) was a sidewalk survey of opinions regarding possible arms reductions by the United States and the Soviet Union. Respondents were asked to evaluate the terms of a nuclear disarmament proposal—a proposal that the interviewer ascribed, depending on experimental condition, to the Soviet Union, to the United States, or to a neutral third party. As predicted, the terms of this plan were seen as unfavorable to the

United States when the Soviets were the putative originator, while the same terms appeared moderately favorable when attributed to a neutral third party, and quite favorable when attributed to the United States[4] (see also related earlier work by Oskamp, 1965a).

More direct evidence for reactive devaluation was subsequently obtained by the same investigators in the context of a campus-wide controversy about Stanford University's divestment of shares in companies doing business in South Africa. In the context of a campus survey, the investigators led subjects to believe in one condition that the university was about to implement a plan for immediate partial divestment, in a second condition that the university was about to implement a delay after which total divestment would occur (unless certain significant steps were taken by the South African government), and in a third "control" condition that the university was merely studying the two plans in question. The students were then asked to evaluate the relevant plans. As predicted, the respondents tended to devalue the "proposed" plan relative to the one that had not been proposed. Further evidence was provided in surveys conducted just before the university finally did offer its proposal (which turned out to be a variant of the "partial divestment" plan) and then again a couple of weeks later. As seen in Figure 1, subjects judged the university's ultimate plan to be a smaller concession after it was offered than before (when it had been merely one of several hypothetical possibilities), whereas an alternative plan calling for the university merely to increase its investment in companies that had left South Africa came to be evaluated more positively.

The tendency to devalue the adversary's concessions and proposals, while undeniably a barrier to dispute resolution, may sometimes be a product of rational deduction or inference. Certainly there is nothing counternormative about treating a proposal's authorship as informative with respect to the balance of advantages and disadvantages that would accrue to its author. ("They wouldn't have offered those terms if those terms didn't advance their interests.") And, where the author in question is presumed to be a foe who seeks to dominate the proposal's recipients, there may be nothing counternormative about also treating such authorship as potentially informative about the proposal's value to the recipient. ("They wouldn't have offered those terms if those terms strengthened our position relative to theirs.")

A recent pilot study run in our laboratory (Ward & Ross, 1993) sheds some light on the role that rational inference of this sort may play in producing reactive devaluation. Subjects who had rated themselves as either supporters of Israel or

---

[4]It is worth noting that although it might have been easy for an artful researcher to contrive an ambiguous proposal well suited to produce divergent interpretations and the predicted reactive devaluation phenomenon, the proposal used in the study was one actually made by President Gorbachev—with the intent of inducing *positive,* not negative, reactions from the recipients.

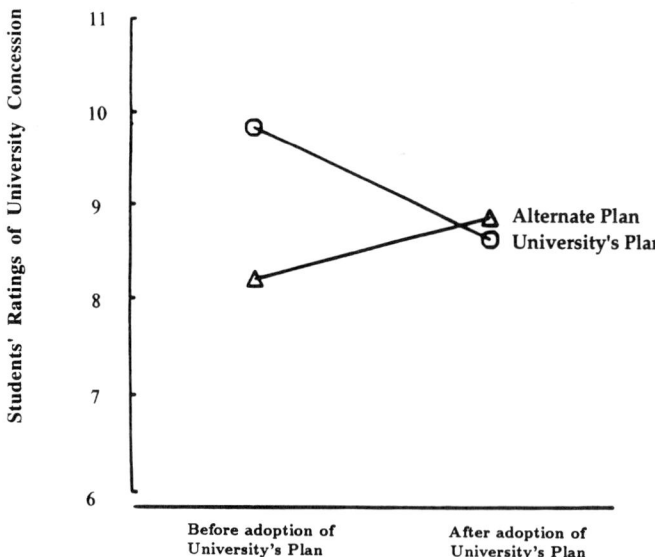

Fig. 1. Students' ratings of university's ("Partial Divestment") plan (○) and alternative ("Reward for Divestment") plan (△) before and after the university announced which plan it would adopt.

neutral with respect to the Arab–Israeli crisis were asked to read and respond to a peace proposal featuring a particular version of the familiar "land for peace" formulation. Half the subjects were told that the proposal had been authored by the Israeli Labor Party, whereas the other half believed it to be of Palestinian authorship. As might be predicted from simple "congruency" or "consistency theory" (Abelson & Rosenberg, 1958; Heider, 1958; Osgood & Tannenbaum, 1955), all subjects, pro-Israelis and neutrals alike, rated the proposal as more favorable to the Palestinians and less favorable to the Israelis when they believed it to be a Palestinian rather than Israeli proposal.

When we probed further, however, by asking subjects to indicate their construals of particular points of the proposal (e.g., "What does limited militarizations mean?" or "How much money is expected to be contributed by the U.S. for resettlement?"), it became clear that in the case of the pro-Israeli partisans an additional, less "mindless" (Langer, 1978) mechanism was playing a role. These partisan subjects went beyond inferences about the proposal's overall favorability to the two sides; unlike the neutrals, they generally went on to construe individual items differently as a function of the proposal's authorship. For example, pro-Israeli subjects reading the Israeli-authored plan construed "limited militarization" of the Occupied Territories to mean something akin to the presence of a typical city police force, whereas pro-Israelis who read the Palestinian-authored plan construed it to be something closer to the presence of a national army. Neutrals, by contrast, generally did not construe or infer different meanings of specific terms or features as a function of putative authorship (i.e., in both conditions they took the term "limited militarization" to indicate a force the size of which was somewhere between the two estimates offered by the pro-Israeli subjects). Unlike the pro-Israeli partisans, these neutrals simply *assumed* or *inferred* that overall the proposal in question must be relatively good for the adversary doing the proposing and relatively bad for the adversary receiving the proposal, without resorting to any deeper or more extensive cognitive processing.

Additional research from our laboratory suggests that in some cases of reactive devaluation another, very different, process may also play a role. This mechanism involves neither mindless changes in assessment nor mindful changes in interpretation. Rather, it involves changes in underlying *preferences*. Reactance theorists have noted that human beings seem inclined, in various circumstances, to reject or devalue whatever is freely available to them, and to covet and strive for whatever is denied them (see J. W. Brehm, 1966; Brehm & Brehm, 1981; also Wicklund, 1974, for theoretical accounts of such "psychological reactance"). Other theorists from various psychological, sociological, and political perspectives (Brock, 1968; Cialdini, 1985; see also Lynn, 1992) have argued that nonavailability signals scarcity and social desirability, which in turn increases both subjective and objective value. Indeed, people may be inclined to devalue whatever is available relative to whatever is unavailable, even when no hostility is perceived on the part of the individual or institution providing access to the opportunities or commodities in question (or, for that matter, even when no human agency seems to be involved). The familiar aphorism that "the grass is always greener on the other side of the fence" nicely captures this source of human unhappiness and frustration, and it is easy to think of anecdotal examples in which we, our children, or our colleagues seem disinclined to "count our blessings" and instead seem to place inordinately high value on precisely those goods, relationships, activities, or opportunities that are denied to us.

A series of role-play studies by Lepper, Ross, Tsai, and Ward (1994) documented this change-of-preference process quite clearly, and at the same time demonstrated further that the reactive devaluation phenomenon depends neither on an adversarial relationship nor on any ambiguity in proposed terms. The subjects in the initial study were social science majors who had been asked to imagine that they had undertaken a summer job with a distinguished professor that ultimately entailed low pay and difficult library research. Then, according to the imaginary scenario, they discovered that the professor was on the verge of publishing a chapter based heavily on their work, for which a hefty royalty was being paid. The fictional professor, however, had offered them neither additional money nor a coauthorship in recognition of their efforts (two rewards that had been vaguely alluded to by the professor as "further possibilities" if the student's efforts led to a publishable article).

Subjects then were asked to imagine writing a particularly polite but firm note to the professor complaining about the lack of fair recognition or compensation (and reminding the professor of the vague assurances regarding additional compensation and recognition offered them at the outset of the project). In response to their letter, the professor in the scenario wrote offering one of two possible concessions—either a "third authorship" (with their name following that of a second author who to the best of their knowledge had contributed little to the project) or a sum of money ($750 in an initial study, $900 in subsequent studies). Finally, the students were asked to assess the attractiveness and value of the two relevant concessions—that is, the one that they had been offered by the professor and the alternative concession that had not been offered.

The predicted reactive devaluation phenomenon was apparent in their evaluations (see Fig. 2). That is, the third authorship seemed more attractive (and more valuable) to the students who had been offered the cash, and the cash seemed more attractive to the students who had been offered the third authorship. The students, it should be noted, gave no evidence of having reinterpreted the meaning or reassessed the objective worth of the relevant concessions. They simply expressed personal preferences and value that favored whichever of the two compromises had not been offered.

A number of follow-up studies by Lepper et al. have extended these findings

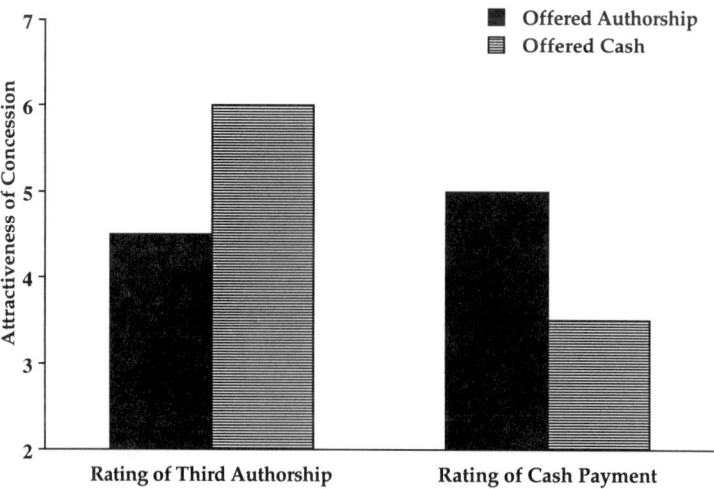

Fig. 2. Ratings of third authorship versus cash payment by students receiving concessionary offer either of authorship or cash.

and manipulated various factors or variables (e.g., the reputation of the professor, the degree of entitlement felt by the student, and whether the professor is male or female) that one might expect to influence the magnitude of reactive devaluation. From such research it has become clear that although many such factors do seem to influence the *degree* of reactive devaluation, the phenomenon remained even when it might be expected to vanish—that is, even when the professor had a reputation for fairness, when the student had never received any prior promises or assurances, and when third parties in fact told the student that either reward was more than was customary for such undergraduate contributions.[5]

IV. Sources of Misattribution and Mistrust: Broader Theoretical Perspectives

The cognitive and motivational processes underlying dissonance, loss aversion, optimistic overconfidence, biased assimilation, and reactive devaluation, we have argued, create immediate barriers to dispute resolution. These same processes, we now argue, compound the difficulties of reaching negotiated settlements by promoting misunderstanding and mistrust. That is, adversaries engaged in bargaining are apt to make overly uncharitable inferences about each other's offers and responses, seeing deviousness and intransigence on the part of the other side, even when that side's offers, counteroffers, and expressions of disappointment and frustration are no less genuine than their own.

Although our research on this topic presently consists mainly of interviews and anecdotal evidence, we have been impressed by a consistent tendency in the accounts offered by seasoned negotiators. First, the negotiators we've encountered seem to hold the conviction that other people engage in more frequent and elaborate strategic ploys than they themselves do. Others, they feel, make completely unrealistic offers and demands, whereas they merely leave themselves a little negotiating room; others exaggerate grossly the difficulty of making the concessions that obviously will be required to consummate a deal, whereas they themselves exaggerate only slightly. Others, they maintain, frequently resort to empty threats, or feign interest in reaching agreement when their main goal is

---

[5]Pilot research conducted in our laboratory (Atkins, Ward, & Lepper, 1994) offered an intriguing (albeit preliminary) demonstration of one technique that *did* prove valuable in overcoming the reactive devaluation barrier. Drawing upon self-affirmation research by Claude Steele (1988), Atkins et al. asked subjects responding to the professor's offer of money or authorship to first describe a personal incident involving a value they had previously ranked as "most important to their self-worth." This self-affirmation manipulation significantly reduced subsequent reactive devaluation of the offered concession (whereas having subjects describe an incident involving a nonimportant value did not).

obstruction and delay; whereas they themselves rarely resort to such tactics, and are guilty only of "fighting fire with fire" or showing appropriate caution in the face of the other side's penchant for less than scrupulous negotiation behavior. More importantly, they insist that the other side's protestations and expressions of disappointment or frustration are insincere, whereas their own are genuine.

To some extent, of course, such claims may be self-serving and manipulative, but we suspect there is something deeper going on. We suspect that, frequently, both sides in the negotiation may be overestimating the other side's penchant for devious tactics and strategies, and underestimating their sincerity, precisely because they do not recognize the extent to which the other side's assessments (and their own as well) have psychological rather than strategic bases.

We should add that we have discussed this suspicion with many practitioners, and their characteristic response is an interesting one. Upon hearing our accounts of various psychological barriers (particularly reactive devaluation), they soon begin to nod in agreement and even furnish wonderfully illustrative examples—although, not coincidentally, almost always examples concerning the biases shown by their adversaries (or, in the case of lawyers, sometimes their clients) rather than themselves. In other words, negotiation practitioners can easily be persuaded to attribute their adversaries' intransigence to psychological processes and biases rather than stubbornness, stupidity, or Machiavellian guile. And this change in attribution can reduce, at least somewhat, practitioners' feelings of enmity and mistrust. What negotiators *cannot* readily be made to do is to see the role of the same processes and biases in their *own* negotiation conduct—a limitation that we shall presently explore in more detail as we turn our attention to broader theoretical perspectives on interpersonal perception.

A. EGO DEFENSIVENESS AND SELF-ENHANCEMENT

A number of researchers have documented the tendency for people to view themselves as more intelligent, more ethical, more fair, and less prejudiced than their peers (Myers, 1990). Additionally, there appear to be several domains in which individuals tend to attribute positive outcomes they achieve to personal qualities while attributing negative ones to external factors beyond their responsibility or control (Gioia & Sims, 1985; Miller & Ross, 1975; Weiner et al., 1971; Whitley & Frieze, 1985, 1986). Furthermore, individuals tend to show consistent biases in estimating the commonness, and normativeness, of their own beliefs and choices. Specifically, actors who make particular choices, exhibit particular preferences, or hold particular beliefs, are inclined to rate those responses as more common—and less revealing of one's idiosyncratic traits and attributes—than do actors who make the opposite choices (Ross, Greene, & House, 1977).

In a classic study, M. Ross and Siccoly (1979) demonstrated that individuals further show systematic (but not systematically self-serving) biases in estimating the magnitude of their own contribution to joint outcomes. More recently, Kunda (1987, 1990) and Dunning (Dunning & Cohen, 1992; Dunning, Meyerowitz, & Holzberg, 1989) have spelled out some of the specific cognitive, perceptual, and motivational processes (including the judicious selection of evaluation dimensions and standards) that could permit the majority of people to perceive themselves as "above average," without exhibiting any gross distortions of perception and judgment. Finally, our colleague, Claude Steele (1992), has done groundbreaking work in showing how people in general, and members of stigmatized groups in particular, selectively identify or "disidentify" with particular achievement domains in order to maintain their self-esteem in the face of threat.

Although there is room for investigators to disagree about whether *sources* of such phenomena are purely motivational or whether cognitive and perceptual factors are playing an important role (see Dawes, 1988; Gilovich, 1991; Kunda, 1987, 1990; Miller & Ross, 1975; Nisbett & Ross, 1980; Ross, 1977), their motivational *consequences* would seem to be rather clear. That is, these and other related phenomena should generally serve to help actors to feel relatively positive about themselves and their life circumstances. Indeed, Shelley Taylor and her colleagues (Taylor, 1983; Taylor & Brown, 1988; Taylor, Collins, Skokan, & Aspinwall, 1989) have argued that cognitive distortions or *illusions*, rather than unbiased accurate assessment, are vital to one's health, happiness, achievement, and overall success in dealing with the ordinary and extraordinary challenges of everyday life.

We do not doubt that a variety of processes and biases, some motivational and some nonmotivational, do indeed serve to enhance people's sense of self-worth and entitlement. (Although we cannot help observe that people also seem at times to show biases in the *opposite* direction—denigrating their own efforts, abilities, or accomplishments in professional, social, or familial roles to a degree that others, as more "objective" observers, would deem unreasonably harsh.) But, as we noted in introducing this section of our chapter, these same processes and biases can create problems when people bargain or negotiate with others. Individuals or groups who have enhanced notions of their "worthiness" (i.e., their contributions to joint outcomes or past successes, their blamelessness for past problems or failures, the quality of their character and capacities, or inevitability of their ultimate triumph) are apt to be unhappy with the compromises and concessions offered by those on the other side of the bargaining table, who do not share their biases (see M. Ross, Thibaut, & Evenbeck, 1971). Indeed, they are apt to be particularly unhappy when they receive proposals from people, on the other side, who have similarly biased notions of their *own* "worthiness." And the parties' mutual expressions of disappointment, unmet expectations, and unsatisfied feelings of entitlement are apt to fuel cycles of enmity and distrust.

B. NAIVE REALISM

We have already discussed several specific ways in which differences in construal can create barriers to dispute resolution. It is now time to consider the problem of construal differences in a somewhat broader context. Intersubjective differences in construal not only can lead parties to reject particular settlement proposals, they can also promote misunderstandings and misattributions that escalate conflict between the bargainers. Consider, for example, the consequences that follow when John and Mary differ markedly in the assumptions about context and meaning they make when they see someone rebuke a ragged individual seeking a handout, or hear a politician endorse "family values," or read about a reported incident of spousal abuse. The two social perceivers will be inclined not only to make different attributions about the relevant actors but also to reach unwarranted conclusions about each other. That is, John, upon seeing Mary react or hearing her express her views, is apt to make attributions about her that presume she has responded to the same event as he did (attributions that might have been quite reasonable if she *had* done so). And Mary, of course, is apt to make similarly erroneous assumptions and inferences upon hearing John's views.

What both perceivers will fail to recognize, we argue, (unless and until they carefully and explicitly probe their two divergent sets of assumptions and construals) is that they have in fact responded to different events, or at least different social constructions of those events. That is, in the terms employed by Solomon Asch (1940), the disagreements in question stem not from differing judgments of the same object, but rather from the fact that they are perceiving and evaluating differing objects of judgment. Moreover, there is a distinct risk that Mary and John will compound the problem when they begin to exchange accusations and even to consider the basis for and implications of those accusations.

The failure of perspective taking, or more specifically, the failure to treat the other person's "surprising" and seemingly "unwarranted" response as a *cue* that the person is responding to a different situation than the one we assume (or at least a different subjective construal of that situation) is a ubiquitous feature of social and political life. Such failures arguably play an important role in promoting the "correspondence bias" (Gilbert & Jones, 1986) or "fundamental attribution error" (Ross, 1977)—that is, the tendency for observers to attribute actions and outcomes to distinguishing personal dispositions of the actor rather than to the situational forces and constraints faced by that actor. Moreover, actor–

observer differences in attribution (Jones & Nisbett, 1971) can be traced in part to the same failure.

It is our more general contention here that these limitations reflect a kind of worldview or lay epistemology that we have characterized as "naive realism" (Ross & Ward, in press; see also Griffin & Ross, 1991). Before exploring the implications for conflict and misunderstanding between individuals and groups, let us set forth the specific features or "tenets" of this naive realism. A naive realist, we propose, holds three related convictions about the relation between his or her subjective experience and the nature of the phenomena that give rise to that subjective experience. For didactic purposes, these convictions or "tenets" are best expressed in first-person terms.

Tenets of naive realism:

1. That I see stimuli and events as they are in objective reality, and that my social attitudes, belief, preferences, priorities, and the like follow from a relatively dispassionate, unbiased, and essentially "unmediated" apprehension of the information or evidence at hand.

2. That other rational social perceivers generally will share my reactions, behaviors, and opinions—provided that they have had access to the same information that gave rise to my views, and provided that they too have processed that information in a reasonably thoughtful and open-minded fashion.

3. That the failure of a given individual or group to share my views arises from one of three possible sources: (a) the individual or group in question may have been exposed to a different sample of information than I was (in which case, provided that the other party is reasonable and open-minded, the sharing or pooling of information will lead us to reach agreement); (b) the individual or group in question may be lazy, irrational, or otherwise unable or unwilling to proceed in a normative fashion from objective evidence to reasonable conclusions; and (c) the individual or group in question may be biased (either in interpreting the evidence, or in proceeding from evidence to conclusions) by ideology, self-interest, or some other distorting personal influence.

The first tenet thus asserts, essentially, that I see things as they are, i.e., that my beliefs, preferences, and resulting responses follow from an essentially "unmediated" perception of relevant stimuli and incorporation of relevant evidence. The second tenet asserts that other rational, reasonable people (provided that they have been exposed to the same stimuli and information as I have, and provided that they "process" that information in a reasonably thoughtful, objective, fashion) will share both my experiences and responses. Together, these tenets relate to the human tendency to assume, often without even considering any alternative, that other social actors and perceivers share one's perspective and one's subjective experience of the objects or events to which one responds. In turn, they dispose people offering behavioral predictions and attributions to make inadequate inferential allowance for the possibility that other social actors and perceivers might be construing or experiencing the relevant events differently—for the possibility that other actors might, in effect, be responding to very different objects of judgment than themselves (see Griffin & Ross, 1991; Ross & Ward, in press).

The third tenet of naive realism, which can essentially be derived from the two earlier ones, concerns the naive realist's possible interpretations of differences in response and disagreement about issues. It is thus this tenet that is most relevant to our present discussion of conflict. We suggest that if the naive realist holds the conviction that he or she sees things "naturally" (i.e., sees them as they "really are," in a relatively "unmediated" or "bottom-up" fashion) then other actors' differing views and responses must reflect something other than a natural, unmediated perception of, and reaction to, that objective reality.

The initial interpretation of such differences in opinion, we suggest, is apt to be relatively "charitable" (i.e., that the other party has not yet been exposed to the "way things really are," or that the other party has not yet been privy to the "real" facts and considerations). Indeed, the naive realist may even be so charitable as to concede that the other party may be privy to additional facts and considerations that could moderate the naive realist's own views. This charitable interpretation of disagreement leads the naive realist to be confident that rational discourse in which information and cogent arguments are freely exchanged will lead to agreement (or at least to a marked narrowing of disagreement). Such confidence, however, is apt to be short-lived, especially in the social-political arena. Repeated attempts at dialogue with those on the "other side" of a contentious issue make us aware that those misguided individuals rarely yield to our attempts at enlightenment. Nor, we soon discover, do our ideological adversaries yield to the efforts of articulate, fair-minded spokespersons who share our views or even to the evidence presented by those few media sources we regard as "balanced" and "responsible."

There is, of course, another, far less charitable interpretation of others' failure to share our views, one involving questions of effort and intellectual capacity. Those who fail, even after being enlightened by us or by other responsible information sources about the real facts and considerations, to arrive at our "truth" (i.e., at the views that we believe follow "naturally" from evidence and logic) may simply be too lazy or too limited in intelligence and common sense to reach the "right" conclusions. This interpretation is comforting, and it's one we sometimes can cling to provided that the dialogue remains limited and the stakes remain low.

There is a third interpretation of disagreement, however, that is more likely—especially where our adversaries are persistent, unyielding, energetic, and outspoken and where the issue is one with hedonic consequences for them or for us. In such cases we are apt to reach the conclusion that those on the other side of the issue are *biased*, that some combination of ideology, self-interest, personal values, idiosyncratic traits, and features of temperament must be either distorting those individuals' construal of relevant information or impairing their capacity to proceed normatively from evidence to conclusions.

A pilot study we conducted during the Persian Gulf War (Ward & Ross, 1991a), provided some evidence of these processes. In the study we presented pro-war and antiwar subjects with written arguments congruent with their own position and then asked them to imagine that a previously uninformed traveler returning to the United States had been unmoved in the face of those specific arguments. As predicted, our subjects were quite willing to make negative attributions, seeing the traveler as "narrow-minded," "hostile," and "stupid." Interestingly, no such negative attributions were made when subjects did not see any specific arguments but instead merely were told to imagine that the traveler in question had remained undecided or neutral after having been exposed to the "best possible arguments" for their side. Apparently, it was the hypothetical traveler's failure to respond "appropriately" to specific concrete stimuli, rather than the simple failure to move in the direction preferred by the subject, that prompted the relevant denigration.

In many domains, the attribution of disagreement to motivated biases on the part of the other side is buttressed by the correlation that generally can be observed between people's social-political beliefs and their individual or collective self-interest. Other people in general, and adversaries in particular (so the naive realist readily observes), rarely hold views or advocate propositions whose acceptance would threaten their economic, social, or psychological well-being. In fact, they generally seem to hold views whose acceptance would plainly advance their individual or collective interests. The naive realist, of course, is quite correct about the direction (if not, as we shall see, the magnitude) of this correlation between motives and beliefs. What generally will be lacking, however, is recognition on the part of the naive realist that his or her own interests, ideological beliefs, and construals of facts and evidence are similarly congruent—and, more importantly, recognition that the relevant congruency could be interpreted in similarly "dynamic" terms.

This willingness to infer bias on the part of those who fail to share one's own views and perspectives has been documented in several studies conducted in our laboratory, and it constitutes a major impediment to the reduction of conflict and misunderstanding. In particular, the efforts of mediators and other third parties are apt to be perceived by the disputants as biased, despite (indeed, because of) their evenhandedness.

Evidence for such perceptions of bias can be found in a pilot study (Ward & Ross, 1991b) conducted during the Senate confirmation hearings for Supreme Court nominee Judge Clarence Thomas, who, it will be recalled, had been accused of sexual harassment by Professor Anita Hill. We asked Thomas supporters and Hill supporters to read and assess one possible account of the events that had supposedly taken place between Thomas and Hill ten years earlier, and to rate the accuracy of their subsequent testimony before the Senate Judiciary Committee. The account, which suggested that Thomas' transgression had been real but exaggerated by Hill, and that both had been less than candid in their testimony, was rated as generally "fair and balanced" by "neutral" subjects. But partisan subjects—pro-Thomas and pro-Hill alike—thought otherwise. Both groups rated the statement as generally biased against the person they supported and in favor of the person supported by the "other side." This pattern of assessments, reminiscent of the tendency for two opposing partisan groups both to see the news media as biased against their side (Vallone, Ross, & Lepper, 1985), suggests again the dilemma faced by impartial mediators who seek to make both sides in a dispute feel that they have received substantive as well as procedural justice.

A second consequence of perceivers' willingness to infer bias on the part of those who hold differing views has also been the subject of recent research conducted in our laboratory. It appears that naive realism, and its attributional consequences, can lead those who participate in or witness ongoing ideological disputes to *overestimate* relevant differences in construal. To understand the source of this overestimation we must look again at the third tenet of naive realism—at the attributional possibilities available to the naive realist who finds that others do not share his or her position on a contentious social issue. Once it is clear that the difference is real and persistent, and not the product either of easily corrected differences in access to information or evidence or of simple inattention or intellectual impairment on the part of those with whom one disagrees, one attributional possibility remains. That possibility involves the distorting influence exerted by ideological bias or self-interest—bias or self-interest, of course, on the part of those with whom one disagrees, rather than oneself.

Although the naive realist's own "bottom-up" construals of issues and events reflect the richness, complexity, ambiguity, and even contradictions of objective reality (or so the naive realist believes), other partisans' "top-down" construals are thought to be a different matter. Other partisans' construals, governed as they are by ideology and self-interest, should manifest a kind of simple, predictable consistency. Specifically, evidence and arguments relevant to beliefs should be construed by others (but not, of course, by the self) in whatever manner serves ideology and self-interest. The result, accordingly, should be an overestimation of the ideological consistency shown by others, particularly by those on the "other side" of a social debate, but perhaps by those on one's own side as well (see Fig. 3).

These predictions were borne out in a pair of studies by Robinson, Keltner, Ward, and Ross (in press) that compared partisan group members' actual differences in construal with their assumptions about such differences. One study dealt

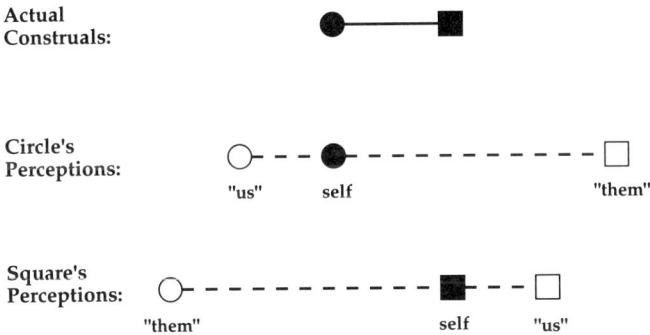

Fig. 3. Actual versus perceived differences in partisan group construals.

with "pro-choice" versus "pro-life" views relevant to the ongoing abortion rights debates (e.g., what kind of abortion "scenarios" and considerations are common versus uncommon; also, what positive consequences and what negative consequences would be likely to follow from a tightening of abortion restrictions, etc.). The second study dealt with "liberal" versus "conservative" construals of specific events in the racially charged Howard Beach incident, in which a Black teenager was fatally injured by an automobile while running away from a group of White pursuers (e.g., who had started and exacerbated the initial confrontation, what had been the intentions and motives of the various participants in the incidents, etc.).

Both sides, as expected, provided many instances of construal differences, but almost invariably the magnitude of such differences was overestimated by the partisans. More specifically, the partisans overestimated the degree of ideological consistency that *both* sides—especially the "other side," but to some extent their own side as well—would show in the assumptions and construals they brought to the relevant issues. What is more, partisans in both studies felt that their own individual views were less driven by ideology than those of other partisans. Not surprisingly, nonpartisan or neutral respondents in the study showed the same tendency to overestimate ideological extremity and congruency in construal as the partisans. That is, partisans and nonpartisans alike significantly overestimated the construal gap between the two sides, and in a sense, underestimated the common ground in the assumptions, beliefs, and values they shared.

Informal interviews with students, incidentally, revealed an additional source of these misperceptions and overestimations beyond naive realism, one that is worth mentioning in light of current discussions of "political correctness." Students shared with us the fact that they rarely acknowledged the degree of ambivalence in their political beliefs—not in talking to their ideological allies (lest their resoluteness come into doubt) and not in talking to their ideological adversaries (lest their "concessions" be exploited or misunderstood). In fact, most students explained that in the interest of avoiding conflict and misunderstanding and being "stereotyped," they generally shunned all potentially contentious political discussion. By doing so, it is apparent, the students also forfeited the opportunity to learn the true complexity (and the shared ambivalence) in each other's views. A possible antidote to naive realism and its attributional consequences—that is, the open, sustained, sympathetic sharing of views and perspectives—was rarely employed by the students. Ironically, in attempting to avoid discomfort and giving offense, many students failed to discover that their particular position on the political spectrum (i.e., that of self-labeled "realistic" liberal, or "compassionate" conservative) was one shared by a great number of their peers.

C. EQUITY ISSUES

The various barriers and biases we have been outlining in this chapter take on particular significance because bargainers and negotiators generally demand more from an agreement than a mere advance in their position over the status quo. They seek, and feel entitled to receive an advance that is fair and appropriate—one that is proportionate to the strength and legitimacy of their claims (see Adams, 1965, Homans, 1961; also Berkowitz & Walster, 1976; McClintock, Kramer, & Keil, 1984; Messick & Cook, 1983; Messick & Sentis, 1979; and Walster, Walster, & Berscheid, 1978). In particular, they demand treatment and terms of settlement that are fair and appropriate *relative* to the treatment and terms received by the "other side." The general implication of such a pursuit should be clear—the set of outcomes that satisfy the parties' equity demands is far narrower than the set offering mere advance over the status quo, especially when assessments of equity are made subject to the assessment biases discussed throughout this chapter. Our particular interest, however, is the interaction between self-interest and equity seeking.

In cases where the parties have an identical basis for their claims (for example, where two partners hold a winning lottery ticket that they purchased jointly), the equitable division will be apparent to all (i.e., a "50/50" split). Neither party, moreover, is likely to propose, much less agree to, any other division. Indeed, it is interesting in this connection to take note of research on the Ultimatum Game, in which (at least in the simplest form of the game) one party is given the opportunity to propose some division of a given purse, and the other party is obliged either to accept that "ultimatum" or to reject it (in which case neither party gains any portion of that purse). Two results from such research are important in terms of our present discussion: First, ultimatums offering the recipient less than 50% of the purse, especially ones offering much less than 50%, are frequently rejected even though the rejecting party thereby forfeits its only opportunity for gain. Second, the most common offer is a 50/50 split, and grossly unequal offers are relatively uncommon, which suggests that the party offering the ultimatum accepts the equity principle, or at least anticipates correctly the other party would rather see the entire purse forfeited than accept a division that it deems too unfair (Guth, Schmittberger, & Schwarze, 1982; Ochs & Roth, 1989).

In most allocation dilemmas outside the laboratory, the requirements of equity often are less obvious and less easily satisfied. As with negotiated agreements, what parties are seeking is generally not an equal advance over the status quo (for example, equal shares of material resources, or equal gains in security) but rather an advance that is proportionate to the weight and legitimacy of their respective claims (see Bazerman, Loewenstein, & White, 1992). This requirement becomes particularly difficult to satisfy when the bases for the contending claims are different in kind. If Jones wrote two-thirds of the chapters in a coauthored text and Smith one-third, or if Jones put up two-thirds of the money for a speculative stock purchase and Smith one-third, they are likely to agree without difficulty or ill will on a similar two-to-one allocation of any returns on their investment. But if Jones wrote more first drafts and did more of the library research, while Smith provided the outlines from which Jones worked and did more of the subsequent revisions and prose polishing, or if Jones provided more of the capital for the joint enterprise while Smith provided more time, effort, and expertise, the search for an equitable allocation of returns is apt to be more difficult and contentious.

The pursuit of equity becomes especially difficult when the contending parties are longstanding adversaries, and the claims in question are not only disparate but subject to dispute (i.e., who started the conflict, who has endured greater wrongs, who made more concessions or exerted more energetic and sincere attempts at conflict resolution in the past, whose present needs and privations are most pressing, who is most likely to prevail in the absence of a negotiated settlement, and so forth) (Bar-Tal, 1993; Bronfenbrenner, 1961; Heradstveit, 1979; Jervis, 1985; Plous, 1985; White, 1977, 1984). Furthermore, a party to a dispute is more apt to insist on such proportionality or equity, rather than mere improvement over the status quo, when it feels that the momentum of history is on its side, that it will continue to grow stronger in the future, and perhaps even be able to impose the settlement terms it "deserves."

Conversely, the search for agreement may be facilitated, and issues of equity may be pointedly avoided, when the relevant parties already enjoy and wish to maintain a positive relationship. For example, longstanding collaborators negotiating future publication royalties (like friends negotiating the payment of a restaurant meal) may readily agree upon simple "equality," that is, equal rather than proportionate shares of the royalties, precisely because such an allocation avoids any consideration of equity or proportionality (and thereby spares the parties any potentially disagreeable discussion of respective claims or relative contributions). Indeed, the "script" in such situations seems quite clear. The party with the stronger claims for a personally advantageous division of cost or benefits (i.e., the colleague who contributed somewhat more to the writing of the book, like the friend who ordered the less-expensive restaurant entrée) is obliged to propose and then to insist over any objections upon simple equality. At the same time, the party who stands to gain from equal rather than equitable division of costs or rewards is obliged to acknowledge the other party's "right" to an unequal division of costs or rewards, then yield when that other party insists on simple equality (ideally, with the latter offering assurances that past and/or future joint activities will "even out" any disparities).

Our discussion of equity seeking suggests a paradox, one that some theorists and practitioners will no doubt find distasteful. On the one hand, many thoughtful analysts have insisted that the art and science of successful dispute resolution demands the discovery—or if necessary the creative construction—of terms that the relevant parties feel are fair and responsive to their underlying needs and concerns, not mere "half-a-loaf" compromises (see Fisher, 1994; Fisher & Ury, 1984; Raiffa, 1982). On the other hand, the analysis offered here suggests that while satisfying participants' sense of fairness or justice in *procedures* is essential (see Lind & Tyler, 1988), the explicit pursuit of fairness or proportionality in outcomes may itself pose a barrier to dispute resolution. To some extent, the resolution of this paradox involves a simple distinction between short-term and long-term perspectives. Agreements that satisfy equity concerns may be more difficult to design, and in many cases may not be achievable; but if they can be achieved they are apt to prove relatively stable (see Pruitt, Peirce, McGillicuddy, Welton, & Castrianno, 1993). Conversely, terms agreed upon that do not satisfy such concerns are apt to come undone in the future, and to create the prospect of renewed hostility (especially if one party or the other increases its power, and feels able to redress the "injustice" of existing arrangements). To some extent, however, satisfaction of the partisans' subjective sense of equity—at least, as an explicit negotiation goal—may simply be an unrealistic and undesirable burden to place on the negotiation process. That is, negotiation may proceed more productively when all that is explicitly sought is the generally obtainable goal of mutual advantage, with no requirement or implication that the disputants thereby concede explicitly or implicitly that the settlement reached reflects the relative merits of their respective cases.

A recent pair of laboratory studies (Diekmann, Samuels, Ross, & Bazerman, 1994) offers a somewhat different and more subtle account of the interplay between equity and self-interest. Both studies confronted subjects with hypothetical "resource allocation" problems. Furthermore, in both studies, the potential recipients of those allocations (i.e., either candidates from two different schools competing for shares of a scholarship fund or managers of two different divisions of a large company seeking shares of a "bonus pool") presented equally strong, albeit rather different, records of accomplishment. Most importantly, both studies contrasted the response of allocators (i.e., those recommending specific splits of the resources in question) and evaluators (i.e., those assessing the fairness of specific splits enacted by others).

The findings from these studies suggested an influence of individual or group interest that was limited but important. That is, allocators tended to opt for "equality" or a "50/50" split, even when they could have pointed to differences in accomplishments or bases for claims if they had sought to justify an unequal split, and subsequently rated all other allocations as unfair. Similarly, evaluators in equal allocation conditions tended to rate the 50/50 splits as perfectly fair (and all other splits as highly unfair), even when they too could have pointed to the differences in accomplishments and claims if they had sought to justify a contention that they, or the representative from their school, deserved the larger share. Only in responding, after the fact, to an *unequal* allocation (e.g., 67% vs. 33%) favoring themselves or a member of their group did subjects' assessments of fairness and perceptions of entitlement show the distorting influence of self-interest (see Fig. 4). Only then did they decide that inequality did little violence to their canons of fairness. And only then did they claim that their own accomplishments, or those of a member of their own group, were more significant and more worthy of financial recognition than those of rival claimants. In sum, tendencies toward fairness, equality, and equity were not consistently overwhelmed by self-interested biases. At the same time, the capacity and willing-

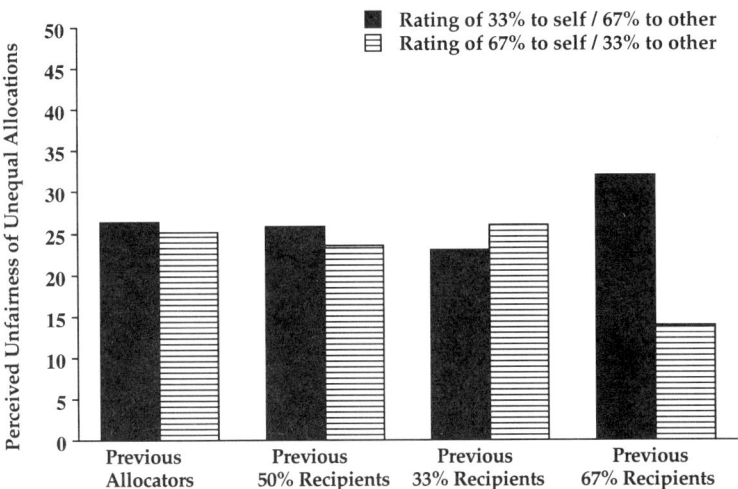

Fig. 4. Rated unfairness of unequal allocations by previous allocators and by previous recipients of equal and unequal allocations.

ness of subjects to justify allocation inequalities that they personally would not have imposed, and personally would not have deemed fair beforehand, revealed a phenomenon that could further exacerbate social conflict involving distributions of wealth, power, and opportunity.

V. Implications for Mediators, Facilitators, and Other Third Parties

The study of barriers and biases, and of exacerbative psychological processes, can do more than help us to understand why negotiations sometimes fail when they should succeed, and why the process of negotiation can escalate rather than attenuate feelings of enmity and mistrust. Such study can also contribute to the analysis and development of techniques for overcoming these barriers and reducing these sources of misunderstanding. Accordingly, we shall conclude this chapter by at least outlining some of the ways that third parties can facilitate efficient bargaining and conflict resolution. Once again, we shall not attempt to be comprehensive in our treatment. (For recent reviews, see Bercovitch & Rubin, 1992; Boardman & Horowitz, 1994; Carnevale & Pruitt, 1992; Kolb, 1994; and Kressel & Pruitt, 1985, 1989). Instead, our emphasis primarily will be on strategies and tactics designed to deal with the specific psychological processes and barriers discussed in this chapter.

A. FRAMING AND CONSTRUAL

Our earlier discussion of specific psychological barriers highlights the importance of subjective interpretation or construal in any bargaining setting. In particular, attempts to promote successful dispute resolution may hinge upon a mediator's success in creating an environment that allows the two sides to construe specific proposals and concessions, and the overall bargaining context, in a manner favorable to efficient bargaining. For example, sophisticated mediators may seek to reduce the inhibiting effects of *loss aversion* by reframing the negotiator's task in a way that makes the costs and risks associated with the conflict-laden status quo more salient—ideally, just as salient as the costs and risks associated with the concessions required to change that status quo. Mediators can further reduce the tendency for the bargainers to view their concessions as losses by inducing them to view the things they will be giving up as "bargaining chips" or "negotiation currency"—something to be exchanged readily (like any other kind of currency) for things one values more (see Kahneman & Tversky, in press).

Mediators and other third parties can also help to protect disputing parties from the optimistic overconfidence that arises when those parties expect others to share their construal of the conflict in which they are involved. Potential litigants, for example, are likely to adopt more similar, and more realistic, assessments once a court-ordered or mutually agreed upon "expert" has examined both sides' contentions and evidence and rendered his or her opinion about the "settlement" value of the case. Other third parties play a similar role—at the risk of being branded as biased or unfair—by giving the parties involved in a dispute more general feedback about the way that their claims are currently being evaluated, or are likely to evaluated, by disinterested parties.

More importantly, perhaps, mediators can endeavor to carefully frame, or if necessary reframe the negotiation process itself. For example, they can frame the endeavor not as an attempt at conflict resolution or redress of injustice but as an exercise in problem solving, (i.e., as an opportunity for each side to trade things they value less than their adversary values them in order to get things they value more; see Fisher, 1994; Raiffa, 1982; Rubin, 1994). In any case, the framing should be one that encourages the parties to move beyond political posturing and recriminations about past wrongs. In a sense, the mediator's framing of the negotiation can turn the parties' attention away from the concerns with equity to the pursuit of enlightened self-interest or group interest. At times, the mediator can even employ semantic framings or labels that lead the parties to construe the negotiation in positive, indeed idealistic terms. In this context, we share the results of a recent study conducted in our laboratory (Ross & Samuels, 1993) that attests to the power of a simple framing or construal manipulation.

1. The Wall Street/Community Game

The Ross and Samuels study essentially pitted the determinative power of a construal manipulation against the predictive power of subjects' reputation for cooperativeness or uncooperativeness. The experiment had two separate phases. In the first phase, dormitory advisors on the Stanford University campus were asked to nominate male undergraduates living in their dorm whom they thought especially likely, or especially unlikely, to cooperate in playing a version of the much-researched Prisoner's Dilemma Game (Rapoport, 1960; see also Dawes, 1991). The dorm advisors then were asked specifically to estimate the probability that their nominees would in fact "play strategy C" (cooperate) rather than "play strategy D" (defect) on the first round of that game. In the second phase of the study, the most likely to cooperate and most likely to defect nominees actually played the game in question—opting, on the first round of the game and then on six subsequent rounds, either to defect (thereby maximizing their own outcome at the expense of the other player and encouraging that player to defect in future rounds) or to cooperate (thereby lowering their own outcome and taking the risk of being exploited in order to reward and encourage cooperation on the part of the other player).

The construal manipulation was a very simple one. On two occasions, in explaining the nature of the game and the payoff matrix it provided, the experimenter referred to it either as the "Wall Street Game" or the "Community Game." Otherwise, all subjects were treated identically. The investigators' concern, of course, was the impact of this difference in labels (and, presumably, the impact of the differing construals or associations evoked by such labels) on subjects' play—especially their choice on the very first round, when no "history" of prior cooperation or defection could influence the subjects' responses or expectations. Two questions were to be answered: How much difference would the label make for the two kinds of players? And how would the influence of the label compare with the influence of the players' nomination status as most likely to cooperate versus most likely to defect?

The results of the study were straightforward and dramatic. The construal manipulation exerted a large and significant impact on subjects' play (see Fig. 5).

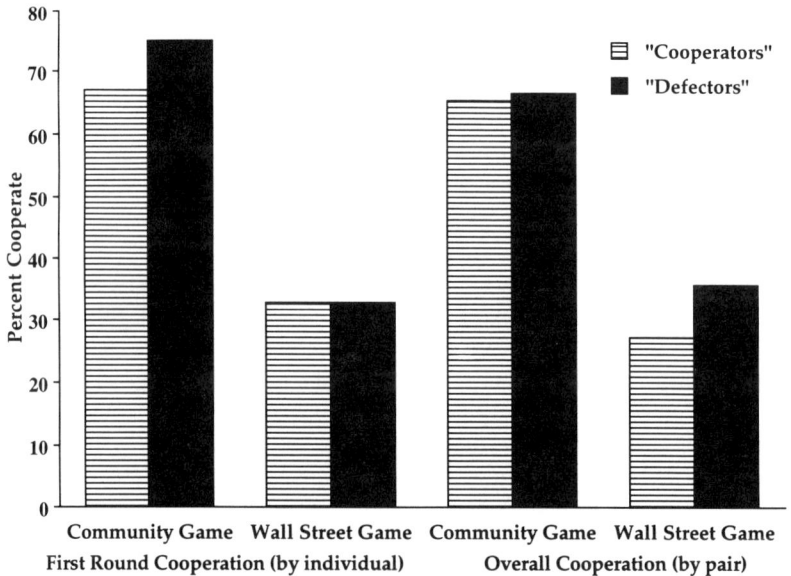

Fig. 5. Percentage of cooperation on first round and over all seven rounds in Community Game versus Wall Street Game.

Only about one-third of players elected to cooperate on round I of the *Wall Street Game,* whereas more than two-thirds elected to cooperate on round I of the *Community Game.* These differences, moreover, persisted on subsequent rounds. The label attached to the game—now buttressed by the tendency for initial mutual cooperation to encourage further cooperation and for initial defection by either player to produce subsequent defection by both players—induced subjects playing the *Community Game* to cooperate more than twice as much overall (and to earn considerably more money) than subjects playing the *Wall Street Game.*

Nomination status or reputation, by contrast, exerted virtually no impact on play. Most likely to cooperate and most likely to defect nominees showed similarly low levels of first-round cooperation in the *Wall Street Game,* and similarly high levels of first-round cooperation in the *Community Game.* Once again, the relevant pattern of responses persisted throughout the subsequent rounds of the game, despite the fact that the dyads always consisted of two subjects with the same most likely to cooperate or most likely to defect status. These findings can be expressed somewhat differently, and perhaps more dramatically. Participants who sought initial and sustained cooperation from the other player would be twice as likely to receive it from a player whose reputation caused him to be nominated as most likely to defect but who happened to be playing the *Community Game,* as from a player whose reputation caused him to be nominated as most likely to cooperate but who happened to be playing the *Wall Street Game.*

Further research is underway to determine exactly why the particular label attached to the game exerted so large an effect—that is, to what extent the label influenced subjects directly (i.e., determined the way subjects felt they ought to play) and to what extent it influenced them indirectly (i.e., by changing subjects' expectations about how the other player would choose to play, or even by altering their beliefs about how the other player would expect *them* to play). But the power of the label—that is to say, its impact on the way the game was construed by the players, what they felt it was "about," and what kinds of real-world situations came to mind as they made their choices—seems indisputable. The manipulation of construal by the experimenter mattered, and it mattered deeply.

What also seems to be beyond question is the fact that the dorm counselors who did the nominating and predicting drastically underestimated the impact of the game label on the subjects' construal and play (and that they also drastically overestimated the predictive value of the impressions they formed about the subjects' personality traits and reputations by observing them in other situations). Indeed, the nominators' probability estimates concerning cooperation or defection suggested that they gave no weight at all to the label in their initial predictions. Mediators who similarly overlook the role that construal plays in negotiations are apt to make a similar error, that is, to worry too much about personalities and reputations and too little about the best way to create an environment that induces participants, regardless of their past deeds and reputations, to bargain efficiently and interpret charitably each other's conciliatory gestures.

B. BUILDING TRUST AND FINDING COMMON GROUND

One of the most obvious and important third-party roles involves the building or rebuilding of trust, and the shift of focus from areas of disagreement to areas of "common ground" (Clark & Marshall, 1981). This role is particularly important in mediating conflicts between groups or peoples with long histories of enmity. Indeed, in such conflicts third parties can take an important step in the direction of these objectives merely by bringing disputants into sustained personal contact, so that they can get beyond stereotypes and discover shared fears and aspirations (Cohen, Kelman, Miller, & Smith, 1977; Doob & Foltz, 1974; Doob, Foltz, & Stevens, 1969; Kelman, 1972, 1993; Kelman & Cohen, 1986). Several studies point to the value of frank, open dialogue between opposing sides— particularly dialogue in which participants talk about their factual assumptions and the complexities of their values, rather than simply defending their positions (see Druckman, Broome, & Korper, 1988; Thompson, 1991; and Walcott, Hopman, & King, 1977). In a sense, such dialogue may be seen as the antidote to the overestimation of extremity and ideological congruency found in the Robinson et al. (in press) study discussed earlier in this chapter.

Even if such dialogue does not lead to agreement, it is likely at least to challenge the partisan's view of the other side as monolithic, unreasoning, unreasonable, and entirely ideologically driven. Such discussions can also permit participants to realize the inconsistencies, uncertainties, and disagreement in their own side's position, thus making them freer to express dissent and entertain new ideas. Indeed, it has been proposed that not only third parties (Rubin, 1980) but also moderates within the rival groups (Jacobson, 1981) have a valuable role to play in this regard—especially in encouraging partisans to get beyond rhetoric and statements of position to the point of discussing underlying interests, assumptions, concerns, and especially sources of uncertainty and ambivalence (see also Fisher et al., 1991; Rubin et al., 1994; Susskind & Cruikshank, 1987).

A particularly interesting development in recent years has been the flourishing of "multi-track diplomacy" (Diamond & McDonald, 1991) and "public peace processes" (Chufrin & Saunders, 1993), through which unofficial peacemaking or dispute resolution initiatives are pursued by nongovernmental organizations (e.g., peace centers, academic and professional organizations, etc.) or groups of citizen elites. Indeed, the path to the dramatic 1993 Israeli–Palestinian accord on Jericho and Gaza was blazed through such initiatives (Rouhana & Kelman,

1994). Our own experience in Palestinian–Israeli and Armenian–Azerbaijanian dialogues (cosponsored by the SCCN and the Foundation for Global Community) is worth noting in this regard. We have seen participants build personal trust and rapport as the conversation gradually shifted from disputes about past wrongdoing to the personal histories that brought the participants to the table with their counterparts on the other side, from charges and countercharges about the present conflict to the participants' vision of the society that they would like to create for their grandchildren.

Beyond seeing the development of warm personal relations, we also have noticed several less obvious benefits from these unofficial initiatives. First, because the participants are not diplomats acting in an official capacity, they are free to explore new and visionary proposals without fearing the "strategic" disadvantages associated with candor and spontaneity. Second, because the meetings are informal, free from the glare of media, and relatively leisurely in their pace, the participants typically can socialize and talk about their families and personal experiences as they take walks, enjoy meals (and, in our conferences, even wash dishes) together, thereby creating personal bonds of respect and friendship that facilitate future contact and joint initiatives. Finally, and perhaps most important, the participants provide each other with invaluable information about priorities and areas of flexibility and potential movement—areas where exchanges of concessions could be sought. By discovering the views of moderates or "peace advocates" in the other camp, the participants are led to more realistic assessments of possibilities and a clearer sense of which of the other side's current demands reflect deeply held, widely shared sentiments and which reflect potential areas for negotiation. These assessments, in turn, get more broadly disseminated when our citizen diplomats return home and share their experiences and impressions with influential colleagues and news media.

C. MANAGING ATTRIBUTIONS

Third parties can play an especially important role in helping adversaries to overcome the specific barrier discussed at greatest length in this chapter, that is, reactive devaluation. One obvious way in which this can be done has already been made apparent in discussing the Stillinger et al. (1990) studies, in which we saw that a proposal offered by the other side becomes less attractive because of its authorship. The implication for mediators and other third parties should be clear, to wit, a proposal originating from one particular side can be made attractive to the recipient if its authorship is concealed, obscured, or even misrepresented.

Experienced diplomats and other mediators have told us that one of the benefits of shuttle diplomacy and other "caucusing procedures" is the opportunity to discover what each side might be willing to give up in trade, and then formulate a plan calling for the exchange of such concessions that is attributed to neither side but is instead represented as the product of the third-party mediator—not as a reflection of what the mediator personally deems fair or proportionate but rather as a reflection of what the mediator understands to be consistent with the parties' differing interests and priorities. Both parties are then invited to treat the proposal merely as a working document that they are free to improve upon, with neither party called upon to defend the relevant document. (Indeed, as might be anticipated from our earlier discussion of perceptions of media and mediator bias, both sides generally *criticize* the document, and in so doing gain the opportunity to "fine tune" their negotiating positions so as to maximize joint gains.)

There is also a subtler role for negotiators and other third parties to play, one that arises from an understanding of the role that attributions play in reactive devaluation. That is, the devaluation in question stems, at least in part, from people's basic tendency to search for *causal attributions* for each other's behavior (Heider, 1958; Jones & Davis, 1965; Kelley, 1967, 1973). Parties in a conflict or bargaining setting are disposed to search for explanations for each other's behavior in general and for the content and timing of each other's concession offers in particular. The recipient of a unilateral concession or proposed trade of concessions is apt to ask, Why is my adversary offering this *particular* concession or proposing this *particular* trade and why *now*? In the absence of other satisfactory answers, the recipient is apt to conclude that the concession is probably less substantial than it might seem on the surface. The problem of unfavorable attributions is probably not limited to evaluations of the terms of an adversary's proposal; it also extends to any form of behavior by the adversary that seemingly might be intended to ameliorate the dispute. Effective measures for conflict reduction, accordingly, require that each side's "attribution problems" be taken into account and, if possible, resolved in a satisfactory manner.

The third-party mediator sometimes can help solve these attribution problems (and, in a sense, also help to reduce some of the dissonance felt by the negotiating parties) merely by explaining to each party, in caucus, the political realities and constraints compelling the other side to make or reject particular proposals. Indeed, this attributional analysis points to the potentially beneficial role of overt, external resolution pressures, such as deadlines or promises of "side payments" by interested third parties in the negotiation process. The existence of such pressures provides the recipient of an attractive package offer or pump-priming concession with an explanation for the adversary's newly demonstrated flexibility, one that precludes the need for reassessing or reconstructing the significance of the various concessions offered and sought in the light of that adversary's willingness to offer them or eagerness to receive them. Indeed, deadlines and other external resolution pressures may provide the negotiating parties with more palatable attributions for their own flexibility (good sense, not weakness or foolishness) and better explanations to offer the constituencies they represent and the critics they must face.

The trade-offs involved in acknowledging external pressures to "settle" are worth noting (Stillinger, 1990, 1991). The knowledge that the other side is being *forced* to offer concessions, and the acknowledgment of this state of affairs by them, may make one less likely to accept their offer on strategic grounds (i.e., strategic intransigence may be encouraged) and less likely to attribute their offer to friendly intent or a change of heart. But the existence of such force, and the adversary's acknowledgment of it, does encourage one to take the concession at face value rather than construing it in whatever manner minimizes its significance. Conversely, the sense that the other side is under no pressure to settle, and/or their explicit claim that they will not yield to such pressure, can aggravate the attributional dilemma we have described, especially when the other side is perceived as hostile (i.e., "If they are offering a concession to us even when they don't have to, it must be trivial to them, and of little value to us"). In short, while insistence on "bargaining from a position of strength," or even claiming such a position, may serve some strategic goals, the bargainer may pay a significant attributional price for doing so. Third-party mediators, or third parties promising to provide additional resources in the event of success or to withdraw them in the event of failure, once again can help to free the antagonists from this dilemma.

Beyond helping the adversaries address attributional dilemmas posed by the other side's willingness to offer or trade concessions, the imposition of a genuine deadline by the mediator, after which the expected outcome of negotiation becomes worse for both parties, can even make dissonance theory work for the negotiation process rather than against it. The two sides will feel less dissonance at now accepting terms that they could have had earlier, perhaps even had more cheaply, because the deadline renders the status quo and the option of continued negotiations less attractive. Indeed, settlement may be facilitated because both parties can *anticipate* the dissonance that they will feel when the deadline expires, or even worse, the dissonance they will feel when they ultimately settle for postdeadline terms that are less attractive than those that were available before that deadline expired.

In a sense, the deadline itself can be "reconstrued" so that it represents not a threatened future loss but a present opportunity for gain. It is important, however, to recognize that deadlines are most likely to be effective aids to negotiation when they are imposed on both parties by the third party (especially if that party is contributing resources to be distributed in the context of a settlement) or by other realities of the situation, not by one party simply threatening the other party with some sanction or future intransigence should the proposal be rejected. But even when the deadline is imposed by one party on the other, it can be productive if it is perceived by the recipient as a product of impending costs or lost opportunities facing the other side, and not as a mere strategic ploy.

D. NEGOTIATION EXPECTATIONS AND IDEOLOGY

Our discussion of conflict resolution would be woefully incomplete if we failed to acknowledge the role of ideology and expectation. Conflict resolution is more likely to be achieved when the antagonists enter the negotiation process with the absolute conviction that such resolution can, must, and will be achieved (and with the confidence that their adversaries share such convictions). By contrast, resolution is least likely to be achieved when the negotiating parties have grave doubts about the possibility of achieving any major "breakthroughs" and accept the likelihood of failure.

When the absolute necessity and the absolute *inevitability* of resolution is accepted by both parties, the possibility of success is greatly enhanced, not only because the parties have a powerful and shared motive to avoid failure, but because they also have a satisfactory explanation for any concessions that they are obliged to make and a satisfactory attribution for apparent concessions by the other side (that is, "we *had* to reach an agreement, and so did *they*").

The origins of this optimistic, even idealistic hypothesis lie in our observation of difficult real-world negotiations that succeed despite the seemingly "intractable" nature of the underlying conflicts in question (see Ross, in press; Ross & Stillinger, 1991). We have in mind both exceptional events (such as the election of a pope) and more ordinary ones (such as the passing of a federal budget). In both cases, the conflicts and divisions are complex and deep, and there is a real sense in which no "solution" can command an authentic majority (much less the two-thirds majority required to elect a pope) whose interests are better served by agreeing to compromise than by continuing to hold out for better terms. But the certainty of relatively timely resolution, buttressed by history and tradition, seems to guarantee that a resolution will be found within the "expected" time period—a resolution that may involve major compromises and minimal satisfaction on the part of many who comprise the necessary majority, but one that is justified by the negotiators (to themselves, as well as to others) by a simple dictum, "we *had* to have a pope" or "we *had* to have a budget."

The implications of this discussion of negotiation ideology and expectation are worth underscoring. When obstacles are formidable, and the sentiment exists that failure is possible or "thinkable," such failure becomes highly likely. Only when failure is "unthinkable" can one be optimistic that the cognitive barriers discussed in this chapter will begin to crumble. We cannot provide third-party mediators with any magic formula to convince negotiators that they have no choice but to succeed, or even that success is inevitable. But we can share the results of a pilot study that suggests that the effort might be worthwhile.

In this simple study (Hollatz & Ross, 1994), liberal and conservative students in a hypothetical but realistic and engaging negotiation task were given the chore of jointly selecting an individual to handle a politically sensitive job—choosing well-known speakers to address current social-political issues. The students had only two candidates, one ultra-liberal, who seemed likely to invite only fellow liberals as speakers, and one ultra-conservative, who seemed likely to invite only fellow conservatives. Furthermore, they knew that failure to agree on a candidate would mean that there would be no speakers invited in the coming academic term. Half the "negotiators" were told simply that they should do their best to reach agreement, and that the experimenter would check their progress in 10 min. The other half were told that, notwithstanding the difficult task, all previous negotiators had readily reached agreement in the allotted 10-min period.

The results were dramatic. In the standard control condition, only 2 out of 12 pairs (17%) reached agreement in the allotted 10-min period (and 5 of the 12 pairs failed to reach agreement even after receiving an additional 5 min). In the experimental or "positive expectations" condition, 11 of 12 pairs (93%) reached agreement within the designated 10-min period. It still remains to be seen whether more substantial (and, ideally, less hypothetical) disputes will similarly yield to such manipulations of positive expectations (L. Ross, 1995). But the suggestion that negotiation expectation or ideology can induce negotiators to succeed in the face of both strategic and psychological barriers, and the opportunity to explore the processes and mechanisms underlying such success, seem worthy of additional research.

E. EDUCATION: BENEFITS OF UNDERSTANDING UNDERLYING PROCESSES

We close our discussion of practical measures to achieve conflict resolution with an optimistic hypothesis about the role of education and insight. Simply stated, we hypothesize that awareness of some of the psychological processes we have outlined—especially the processes of biased construal and reactive devaluation that make parties respond coolly to concessions, compromise packages, and other harmony-seeking overtures—will forestall them or weaken their impact.

In a sense, we are proposing that adversaries who have been "debriefed" about social and psychological processes that limit their capacity to negotiate compromises that are in their own best interests will have a useful tool for self-appraisal and for educating relevant constituencies (see Ross, Lepper, & Hubbard, 1975; also Lord, Lepper, & Preston, 1984). Similarly, we feel that such insights about process will serve third-party mediators well—both in helping them to define their roles and in helping to overcome the pitfalls facing the adversaries. Finally, and most generally, we think that education and insight about barriers to conflict resolution will aid people of goodwill in designing conflict-resolution strategies and tactics that allow the adversaries either to avoid the barriers in question or to overcome them.

References

Abelson, R. P., & Rosenberg, M. J. (1958). Symbolic psycho-logic: A model of attitudinal cognition. *Behavioral Science, 3,* 1–13.

Adams, J. S. (1965). Inequity in social exchange. In L. Berkowitz (Ed.), *Advances in experimental social psychology* (Vol. 2, pp. 267–299). New York: Academic Press.

Alpert, M., & Raiffa, H. (1982). A progress report on the training of probability assessors. In D. Kahneman, P. Slovic, & A. Tversky (Eds.), *Judgment under uncertainty: Heuristics and biases* (pp. 294–305). Cambridge: Cambridge University Press.

Aronson, E. (1969). The theory of cognitive dissonance: A current perspective. In L. Berkowitz (Ed.), *Advances in experimental social psychology* (Vol. 4, pp. 1–34). New York: Academic Press.

Arrow, K. (1951). *Social choice and individual values.* New Haven, CT: Yale University Press.

Arrow, K. (in press). Information acquisition and the resolution of conflict. In K. Arrow, R. Mnookin, L. Ross, A. Tversky, & R. Wilson (Eds.), *Barriers to the negotiated resolution of conflict.* New York: Norton.

Arrow, K., Mnookin, R., Ross, L., Tversky, A., & Wilson, R. (Eds.). (in press). *Barriers to the negotiated resolution of conflict.* New York: Norton.

Asch, S. E. (1940). Studies in the principles of judgments and attitudes: II. Determination of judgments by group and by ego standards. *Journal of Social Psychology, 12,* 433–465.

Atkins, D., Ward, A., & Lepper, M. (1994). *Reducing reactive devaluation with a self-affirmation.* Unpublished manuscript, Stanford University, Palo Alto, CA.

Bar-Tal, D. (1993). American convictions about conflictive U.S.A.–U.S.S.R. relations: A case of group beliefs. In S. Worchel & J. A. Simpson (Eds.), *Conflict between people and groups* (pp. 193–213). Chicago: Nelson-Hall.

Bazerman, M., & Neale, M. (in press). The role of fairness considerations and relationships in a judgmental perspective of negotiation. In K. Arrow, R. Mnookin, L. Ross, A. Tversky, & R. Wilson (Eds.), *Barriers to the negotiated resolution of conflict.* New York: Norton.

Bazerman, M. H. (1990). *Judgment in managerial decision making* (2nd ed.). New York: John Wiley and Sons.

Bazerman, M. H., Loewenstein, G. F., & White, S. B. (1992). Psychological determinants of utility in competitive contexts: The impact of elicitation procedures. *Administrative Science Quarterly, 37,* 220–240.

Benton, A. A., Kelley, H. H., & Liebling, B. (1972). Effects of extremity of offers and concession rate on the outcomes of bargaining. *Journal of Personality and Social Psychology, 24,* 73–83.

Bercovitch, J., & Rubin, J. Z. (1992). *Mediation in international relations.* London: Macmillan.

Berkowitz, L., & Walster, E. (1976). Equity theory: Towards a general theory of social interaction. In L. Berkowitz & E. Walster (Eds.), *Advances in experimental social psychology* (Vol. 9). New York: Academic Press.

Boardman, S. K., & Horowitz, S. V. (1994). Constructive conflict management and social problems: An introduction. *Journal of Social Issues, 50,* 1–12.

Brehm, J. W. (1966). *A theory of psychological reactance.* New York: Academic Press.

Brehm, J. W., & Cohen, A. R. (1962). *Explorations in cognitive dissonance.* New York: John Wiley.

Brehm, S., & Brehm, J. W. (1981). *Psychological reactance: A theory of freedom and control.* New York: Academic Press.

Brenner, L. A., Koehler, D. J., & Tversky, A. (1993). *On the evaluation of one-sided evidence.* Unpublished manuscript, Stanford University, Palo Alto, CA.

Brock, T. C. (1968). Implications of commodity theory for value change. In A. G. Greenwald, T. C. Brock, & T. M. Ostrom (Eds.), *Psychological foundations of attitudes* (pp. 243–275). New York: Academic Press.

Bronfenbrenner, U. (1961). The mirror image in Soviet-American relations. *Journal of Social Issues, 17,* 45–56.
Bruner, J. S. (1957). Going beyond the information given. In H. Gruber, K. R. Hammond, & R. Jesser (Eds.), *Contemporary approaches to cognition* (pp. 41–69). Cambridge, MA: University Press.
Carnevale, P. J., & Pruitt, D. G. (1992). Negotiation and mediation. *Annual Review of Psychology, 43,* 531–582.
Chufrin, G. I., & Saunders, H. H. (1993). A public peace process. *Negotiation Journal, 9,* 155–177.
Cialdini, R. B. (1985). *Influence.* Glenview, IL: Scott, Foresman, and Co.
Clark, H. H., & Marshall, C. R. (1981). Definite reference and mutual knowledge. In A. K. Joshi, B. Webber, & I. Sag (Eds.), *Linguistic structure and discourse setting* (pp. 10–63). Cambridge: Cambridge University Press.
Cohen, S. P., Kelman, H. C., Miller, F. D., & Smith, B. L. (1977). Evolving intergroup techniques for conflict resolution: An Israeli-Palestinian pilot workshop. *Journal of Social Issues, 33,* 165–189.
Dawes, R. M. (1988). *Rational choice in an uncertain world.* San Diego, CA: Harcourt Brace Jovanovich.
Dawes, R. M. (1991). Social dilemmas, economic self-interest, and evolutionary theory. In D. R. Brown & J. E. Keith Smith (Eds.), *Frontiers of mathematical psychology: Essays in honor of Clyde Coombs* (pp. 53–79). New York: Springer-Verlag.
Diamond, L., & McDonald, J. (1991). *Multi-track diplomacy: A systems guide and analysis* (Report No. 3, June 1991). Grinnell, Iowa: Iowa Peace Institute.
Diekmann, K. A., Samuels, S. M., Ross, L., & Bazerman, M. H. (1994). *Self-interest and fairness in problems of resource allocation.* Unpublished manuscript, Northwestern University, Evanston, IL.
Doob, L. W., & Foltz, W. J. (1974). The impact of a workshop upon grass-roots leaders in Belfast. *Journal of Conflict Resolution, 18,* 237–256.
Doob, L. W., Foltz, W. J., & Stevens, R. B. (1969). The Fermeda workshop: A different approach to border conflicts in Eastern Africa. *Journal of Psychology, 73,* 249–266.
Druckman, D., Broome, B. J., & Korper, S. H. (1988). Value differences and conflict resolution. *Journal of Conflict Resolution, 32,* 489–510.
Dunning, D., & Cohen, G. (1992). Egocentric definitions of traits and abilities in social judgment. *Journal of Personality and Social Psychology, 63,* 341–355.
Dunning, D., Griffin, D. W., Milojkovic, J., & Ross, L. (1990). The overconfidence effect in social prediction. *Journal of Personality and Social Psychology, 58,* 568–581.
Dunning, D., Meyerowitz, J. A., & Holzberg, A. D. (1989). Ambiguity and self-evaluation: The role of idiosyncratic trait definitions in self-serving assessments of ability. *Journal of Personality and Social Psychology, 57,* 1082–1090.
Festinger, L. (1957). *A theory of cognitive dissonance.* Stanford, CA: Stanford University Press.
Fischhoff, B., Slovic, P., & Lichtenstein, S. (1977). Knowing with certainty: The appropriateness of extreme confidence. *Journal of Experimental Psychology: Human Perception and Performance, 3,* 552–564.
Fisher, R., & Ury, W. (1984). *Getting to YES: Negotiating agreement without giving in.* New York: Penguin.
Fisher, R., Ury, W., & Patton, B. (1991). *Getting to YES: Negotiating agreement without giving in* (2nd. ed.). New York: Penguin.
Fisher, R. J. (1994). Generic principles for resolving intergroup conflict. *Journal of Social Issues, 50,* 47–66.
Fiske, S. T., & Taylor, S. E. (1991). *Social cognition* (2nd ed.). New York: McGraw-Hill, Inc.
Follett, M. P. (1942). *Dynamic administration: The collected papers of Mary Parker Follett.* H. C. Metcalf and L. Urwick (Eds.). New York: Harper & Row.

Gilbert, D. T., & Jones, E. E. (1986). Perceiver-induced constraint: Interpretations of self-generated reality. *Journal of Personality and Social Psychology, 50,* 269–280.

Gilovich, T. (1991). *How we know what isn't so: The fallibility of human reasoning in everyday life.* New York: Free Press.

Gilson, R. J., & Mnookin, R. H. (in press). Competition and cooperation among litigants: A barrier to dispute resolution. In K. Arrow, R. Mnookin, L. Ross, A. Tversky, & R. Wilson (Eds.), *Barriers to the negotiated resolution of conflict.* New York: Norton.

Gioia, D. T., & Sims, H. P. (1985). Self-serving bias and actor-observer differences in organizations: An empirical analysis. *Journal of Applied Social Psychology, 15,* 547–563.

Griffin, D., & Ross, L. (1991). Subjective construal, social inference, and human misunderstanding. In M. P. Zanna (Ed.), *Advances in experimental social psychology* (Vol. 24, pp. 319–359). San Diego, CA: Academic Press.

Guth, W., Schmittberger, R., & Schwarze, B. (1982). An experimental analysis of ultimatum bargaining. *Journal of Economic Behavior and Organization, 3,* 367–388.

Hastorf, A., & Cantril, H. (1954). They saw a game: A case study. *Journal of Abnormal and Social Psychology, 49,* 129–134.

Heider, F. (1958). *The psychology of interpersonal relations.* New York: Wiley.

Heradstveit, D. (1979). *The Arab-Israeli conflict: Psychological obstacles to peace.* Oslo, Norway: Universitetsforlaget. Distributed by Columbia University Press.

Hollatz, M., & Ross, L. (1994). *The role of expectations in mediating success vs. failure in difficult negotiations.* Unpublished manuscript, Stanford University, Palo Alto, CA.

Homans, B. C. (1961). *Social behavior: Its elementary forms.* New York: Harcourt Brace Jovanovich.

Jacobson, D. (1981). Intraparty dissensus and interparty conflict resolution. *Journal of Conflict Resolution, 25,* 471–494.

Jervis, R. (1985). Perceiving and coping with threat: Psychological perspectives. In R. Jervis, R. N. Lebow, & J. Stein (Eds.), *Psychology and deterrence* (pp. 13–23). Baltimore, MD: John Hopkins University Press.

Jones, E. E., & Davis, K. E. (1965). From acts to dispositions: The attribution process in person perception. In L. Berkowitz (Ed.), *Advances in experimental social psychology* (Vol. 2, pp. 219–266). New York: Academic Press.

Jones, E. E., & Nisbett, R. E. (1971). The actor and the observer: Divergent perceptions of the causes of behavior. In E. E. Jones, D. Kanouse, H. H. Kelley, R. E. Nisbett, S. Valins, & B. Weiner (Eds.), *Attribution: Perceiving the causes of behavior* (pp. 79–94). Morristown, NJ: General Learning Press.

Kahneman, D., & Tversky, A. (1973). On the psychology of prediction. *Psychological Review, 80,* 237–251.

Kahneman, D., & Tversky, A. (1979). Prospect theory: An analysis of decision under risk. *Econometrica, 47,* 263–291.

Kahneman, D., & Tversky, A. (1984). Choices, values, and frames. *American Psychologist, 39,* 341–350.

Kahneman, D., & Tversky, A. (in press). Conflict resolution: A cognitive perspective. In K. Arrow, R. Mnookin, L. Ross, A. Tversky, & R. Wilson (Eds.), *Barriers to the negotiated resolution of conflict.* New York: Norton.

Kelley, H. H. (1967). Attribution theory in social psychology. In D. L. Vine (Ed.), *Nebraska Symposium on Motivation* (pp. 192–238). Lincoln, NE: University of Nebraska Press.

Kelley, H. H. (1973). The process of causal attribution. *American Psychologist, 28,* 107–128.

Kelman, H. C. (1972). The problem-solving workshop in conflict resolution. In L. Merritt (Ed.), *Communication in international politics* (pp. 168–204). Urbana, IL: University of Illinois Press.

Kelman, H. C. (1993). Coalitions across conflict lines: The interplay of conflicts within and between the Israeli and Palestinian communities. In S. Worchel & J. A. Simpson (Eds.), *Conflict between people and groups* (pp. 236–258). Chicago: Nelson-Hall.

Kelman, H. C., & Cohen, S. P. (1986). Resolution of international conflict: An interactional approach. In S. Worchel & W. G. Austin (Eds.), *Psychology of intergroup relations* (pp. 323–342). Chicago: Nelson-Hall.

Kolb, D. M. (1994). *When talk works: Profiles of working mediators*. San Francisco, CA: Jossey-Bass.

Kressel, K. & Pruitt, D. G. (Eds.). (1985). The mediation of social conflict. *Journal of Social Issues, 41*(2).

Kressel, K., & Pruitt, D. G. (1989). *Mediation research: The process and effectiveness of third-party intervention*. San Francisco, CA: Jossey-Bass.

Kunda, Z. (1987). Motivated inference: Self-serving generation and evaluation of causal theories. *Journal of Personality and Social Psychology, 53*, 636–647.

Kunda, Z. (1990). The case for motivated reasoning. *Psychological Bulletin, 108*, 480–498.

Langer, E. J. (1978). Rethinking the role of thought in social interaction. In J. H. Harvey, W. I. Ickes, & R. Kidd (Eds.), *New directions in attribution research* (Vol. 2, pp. 35–58). Hillsdale, NJ: Erlbaum.

Lax, D. A., & Sebenius, J. K. (1986). *The manager as negotiator: Bargaining for cooperation and competitive gain*. New York: Free Press.

Lepper, M., Ross, L., Tsai, J., & Ward, A. (1994). *Mechanisms of reactive devaluation*. Unpublished manuscript, Stanford University, Palo Alto, CA.

Lind, E. A., & Tyler, T. R. (1988). *The social psychology of procedural justice*. New York: Plenum.

Loewenstein, G., Issacharoff, S., Camerer, C., & Babcock, L. (1993). Self-serving assessments of fairnes and pretrial bargaining. *Journal of Legal Studies, 22*, 135–159.

Lord, C. G., Lepper, M. R., & Preston, E. (1984). Considering the opposite: A corrective strategy for social judgment. *Journal of Personality and Social Psychology, 47*, 1231–1243.

Lord, C. G., Ross, L., & Lepper, M. R. (1979). Biased assimilation and attitude polarization: The effects of prior theories on subsequently considered evidence. *Journal of Personality and Social Psychology, 37*, 2098–2109.

Lynn, M. (Ed.). (1992). The psychology of unavailability: Explaining scarcity & cost effects on value. *Basic and Applied Social Psychology, 13*(1).

McClintock, C. G., Kramer, R. M., & Keil, L. J. (1984). Equity and social exchange in human relationships. In L. Berkowitz (Ed.), *Advances in experimental social psychology* (Vol. 17, pp. 183–228). New York: Academic Press.

Messick, D. M., & Cook, K. S. (Eds.). (1983). *Equity theory: Psychological and sociological perspectives*. New York: Praeger.

Messick, D. M., & Sentis, K. P. (1979). Fairness and preference. *Journal of Experimental Social Psychology, 15*, 418–434.

Miller, D. T., & Ross, M. (1975). Self-serving biases in attribution of causality: Fact or fiction? *Psychological Bulletin, 82*, 213–225.

Mnookin, R. (1993). *Why negotiations fail: An exploration of barriers to the resolution of conflict* (Report No. 30). Stanford, CA: Stanford University: Stanford Center on Conflict and Negotiation.

Mnookin, R., & Ross, L. (in press). Strategic, psychological, and institutional barriers: An introduction. In K. Arrow, R. Mnookin, L. Ross, A. Tversky, & R. Wilson (Eds.), *Barriers to the negotiated resolution of conflict*. New York: Norton.

Mnookin, R., & Wilson, R. (1989). Rational bargaining and market efficiency: Understanding Pennzoil v. Texaco. *Virginia Law Review, 75*, 295.

Myers, D. G. (1990). *Social psychology* (3rd ed.). New York: McGraw-Hill, Inc.

Neale, M. A., & Bazerman, M. H. (1991). *Cognition and rationality in negotiation*. New York: The Free Press.

Nisbett, R. E., & Ross, L. D. (1980). *Human inference: Strategies and shortcomings of social judgment*. New Jersey: Prentice-Hall, Inc.

Ochs, J., & Roth, A. E. (1989). An experimental study of sequential bargaining. *American Economic Review, 79*, 335–385.

Osgood, C. E. (1962). *An alternative to war or surrender*. Urbana, IL: University of Illinois Press.

Osgood, C. E., & Tannenbaum, P. H. (1955). The principle of congruity in the prediction of attitude change. *Psychological Review, 62*, 42–55.

Oskamp, S. (1965a). Attitudes toward U.S. and Russian actions: A double standard. *Psychological Reports, 16*, 43–46.

Oskamp, S. (1965b). Overconfidence in case-study judgments. *Journal of Consulting Psychology, 29*, 261–265.

Panofsky, W. (in press). Barriers to negotiated arms control. In K. Arrow, R. Mnookin, L. Ross, A. Tversky, & R. Wilson (Eds.), *Barriers to the negotiated resolution of conflict*. New York: Norton.

Plous, S. (1985). Perceptual illusions and military realities: A social-psychological analysis of the nuclear arms race. *Journal of Conflict Resolution, 29*, 363–389.

Png, I. (1983). Strategic behavior in suit, settlement, and trial. *Bell Journal of Economics, 14(2)*, 539–550.

Pratt, J. & Zeckhauser, R. (Eds.). (1985). *Principals and agents: The structure of business*. Boston: Harvard Business School.

Pruitt, D. G., Peirce, R. S., McGillicuddy, N. B., Welton, G. L., & Castrianno, L. M. (1993). Long-term success in mediation. *Law and Human Behavior, 17*, 313–330.

Rachlinski, J. (1994). *Prospect theory and the economics of litigation*. Unpublished doctoral dissertation, Stanford University, Palo Alto, CA.

Raiffa, H. (1982). *The art and science of negotiation*. Cambridge, MA: Harvard University Press.

Rapoport, A. (1960). *Fights, games, and debates*. Ann Arbor, MI: University of Michigan Press.

Robinson, R. J., Keltner, D., Ward, A., & Ross, L. (in press). Actual versus assumed differences in construal: "Naive realism" in intergroup perception and conflict. *Journal of Personality and Social Psychology*.

Ross, L. (1977). The intuitive psychologist and his shortcomings: Distortions in the attribution process. In L. Berkowitz (Ed.), *Advances in experimental social psychology* (Vol. 10, pp. 173–220). New York: Academic Press.

Ross, L. (in press). Reactive devaluation in negotiation and conflict resolution. In K. Arrow, R. Mnookin, L. Ross, A. Tversky, & R. Wilson (Eds.), *Barriers to the negotiated resolution of conflict*. New York: Norton.

Ross, L., Greene, D., & House, P. (1977). The false consensus effect: An egocentric bias in social perception and attribution processes. *Journal of Experimental Social Psychology, 13*, 279–301.

Ross, L., Lepper, M. R., & Hubbard, M. (1975). Perseverance in self-perception and social perception: Biased attributional processes in the debriefing paradigm. *Journal of Personality and Social Psychology, 32*, 880–892.

Ross, L., & Samuels, S. M. (1993). *The predictive power of personal reputation vs. labels and construal in the Prisoner's Dilemma game*. Unpublished manuscript, Stanford University, Palo Alto, CA.

Ross, L., & Stillinger, C. (1991). Barriers to conflict resolution. *Negotiation Journal, 8*, 389–404.

Ross, L., & Ward, A. (in press). Naive realism: Implications for misunderstanding and divergent perceptions of fairness and bias. In T. Brown, E. Reed, & E. Turiel (Eds.), *Values and knowledge*. Hillsdale, NJ: Erlbaum.

Ross, M., & Sicoly, F. (1979). Egocentric biases in availability and attribution. *Journal of Personality and Social Psychology, 37*, 322–336.

Ross, M., Thibaut, J., & Evenbeck, S. (1971). Some determinants of the intensity of social protest. *Journal of Experimental Social Psychology, 7,* 401–418.

Rouhana, N. N., & Kelman, H. C. (1994). Promoting joint thinking in international conflicts: An Israeli-Palestinian continuing workshop. *Journal of Social Issues, 50,* 157–178.

Rubin, J. Z. (1980). Experimental research on third-party intervention in conflict: Toward some generalizations. *Psychological Bulletin, 87,* 379–391.

Rubin, J. Z. (1994). Models of conflict management. *Journal of Social Issues, 50,* 33–45.

Rubin, J. Z., Pruitt, D. G., & Kim, S. H. (1994). *Social Conflict* (2nd ed.). New York: McGraw-Hill.

Schank, R. C., & Abelson, R. P. (1977). *Scripts, plans, goals, and understanding: An inquiry into human knowledge structures.* Hillsdale, NJ: Erlbaum.

Sebenius, J. (in press). Dealing with blocking coalitions and related barriers to agreement: Lessons from negotiations on the oceans, the ozone, and the climate. In K. Arrow, R. Mnookin, L. Ross, A. Tversky, & R. Wilson (Eds.), *Barriers to the negotiated resolution of conflict.* New York: Norton.

Steele, C. M. (1988). The psychology of self-affirmation: Sustaining the integrity of the self. In L. Berkowitz (Ed.), *Advances in Experimental Social Psychology* (Vol. 21, pp. 261–302). San Diego: Academic Press.

Steele, C. M. (1992, April). Race and the schooling of black Americans. *The Atlantic Monthly,* 68–78.

Stillinger, C. (1990). *Overcoming attributional barriers to conflict resolution.* Unpublished doctoral dissertation, Stanford University, Palo Alto, CA.

Stillinger, C. (1991). *Solving the attribution problem in social negotiation.* Unpublished manuscript, Stanford University, Palo Alto, CA.

Stillinger, C., Epelbaum, M., Keltner, M., & Ross, L. (1990). *The reactive devaluation barrier to conflict resolution.* Unpublished manuscript, Stanford University, Palo Alto, CA.

Susskind, L. (in press). Barriers to effective environmental treaty-making. In K. Arrow, R. Mnookin, L. Ross, A. Tversky, & R. Wilson (Eds.), *Barriers to the negotiated resolution of conflict.* New York: Norton.

Susskind, L., & Cruikshank, J. (1987). *Breaking the impasse.* New York: Basic Books.

Susskind, L. E. (1994). *Environmental diplomacy: Negotiating more effective global agreements.* New York: Oxford University Press.

Taylor, S. E. (1983). Adjustment to threatening events: A theory of cognitive adaptation. *American Psychologist, 38,* 1161–1173.

Taylor, S. E., & Brown, J. D. (1988). Illusion and well-being: A social psychological perspective on mental health. *Psychological Bulletin, 103,* 193–210.

Taylor, S. E., Collins, R. L., Skokan, L. A., & Aspinwall, L. G. (1989). Maintaining positive illusions in the face of negative information: Getting the facts without letting them get to you. *Journal of Social and Clinical Psychology, 8,* 114–129.

Thomas, K. W., & Pondy, L. R. (1977). Toward an "intent" model of conflict management among principal parties. *Human Relations, 30,* 1089–1102.

Thompson, L. L. (1991). Information exchange in negotiation. *Journal of Experimental Social Psychology, 27,* 161–179.

Vallone, R. P., Ross, L., & Lepper, M. R. (1985). The hostile media phenomenon: Biased perceptions and perceptions of bias in media coverage of the "Beirut Massacre." *Journal of Personality and Social Psychology, 49,* 577–585.

Walcott, C., Hopmann, P. T., & King, T. D. (1977). The role of debate in negotiation. In D. Druckman (Ed.), *Negotiations: Social-psychological perspectives.* Beverly Hills, CA: Sage.

Walster, E., Walster, G. W., & Berscheid, E. (1978). *Equity: Theory and research.* Boston, MA: Allyn and Bacon.

Ward, A., & Ross, L. (1991a). *Attributions about "persuaded" and "non-persuaded" others.* Unpublished manuscript, Stanford University, Palo Alto, CA.

Ward, A., & Ross, L. (1991b). *Perceptions of bias in response to the "Judge Thomas–Anita Hill" affair.* Unpublished manuscript, Stanford University, Palo Alto, CA.

Ward, A., & Ross, L. (1993). *Reactive devaluation of an Israeli-Palestinian peace proposal.* Unpublished manuscript, Stanford University, Palo Alto, CA.

Weiner, B., Frieze, I., Kukla, A., Reed, L., Rest, S., & Rosenbaum, R. M. (1971). Perceiving the causes of success and failure. In E. E. Jones, D. Kanouse, H. H. Kelley, R. E. Nisbett, S. Valins, & B. Weiner (Eds.), *Attribution: Perceiving the causes of behavior* (pp. 95–120). Morristown, NJ: General Learning Press.

White, R. (1984). *Fearful warriors: A psychological profile of U.S.–Soviet relations.* New York: Free Press.

White, R. K. (1977). Misperception in the Arab–Israeli conflict. *Journal of Social Issues, 33,* 190–221.

Whitley, B. E., & Frieze, I. H. (1985). Children's causal attributions for success and failure in achievement settings. A meta-analysis. *Journal of Educational Psychology, 77,* 608–616.

Whitley, B. E., & Frieze, I. H. (1986). Measuring causal attributions for success and failure: A meta-analysis of the effects of question wording style. *Basic and Applied Social Psychology, 7,* 35–51.

Wicklund, R. A. (1974). *Freedom and reactance.* Potomac, MD: Erlbaum.

Wilson, R. (in press). Strategic and informational barriers to negotiation. In K. Arrow, R. Mnookin, L. Ross, A. Tversky, & R. Wilson (Eds.), *Barriers to the negotiated resolution of conflict.* New York: Norton.

Zeckhauser, R., & Parson, E. (in press). Cooperation in the unbalanced commons. In K. Arrow, R. Mnookin, L. Ross, A. Tversky, & R. Wilson (Eds.), *Barriers to the negotiated resolution of conflict.* New York: Norton.

INDEX

A

Abuse, responsibility judgments, 13–15
Adolescents
  self-esteem, 94–95, 98
  socialization based on bodily experiences, 163–166
Affective state, causality, 9–11
Afterimages, chromatic, 183–185
Aggression, 30–32
AIDS, perceived responsibility, 1–6, 8, 12–14
Alcohol use, gender differences, 168
Altruism, social motivation, 26–30
Alzheimer's disease, responsibility judgments, 13–15
Anger
  responsibility, 21–25, 29, 42
  self-esteem stability, 100–101, 114–116
Assimilation, stereotype maintenance, 211–216
Associative network model, informal interaction, 83
Athletic effort reporting, gender differences, 154–156
At-risk children, 32, 38–40
Attention
  conversational norm violations, 78–79
  gender differences, 161
  stereotype maintenance, 216–219
Attractiveness, self-esteem stability, 98–99
Attributional processes, 203–210, 293–295
Auditory perception, 185–186
Awareness, *see also* Perception
  body, gender differences, 165

B

Bargaining strategies, dispute resolution, 262–263
Bias
  perception of, in dispute resolution, 281–284
  stereotype maintenance, 211

Blame, 41–42
Blindness, responsibility judgments, 13–14
Blood glucose, interoceptive study, 151–152, 154
Blood pressure, interoceptive study, 151, 152, 155
Bodily state, perceptual cue use, gender differences, 143–170
Body awareness, gender differences, 165
Body fat, internal signal detection and, 153
Brain, gender differences, 162–163
Buss–Durkee Hostility Inventory, 114, 115

C

Cancer, responsibility judgments, 13–14
Causality, 7–20
  controllable vs. uncontrollable, 12–15
  mitigation circumstances, 15–19
  personal vs. impersonal, 7–12
  political ideology and perceived causality, 11–12, 15
Cerebral hemispheric lateralization, gender differences, 162–163
Child abuse, responsibility judgments, 13–15
Children
  at risk, *see* At-risk children
  self-esteem, 94–95, 99–101
    early childhood experiences, 104–107
  socialization based on bodily experiences, 163–166
Chromatic afterimages, 183–185
Communication
  anatomical names of genitals, 165
  conflict resolution, 256–257
  conversational norms, 69–70
    violation effects, 70–79
  deception, 58–59
  emotional, 74–75
  gender differences, 161–163, 170
  humor, 72–74
  information processing in social contexts, 49–87

memory, 75–77
narrative, 84–85
nonverbal, gender differences, 161–163
speech style, 55–58
uncertainty, 55–58
Competence, self-esteem stability, 98–99
Conceptual processes, stereotypes, 195–224
Conditional positive regard, self-esteem, 105
Conflict, *see also* Dispute resolution
  gender difference, 168
Construal, dispute resolution, 268–270, 288–292
Contextual cues, 66–68
Contingent self-esteem, 103, 105
Contrast, stereotype maintenance, 211–216
Controllable causality, 12–15, 19–20
Conversational norms, 69–70
  emotional communication, 74–75
  humor, 72–74
  violation effects
    information, attention to, 78–79
    information, interpretation, 70–75
    memory, 75–77
Couples
  emotional communication, 74–75
  interpersonal conflict, gender differences, 168
Cues, contextual, 66–68
Cue use, internal state, gender differences, 143–170

D

Deception, dispute resolution, 260–262
Depression, self-esteem, 121–127
Diabetics, interoceptive blood-glucose study, 151–152, 154
Dieting, gender differences, 164, 165
Dispositional causality, 8–9
Dispute resolution
  equity issues, 284–288
  institutional barriers, 256–260
  negotiation expectations, 296–297
  psychological barriers, 255–256, 263–297
    dissonance reduction, 263–265
    divergent construal, 268–270, 288–292
    loss aversion, 266–268
    mistrust, 275–288
    overconfidence, 265–266, 289
    reactive devaluation, 270–275, 293–294
  strategic barriers, 260–263
  third-party mediators, 288–297
Dissonance reduction, dispute reduction, 263–265
Divergent construal, dispute resolution, 268–270, 288–292
Drug abuse, responsibility judgments, 13–15
Drug use, gender differences, 168

E

Early childhood, unstable self-esteem from early experiences, 104–107
Eating, gender differences, 164, 165
Eating disorders, gender differences, 164
Ego defensiveness, dispute resolution, 276–278
Ego-involvement, self-esteem, 97–103
Elaborative processing, 192–201
Emotion
  negative and positive, perceived causality, 9–11
  theories, 169–170
Emotional communication, 74–75
Emotion reporting, gender differences, 154–156
Encoding, 180–181
  stereotype maintenance, 177–241
Equity issues, dispute resolution, 284–288
Excuse making, 34–40
  at-risk children, 38–40
  self-esteem, 116–117, 121
Expectancy, social perception, 182–183
Expectancy deviations
  pragmatic information processing, 68–79
  prejudice as encoding process, 223–226
External cues, gender differences, 143–170

F

Facial feedback, gender differences, 168
Facilitators, dispute resolution, 288–297
Failure, depression and, 125–127
Fat, body, internal signal detection and, 153
Feedback
  bodily, gender differences, 143–170
  self-esteem, 104–106, 112, 117–120
  parental feedback, 106–107
Field dependence, gender differences, 159, 168
Five-Factor Inventory, 127, 129–131

G

Gedanken experiments, 7, 12
Gender differences
  alcohol use, 168
  bodily experiences, 163–166
  brain, hemispheric lateralization, 162–163
  dieting, 164, 165
  drug use, 168
  eating, 164, 165
  eating disorders, 164
  emotion reporting, 154–156
  facial feedback, 168
  field dependence, 159, 168
  genitals, anatomic names, 165
  interpersonal conflict, 168
  motion sickness, 168
  nonverbal communication, 161–163
  perceiving internal state, 143–170
  self-esteem and parental feedback, 106–107
  sexual arousal, 164–165
  sexuality, 165, 167
  socialization, 163–166
  social status, 160–162
  spatial navigation, 157–158
  spatial reasoning, 167
  zero gravity, 168
Gender-role stereotype, emotional conversation, 74–75
Genitals, anatomic names, gender differences, 165
Glucose, blood, interoceptive study, 151–152, 154

H

Heartbeat perception, gender differences, 145–147, 155, 162
Heart disease, responsibility judgments, 13–14
Hemispheric lateralization, cerebral, gender differences, 162–163
High self-esteem, 93, 110–111, 127–132
  depression, 122
HIV-positive, perceived responsibility, 1–6, 8, 12–14
Homosexuality, responsibility judgments, 15
Hostility
  Buss–Durkee Hostility Inventory, 114, 115
  expression, in emotional communication, 74–75
  proneness, and self-esteem, 114–116, 120–121
Humor, informal conversation, 72–74

I

Identification, stereotype maintenance, 206–210
Imagery experiments, 183–185
Impression formation, 81
  conversational norm violations, 78–79
  narrative communication, 84–85
  pragmatic information, 60–65
Impression revision, perceptual revision, 188–192
Incongruent information, encoding, 197–203
Inferential processes, stereotype maintenance, 206–210
Informal conversation, humor, 72–74
Information processing
  attentional processes, 216–219
  attributional processes, 203–210
  automatic activation, 220–223
  conceptual processes, 195–224
  divergent construal, 268–270, 288–292
  encoding, 180–181, 189–241
  expectancy deviations, 68–79
  individual differences, 80–83
  perceptual cue use, gender differences, 143–170
  perceptual processes, 181–185
  in social contexts, 49–87
Informativeness, 70–72
Internal cues, gender differences, 143–170
Interoception, gender differences, 145–156, 162, 164, 166
Interpersonal conflict, gender difference, 168

J

Johnson, Magic, AIDS and social responsibility, 1–6, 8, 12

L

Litigation
  barriers to resolution
    institutional, 256–260
    psychological, 255–256, 263–297
    strategic, 260–263

equity issues, 284–288
negotiation expectations, 296–297
third-party mediators, 288–297
Locus of causality, 8
Loss aversion, dispute resolution, 266–268, 288
Love, expression, in emotional communication, 74–75
Low self-esteem, 94, 112–114, 127–131, 133–134
  depression, 122
  excuse making, 122

M

Media, informativeness, effect on responses to information, 70–72
Mediators, dispute resolution, 288–297
Memory
  conversational norm violations, effect on, 75–77
  incongruency effect, 197–203
Men, *see also* Gender differences
  cerebral hemispheric lateralization, 162–163
  dieting, 164, 165
  eating, 164, 165
  emotional communication, 74–75
  genitals, anatomic names, 165
  interpersonal conflict, gender differences, 168
  menstruation, 163–164
  perceiving internal state, gender differences, 143–170
  self-esteem and parental feedback, 106–107
  socialization based on bodily experience, 163–166
  social status, 160–162
Menstruation, socialization, 163–164
Minorities, stereotype maintenance, encoding processes, 177–241
Mistrust, dispute resolution, 275–288
Mitigating circumstances, causality, 15–19
Modesty, memory, effect on, 75–77
Motion sickness, gender differences, 168
Motivation
  altruism, 26–30
  blame, 41–42
  communication of pragmatic meaning, 52–68
  repsonsibility and action, 21–25, 42–43

self-enhancement and self-protection strategies, 108–114
self-esteem, 101

N

Naive realism, dispute resolution, 278–284
Narrative communication, 84–85
Negative emotions, perceived causality, 9–11
Negotiation, barriers to resolution
  institutional, 256–260
  psychological, 255–256, 263–297
  strategic, 260–263
  equity issues, 284–288
  negotiation expectations, 296–297
  third-party mediators, 288–297
NEO-PI, 129–130
Neuroticism, 130
Noncontingent feedback, self-esteem, 104–105
Nonverbal communication, gender differences, 161–163

O

Obesity, responsibility judgments, 13–15
Opinion surveys, pragmatic information, 65–68
Overconfidence, dispute resolution, 265–266, 289

P

Paraplegia, responsibility judgments, 13–14
Parental feedback, self-esteem, 106–107
Partners
  emotional communication, 74–75
  interpersonal conflict, gender differences, 168
Pathos, 23–24, 29, 42
Perception
  auditory, 185–186
  body awareness, gender differences, 165
  heartbeat, gender differences, 145–147, 155, 162
  Self-Perception Profile, 127
  social, stereotypes, 182–183
Perceptual cue use, internal state, gender differences, 143–170
Perceptual processes, 181
  stereotypes, 182–241

Perfectionism, self-esteem and, 107
Personal causality, 7–12, 19–20
Physical attractiveness, self-esteem stability, 98–99
Physical exertion reporting, gender differences, 154–156
Physiological state, perceptual cue use, gender differences, 143–170
Politeness, memory, effect on, 75–77
Political ideology, perceived causality, 11–12, 15
Positive emotions, perceived causality, 9–11
Poverty, political ideology and perceived causality, 11–12
Pragmatic information processing
    expectancy deviations, 68–79
    individual differences, 80–83
Pragmatic meaning, 51–68
    emotional communication, 74–75
    humor, 72–74
    memory, 75–77
Prejudice, 179
    automatic activation of stereotypes, 220–223
    as encoding process, 201–203, 224–236
Pride, self-esteem, 129
Processing, see also Information processing
    elaborative, 192–201
Puberty, socialization, based on bodily experiences, 163–166
Public media, informativeness, 70–72

Q

Questionnaires, pragmatic information, 65–68

R

Race, stereotype maintenance, encoding processes, 177–241
Rats, spatial navigation experiments, 157
Reactive devaluation, dispute resolution, 270–275, 293–294
Rejection, 32–34
Responsibility, 1–43
    aggression, 30–32
    altruism, 26–30
    anger, 21–25, 29, 42
    at-risk children
        aggression, 32
        excuses, 38–40
    blame, 41–42
    causality, 7–20
        controllable vs. uncontrollable, 12–15
        mitigating circumstances, 15–19
        personal vs. impersonal, 7–12
    excuse giving, 34–40
    impression management, 34–40
    rejection, 32–34
    sympathy, 23–25, 29, 42
Rod and frame test, 159, 167

S

Secrecy, dispute resolution, 260–262
Self-appraisal, 97–99, 127–131
Self-concept, 98–99
    impoverished, 103–104, 112
Self-description, 63–65
Self-enhancement strategies, 108–114, 120, 135
    dispute resolution, 276–278
Self-esteem, 93–135; see also High self-esteem; Low self-esteem
    adolescents, 94–95, 98
    adults, 96, 99–100, 107
    anger-proneness, 100–101, 114–116, 120–121
    children, 94–95, 99–101
    depressive symptomatology, 121–127
    ego-involvement, 97–103
    excuse making, 116–117, 121
    feedback, 104–106, 112, 117–120
    hostility-proneness, 114–116, 120–121
    parental feedback, 106–107
    perfectionism, 107
    pride, 129
    self-enhancement and self-protection strategies, 108–114
    stability, 94–97, 111, 120–121, 127–135
Self-Perception Profile, 127
Self-protection strategies, 108–114, 120, 135
Self-report methods, gender differences, 148–150
Sex-role stereotype, emotional conversation, 74–75
Sexual arousal, gender differences, 164–165
Sexual dysfunction, 167
Sexuality, gender differences, 165, 167
Sexual orientation, responsibility judgments, 15

Signal-detection methods, gender differences, 146–150, 162
Situational causality, 7–12
Social acceptance, self-esteem stability, 98–99
Social information processing, 49–87
  gender differences, 160–166
Socialization, based on bodily experience, 163–166
Social motivation, altruism, 26–30
Social perception, stereotypes, 182–183
Social status, gender differences, 160–162
Spatial navigation, gender differences, 157–158
Speech style
  communication of uncertainty, 55–58
  deception, 58–59
Spouses
  emotional communication, 74–75
  interpersonal conflict, gender differences, 168
Stability, self-esteem, 94–97, 111, 120–121, 127–135
  depression, 122–127
Stable self-esteem
  anger and hostility proneness, 114–116, 120–121
  excuse making, 116–117, 121
Stereotypes, 178–179
  accuracy, 238–239
  attributional processes, 203–210
  automatic activation, 220–223
  conceptual processes, 195–224
  encoding processes in stereotype maintenance, 177–241
  perceptual processes, 182–241
  sex-role, emotional communication, 74–75
Stigma
  causal controllability, 13–15
  responsibility, 1–6, 8
Stress, depression, 122–124
Substance abuse, responsibility judgments, 13–15
Surveys, pragmatic information, 65–68
Sympathy, responsibility, 23–25, 29, 42
Symptom reporting, gender differences, 154–156

T

Third party mediators, dispute resolution, 288–297

TOSCA, 129, 130
Trust, dispute resolution, 275–288, 292–293

U

Ultimate attribution error, 205
Uncertainty, speech style and, 55–58
Unconditional positive regard, self-esteem, 105
Uncontrollable causality, 12–15, 19–20
Unstable self-esteem, 94, 97, 103–104, 111, 120–121, 127–131, 132–135
  adults, 107
  anger and hostility proneness, 114–116, 120–121
  children, 99–101
  depression, 122–127
  early childhood experiences, 104–107
  excuse making, 116–117, 121

V

Vestibular disturbance, gender difference, 168
Vietnam War syndrome, responsibility judgments, 13–14

W

Witticisms, informal conversation, 72–74
Women, *see also* Gender differences
  cerebral hemispheric lateralization, 162–163
  dieting, 164, 165
  eating disorders, 164
  emotional communication, 74–75
  genitals, anatomic names, 165
  interpersonal conflict, gender differences, 168
  menstruation, 163–164
  perceiving internal state, gender differences, 143–170
  self-esteem and parental feedback, 106–107
  sexual dysfunction, 167
  socialization based on bodily experience, 163–166
  social status, 160–162
  spectatoring, 167

Y

Youth at risk, *see* At-risk children

Z

Zero gravity, gender differences, 168

CONTENTS OF OTHER VOLUMES

Volume 1

Cultural Influences upon Cognitive Processes
Harry C. Triandis
The Interaction of Cognitive and Physiological Determinants of Emotional State
Stanley Schachter
Experimental Studies of Coalition Formation
William A. Gamson
Communication Networks
Marvin E. Shaw
A Contingency Model of Leadership Effectiveness
Fred E. Fiedler
Inducing Resistance to Persuasion: Some Contemporary Approaches
William J. McGuire
Social Motivation, Dependency, and Susceptibility to Social Influence
Richard H. Walters and Ross D. Purke
Sociability and Social Organization in Monkeys and Apes
William A. Mason
Author Index—Subject Index

Volume 2

Vicarious Processes: A Case of No-Trial Learning
Albert Bandura
Selective Exposure
Jonathan L. Freedman and David O. Sears
Group Problem Solving
L. Richard Hoffman
Situational Factors in Conformity
Vernon L. Allen
Social Power
John Schopler
From Acts to Dispositions: The Attribution Process in Person Perception
Edward E. Jones and Keith E. Davis
Inequality in Social Exchange
J. Stacy Adams
The Concept of Aggressive Drive: Some Additional Considerations
Leonard Berkowitz
Author Index—Subject Index

Volume 3

Mathematical Models in Social Psychology
Robert P. Abelson
The Experimental Analysis of Social Performance
Michael Argyle and Adam Kendon
A Structural Balance Approach to the Analysis of Communication Effects
N. T. Feather
Effects of Fear Arousal on Attitude Change: Recent Developments in Theory and Experimental Research
Irving L. Janis
Communication Processes and the Properties of Language
Serge Moscovici
The Congruity Principle Revisited: Studies in the Reduction, Induction and Generalization of Persuasion
Percy H. Tannenbaum
Author Index—Subject Index

Volume 4

The Theory of Cognitive Dissonance: A Current Perspective
Elliot Aronson
Attitudes and Attraction
Donn Byrne
Sociolinguistics
Susan M. Ervin-Tripp
Recognition of Emotion
Nico H. Frijda
Studies of Status Congruence
Edward E. Sampson
Exploratory Investigations of Empathy
Ezra Stotland

The Personal Reference Scale: An Approach to Social Judgment
Harry S. Upshaw
Author Index—Subject Index

Volume 5

Media Violence and Aggressive Behavior: A Review of Experimental Research
Richard E. Goranson
Studies in Leader Legitimacy, Influence, and Innovation
Edwin P. Hollander and James W. Julian
Experimental Studies of Negro-White Relationships
Irwin Katz
Findings and Theory in the Study of Fear Communications
Howard Leventhal
Perceived Freedom
Ivan D. Steiner
Experimental Studies of Families
Nancy E. Waxler and Elliot G. Mishler
Why Do Groups Make Riskier Decisions than Individuals?
Kenneth L. Dion, Robert S. Baron, and Norman Miller
Author Index—Subject Index

Volume 6

Self-Perception Theory
Daryl J. Bem
Social Norms, Feelings, and Other Factors Affecting Helping and Altruism
Leonard Berkowitz
The Power of Liking: Consequences of Interpersonal Attitudes Derived from a Liberalized View of Secondary Reinforcement
Albert J. Lott and Bernice E. Lott
Social Influence, Conformity Bias, and the Study of Active Minorities
Serge Moscovici and Claude Faucheux
A Critical Analysis of Research Utilizing the Prisoner's Dilemma Paradigm for the Study of Bargaining
Charlan Nemeth
Structural Representations of Implicit Personality Theory
Seymour Rosenberg and Andrea Sedlak
Author Index—Subject Index

Volume 7

Cognitive Algebra: Integration Theory Applied to Social Attribution
Norman A. Anderson
On Conflicts and Bargaining
Erika Apfelbaum
Physical Attractiveness
Ellen Bersheid and Elaine Walster
Compliance, Justification, and Cognitive Change
Harold B. Gerard, Edward S. Connolley, and Roland A. Wilhelmy
Processes in Delay of Gratification
Walter Mischel
Helping a Distressed Person: Social, Personality, and Stimulus Determinants
Ervin Staub
Author Index—Subject Index

Volume 8

Social Support for Nonconformity
Vernon L. Allen
Group Tasks, Group Interaction Process, and Group Performance Effectiveness: A Review and Proposed Integration
J. Richard Hackman and Charles G. Morris
The Human Subject in the Psychology Experiment: Fact and Artifact
Arie W. Kruglanski
Emotional Arousal in the Facilitation of Aggression through Communication
Percy H. Tannenbaum and Dolf Zillman
The Reluctance to Transmit Bad News
Abraham Tesser and Sidney Rosen
Objective Self-Awareness
Robert A. Wicklund
Responses to Uncontrollable Outcomes: An Integration of Reactance Theory and the Learned Helplessness Model
Camille B. Wortman and Jack W. Brehm
Subject Index

Volume 9

New Directions in Equity Research
Elaine Walster, Ellen Bersheid, and G. William Walster
Equity Theory Revisited: Comments and Annotated Bibliography
J. Stacy Adams and Sara Freedman

The Distribution of Rewards and Resources in Groups and Organizations
Gerald S. Leventhal
Deserving and the Emergence of Forms of Justice
Melvin J. Lerner, Dale T. Miller, and John G. Holmes
Equity and the Law: The Effect of a Harmdoer's "Suffering in the Act" on Liking and Assigned Punishment
William Austin, Elaine Walster, and Mary Kristine Utne
Incremental Exchange Theory: A Formal Model for Progression in Dyadic Social Interaction
L. Lowell Huesmann and George Levinger
Commentary
George C. Homans
Subject Index

Volume 10

The Catharsis of Aggression: An Evaluation of a Hypothesis
Russell G. Geen and Michael B. Quanty
Mere Exposure
Albert A. Harrison
Moral Internalization: Current Theory and Research
Martin L. Hoffman
Some Effects of Violent and Nonviolent Movies on the Behavior of Juvenile Delinquents
Ross D. Parke, Leonard Berkowitz, Jacques P. Leyens, Stephen G. West, and Richard Sebastian
The Intuitive Psychologist and His Shortcomings: Distortions in the Attribution Process
Lee Ross
Normative Influences on Altruism
Shalom H. Schwartz
A Discussion of the Domain and Methods of Social Psychology: Two Papers by Ron Harre and Barry R. Schlenker
Leonard Berkowitz
The Ethogenic Approach: Theory and Practice
R. Harre
On the Ethogenic Approach: Etiquette and Revolution
Barry R. Schlenker
Automatisms and Autonomies: In Reply to Professor Schlenker
R. Harre
Subject Index

Volume 11

The Persistence of Experimentally Induced Attitude Change
Thomas D. Cook and Brian F. Flay
The Contingency Model and the Dynamics of the Leadership Process
Fred E. Fiedler
An Attributional Theory of Choice
Andy Kukla
Group-Induced Polarization of Attitudes and Behavior
Helmut Lamm and David G. Myers
Crowding: Determinants and Effects
Janet E. Stockdale
Salience: Attention, and Attribution: Top of the Head Phenomena
Shelley E. Taylor and Susan T. Fiske
Self-Generated Attitude Change
Abraham Tesser
Subject Index

Volume 12

Part I. Studies in Social Cognition

Prototypes in Person Perception
Nancy Cantor and Walter Mischel
A Cognitive-Attributional Analysis of Stereotyping
David L. Hamilton
Self-Monitoring Processes
Mark Snyder

Part II. Social Influences and Social Interaction

Architectural Mediation of Residential Density and Control: Crowding and the Regulation of Social Contact
Andrew Baum and Stuart Valins
A Cultural Ecology of Social Behavior
J. W. Berry
Experiments on Deviance with Special Reference to Dishonesty
David P. Farrington
From the Early Window to the Late Night Show: International Trends in the Study of Television's Impact on Children and Adults
John P. Murray and Susan Kippax
Effects of Prosocial Television and Film Material on the Behavior of Viewers
J. Phillipe Rushton
Subject Index

Volume 13

People's Analyses of the Causes of Ability-Linked Performances
John M. Darley and George R. Goethals
The Empirical Exploration of Intrinsic Motivational Processes
Edward I. Deci and Richard M. Ryan
Attribution of Responsibility: From Man the Scientist to Man as Lawyer
Frank D. Fincham and Joseph M. Jaspars
Toward a Comprehensive Theory of Emotion
Howard Leventhal
Toward a Theory of Conversion Behavior
Serge Moscovici
The Role of Information Retrieval and Conditional Inference Processes in Belief Formation and Change
Robert S. Wyer, Jr. and Jon Hartwick
Index

Volume 14

Verbal and Nonverbal Communication of Deception
Miron Zuckerman, Bella M. DePaulo, and Robert Rosenthal
Cognitive, Social, and Personality Processes in the Physiological Detection of Deception
William M. Waid and Martin T. Orne
Dialectic Conceptions in Social Psychology: An Application to Social Penetration and Privacy Regulation
Irwin Altman, Anne Vinsel, and Barbara B. Brown
Direct Experience and Attitude–Behavior Consistency
Russell H. Fazio and Mark P. Zanna
Predictability and Human Stress: Toward a Clarification of Evidence and Theory
Suzanne M. Miller
Perceptual and Judgmental Processes in Social Contexts
Arnold Upmeyer
Jury Trials: Psychology and Law
Charlan Jeanne Nemeth
Index

Volume 15

Balance, Agreement, and Positivity in the Cognition of Small Social Structures
Walter H. Crockett
Episode Cognition: Internal Representations of Interaction Routines
Joseph P. Forgas
The Effects of Aggressive-Pornographic Mass Media Stimuli
Neil M. Malamuth and Ed Donnerstein
Socialization in Small Groups: Temporal Changes in Individual–Group Relations
Richard L. Moreland and John M. Levine
Translating Actions into Attitudes: An Identity-Analytic Approach to the Explanation of Social Conduct
Barry R. Schlenker
Aversive Conditions as Stimuli to Aggression
Leonard Berkowitz
Index

Volume 16

A Contextualist Theory of Knowledge: Its Implications for Innovation and Reform in Psychological Research
William J. McGuire
Social Cognition: Some Historical and Theoretical Perspectives
Janet Landman and Melvin Manis
Paradigmatic Behaviorism: Unified Theory for Social-Personality Psychology
Arthur W. Staats
Social Psychology from the Standpoint of a Structural Symbolic Interactionism: Toward an Interdisciplinary Social Psychology
Sheldon Stryker
Toward an Interdisciplinary Social Psychology
Carl W. Backman
Index

Volume 17

Mental Representations of Self
John F. Kihlstrom and Nancy Cantor
Theory of the Self: Impasse and Evolution
Kenneth J. Gergen
A Perceptual-Motor Theory of Emotion
Howard Leventhal

Equity and Social Change in Human Relationships
Charles G. McClintock, Roderick M. Kramer, and Linda J. Keil
A New Look at Dissonance Theory
Joel Cooper and Russell H. Fazio
Cognitive Theories of Persuasion
Alice H. Eagly and Shelly Chaiken
Helping Behavior and Altruism: An Empirical and Conceptual Overview
John F. Dovidio
Index

Volume 18

A Typological Approach to Marital Interaction: Recent Theory and Research
Mary Anne Fitzpatrick
Groups in Exotic Environments
Albert A. Harrison and Mary M. Connors
Balance Theory, the Jordan Paradigm, and the Wiest Tetrahedon
Chester A. Insko
The Social Relations Model
David A. Kenny and Lawrence La Voie
Coalition Bargaining
S. S. Komorita
When Belief Creates Reality
Mark Snyder
Index

Volume 19

Distraction–Conflict Theory: Progress and Problems
Robert S. Baron
Recent Research on Selective Exposure to Information
Dieter Frey
The Role of Threat to Self-Esteem and Perceived Control in Recipient Reaction to Help: Theory Development and Empirical Validation
Arie Nadler and Jeffrey D. Fisher
The Elaboration Likelihood Model of Persuasion
Richard E. Petty and John T. Cacioppo
Natural Experiments on the Effects of Mass Media Violence on Fatal Aggression: Strengths and Weaknesses of a New Approach
David P. Phillips

Paradigms and Groups
Ivan D. Steiner
Social Categorization: Implications for Creation and Reduction of Intergroup Bias
David A. Wilder
Index

Volume 20

Attitudes, Traits, and Actions: Dispositional Prediction of Behavior in Personality and Social Psychology
Icek Ajzen
Prosocial Motivation: Is It Ever Truly Altruistic?
C. Daniel Batson
Dimensions of Group Process: Amount and Structure of Vocal Interaction
James M. Dabbs, Jr. and R. Barry Ruback
The Dynamics of Opinion Formation
Harold B. Gerard and Ruben Orive
Positive Affect, Cognitive Processes, and Social Behavior
Alice M. Isen
Between Hope and Fear: The Psychology of Risk
Lola L. Lopes
Toward an Integration of Cognitive and Motivational Perspectives on Social Inference: A Biased Hypothesis-Testing Model
Tom Pyszczynski and Jeff Greenberg
Index

Volume 21

Introduction
Leonard Berkowitz

Part I. The Self as Known

Narrative and the Self as Relationship
Kenneth J. Gergen and Mary M. Gergen
Self and Others: Studies in Social Personality and Autobiography
Seymour Rosenberg
Content and Process in the Experience of Self
William J. McGuire and Claire V. McGuire
Information Processing and the Study of the Self
John F. Kihlstrom, Nancy Cantor, Jeanne Sumi Albright, Beverly R. Chew, Stanley B. Klein, and Paula M. Niedenthal

Part II. Self-Motives

Toward a Self-Evaluation Maintenance Model of Social Behavior
Abraham Tesser

The Self: A Dialectical Approach
Carl W. Backman

The Psychology of Self-Affirmation: Sustaining the Integrity of the Self
Claude M. Steele

A Model of Behavioral Self-Regulation: Translating Intention into Action
Michael F. Scheier and Charles S. Carver

Index

Volume 22

On the Construction of the Anger Experience: Aversive Events and Negative Priming in the Formation of Feelings
Leonard Berkowitz and Karen Heimer

Social Psychophysiology: A New Look
John T. Cacioppo, Richard E. Petty, and Louis G. Tassinary

Self-Discrepancy Theory: What Patterns of Self-Beliefs Cause People to Suffer?
E. Tory Higgins

Minding Matters: The Consequences of Mindlessness-Mindfulness
Ellen J. Langer

The Tradeoffs of Social Control and Innovation in Groups and Organizations
Charlan Jeanne Nemeth and Barry M. Staw

Confession, Inhibition, and Disease
James W. Pennebaker

A Sociocognitive Model of Attitude Structure and Function
Anthony R. Pratkanis and Anthony G. Greenwald

Introspection, Attitude Change, and Attitude–Behavior Consistency: The Disruptive Effects of Explaining Why We Feel the Way We Do
Timothy D. Wilson, Dana S. Dunn, Dolores Kraft, and Douglas J. Lisle

Index

Volume 23

A Continuum of Impression Formation, from Category-Based to Individuating Processes: Influences of Information and Motivation on Attention and Interpretation
Susan T. Fiske and Steven L. Neuberg

Multiple Processes by Which Attitudes Guide Behavior: The MODE Model as as Integrative Framework
Russell H. Fazio

PEAT: An Integrative Model of Attribution Processes
John W. Medcof

Reading People's Minds: A Transformation Rule Model for Predicting Others' Thoughts and Feelings
Rachel Karniol

Self-Attention and Behavior: A Review and Theoretical Update
Frederick X. Gibbons

Counterfactual Thinking and Social Perception: Thinking about What Might Have Been
Dale T. Miller, William Turnbull, and Cathy McFarland

Index

Volume 24

The Role of Self-Interest in Social and Political Attitudes
David O. Sears and Carolyn L. Funk

A Terror Management Theory of Social Behavior: The Psychological Functions of Self-Esteem and Cultural Worldviews
Sheldon Solomon, Jeff Greenberg, and Tom Pyszczynski

Mood and Persuasion: Affective States Influence the Processing of Persuasive Communications
Norbert Schwarz, Herbert Bless, and Gerd Bohner

A Focus Theory of Normative Conduct: A Theoretical Refinement and Reevaluation of the Role of Norms in Human Behavior
Robert B. Cialdini, Carl A. Kallgren, and Raymond R. Reno

The Effects of Interaction Goals on Person Perception
James L. Hilton and John M. Darley

Studying Social Interaction with the Rochester Interaction Record
Harry T. Reis and Ladd Wheeler

Subjective Construal, Social Inference, and Human Misunderstanding
Dale W. Griffin and Lee Ross
Index

Volume 25

Universals in the Content and Structure of Values: Theoretical Advances and Empirical Tests in 20 Countries
Shalom H. Schwartz
Motivational Foundations of Behavioral Confirmation
Mark Snyder
A Relational Model of Authority in Groups
Tom R. Tyler and E. Allan Lind
You Can't Always Think What You Want: Problems in the Suppression of Unwanted Thoughts
Daniel M. Wegner
Affect in Social Judgments and Decisions: A Multiprocess Model
Joseph Paul Forgas
The Social Psychology of Stanley Milgram
Thomas Blass
The Impact of Accountability on Judgment and Choice: Toward a Social Contingency Model
Philip E. Tetlock
Index

Volume 26

Attitudes toward High Achievers and Reactions to Their Fall: Theory and Research Concerning Tall Poppies
N. T. Feather
Evolutionary Social Psychology: From Sexual Selection to Social Cognition
Douglas T. Kenrick
Judgment in a Social Context: Biases, Shortcomings, and the Logic of Conversation
Norbert Schwarz
A Phase Model of Transitions: Cognitive and Motivational Consequences
Diane N. Ruble
Multiple-Audience Problems, Tactical Communication, and Social Interaction: A Relational-Regulation Perspective
John H. Fleming
From Social Inequality to Personal Entitlement: The Role of Social Comparisons, Legitimacy Appraisals, and Group Membership
Brenda Major
Mental Representations of Social Groups: Advances in Understanding Stereotypes and Stereotyping
Charles Stangor and James E. Lange
Index

ISBN 0-12-015227-4